DIEM'S FINAL FAILURE

DIEM'S FINAL FAILURE

PRELUDE TO

AMERICA'S WAR

IN VIETNAM

Philip E. Catton

UNIVERSITY PRESS OF KANSAS

Published by the University Press of Kansas (Lawrence, Kansas 66049), which was
organized by the Kansas Board of Regents and is operated and funded by Emporia
State University, Fort Hays State University, Kansas State University, Pittsburg State
University, the University of Kansas, and Wichita State University

Library of Congress Cataloging-in-Publication Data

Catton, Philip E.
  Diem's final failure : prelude to America's War in Vietnam / Philip E.
Catton.
      p. cm.—(Modern war studies)
Includes bibliographical references and index.
  ISBN 0-7006-1220-3 (cloth : alk. paper)
  1. Vietnam (Republic)—Politics and government. 2. Ngo, Dinh Diem,
1901–1963. 3. Vietnam (Republic)—Foreign relations—United
States. 4. United States—Foreign relations—Vietnam (Republic) I.
Title. II. Series.
  DS556.9 .C37 2003
  959.704'31—dc21   2002008243

British Library Cataloguing in Publication Data is available.

Printed in the United States of America

10 9 8 7 6 5 4 3 2 1

The paper used in this publication meets the minimum requirements of the American
National Standard for Permanence of Paper for Printed Library Materials Z39.48-1984.

TO MY PARENTS

Geoffrey and Margaret Jean Catton

Contents

Preface and Acknowledgments   ix

Introduction   1

1. A Shotgun Wedding   5

2. The Ngos, Nationalism, and Nation Building   25

3. Land Reform, Land Development, and Agrovilles   51

4. Origins of the Strategic Hamlet Program   73

Photo Gallery   99

5. Theory and Practice   117

6. Competitive Cooperation   141

7. Binh Duong Province: Case Study of a Program in Trouble   163

8. The Reckoning   185

Conclusion   209

Notes   213

Bibliography   273

Index   289

Preface and Acknowledgments

This book began as a graduate student paper on the Strategic Hamlet program in South Vietnam in the period 1961–1963. The research for the project raised a number of intriguing questions about the character of the Diem regime, encouraging me to undertake a more detailed treatment of the topic in my doctoral dissertation. This present study builds on the dissertation; it seeks to reexamine the course of U.S.–Vietnamese relations from 1954 to 1963 and shed new light on the Diem government, whose historical reputation has remained largely unchanged for more than three decades.

To do so, I have drawn extensively on Vietnamese-language materials, as well as sources available in English. Unless otherwise indicated, all translations are mine, although I have sought to check the interpretation of troublesome passages with native speakers. At this point, I should also say a brief word about terminology. In the text, I have employed the English-language equivalents of significant Vietnamese terms, not all of which are exact translations. For example, the Vietnamese term *Khu Tru mat* literally means "populous zone," but the term "agroville" was also used at the time and is commonly employed in current studies. I have generally used given names to refer to individual Vietnamese persons (e.g., "Diem" rather than "Ngo"). For place names, I have kept the Vietnamese division of words (e.g., "Ban Me Thuot" rather than "Banmethuot"), except for familiar names like Saigon, Hanoi, and Vietnam.

In the course of completing this study, I have incurred many debts, which I am pleased to have this opportunity to acknowledge formally. I received financial support from a number of sources: Ohio University's Department of History, Contemporary History Institute, Graduate Council, and John Houk Memorial Committee; the U.S. Army Military History Institute; the Lyndon B. Johnson Library; and the Society for Historians of American Foreign Relations.

As I sought to flesh out my ideas and gather information, various people offered helpful advice and suggestions. I thank, in particular, Robert Brigham, Pierre Brocheux, Debbie Cramer, Dinh D. Vu, Do Mau, Chris Goscha, Daniel Hémery, Hoang Van Lac, Hue-Tam Ho Tai, David Marr, Douglas Pike, Ralph Smith, Stein Tønnesson, Tran Ngoc Chau, William Turley, and

Vu Ngu Chieu. In addition, several of the above provided invaluable assistance in the planning of a research trip to Vietnam. For their support for this adventure, I also wish to thank Lady Borton, Thomas Engelbert, Ha Minh Hong, Judith Henchy, Ho Sy Khoach, Kurt Leffler, Nguyen Huu Nguyen, Nguyen Van Lich, Mark Sidel, and Thaveeporn Vasavakul.

Of the many archivists and librarians who assisted me in my research, I would like to single out Jeff Ferrier, Douglas Pike, Cliff Snyder, David Keogh, Robert Wardle, and the staffs at Archives II and the General Sciences Library in Ho Chi Minh City. I am indebted to Do Mai Linh, Hoang Chau, and Tran Van Quyen, who helped in drafting correspondence in Vietnamese, transcribing taped interviews, and checking certain translations. Mike Floyd showed great skill and patience in putting together the illustrations for the book. I am also grateful to the following for their intellectual, material, or moral support at various points over this long haul: Penny and Stuart Ager, Ole Beck-Peterson, Matt Bird, Gary Bodinar, Gina and Paul Butler, Todd Davis, Simon and Alice Davis, Harry Dickinson, David Evans, Sabrina Figueroa, Scott Gates, Chris Jensen, Michael Lowry, Doug Macdonald, Soo and Phil Nash, Chris Parry, Philippe Peycam, Andy Rotter, Sato Yoko, Jim Sheehan, Heather, Joyce and Bill Slough, and graduate students at Cornell University's Southeast Asia program.

I owe special thanks to the members of my dissertation committee—Marvin Fletcher, Takaaki Suzuki, Chester Pach, and William Frederick—particularly to the last two. William Frederick introduced me to Southeast Asia and encouraged me to be ambitious for this study. Chester Pach served as my dissertation adviser. As well as reading numerous drafts of my work, he provided steady support throughout my time in graduate school. Finally, I thank Mike Briggs at the University Press of Kansas for helping to bring this project to fruition.

Parts of the introduction and chapters 1 and 2 appeared as "Trying to Hustle the East: U.S. Relations with the Ngo Dinh Diem Government," in *The Cultural Turn: Essays in the History of U.S. Foreign Relations,* ed. Frank A. Ninkovich and Liping Bu (Chicago: Imprint Publications, 2001), 181–99. Part of chapter 5 appeared as "Counter-Insurgency and Nation-Building: The Strategic Hamlet Programme in South Vietnam, 1961–1963," *International History Review* (December 1999): 918–40.

DIEM'S FINAL FAILURE

South Vietnam—Provincial and Corps boundaries circa 1962–1963 (adapted from maps contained in South Vietnam Provincial Maps 9/67, Doc. 1, Country File— Vietnam, Box 180/181, National Security File, Lyndon B. Johnson Library).

Introduction

Five days before the coup of November 1, 1963, President Ngo Dinh Diem and Ambassador Henry Cabot Lodge attended the opening of an atomic research laboratory in the highland city of Da Lat. This was their first meeting for a month, a reflection of the recent and rapid downward spiral in U.S.–Vietnamese relations. The atmosphere was cordial, even though both men were well aware that the United States was involved in a plot to overthrow Diem's government. En route, the president gave the ambassador a running commentary on the passing terrain and the achievements of his regime. Even during the last leg of the journey, when the noise of the helicopter's rotor blades prevented talking, Diem continued his dissertation by writing messages on a large pad of paper. Lodge described the president as "very likeable," but there was no meeting of minds when it came to discussing the issues currently plaguing U.S.–Vietnamese relations. Diem either sidestepped the ambassador's questions or replied, "I will not give in." "Isn't there some one thing you may think of that is within your capabilities to do and that would favorably impress U.S. opinion[?]" Lodge asked finally. Diem gave the ambassador "a blank look and changed the subject."[1]

The encounter illustrates the clash of wills that, within days, led to Diem's overthrow and assassination. In a broader sense, it captures the key characteristic of a nine-year relationship replete with such episodes. At bottom, the Diem–Lodge exchange shows that the Vietnamese and the Americans simply did not understand one another, as was apparent from each man's reaction to their encounter. Diem thought the meeting was a success. Endless monologues were his preferred mode of communicating with the Americans, who, he believed, knew little about his regime or country. "At last," he observed after their meeting, "Mr. Lodge understands what I am trying to do." The latter's reaction was quite different, however. Lodge found the conversation "frustrating." He described Diem as "a nice, good man who [is] living a good life by his own lights," but also someone "who is cut off from the present, who is living in the past, who is truly indifferent to people as such and who is simply unbelievably stubborn."[2] The two partners were talking past, not to, one another. Although they were allies, their concerns and interests were far from identical.

thesis

*

    This book examines these differing perspectives and the way in which
they shaped the course of events in the period 1954–1963; it devotes particular attention to the policies of the Diem regime, which receive short shrift in
most historical accounts. Its thesis is that the conflict in U.S.–Vietnamese
relations represented a clash between visions of nation building and methods
of modernizing South Vietnam. Thus, it takes issue with the current literature's view of Diem, which generally portrays him as the "Last Confucian,"[3]
a dyed-in-the-wool reactionary, who stymied U.S. attempts to reform his
regime in order to preserve an old-fashioned autocracy. In fact, Diem held
his own ideas about the best way for South Vietnam to move ahead, conceptions that proved to be deeply flawed but that were nevertheless forward looking and, in their own way, thoroughly modern. His approach led to conflict
with Washington because the Americans harbored quite different ideas about
the most appropriate way to solve the south's problems. In short, Diem was a
modern nationalist, rather than a traditional mandarin, and it was his determination to push ahead with his own nation-building agenda that was a major
source of the tension in U.S.–Vietnamese relations.
    The current view of Diem as the reactionary mandarin is a long-standing
one that reflects the general neglect of the South Vietnamese side of the story
in the historiography of the Vietnam War.[4] Although much has been written
about the South Vietnamese president, most books look at the period 1954–
1963 from an American perspective, tracing the trials and tribulations of U.S.
policy. Thus, they deal with Diem's government as part of an episode in
American history, or an "American tragedy" as the title of one recent book
posits.[5] Relegated to the sidelines in this fashion, Diem often appears as more
of a two-dimensional, cardboard cutout than a real actor in the drama.
    Of course, there is a growing body of literature that does seek to put the
Vietnamese side of the story center stage, so that the country's people are no
longer treated merely as "passive bystanders in a historical process engineered
elsewhere."[6] Yet while these works do shed new light on the indigenous
dynamics of the conflict, they tend to concentrate on the war's eventual winners, the Vietnamese communists. The losers, the Diem government and its
successors, do not feature much in such accounts, except as bit-part players
in the story of the "communist road to power."[7]
    Consequently, our view of Diem remains underdeveloped and largely fixed
in time. It reflects the enduring influence of interpretations put forward in the
early histories of the conflict, many of them journalistic "first drafts of history" like those of David Halberstam, Joseph Buttinger, Frances FitzGerald,
and Stanley Karnow.[8] Certain abiding images that we associate with Diem
have also served to bolster the written word, especially the fiery suicide of the
Buddhist monk, Thich Quang Duc, which came to symbolize the political

and moral bankruptcy of the Saigon regime. These interpretations and images have helped set Diem's reputation in stone, establishing a portrait of his government that writers have seen little reason to reexamine. The Ngo family's "repressive ways are so well known that they need no discussion here," commented one historian as an explanation of the regime's character.[9] While no reasonable judge would wish to suggest that Diem's South Vietnam was a practicing democracy, his government's goals and methods deserve closer attention than such quick dismissals if we are to better understand the dimensions of the Vietnam conflict in this period.

To reexamine the Saigon regime, this book draws extensively on Vietnamese-language sources, including new materials from the Vietnamese archives, which provide us with a much fuller and richer picture, especially of some of Diem's major programs. In addition, the book is based on the copious quantities of primary materials that are now available in the English language. Although these sources frequently illuminate a side to the Diem regime at odds with the prevailing image, historians have passed rapidly over such evidence. Not only do their topical concerns generally lie elsewhere; they have also tended to treat the pronouncements of the Ngos as mere propaganda, or too confusing to be taken seriously. Yet this evidence reveals a good deal about the preoccupations of the Saigon government, if we reexamine it carefully and from a fresh perspective. In particular, we need to analyze the Diem regime on its own terms, and in the context of modern Vietnamese history, not just the history of U.S. foreign relations.

That said, this book is an attempt to further our understanding of Diem and his regime, not to turn a demon into a saint. Bernard Fall, the veteran observer of the Vietnam conflict, once noted that information about the South Vietnamese leader consisted "either of totally uncritical eulogy or of equally partisan condemnation."[10] In seeking to revise the current image of Diem, this study is certainly not an attempt to eulogize the former president, for his shortcomings are plain to see. While he was no hopeless reactionary, neither did he appear capable of building a nation south of the Seventeenth Parallel. He did articulate a vision of a modern Vietnam, but, as we shall see, his government encountered enormous problems in attempting to translate its ideas into practice. This failing was especially evident in the implementation of the Strategic Hamlet program, the last and most ambitious of the regime's nation-building schemes.

In turn, Diem's inability to knit together a strong state in South Vietnam precipitated the breakdown of relations between Saigon and Washington. The course of the U.S.–Vietnamese relationship was inextricably bound up with the progress of Diem's efforts at nation building, particularly in staving off a communist takeover. His lack of success in establishing an effective government and quelling a burgeoning communist challenge inevitably aggravated tensions with the United States, exposing the two partners' conflicting ideas about the type of policies that ought to be pursued in South Vietnam. Eventually, the Americans encouraged Diem's overthrow in an attempt to find a more effective and compliant client. As we now know, this move actually heralded a process of increasing U.S. intervention in Vietnamese affairs, for, if anything, South Vietnam's new leaders proved even less capable than their predecessor. By 1965, the Americans felt compelled to engage in a massive military escalation of the conflict in an attempt to save the south from collapse.

Diem's failings, then, decisively shaped the course of events in Vietnam. His overthrow represented the defeat of his government's efforts to promote a noncommunist and specifically Vietnamese program of nation building; one that would keep South Vietnam's U.S. ally at arm's length and establish a state capable of standing on its own two feet without the need for foreign backing. That defeat paved the way for the Americanization of the conflict because it was far more difficult for Washington to contemplate the loss of the south in 1964–1965 than it had been at the outset of the U.S.–Vietnamese relationship in 1954–1955. The following pages tell the story of Diem's failure, the prelude to America's war in Vietnam.

1

A Shotgun Wedding

Like all alliances, the U.S.–Diem relationship was a marriage of convenience, a partnership based on the fear of a common enemy. That enemy was the Viet Minh, the communist-led movement that had spearheaded the fight against French colonial rule. In May 1954, Viet Minh forces had finally brought the curtain down on the First Indochina War by overpowering the French garrison at Dien Bien Phu. The battle signaled the end of France's colonial adventure in Indochina, but the agreements at the Geneva Conference in July denied the Vietnamese communists the full fruits of victory by temporarily dividing Vietnam in two. It was into this political maelstrom that Diem stepped in the summer of 1954, returning from exile to take charge of what was left of the French-sponsored Associated State of Vietnam. The new premier looked to the United States to help prevent a Viet Minh takeover of the entire country, while U.S. officials looked to Diem to establish an anticommunist bastion south of the Seventeenth Parallel.[1]

Washington's decision to back Diem represented a desperate gamble. The chances of salvaging something from the wreckage of the French collapse appeared slim, even though the Geneva settlement's two-year deadline for unifying elections offered a little breathing space. Moreover, U.S. officials knew little about their prospective new client and were not wholly impressed with what they did know. In this sense, the U.S.–Diem relationship began with all the haste of a shotgun wedding.

Diem did not possess the popular profile of his chief rival, Ho Chi Minh, but he was a well-known figure among the Vietnamese elite.[2] Born in 1901, in central Vietnam, he came from a prominent Catholic and mandarin family. He was a driven man, energetic, puritanical, and intensely studious. Under the patronage of Nguyen Huu Bai, adviser to the court at Hue, he had risen rapidly within the colonial administration, becoming a provincial governor at the age of just twenty-eight. In 1932, this meteoric rise brought him to the attention of Emperor Bao Dai, newly returned from France and briefly consumed by a youthful enthusiasm for reform. Eager to shake up the mandarinate and establish a modern constitutional monarchy, Bao Dai brought Diem to Hue and in May 1933 catapulted him over more senior figures into the position of minister of the interior. Within months, however, Diem resigned. According to French reports, he accused the colonial power of violating the protectorate treaty of 1884 and blocking reforms. To remain at his post under these circumstances, Diem told Bao Dai, would be a "deplorable comedy." His resignation established an enduring reputation for stubborn integrity and uncompromising nationalism.[3]

This principled obstinacy would keep Diem from holding high office again for over twenty years. While he remained politically active, his aversion to compromise served to thwart his evident ambition. His ardent patriotism encouraged the Japanese to look elsewhere when they sought to form a compliant Vietnamese government at the tail end of the Second World War;[4] his vehement anticommunism led him to reject an offer to become part of Ho's fledgling administration in 1946;[5] and, after the outbreak of the First Indochina War, he refused to join an anticommunist government under Bao Dai, unless the French granted Vietnam the status of a dominion.[6] Like a man in a strobe light, Diem flickers in and out of the events of this period, appearing and disappearing as his political prospects alternately brightened and dimmed.

In 1950, Diem left Vietnam to begin a four-year-long, self-imposed exile. Not only was his name on a Viet Minh hit list, but he also lacked a proper platform for his brand of anticommunist nationalism. With the Viet Minh on one side and the French on the other, he observed, his opposition to both communism and collaboration left him in a political no-man's land.[7] Exile did not kill his ambition, however. Indeed, Diem found a far more receptive audience for his message outside the country, especially in political circles in the United States. He would spend over two years in America, living mainly at the Maryknoll Mission Society's seminaries in New York and New Jersey. From these retreats, he undertook trips to preach the cause of an anticommunist, nationalist alternative to the Viet Minh and the Franco–Bao Dai government; he also met with U.S. officials and created an impressive network of contacts among journalists, academics, politicians, and Catholic clergymen. Diem's "third way" was music to the ears of many Americans, who were not only hostile to the Viet Minh but also deeply troubled by U.S. support for French colonialism.[8]

There has been a good deal of speculation about the role that these American connections may have played in Diem's elevation in June 1954 to the premiership of the State of Vietnam. Some accounts argue that U.S. officials or Diem's American supporters prevailed on Bao Dai, the chief of state, to make the appointment. Others suggest that the former emperor or the French expected the State of Vietnam to collapse and chose Diem as the fall guy, a suspicion also entertained by the new premier himself. The most persuasive thesis is that Diem was not an American protégé, at least not in the sense of having being handpicked by the United States, but that his U.S. connections did loom large in Bao Dai's thinking when the latter came to choose a new prime minister.[9] As France's will to continue the war in Indochina collapsed in the spring of 1954, Bao Dai desperately sought to solicit U.S. support for his beleaguered state. To do so, he had to jettison his regime's discredited Francophile incumbents and find a viable alternative: a new government that might not only rally noncommunist nationalists but also pass muster with the Americans. Shortly after the fall of Dien Bien Phu, he began to inquire about the possibility of U.S. support and put forward Diem, who was now in Paris, as a potential candidate for premier.[10]

Diem must have appeared to Bao Dai as an obvious choice, although there was certainly no love lost between the two Vietnamese. The ex-emperor regarded Diem as too stubborn by half and possessing a wildly inflated opinion of his personal popularity; the ex-minister viewed Bao Dai as a man of weak and dissolute character, incapable of asserting real independence for Vietnam. "All Bao Dai's public life and previous conduct," Diem wrote in a paper sent to Justice William O. Douglas in July 1953, "only too clearly demonstrate that he has always willingly and consciously preferred subordination to France rather than dependence on his people."[11] Nevertheless, both men sought to suppress their distaste for one another. Diem had refused Bao Dai's offers of the premiership in the past, but this time he would be taking charge of a virtually independent country at what he described as a decisive moment in its history.[12] Bao Dai, meanwhile, needed a person with Diem's credentials: a committed anticommunist who was also untainted by collaboration with colonialism; a leader who could pick up the soiled banner of noncommunist nationalism and, at the same time, enlist U.S. backing to supplant the French.

Bao Dai had read the general drift of U.S. policy well. As Secretary of State John Foster Dulles told the U.S. delegation to the Geneva Conference: "If we are to take [an] active part in [the] Indochina war, we must work toward [the] rapid establishment of [an] authentic Vietnamese nationalist government." Yet Dulles made no mention of Diem at this time, outlining instead the potential role that Bao Dai might play in the future.[13] In addition, the U.S. response to the latter's overtures, including Diem's proposed elevation, was cautious and noncommittal. For one thing, the Americans were not entirely sure that Diem really represented Bao Dai's choice for premier because their point of contact with the former emperor was an interested party, Ngo Dinh Luyen, one of the candidate's brothers.[14] Following a recommendation from the U.S. delegation in Geneva, the American embassy in Paris organized a meeting with Diem on May 24. The purpose was to determine the premier-designate's views and the general lay of the land, however, not to pledge U.S. support.[15] The initiative for Diem's appointment remained Bao Dai's, although Washington may, in effect, have reassured him by not actively seeking to veto his choice. In short, Diem became premier by default rather than design on the part of the United States.

Of course, given his activities during the First Indochina War, this new standard-bearer of the anticommunist cause was not an entirely unfamiliar figure to the Americans. U.S. officials held decidedly mixed opinions, however, about Diem's fitness for office. On the one hand, they praised his nationalism, honesty, sincerity, and courage; they also reported that he possessed a modicum of personal prestige and political support among his fellow countrymen that could not be matched by other noncommunist Vietnamese. "There is no other man known to us or to [the] best French observers to replace, with any chance of success at this moment, Diem as head of government," concluded Donald R. Heath, the ambassador in Saigon, in July 1954.[16] In addition, and critical to the entire thrust of U.S. policy, Diem's staunch anticommunism meant that Washington need not fear some kind of rapprochement between the embattled State of Vietnam and the triumphant Viet Minh. This possibility was entertained by at least one of his rivals for the premiership, Buu Hoi, a cousin of Bao Dai's.[17]

At the same time, some of Diem's other qualities—his obstinacy, self-righteousness, and lack of experience—were a cause for concern among American officials. Heath stated that "there was some doubt, in view of his personal intransigence, whether he could organize and lead a governmental team." Robert McClintock, the Saigon embassy's chargé d'affaires, noted that Diem exhibited "a narrowness of view and of egotism which will make him a difficult man to deal with." He was a "messiah without a message," McClintock added. "His only formulated policy is to ask immediate American assistance in every form including refugee relief, training of troops and armed military intervention." Perhaps Douglas C. Dillon, the ambassador in Paris, best captured the ambivalence of U.S. officials in a report that followed his embassy's contacts with the budding premier in May 1954. He described Diem as a "yogi-like mystic," who impressed his American listeners "only because the standard set by his predecessors is so low."[18]

All these hopes and fears were about to be put to the sternest of tests. When Diem returned to Vietnam, he was a king without a kingdom; the northern half of the country was in the hands of the Viet Minh and the southern half in chaos. Colonel Edward Lansdale, the head of the CIA's Saigon Military Mission, found a lonely and isolated figure at his first meeting with the new leader in June 1954. Washington had ordered Lansdale to repeat in Vietnam the success he had achieved in the Philippines in helping to foster a viable nationalist alternative to communism. The colonel duly pitched up at the premier's palace the day after Diem arrived in Saigon in order to offer his services. He met no guards or reception, just a "few harried-looking people" wandering around the hallways. Told Diem was upstairs, he found a "middle-aged Vietnamese" in a small office and asked him where he could find the premier. "I am Ngo dinh Diem," the man replied.[19] This gap between Diem's formal status and actual situation persisted for much of his first year in power, his authority existing largely on paper and not extending much beyond the walls of his new residence. "Vietnam in those days," recalled Diem, "was as chaotic and shaky as France was at the time of Joan of Arc."[20]

Quite apart from the threat posed by the communists, there were a number of organizations that resisted Diem's efforts to establish his authority. The Binh Xuyen, Vietnam's answer to the *Cosa Nostra*, ran Saigon-Cholon's lucrative vice rackets and the city's police force; the politico-religious sects of the Cao Dai and Hoa Hao held sway over large parts of the countryside west of the capital as well as possessing sizable private armies. For these groups, the colonial order had brought financial rewards and a measure of political autonomy, so Diem's new order jeopardized a rather agreeable status quo.[21] To make matters worse, the new premier could not even count on the loyalty of his own army to rein in these challengers because General Nguyen Van Hinh, its chief of staff, repeatedly threatened to remove him.[22] Behind much of Hinh's politicking, as well as that of the other groups, lay the French and Bao Dai, who stirred the murky political waters in order to extract some advantage from their dwindling power and influence. Consequently, Diem found his authority hamstrung. The situation was "truly horrible," observed Wesley Fishel, a close confidant of the premier, assigned at that time to the United States Operations Mission (USOM) in Saigon. "I would say without hesitation that historians will rank the mess Diem inherited from his predecessors and the French with the worst since God knows when."[23]

Against the odds, Diem eventually brought a semblance of order out of this chaos. U.S. moral and monetary support proved invaluable in this regard as the noncommunist forces arrayed against him either chose to reconcile themselves to the emergence of the new, American-backed order, or lacked the wherewithal to resist it. Diem's success also stemmed from some of those personal characteristics that U.S. officials had identified earlier: his stubborn determination, sense of mission, and reluctance to compromise. He was not a politician, revealing a visceral aversion to the whole idea of political give-and-take. As he told Ambassador Heath, "he was 'no good at such negotiations.' He didn't like to make deals and 'to buy' support by concessions and favors." He left to others what deal making there was to be done, although he never really considered meeting his opponents halfway.[24] Instead, he sought to marginalize or defeat them, putting himself firmly in control by mid-1955. A few months later, in a thoroughly stage-managed referendum, he deposed Bao Dai as chief of state and assumed the presidency of the new Republic of Vietnam (RVN).

Diem's victory was a close-run thing, however, and the very qualities that helped him to triumph were a cause for deep concern among many Americans. His performance in the period 1954–1955 actually convinced a number of U.S. officials that he was simply not up to the job of building a new nation in southern Vietnam. Heath's cables from Saigon in the autumn of 1954 expressed increasing exasperation with the narrow base of Diem's government, the premier's inability to delegate authority, and his refusal to compromise politically with opponents. "Everyone in [the] Embassy is convinced," the ambassador reported in October, "that Diem cannot organize and administer [a] strong government."[25]

General J. Lawton Collins took up the same charge soon after assuming the post of President Eisenhower's special representative in Vietnam in November 1954. Collins formulated a seven-point program to help bolster the premier's position, including the creation of a broadly based and representative government. By April 1955, however, the general concluded that Diem was a lost cause and recommended that Washington look for alternative leadership: "During the five months that I have been here I have come to admire Diem greatly in many ways. He has valuable spiritual qualities, is incorruptible, is a devoted Nationalist, has great tenacity. However, these very qualities, linked with his lack of practical political sense, his inability to compromise, his inherent incapacity to get along with other able men, and his tendency to be suspicious of the motives of anyone who disagrees with him, make him practically incapable of holding this government together."[26]

Washington was reluctant to accept Collins's recommendation. Dulles, backed by Eisenhower, believed that much of the blame for the chaos in the south rested with the failure of the departing French to provide the new Vietnamese government with adequate support. While acknowledging Diem's shortcomings, moreover, Dulles argued that no other leader could garner comparable support within Vietnam or the United States Congress.[27] Nevertheless, Collins stuck to his guns and his advice carried great weight in Washington. Consequently, the wheels of a change in policy were already in motion when Diem won a dramatic reprieve with a military victory over the Binh Xuyen at the end of April 1955.[28]

The premier's eleventh-hour success in consolidating his authority transformed both his political position and reputation. "Overnight, in the eyes of most American officials and much of the U.S. press," commented one historian, "Diem was metamorphosed from a stubborn, narrow, politically maladroit failure into a wise and clever hero." So was born the legend of the "tough miracle man of Asia."[29] Dulles informed Collins on May 1 that the premier's triumph over the Binh Xuyen ruled out any plans to replace him. "For us at this time to participate in a scheme to remove Diem," he stated, "would not only be domestically impractical but highly detrimental [to] our prestige in Asia." Dulles's stance represented the "point of no return" in the U.S.–Vietnamese relationship; the moment when the United States pledged itself to backing the Diem government.[30]

This commitment tended to lock Washington into the defense of the south. With it went the opportunity for U.S. policy makers to blame the situation in Vietnam on French colonialism and wash their hands of the whole sorry mess. From this point on, successive presidents believed that U.S. honor and credibility was at stake there and found it increasingly difficult to contemplate a diplomatic withdrawal.[31] Yet America's relationship with Diem was evidently conceived in doubt. The events of 1954–1955 demonstrated that the U.S. interest in preserving an anticommunist South Vietnam was not necessarily synonymous with unqualified support for Diem's leadership. The policy debate in this period had revolved around the question of whether the United States could achieve its goals with Diem at the helm; some U.S. officials thought it could, while others did not. U.S. support for his leadership, therefore, evidently depended on his ability to satisfy Washington's concerns. Like a prisoner on probation, his future rested on his good conduct, as defined by his new superpower patron.

The contingent quality of American backing for Diem was thus clear from the very beginning of the U.S.–Vietnamese relationship, years before the United States connived in his overthrow. Eisenhower had made the basic quid pro quo explicit in his first letter to the Vietnamese premier in October 1954. The president stated that Diem could count on U.S. assistance "provided that your Government is prepared to give assurances as to the standards of performance it would be able to maintain in the event such aid were supplied."[32] Implicit in this offer was the threat to withdraw U.S. support if he proved incapable of meeting the required "standards of performance." Dulles took the logic of the patron–client relationship one step further in a press conference in May 1955, when he noted that, as long as Diem appeared to fit the bill, "we don't seem to see any particular reason to throw him out." In other words, the new premier would do for now, providing he came up with the goods and in the absence of someone more suitable.[33]

Henry Cabot Lodge, the last U.S. ambassador to Diem's Vietnam, argued that the quid pro quo is a perfectly normal feature of alliance diplomacy. "I think we have an absolute right frankly to use legitimate pressure and influence as part of a bargain with another government," he observed, "just as they have a right to bargain with us. When people accept our help, we have a right to make stipulations if we want to. The other party doesn't have to accept them. In conducting our foreign relations, we have our own purposes, of course. The recipient government must decide whether our purposes and theirs coincide."[34] Lodge's generalities, however, raised more questions than they answered when it came to the particulars of the U.S.–Vietnamese relationship. What, for example, constituted legitimate U.S. pressure on the Diem government if the latter refused American demands? When did such pressure begin to infringe on Vietnamese sovereignty and independence? Did a patron ultimately have the right to seek the removal of a recalcitrant client? At what point, in short, did the actions of a patron toward a client cross over the line that separated advice and support from unwarranted intervention and a thinly disguised neocolonialism?[35]

Such questions proved deeply troubling to many Americans. On the one hand, they had no desire to exercise the kind of colonial control over the Vietnamese so recently relinquished by the French, nor did they want to be seen to be pushing around a newly independent nation. On the other hand, they found it difficult to maintain a hands–off approach because Diem not only repeatedly rejected their advice but also pursued policies that many Americans saw as a threat to the very survival of an anticommunist South Vietnam, the sine qua non of U.S. policy. U.S. officials appreciated that the need to work through an indigenous government placed limits on their influence in Vietnam. Yet how could they afford to adhere to traditional American principles—anticolonialism, self–determination, nonintervention—in the case of a client whose policies threatened to increase his vulnerability to a communist takeover?

This dilemma proved inescapable. The early criticisms of Diem made by Collins and others were merely a dress rehearsal for the charges that Americans would level at his regime until events finally came to a head in 1963. After consolidating his position, Diem proceeded to adopt policies that Washington found increasingly worrisome. In particular, U.S. officials fretted about his efforts to concentrate power, which undermined popular support for his regime and appeared to preclude the development of any real political freedom in South Vietnam. Although Diem's government exhibited all the outward trappings of a republic, it was certainly no advert for liberal democracy. One American observer described the RVN's political system as "an executive–authoritarian model qualified by certain democratic features." Saigon wits were less diplomatic; they labeled it a "Diemocracy," one–man rule behind a democratic facade.[36]

Diem's intention to play the key role in shaping the nation's future was evident, in formal terms, in the RVN's constitution that was promulgated in October 1956. This provided for a powerful presidency rather than a parliamentary system, which limited the autonomy of executive departments and the other branches of government. As Daniel Anderson, counselor at the U.S. embassy, observed, the presidency would exercise "virtually unhindered predominance in the management of national affairs." Moreover, while the document contained "most of those basic freedoms that have come to be accepted in western democracies," it also specifically enumerated the "police power reservations" that placed limits on these civil rights. Anderson likened parts of the new constitution to the 1946 Democratic Republic of Vietnam's, noting that several members of the drafting committee had also participated in the drawing up of that earlier charter. The resulting political framework, he concluded, was "a fairly realistic though somewhat unflattering self-portrait of the present regime."[37]

The constitution did lay the foundations for democratic development in South Vietnam, but the president appeared unwilling to build on them. Such was the fate of the RVN's National Assembly. Elections for a constituent assembly were first held in March 1956. Although the return of an overwhelmingly pro-Diem body may not have involved the actual stuffing of ballot boxes—indeed, there were several surprise victories for independents—the elections violated a number of normal democratic conventions.[38] U.S. officials were inclined to reserve judgment on the question of what all this portended for the future. In fact, the events of 1956 set the standard, as became evident in the succeeding election of 1959.[39] Not surprisingly, the legislature that emerged from this kind of electoral process tended to be of the rubber stamp variety. "Never has it rejected or seriously changed any legislation the Presidency asked for," commented Robert Scigliano, formerly of the Michigan State University Vietnam Advisory Group, "and never has it originated important legislation on its own initiative."[40]

Diem's determination to exercise strong leadership was also mirrored in his efforts to reorganize local administration and establish the writ of the central government down to the village level. The 1956 constitution did not deal with provincial arrangements, which Diem was in the process of changing by executive fiat. Shortly after coming to power, he had moved to centralize authority and limit local autonomy by abolishing the powerful regional governorships that had existed under Bao Dai, replacing them with regional delegates who possessed greatly reduced powers. Government directives in 1956 established the province chiefs, who would be appointed by the president, as the main representatives of the central government. These officials also exercised greater control over local administration; for example, they would be

responsible for appointing village councils, which was a reversal of a tradition of grassroots autonomy that dated back to the fifteenth century.[41]

The regime sought in other ways as well to bridge the gap that traditionally separated rural Vietnamese from their rulers. It organized "mutual-aid
family groups," the linking of several households into administrative units,
in order to improve security, the transmission of government policy, and communal solidarity.[42] Saigon also created a series of mass movements or parties
to extend its political reach. Several organizations spearheaded this drive during the first years of the regime, notably the National Revolutionary Movement and the Citizens Group. These associations enrolled hundreds of
thousands of people in their various branches—in fact, most of the population in those areas of the country where they were most fully developed. They
engaged in numerous propaganda activities, mobilized workers and peasants
for public works projects, and sought to root out alleged subversive elements
among the population.[43] Their purpose was to create the political tissue that
would connect the new government in Saigon with the farthest-flung corners of the new southern state.

As critics frequently pointed out, such mass movements were more reminiscent of politics in a people's republic than a democracy; they were cre-
ations of the state rather than reflections of the popular will. Behind them,
moreover, in imitation of the "front" strategy employed by the communists,
lay the Revolutionary Personalist Workers' Party *(Can Lao Nhan Vi Cach
Mang Dang)*, the Diem regime's copy of a Leninist vanguard. Like its communist counterpart, the Can Lao was a semicovert party complete with
"cadres" and cell structures, which numbered about sixteen thousand members according to a report by the U.S. embassy in 1959. Its role was to infiltrate the upper echelons of the regime's other political organizations, so as to
control and direct them on behalf of the government. As one U.S. diplomat
reported, the party was "an elite steering group composed of members, frequently the officers, of the other political or quasi-political groups." Since
most Can Lao personnel held positions within the regular organs of the state,
both civil and military, the party also provided the ever-suspicious Ngo family with a network of informers to keep watch within its own administration.[44]

These arrangements effectively created a "state within a state," a shadow
regime that operated behind the visible political architecture of the new republic. Nguyen Thai, the former editor of the *Vietnam Press*, called this phenomenon the "invisible family government," because the figures wielding
most power within it were members of the Ngo clan, who exercised a degree
of influence out of all proportion to their official positions.[45] That the president should rely so heavily on his kin is not particularly surprising. Both the
traditions of court intrigue and, more recently, the internecine nature of anti-

colonial politics positively encouraged the suspicion of others. Loyalty and trust, therefore, were valuable commodities. Diem filled the key posts in his new regime with people known to him personally, or those who had already demonstrated support for his cause—figures such as Nguyen Huu Chau, Tran Chanh Thanh, Tran Kim Tuyen, Tran Quoc Buu, Tran Van Do, and Vo Van Hai. He would place most faith and power, however, in the hands of his immediate family, especially his band of brothers.[46]

Diem had four surviving brothers; the fifth and eldest, Ngo Dinh Khoi, was murdered by the Viet Minh in 1945.[47] Two of them, Ngo Dinh Luyen and Ngo Dinh Thuc, generally wielded power on the margins. Luyen was the youngest and the least influential. Although he had played a prominent part in Diem's accession to power, his influence waned rapidly thereafter. His diplomatic "exile"—he served as the RVN's ambassador to several European states—perhaps reflected the rest of the family's distaste for Luyen's more liberal political ideas.[48] Ngo Dinh Thuc was the eldest, the bishop of Vinh Long, and a rising star in the Catholic Church. His official position distanced him from the day-to-day running of the regime, but also enabled him to serve as a mediator in its internal squabbles as well as a conduit for its more moderate critics. On those occasions when he chose to use it, his voice carried great weight with the president. Diem was indebted to Thuc for the latter's support during his years in the political wilderness; he also showed the bishop the deference that was due to an older brother.[49]

Diem's other two siblings, Ngo Dinh Can and Ngo Dinh Nhu, were the regime's real political heavyweights. The former was the custodian of the Ngo family residence in Hue and the political boss of central South Vietnam, controlling affairs from Ninh Thuan province northwards to Quang Tri on the Seventeenth Parallel.[50] For the brutal fashion in which he dealt with the regime's political opponents—communist and noncommunist alike—Can earned the pejorative title of "Lord of the Manor," and he did run the center like a fiefdom; he filled the government posts in the region with his protégés and nothing could be done there without his support. Yet Can also remained something of an enigma. Apart from a virulent anticommunism—much of it apparently a consequence of his eldest brother's murder in 1945—his political ideas were vague and undefined. He was reputedly a xenophobe and certainly much less cosmopolitan than his other brothers; he dressed in traditional clothes, chewed betel, and was something of a recluse. Robert Barbour, the U.S. consul in Hue, who finally met the elusive Can after several unsuccessful attempts, described him as a "mysterious *eminence grise* [power behind the throne]."[51]

In a sense, Can's parochialism was the secret of his success. While his brothers had flown the family nest, he remained in Hue, taking care of the family's property and its matriarch, Mrs. Ngo Dinh Kha. From this base, he developed a network of supporters, many of them Catholics, to promote the exiled Diem's political aspirations. He proved an adept organizer, creating a political movement that, in 1954, provided the embattled new premier with a measure of support in areas distant from Saigon. Can subsequently extended his authority through the expansion of the new government's mass movements and the influence of the Can Lao.[52] By controlling the regional branches of these organizations, he was able to run a tight ship in central Vietnam. At the same time, his local autonomy, which ran counter to the regime's general efforts to centralize power, created some tension between Hue and Saigon over questions of political jurisdiction and patronage. This fractured the unity of organizations like the Can Lao, a problem exacerbated by the sibling rivalry that existed between Can and the president's right-hand man, Ngo Dinh Nhu.[53]

Nhu's official title was "Political Counselor" to the president. In fact, as Robert McClintock concluded at the end of June 1954, he "quite evidently serves as an informal co–Prime Minister."[54] Like Can, Nhu's influence stemmed in part from the active role he had played in Diem's rise to power. In the early 1950s, he had promoted his brother's cause among Vietnamese intellectuals, publishing a monthly journal, *Xa-Hoi*, which echoed Diem's call for a "third way" between communism and colonialism. He had also dabbled in political organization, allying himself with Tran Quoc Buu's trade union movement as well as establishing an embryonic party that would become the Can Lao. As the roof began to cave in on French colonialism in 1953–1954, Nhu organized these political forces to lobby on Diem's behalf. Consequently, when Diem returned to Vietnam as premier, he naturally looked to Nhu for assistance, both to reward these efforts and draw on the latter's knowledge of the political scene. In addition, Diem's respect for Nhu's educational credentials—he was a graduate of France's Ecole de Chartres—served to enhance his brother's reputation in the eyes of the premier. The counselor's standing as the family's intellectual and the regime's "ideas" man helped to make him the most influential of Diem's siblings.[55]

The source of Nhu's influence was also institutional. As the regime's intelligence and security chief, he drew on the resources of the Service for Political and Social Research, an office housed in the presidential palace and headed by Tran Kim Tuyen, a northern Catholic and Nhu's former private secretary. Despite its innocuous sounding title, the service was the nerve center of the regime's informal political apparatus, through which Nhu could direct the activities of the RVN's extragovernmental organizations. The service, noted a former palace insider, provided Nhu with "the miniature *real* government which guides, directs, supervises and controls the *official* government appointed by Ngo-dinh Diem." It also enabled him, through the use of its biographical files, to influence Diem's choice of appointments to official positions. By exploiting all these powers, Nhu made himself indispensable; he was the premier's eyes and ears, his chief source of intelligence, and his hatchet man. He used his position to monopolize political access to the president, isolating his brother from alternative sources of advice and information. Ultimately, remarked the journalist Robert Shaplen, the counselor would become the regime's Rasputin.[56]

No discussion of Nhu would be complete without mention of his equally notorious wife, Tran Le Xuan, more commonly referred to as Madame Nhu; Shaplen described her as a combination of Eleanor Roosevelt and Marie Antoinette, politically prominent but self-destructive.[57] She was the palace's first lady, serving as the bachelor president's official hostess, and held a seat in the 123-member National Assembly. She was also the self-appointed standard-bearer for Vietnamese women, presiding each year over a celebration of the Trung Sisters, the Vietnamese heroines who had led an unsuccessful revolt against Chinese rule in the first century A.D.[58] Like other members of the Ngo family, Madame Nhu possessed a degree of influence that far exceeded her official positions because she could exploit the regime's "invisible family government" to promote her interests. She was quick to do so. As the U.S. embassy's John Mecklin recalled, she "simply issued orders, often on impulse by telephone, on virtually any subject to virtually anyone she wanted, from ministers and generals on down."[59]

Madame Nhu fulfilled with a vengeance Lord Acton's axiom about the corrosive qualities of power. Of all the members of the Ngo family, noted journalist David Halberstam, she was the only one who seemed to enjoy her political position and the exercise of power.[60] Her megalomania and shocking public outbursts, most notably her reference to the Buddhist self-immolations of 1963 as "barbecues," acted as a lightning rod for the government's critics, foreign and domestic. Diem, who did not entirely approve of his sister-in-law, was not party to some of her activities; he also appeared reluctant to restrain some of those of which he was aware, even as Madame Nhu wrought increasing damage on the government's reputation.[61] "The help she gave the failing Diem regime," Joseph Buttinger later observed, "was the help rendered a drowning man by a rock tied to his neck."[62] Last but not least in the regime's cast of characters, Madame Nhu came to symbolize what a growing number of Americans judged to be an unstable, perhaps irredeemable, family despotism.

Despite the warnings of Collins and other U.S. officials, however, that judgment of the regime's character lay in the future. At the outset of its relationship with Saigon, the Eisenhower administration suppressed any lingering doubts about Diem's political style. Washington sought to give the new Vietnamese premier some room for maneuver and operate a hands-off approach toward his regime. As Dulles reported to Eisenhower in May 1955: "The French seemed to think that all we need to do is to crack the whip. I keep emphasizing that if that is the case, then the situation would be hopeless because he could never gain the confidence of his own people." Washington could not dictate to Diem, the secretary of state told French officials, because he would not listen and, moreover, any "man who would blindly accept U.S. bidding would not be worth supporting."[63] In addition, the Eisenhower administration wanted to see Diem establish a strong state in South Vietnam, to which end it was prepared to tolerate the regime's authoritarian practices.

As one scholar has argued, Republican policy makers have often shown more willingness than their Democratic counterparts to accept the less-than-democratic character of client states. This is not due to any lack of attachment to American ideals, but because, when faced with the possibility of radical unrest or communist subversion, they have generally assigned priority to the values of order and stability over democracy. Republicans have sought to "bolster" client regimes, preferring strong governments that could maintain control; Democrats have tended to try to "reform" them, calling for a variety of democratically oriented changes that would address the causes of political unrest.[64] The "bolstering" approach certainly prevailed in the early years of the U.S.–Vietnamese relationship. The development of "strong stable executive leadership in Vietnam should have priority," Dulles informed Frederick Reinhardt, U.S. ambassador to South Vietnam, in October 1955. "Such representative and constitutional processes should be developed to [the] extent that they do not weaken central authority." According to Edward Lansdale, U.S. officials even encouraged the growth of the Can Lao because it would buttress the new regime. After all, Reinhardt recalled, Diem was trying to forge a new state in extraordinarily difficult circumstances, not "running a Jeffersonian democracy."[65]

By 1960, however, even the Eisenhower administration would find it difficult to stick to a policy that increasingly appeared to be "bolstering" failure in South Vietnam. The rekindling of the communist insurgency revived the doubts about Diem's leadership that U.S. officials had first expressed in the period 1954–1955; indeed, in the dying days of the Republican presidency, Elbridge Durbrow, Reinhardt's successor as ambassador, resurrected the issue of finding a suitable replacement for Diem.[66] While Washington would again shy away from this option, the question of the Vietnamese premier's leadership never stayed far from the surface of U.S. policy debates after John F. Kennedy entered office in 1961. The United States had helped to establish Diem in power in 1954 in order to build an anticommunist state in South Vietnam; and it was prepared to remove him to prevent the failure of that project.

There could be no more vivid demonstration of the qualified nature of Washington's commitment to Diem than this readiness to contemplate removing him from power. At the same time, the willingness to resort to this ultimate sanction reveals a good deal about the biases and prejudices that shaped the evolution of American policy. Diem's failings were legion and manifest, but Washington's view of them tells us as much about the attitudes of U.S. policy makers as it does about the weaknesses of the Saigon regime. The U.S.– Vietnamese relationship was neither a colonial one nor an alliance of equals, yet the Americans frequently behaved in a manner more akin to the former than the latter. Although they would indignantly reject the comparison, there were striking similarities between the views of U.S. officials and those held by the recently departed French. Both denigrated the capabilities of the Vietnamese and both believed they knew what was best for their charges.

Stereotypes of Vietnamese incapacity, and a corresponding assumption of American superiority, pervaded official U.S. thinking in the 1950s and 1960s. Policy makers imagined the Vietnamese to be people who were innately incapable and badly in need of U.S. tutelage. "Americans did tend to regard Vietnam," observed Arthur Schlesinger, Jr., an adviser to the Kennedy White House, "as a 'young and unsophisticated' nation, populated by affable little men, unaccustomed to the modern world, who, if sufficiently bucked up by instruction and encouragement, might amount to something." Like a frustrated adult instructing a wayward child, Washington saw itself as helping to guide people that appeared to be hopelessly or willfully negligent.[67]

Such paternalism, so reminiscent of the colonial mentality, was nourished by America's own imperial experiences. "The need for enlightened tutelage," a historian has noted, "was a lasting lesson which American officials had learned from their Philippine encounter." Certainly, this attitude was not confined to U.S. views of the Vietnamese. As Americans watched the great changes transforming the southern half of the globe after 1945, they displayed a generally low opinion of the capacity of developing states for self-government as well as a corresponding insensitivity toward Third World nationalism. In China, for example, as one scholar explains, negative U.S. images of Chiang Kai-shek, another of America's East Asian clients, fed off the "well entrenched conviction that 'native' leaders were not equal to the challenges of the modern world."[68] Yet perhaps such prejudices exercised even greater influence in the case of Vietnam because of Diem's absolute dependence on American support. Carved out of the ruins of the French defeat in Indochina, the Republic of Vietnam would not have existed or continued to survive without U.S. backing. This basic feature of the patron–client relationship increased Washington's sense of proprietary interest in the Ngos as well as its exasperation at their failure, as one presidential adviser put it, "to do things they ought to do but don't want to do."[69]

The companion to this impatient condescension was the faith that Americans held in their own recipes for nation building in Vietnam. Unconsciously or otherwise, U.S. officials approached the problems of insurgency and development with a set of preconceived ideas and policy prescriptions that reflected their confidence in American goals and values. "You should know one thing at the beginning," Edward Lansdale informed readers in the introduction to his memoir. "I took my American beliefs with me into these Asian struggles, as Tom Paine would have done."[70] This faith in America's mission, and the universal applicability of its values, found easy expression in the country's rise to globalism after 1945. "Americans who wanted to bring the blessings of democracy, capitalism, and stability to everyone," commented one historian, "meant just what they said—the whole world, in their view, should be a reflection of the United States."[71] When it came to the Third World, such images of the nation's Manifest Destiny provided the ideological glue for an updated version of the old colonial "civilizing mission."

American conceptions of political change in the Third World drew deeply on a series of culturally conditioned assumptions. Harking back to their own country's experiences of revolution and nation building, Americans expected that the process of postcolonial development would be a relatively easy, painless, and orderly transition, in which societies moved with reasonable dispatch from a state of "backwardness" toward "modernity." The U.S. role in this scheme of things was to oversee the transition; to provide the advice and support that would overcome poverty and desperation, silencing the siren calls of communism that threatened to derail the "natural" process of change. The end result would be the establishment of societies that, in their essential economic and political features, resembled the United States: modern capitalist democracies, pro-American and anticommunist. Even when confronted by the failure of most developing states to conform to these rosy assumptions, U.S. officials could not shake off the powerful hold that such expectations exercised over their thinking.[72]

Theories from the social sciences helped to articulate and buttress policy makers' assumptions, as they did across a whole range of public policy issues in the early postwar period. "The liberalism of the 1950s and 1960s," remarked Godfrey Hodgson, "saw political action as almost the executive arm of social science."[73] Walt Rostow personified this connection between academic theory and policy practice by moving from Boston's MIT to the

Kennedy White House. According to Rostow and other gurus of "modernization" theory, underdeveloped states went through a natural transition from being "traditional" to becoming "modern" societies. Communist insurgents, meanwhile, sought to take advantage of the stresses and strains that accompanied this process in an attempt to hijack it for their own diabolical ends. Thus, it was America's duty to step into the breach and help guide the Third World along the road to a bright and modern, American-style future. "Modern societies must be built, and we are prepared to help build them," Rostow asserted, with the expectation that developing states would "choose their own version of what we would recognize as a democratic, open society."[74]

In their role as the managers of change, the Americans expected Diem to adopt the kind of policies that they believed would promote this preferred path to modernity. Several caveats are in order before we elucidate these U.S. policy prescriptions. First, as the debate between the "bolstering" and "reforming" of clients suggests, U.S. policy makers were prepared, at least in the short term, to countenance regimes that diverged from the democratic ideal if that promised to stave off the prospect of communist revolution. During the Cold War, successive U.S. administrations supported an array of authoritarian governments that ignored the niceties of democratic politics but proved tough on communism. "With few exceptions," noted Robert Packenham, a former official of the Agency for International Development (AID), "the United States has supported liberal, constitutional forces or governments where 'possible,' and authoritarian, anti-Communist ones where 'necessary.' "[75] President Kennedy best expressed this calculation in his assessment of the political unrest in the Dominican Republic in 1961. Washington had three choices, he stated, in descending order of preference: a democratic government, the maintenance of the incumbent dictatorship, or a Castro regime. "We ought to aim at the first," Kennedy argued, "but we really can't renounce the second until we are sure that we can avoid the third."[76]

The second caveat is that the direction of U.S. policy was never simply a matter of either "bolstering" or "reforming" a client government, for, at any particular moment in time, there were bureaucratic divisions over which of these approaches should receive priority. American policy in Vietnam was often a product of the conflicting concerns of the various agencies that contributed to it, each with its own organizational imperatives.[77] These differing bureaucratic interests became especially evident as progress in South Vietnam stalled in the latter part of the 1950s. For example, Ambassador Durbrow's end-of-year report to Washington in 1957 expressed the belief that Diem needed to do more to broaden his political appeal; General Samuel T. Williams, chief of the U.S. Military Assistance Advisory Group (MAAG), refused to endorse this recommendation, arguing that security considerations should take priority over political reforms.[78] By 1960, such conflicting perspectives clearly divided many policy makers in Washington as well as in the field.[79]

Notwithstanding these caveats, there was an underlying theme, or cumulative thrust, to American policy in Vietnam. At bottom, U.S. officials wanted to divert Diem from what they increasingly regarded as his *excessive* concentration of power, not only in the central government but also within the walls of the presidential palace itself. This goal was one to which almost all Americans could in general subscribe, however much they might disagree over the particular priorities of policy. The devolution of power fitted the democratic model that represented the ultimate ideal; it also promised to promote administrative efficiency and boost the regime's political appeal, which were Washington's more immediate aims.

Even during the most indulgent phase of the U.S.–Vietnamese relationship, American officials wanted Diem's government not only to establish order but also to gradually move in a liberal direction. U.S. officials actually saw these two elements as intertwined. As Ambassador Reinhardt noted in December 1955, the goals of democratization and political stability were not mutually exclusive, for a "certain minimum degree of liberty is probably a necessary ingredient for developing strong popular support [for the government], without which no lasting stability can be achieved."[80] For the Americans, the emerging problem in South Vietnam was not so much Diem's dictatorial tendencies as his suffocating and self-defeating brand of authoritarianism, which reduced the regime's effectiveness as well as the prospects for achieving long-term stability.

U.S. proposals to remedy this shortcoming focused on a series of related concerns. First, American officials wanted to improve the administrative performance of the Saigon regime, both on the battlefield and in the delivery of government services. Diem's system of administration can only be described as dysfunctional. For one thing, the president was a slow and cautious decision maker, so the concentration of power at the center resulted in unresponsive and sluggish government. Diem compounded the problem by interfering in routine matters of state and overriding the authority of subordinates; other members of the "invisible family government" issued orders as well, sometimes of a competing and contradictory nature, without any respect for formal chains of command. The result of all this was a confused and chaotic government, prone to administrative paralysis; and uncertain, demoralized officials, who spent their time attempting to divine the desires of their masters rather than seeing to the affairs of state.[81] The Americans deplored this situation, pressing the palace to delegate more authority and straighten out its administrative procedures. Walt Rostow argued that the key to the effective administration of South Vietnam lay in devolving power to a new generation of "modernizing students, technicians, and soldiers."[82]

The desire to tap the talents of these groups, and simultaneously generate popular backing for the government, was also evident in U.S. calls for liberalization, or "broadening the base" of the Saigon regime. U.S. officials wanted Diem to breathe some real democratic life into his "Diemocracy" by such measures as upholding a free press, encouraging a more positive role for the national legislature, and bringing opposition figures into the cabinet. Although the Americans appreciated Diem's need for strong government, they argued that his brand of authoritarianism was inherently unstable; it isolated the palace from reality, encouraged political and financial corruption, and threatened to strangle any nascent moves toward democracy. Above all, U.S. officials worried about the impact of Diem's autocracy on the south's intellectual and professional classes, the elite to which the Americans looked to manage the modernization of the country. Members of that elite, such as Truong Nhu Tang and Bui Diem, have argued that Diem's politics of exclusion blew a real opportunity after the Geneva Conference to rally patriotic sentiment behind a southern government. Instead, and to the chagrin of the Americans, the south's best and brightest drifted into an unhelpful passivity, threw their energies into sniping at the regime, or even joined the communists.[83]

Finally, the Americans wanted Diem to do more to satisfy the "rising expectations" of the rural masses. This concern would grow as the security situation in the countryside deteriorated, but even in the late 1950s American officials recognized the issue's importance. While much of his attention focused on politics at the elite level, Ambassador Durbrow repeatedly emphasized that broad backing for Diem ultimately depended on his ability to improve the popular welfare through social and economic development. "Progress, which is demanded in Viet Nam as throughout Asia, is perhaps the touchstone of the regime's enduring viability," he stated in December 1957. If Diem would devote more attention to bettering the lot of his country's population, argued the ambassador, economic and social progress would create stability, counter the appeal of communism, and promote democracy.[84]

Taken together, these proposals represented the American solution for South Vietnam's problems, the prescriptions that U.S. officials expected Diem to heed in return for their advice and support. Yet it was at this point that U.S. plans for nation building in South Vietnam ran into difficulties, for Diem proved to be a notoriously uncooperative ally. Far from playing the part of a grateful supplicant, the Ngos deeply resented their dependence on the United States and their treatment at Washington's hands. They were staunch nationalists, who were determined to assert their sovereign rights; they doubted the wisdom and steadfastness of the Americans; and they possessed their own vision of nation building, which diverged in significant respects from the route to modernity favored by the United States. The shotgun wedding between Saigon and Washington set the stage for an extraordinarily stormy relationship. As John Mecklin remarked, "There probably had never before in American foreign affairs been a phenomenon comparable to our relations with the Ngo Dinh family. It was like dealing with a whole platoon of de Gaulles."[85]

2

The Ngos, Nationalism,
and Nation Building

Saigon's view of the U.S.–Vietnamese relationship was, in many ways, a mirror image of Washington's. The Americans needed the Diem regime to hold the line in Southeast Asia but viewed their client with a distinctly jaundiced eye; for their part, the Ngos regarded the United States as an indispensable but far from ideal patron. U.S. officials expected the regime to govern South Vietnam according to certain precepts and to accept their advice in return for U.S. assistance; the palace believed that it knew what was good for the country and certainly had no intention of bowing, or being seen to bow, to American demands. Coming from quite different worlds, the Americans and Vietnamese did not view events in the same way or agree about the best way forward for South Vietnam. Ngo Dinh Nhu simply described the U.S.–Vietnamese relationship as a "clash of civilisations."[1]

At the heart of this clash lay the patriotic sensibilities of the Ngos. Perhaps there was no Third World client that found its dependence on a foreign patron quite as insufferable as did the Diem regime. The palace's incumbents came from a culture that was steeped in a tradition of resistance to outside control, which the Vietnamese traced back two thousand years to their first revolts against Chinese rule. That tradition, and its latent xenophobia, was one of the defining characteristics of Vietnamese nationalism.[2] "Diem and others," observed Ambassador Elbridge Durbrow, "do not basically trust most foreigners." As Nhu told foreign dignitaries at a diplomatic reception in 1963: "There exists in the Vietnamese people a sensitivity about sovereignty and a mistrust not only of the Chinese but of all occupants and colonizers, all!" Nhu's thinly veiled reference to the regime's U.S. ally was not lost on his listeners.[3]

   The circumstances that surrounded the winning of Vietnamese independence only served to sharpen this prickly patriotism. While they appreciated the need for U.S. support, the presence of the Americans in Vietnam, so soon after the departure of the French, embarrassed and irritated the Ngos. Like the leaders of other states emerging from the shadows of colonial rule, they were jealous of their country's newly won independence and very sensitive to any real or perceived infringements of its sovereignty. They disliked their reliance on foreign support and resented U.S. efforts to tell them what to do. "If you order Vietnam around like a puppet on a string," Diem once asked journalist Marguerite Higgins, "how will you be different—except in degree—from the French?"[4]

Diem's concern was not only a matter of salving injured pride; he believed that his government's survival depended on his ability to assert its independence and convince his compatriots of its nationalist credentials. His reading of the fate of the "Bao Dai solution" made clear the perils of being branded as a collaborator. He had argued during the First Indochina War that Bao Dai's collaboration with the colonial power fatally compromised the cause of noncommunist nationalism, while France's stubborn refusal to admit defeat enabled the Vietnamese communists to strengthen their hold over the anticolonial movement. "The bulk of the [anticolonial] opposition, which Ho Chi Minh and his followers maneuver to lead," he told an audience at Cornell University in February 1953, "comes from people deeply and sincerely anticommunist." If the communists had been unable to agitate on the nationalist issue, he reasoned, they would never have succeeded in generating a popular base of support.[5] Bao Dai's failure to escape the clutches of the French, and the taint of treason, offered an object lesson to the Ngos: too close an association with an outside power would play into the hands of their communist rivals.

This lesson could not be ignored after 1954, for the political geography of postcolonial Vietnam inevitably raised questions about the legitimacy of Diem's government. By temporarily dividing the country at the Seventeenth Parallel, the framers of the Geneva accords brought one Indochina war to a close but laid the foundations for a second, leaving communist and noncommunist Vietnamese to settle the question of who was to lead an independent Vietnam. "Now we must face up to the situation," announced Tran Van Do, the head of the State of Vietnam's delegation, upon his return from Geneva. "The competition begins between the South and the North."[6] When Diem subsequently refused to support nationwide elections, scheduled for 1956, he scuppered any chance of peaceful reunification and turned Vietnam's division into a permanent split. The emergence after 1954 of two competing successor states, the Republic of Vietnam and the Democratic Republic of Vietnam (DRVN), thus set the stage for a struggle over which of them could legitimately claim to represent the "just cause" *(chinh nghia)*.

Not that Diem felt the need to make any apologies for his regime or this state of affairs; in fact, he blamed the French and the communists for the country's partition and the conflict that he believed would inevitably follow from it. When he assumed the premiership of the State of Vietnam, he had expected to inherit the whole of the country. He bitterly criticized the French decision to abandon the north to the Viet Minh after Dien Bien Phu; and he was outraged by the Franco–Viet Minh carve-up of the country at Geneva. In his view, partition flew in the face of his legal and moral claim to represent a unified independent nation. Given his regional prejudices as a native of central Vietnam, he also felt that he had been left with the least patriotic and industrious section of the country. His delegation, excluded at Geneva from the behind-the-scenes deliberations of the main players, refused to sign the final agreements.[7] Nor did Diem feel bound to submit to the call for unifying elections, which, he argued, would merely give the communists the opportunity to cheat their way into power.[8]

Diem harbored no doubts about his right to lead an independent Vietnam, a role that he approached with a messianic sense of mission. He told the U.S. embassy's Paul Kattenburg that, from an early age, he believed himself "predestined for leadership." He certainly had "a lively appreciation of himself," reported Robert McClintock. After a trip to northern Vietnam in the summer of 1954, amid the chaos of France's crumbling position in Indochina, Diem informed McClintock that "only his presence in Hanoi had prevented [the] populace from stampeding" and his arrival there "had been welcomed as that of a saviour." This "grade-A Messiah complex," as another U.S. official put it, helped to sustain Diem at the most difficult of times during his first year in office. Cao Van Luan, a Catholic priest and confidant of the Ngos, recalled that the premier was determined to stay the course during this period because he regarded himself as the last hope for saving his country from communism.[9]

For Diem, the Vietnamese communists were bogus patriots. Saigon attacked them for being the servants of Moscow and Peking, in thrall to a foreign ideology that was "alien to the national character as well as to the most ancient traditions of the country." They were traitors, the Diem regime asserted: in 1945, Ho Chi Minh hid his ideological affiliations and hijacked the movement for national liberation; a year later, he agreed to the return of the colonial power; and, at Geneva, he colluded with the French to cut the country in half.[10] While such charges smack of propagandistic bombast, they rather accurately reflect the quasi-religious intensity of the palace's beliefs, no doubt nourished by the virulent anticommunism of Vietnamese Catholicism. Indeed, Diem described his contest with Hanoi in almost apocalyptic terms. "If the Viet-Minh win out in this contest," he declared, "our beloved country will disappear and it will be only mentioned as a Southern province of Communist China. Moreover, the

Vietnamese people will eternally live under the yoke of a dictatorship, inspired by Moscow and denying religion, fatherland and family."[11]

In this life-or-death struggle, where nationalist credentials might be as important as military divisions, Diem was naturally anxious to demonstrate his moral claims to leadership. The U.S. presence in South Vietnam, however, fueled communist charges that he was merely an imperial puppet and the leader of an illegitimate rump state. Hanoi pigeonholed Diem as another traitor in a long line of wretched individuals in Vietnamese history who had sold out their country to foreign invaders; the Ngos and their supporters were reactionaries, and the puppets of French, Japanese, and now U.S. colonialism. The communists referred to them as *tay sai* ("lackeys") and the regime as *My-Diem* ("American-Diem").[12] The latter tag plagued the palace. According to Robert Scigliano, this epithet had become so thoroughly established by the late 1950s "that Vietnamese government officials have been addressed, with all respect, as *My-Diem* by peasants doing business with them."[13] No such association, redolent as it was of a colonial relationship, seemed more politically damaging to Diem, challenging his regime's claim to the mantle of postcolonial Vietnamese nationalism.

Not surprisingly, Diem was obsessed with the specter of collaboration. Perhaps this acute sensitivity explains the chronological gaps that are evident in the hagiographies and official biographies of the time, which generally gloss over events that might "complicate" a nationalist narrative, such as Diem's wartime relationship with the Japanese or his negotiations with the French in the late 1940s.[14] While these episodes do not impugn his patriotism—after all, he set too high a price for his cooperation—the attempt to brush over them does suggest a fixation with his political credentials. In turn, this obsession helps explain the highly strung nationalism of the Ngos and their peculiar obduracy when it came to dealing with the Americans. The palace's incumbents were not just nationalists; they were self-consciously nationalistic. As William Colby, one-time CIA station chief in Saigon, remarked, the Ngos and their supporters believed it essential "not only to demonstrate their sovereignty and independence to the Vietnamese people; for the demonstration to be convincing, to ensure that they really represented a nationalist cause, they had to demonstrate it to themselves as well."[15]

Given the premium they placed on their sovereign rights, the Ngos bridled at the character of the patron–client relationship. They expected the Americans to treat them as partners and certainly not as puppets. Besides, they believed that their contribution to the alliance fully justified such treatment, for the Republic of Vietnam, as its foreign minister, Vu Van Mau, explained, had "the sad privilege of keeping the watch at the gates of the Red Empire." Diem noted that, in manning the ramparts of the Free World, the Vietnamese had "accepted very heavy sacrifices in order to defend not only their territory, but also the liberty and independence of more privileged countries situated outside the friction zone of the two worlds."[16] He also argued, in terms that must have warmed the cockles of John Foster Dulles's heart, that his steely example helped discourage the spread of neutralism among the RVN's "capricious" and "timid" neighbors in South and Southeast Asia.[17]

The Ngos felt that this kind of support was invaluable to the United States because they did not believe their ally possessed much political savvy of its own. According to Wesley Fishel and William Henderson, two of his early U.S. supporters, Diem "had little confidence in the soundness of American judgments on Vietnamese problems." Several meetings with U.S. officials during his exile in the United States convinced him that his hosts did not understand what was going on in Vietnam. In a letter to Justice Douglas in November 1953, he described U.S. policy in Indochina as naïve. The French, he argued, were hoodwinking the Americans into supporting them by suggesting that otherwise they would withdraw from Indochina; meanwhile, U.S. support merely fueled France's illusion that it could achieve a military victory. Later, other aspects of U.S. policy, such as Washington's willingness to tolerate neutralism and lavish aid on nonaligned countries, reinforced Diem's doubts about his ally.[18]

The president's brother Nhu also nourished these concerns. The counselor was a vain and arrogant man, who, in the words of one foreign observer, "had picked up, as part of the legacy of French scholasticism, an exaggerated esteem for his own intuition and eloquence."[19] He shared the distaste of many of Vietnam's French-educated intellectuals for the rich and brash Anglo-Saxons, whom he considered to be dull and unsophisticated. Although the French had been the colonial masters, Nhu told Lieutenant Colonel Nguyen Van Chau, at least they had understood Vietnam, whereas the United States "helps us with a lot of money but doesn't know anything about Vietnamese affairs." Diem's brother believed most foreigners, "with the exception of certain Frenchmen, to be fundamentally naïve and not to understand Vietnamese problems," commented Fishel.[20] Under the circumstances, and since Diem and Nhu harbored no doubts about their own ability, the Ngos thought that their less-than-competent ally should be suitably grateful to have such able lieutenants to take care of U.S. interests in Southeast Asia.

These concerns about the dependability of the Americans show that Saigon fully reciprocated Washington's reservations about the U.S.–Vietnamese relationship. The Ngos saw themselves not only as full partners in the alliance but also as the more reliable half of that partnership. In fact, they doubted America's staying power in Vietnam and questioned the commitment of the Americans, especially in an age of nuclear weapons. Admiral Arthur Radford, chairman of the joint chiefs, told a meeting of the National Security Council in June 1956 that "the Vietnamese authorities entertained genuine doubts as to whether the United States would actually intervene to assist Vietnam if it were the victim of Communist aggression." Diem feared that one day, if push came to shove, the United States would trade South Vietnam for peace with the communist bloc. Washington's less than wholehearted support for his position in the period 1954–1955 only served to fuel such suspicions. "Deep down, he seems always to have harbored a stereotype of Americans as politically naïve and incurably softhearted," concluded Fishel and Henderson. "He was gravely concerned as to the constancy of United States policy in protracted struggle against the Communists."[21]

As well as doubting America's long-term commitment to South Vietnam, the Ngos also complained about the nature of the support that they currently received from the United States. First, they criticized the amount of aid provided by their patron. They considered the Americans to be parsimonious and were particularly incensed by the proposed cuts in the U.S. aid budget for 1958. Diem told General Williams that the cuts made him "really angry"; he had hoped South Vietnam would be largely self-sufficient within five years but the lack of adequate U.S. assistance "paralyzes progress." Given the contribution that he believed he made to the anticommunist cause, Diem bitterly resented the extent of American support. Nor could he understand why Washington would impose cuts on a loyal ally while continuing to provide financial aid to neutral nations like Cambodia.[22]

In addition, the palace disapproved of the procedures associated with the delivery of American assistance. Its chief target was the Commodity Import Program, a method of import subsidization that constituted by far the largest element of U.S. economic aid to South Vietnam. The program generated local currency for the regime's use: licensed Vietnamese traders imported goods paid for by the United States and, in exchange, put RVN piasters into a "counterpart" fund made available to the Saigon government. Although this process restrained the inflationary effect of dollar aid, the Ngos argued that it was too time-consuming and did not deliver money in sufficient amounts or quickly enough to meet the needs of a newly developing country. They complained, moreover, that the Americans employed unnecessarily strict controls over the uses to which counterpart funds were put; U.S. regulations for the planning and administration of economic projects delayed their implementation and undermined the regime's ability to make effective use of U.S. support. The Ngos preferred the looser arrangements that characterized U.S. assistance for the RVN's military budget, whereby the Americans handed over the money to the Vietnamese with minimal checks on the way it was spent.[23]

Finally, the Diem regime criticized the type of aid it received, with the Commodity Import Program again singled out for attack. On the one hand, the palace was well aware that the program helped foster support for the regime, both among licensed traders, who made considerable profits, and the urban middle class, which was able to purchase the consumer goods that made up most of the imports.[24] At the same time, the Ngos feared that the program might prove detrimental to the long-term health of the country because the importation of consumer, rather than capital, goods created the illusion of prosperity while hampering the development of local industry. U.S. stipulations that capital equipment could only be imported for privately run businesses exacerbated the problem. The current type of assistance "perpetuates dependence upon this aid," complained Tran Van Chuong, the RVN's ambassador to Washington, in a June 1956 memorandum to the State Department. "American aid would be most valuable if it were partly devoted to promoting [the] country's industrial possibilities." The regime wanted U.S. support to help lay the foundations for real, self-sustaining growth as a necessary step toward South Vietnam's economic independence. As Diem told the former MAAG chief, General John W. O'Daniel, "We cannot survive as a nation without industrialization."[25]

At bottom, these various complaints reflected Saigon's fear that the nature of U.S. assistance might reduce South Vietnam to the status of a permanent mendicant, dependent on foreign charity, and on a superpower patron that was both overbearing and unreliable. Without adequate aid, of the right sort, delivered as expeditiously as possible, South Vietnam could not reach the point of economic takeoff. Instead, it would remain attached indefinitely to an American IV. Vu Van Mau likened the situation to a convalescent who received sufficient treatment to stay alive but not enough to make a proper recovery. Nhu employed a similar analogy during an April 1957 visit to Washington, when he told U.S. officials that, if the Vietnamese were not careful, "American aid could become a sort of opium paralyzing the country." In discussions with the regime's own officials, the counselor often compared dependency to the condition of childhood; it meant a lack of maturity and independence, and it could not go on indefinitely because one's parents would not always be around to help.[26]

For the intensely nationalistic Ngos, this state of affairs was intolerable. Without economic independence, the country's political independence would lack substance.[27] Continued reliance on the Americans would also bolster communist charges that the south was merely an imperial appendage, especially if North Vietnam succeeded in developing its own economy successfully. The Ngos felt a keen sense of being in economic competition with the north, a contest that they saw as intimately related to the struggle of the two Vietnams for political legitimacy. In a paper given to General O'Daniel in the autumn of 1956, Diem stated that "the threat of economic competition unleashed by the Communists is a matter of profound concern to me" and he would have to do for his people "certainly no less than the Communists intend doing for theirs." Yet the Ngos argued that the nature of U.S. aid put them at a competitive disadvantage; while the communist bloc liberally dispensed aid to its allies, America's friends labored under the limitations of U.S. support.[28] Saigon's solution was simple; it wanted more money and less interference with the way it was spent. "We would prefer untied long-time loans at low interest rates and in large amounts," declared a February 1959 article in the *Times of Viet Nam*, the regime's English-language mouthpiece. "Give us the money for economic aid and we will know how to spend it best" was the way Ambassador Durbrow characterized the palace's position.[29]

Of course, this desire for freedom of action was not limited to the issue of aid. The Ngos resented all forms of "interference" in their sovereign affairs, especially U.S. attempts to press American policy prescriptions on South Vietnam. As they consolidated their position and grew in confidence, noted Ambassador Reinhardt in December 1956, they were, in fact, increasingly disinclined to accept U.S. advice.[30] They wanted American backing with no strings attached—aid without conditions, as Nhu told one U.S. official, "the same way you help Tito without interfering in his affairs."[31]

The Ngos regarded Washington's attempts to push its ideas on the regime as high-handed and the advice itself as wrongheaded. Diem saw no alternative, at least in the short term, to his style of government. Nothing that the Americans told him could shake his belief that his brand of centralized rule was the only way to hold the fragile southern state together. He promised that the regime would gradually introduce more political freedoms; indeed, the Ngos spoke of ultimately creating a decentralized system of government, which they deemed to be consonant with a tradition of village democracy in Vietnam. As we shall see, this idea formed the kernel of the later Strategic Hamlet program. Yet, for the foreseeable future, argued Diem, there must be a strong guiding hand at the top. "I am not content to wait for the chaos around me to turn into order of its own accord," he declared. "I am going to try to bring order out of chaos myself."[32]

Not surprisingly, U.S. efforts to persuade the palace to delegate more authority found little favor. Diem defended his centralization of power, and constant interference in administrative matters, on the grounds that his own subordinates were simply not up to the job. "They are, for the most part, honest men," he explained to Wesley Fishel and others in a meeting in August 1957, "but you understand that in Vietnam in the last ten years we have had no training of *fonctionnaires* which has been sufficient to turn out men who understand even the routine of their jobs. The average fonctionnaire is incompetent."[33] In addition, the Ngos were acutely sensitive to the way in which changes in the regime's organizational arrangements might threaten their political preeminence. Diem sought to keep the levers of power close to home because he doubted the loyalty of others, especially his own armed forces. General Hinh's behavior in 1954 was not the only occasion when he had good reason to question the forces' loyalties: several paratrooper units would attempt a coup in November 1960 and two renegade air force pilots bombed the presidential palace in February 1962.[34]

The Ngos regarded U.S. proposals to liberalize the regime as equally misguided. As an RVN study document noted, the communists would not be defeated just because "freedom of the press and freedom to establish political parties are proclaimed in Saigon; nor will the adversary withdraw out of fear or panic!"[35] The Ngos believed that such measures not only were irrelevant to South Vietnam's real problems but also would exacerbate them. They held little but contempt for the south's urban elite, the prospective beneficiaries of any broadening of the government's base; they regarded its members as talentless, self-interested, disloyal, and tainted by collaboration with the French. True to form, Diem observed, these people showed a lack of patriotic commitment to the new republic and an unhealthy intimacy with the new foreigners, the Americans.[36] Since the U.S. embassy picked up a good deal of information about the regime from contacts with members of this elite, American advice was doubly damned in the eyes of the palace; it not only came from the mouths of foreigners but also seemed to parrot the views of the regime's domestic critics.[37]

Finally, the Ngos cold-shouldered American suggestions about how to win peasant support. Diem certainly shared U.S. concerns about meeting the "rising expectations" of the masses, as was evident from the priority that the palace placed on competing economically with the DRVN. Yet, as we shall see, the Ngos believed that the population must participate actively in the process of national reconstruction, rather than merely being the passive beneficiary of economic aid and progress. They argued that, given the RVN's limited resources, the people had to play an active part in building the country—unless, that is, South Vietnam chose to depend on American largesse. In their view, however, such reliance was incompatible with national sovereignty and sapped the very moral fiber that was required to construct a new society. If the people became dependent on outside support, or overly reliant on their own government for that matter, how would they ever be able to nurture the personal and collective strength necessary to develop a modern independent nation? "Our freedom," Nhu proclaimed, "is the result of our struggle, not a gift from Santa Claus, from our government or from any foreign government."[38] This line of thinking put the Ngos squarely at odds with the Americans, who wanted the regime to emphasize what it could do for the people rather than vice versa.

All these disagreements placed enormous strain on U.S.–Vietnamese relations. The Ngos not only took a dim view of being dependent on the Americans and exposed, as a result, to U.S. policy prescriptions; they also considered the nature of U.S. advice and support to be a threat to the future of South Vietnam. To the palace's incumbents, the patron–client relationship was both dishonorable and dangerous; it symbolized the current limits of the nation's independence and threatened to suffocate the south's efforts to overcome those limits. Compounding the natural resentment that the Ngos felt at their client status was the fear that American backing might ultimately jeopardize the south's survival by derailing their plans for nation building.

What exactly were these plans for nation building? After all, most commentators have not credited Diem with possessing any agenda of this sort and certainly nothing to compare with the revolutionary program of his communist challengers. The prevailing image we have of the RVN president is of a man out of his time, a power-hungry autocrat who sought to rule by the outdated precepts of a defunct political order. "He was the heir to a dying tradition," wrote William Turley, "member of an elite that had been superbly prepared by birth, training, and experience to lead a Vietnam that no longer existed." Here was no modernizer; in the circumstances of a society in the throes of revolutionary change, Diem was merely a patriot without a program. "His love for his country in the abstract was profound, but he was an elitist who had little sensitivity to the needs and problems of the Vietnamese people," argued George Herring. "He had no blueprint for building a modern nation or mobilizing his people."[39]

According to some of the defining histories of the Diem period, if the palace did possess a political program, then it was one aimed at trying to re-create the past rather than build for the future. Jean Lacouture described the RVN president as having "an attachment to the ancient society of Annam—high aristocracy, closed castes, intellectual hierarchies, its cohesive families, its disdain of strangers, its hatred of China. He wanted to revive the old order, the ancient morality, the respect for the master, the rule of the closed city." Frances FitzGerald developed this interpretation most fully in her Pulitzer Prize–winning book on Vietnam, where she portrayed Diem as a Confucian/Catholic reactionary, violently opposed to things modern and Western, and bent on restoring a traditional version of Vietnamese kingship.[40]

There is usually no smoke without fire. Although these views of Diem are wide of the mark in important respects, they do highlight certain salient features of his government. Diem was, indeed, a conservative person who felt intense pride in his country's history and its Confucian tradition. "I know that some Americans try to tarnish me by calling me a mandarin," he told Marguerite Higgins. "But I am proud of being a mandarin."[41] His reverence for the past exercised a good deal of influence over the character of his government, whereas his rivals' adoption of Marxism-Leninism marked a self-conscious rejection of tradition. As a family-run operation, moreover, the Saigon regime looked remarkably like some old-fashioned imperial dynasty. Diem's autocratic behavior reinforced the resemblance, as did his remoteness from the lives of ordinary Vietnamese, in stark contrast to his chief rival, "Uncle Ho."

Yet stereotypes of the Saigon regime's stultifying conservatism obscure as much as they reveal. Diem was not a patriot without a program, nor was he an old-fashioned "Oriental" despot. The president and his chief adviser, Counselor Nhu, are better described as conservative modernizers. The prevailing image of Diem's government is one-dimensional and so too is the broader view of the Vietnamese conflict that it encourages. A black-and-white picture of traditional autocrats versus modern communists draws too sharp a distinction between the warring factions. As one historian of Vietnam has pointed out, in any revolutionary confrontation, the difference between the sides "may be only a matter of degree." To view the struggle as pitting "an ancien régime whose ideas are all out-of-date and detached from reality" against challengers who are "attuned to only the most contemporary historical developments" would be a "gross oversimplification."[42] Or, to put it another way, the Diem regime ignored the realities of the modern world no more than the communists escaped the pull of tradition.

In assessing the nature of Diem's conservatism, we need to set it in the stream of modern Vietnamese nationalism, which was a phenomenon that looked forward as well as backward. Nationalism is often regarded as a regressive trait, an "infantile yearning" for parental reassurance according to two observers of the twentieth-century, European variety.[43] Students of the Vietnamese kind, however, have emphasized not just its nostalgic aspects—myths and memories—but also its broadly progressive qualities. These forward-looking impulses followed from the challenge presented to the country's traditions and institutions by France's subjugation of Vietnam in the nineteenth century. "Harmony received a severe blow in the period of French conquest," wrote the historian David Marr. "If evil barbarians could subjugate good believers in the *Dao,* then there was something profoundly wrong, either with the world or with the previous way of looking at it." Colonial control also brought about massive socioeconomic changes that further shook people's faith in the values of the old order. Defeat and despair thus led the Vietnamese to engage in a critical examination of their own society as well as foreign ideas and methods. The type of nationalism that emerged from this process aimed at overcoming not only the colonial power but also the societal weaknesses that colonialism had made manifest.[44]

This soul-searching encouraged the growth of a new political consciousness among an emergent Vietnamese intelligentsia in the period 1920–1945. Members of this group came to believe in the need for a transformation of the country. The characteristics of this new society "meant different things to different people," Marr noted, but "it generally encompassed mastery over nature, a spirit of civic responsibility, full development of the individual's mental, physical, and moral faculties, and the ability of Vietnamese to stand proud among other peoples of the world." For all their differences, intellectuals also agreed "that there could be no return to the past, and that critical, informed discussion of future political, socio-economic, and cultural changes was essential to the survival and development of the nation."[45] This preoccupation with change helps to explain why both communist and noncommunist Vietnamese so readily employed the term "revolution" after 1954 to describe their approaches to solving their country's problems.[46]

Above all, the Vietnamese intelligentsia focused on the problem of group cohesion and unity *(doan the* and *doan ket)*. Commentators from across the political spectrum argued that the country had lost its independence because of a lack of national consciousness and an absence of the kind of organized social structures that could connect the individual/family with the rest of society. Traditional Confucian homilies, which described the country as the family writ large, had obviously proved to be a weak reed in the face of colonialism's advance.[47] When the West encountered East Asia, one scholar remarked, the peasant was "standing stock still, his feet stuck politically in the mud of the paddy-field, while the Emperor sat above on his throne, resplendent in imperial robes, but without any civil underclothing beneath the facade of bureaucratic rule."[48] The search was on, therefore, to foster the group solidarity that would overcome this lack of social cohesion and lay the foundations for the development of a modern independent state.

Such concerns animated the Diem regime as much as they did its communist rival. Diem may have been a conservative, but his thinking fell squarely within the broadly progressive confines of modern Vietnamese nationalism; it was forward-looking, concerned with change, and determined to strengthen the country. He recognized that the overthrow of French colonialism was not an end in itself, for Vietnam would remain underdeveloped, a condition that the Ngos found humiliating. The country's struggle, he pointed out in a statement in June 1949, was not only for "national independence" but also a "social revolution" that would transform the living conditions of the Vietnamese population. He told Wesley Fishel in the summer of 1953 that "my country needs vast reforms in every field," a call he repeated a year later upon his return to Vietnam when he proclaimed the need for a "complete revolution . . . in all the branches of the organization and the activity of the state."[49] Diem's thinking certainly drew deeply on older ideas and customs, but he set out in 1954 to build a version of a modern nation rather than recreate a copy of the precolonial past. Although reared in a conservative tradition, Frederick Reinhardt commented, Diem was "far too intelligent and forward-looking" to remain its prisoner.[50]

The Ngos possessed a sense of historical change that militated against mere revivalism. Diem argued that the "central historic movement of the Twentieth Century" was the "march toward political and economic liberation" of the Asian masses. Governments had to respond positively to this development, he stated, or face the wrath of a disaffected populace. The Vietnamese people, like their Asian neighbors, "have become embittered and impatient," he noted during his visit to the United States in 1957. "They want to catch up rapidly with the advanced western nations, and some are even prepared to accept totalitarian measures in order to achieve this end." Vietnam was in a particularly difficult position, Nhu explained to U.S. officials. Not only was its economy in a shambles after years of war; the country's geographical position also made it a prime target for the communist bloc, whose goal was to exploit popular dissatisfaction in order to win over the Asian peasantry.[51]

Given this state of revolutionary tension, standing pat was not an option, as was demonstrated, Diem believed, by Chiang Kai-shek's failure to win over the Chinese masses.[52] "The nationalism that would surrender to reaction is doomed," he declared at the start of his government, "just as nationalism which allies itself with communism is bound to end up in treason."[53] Like the leaders of other newly independent states, the issue for Diem was not how to get back to Vietnam's precolonial roots but what route to take to a modern future. He believed that he was engaged in a titanic struggle to wrench the country into the twentieth century and out of the clutches of the Marxist-Leninists.

Saigon described itself as engaged in a battle against three "enemies": "Communism, Underdevelopment, and Disunity," or sometimes "Colonialism, Feudalism, and Communism." "Communism" presented the most obvious threat, the palace opined, and its assault on the south aggravated the RVN's other problems. The regime attributed "Underdevelopment," the second of its "enemies," to the legacies of feudalism and colonialism; Vietnam was technically and economically backward, while its people were poor and ignorant. Like most of its neighbors, stated Vu Van Mau, the country was "still mainly at the stage of 'vegetal civilization,' " a condition that stymied progress and facilitated communist subversion. Finally, there was the problem of "Disunity," not just in the sense of a divided country but also divided minds. Diem spoke of the difficulty of trying to govern a society that lacked an ideological consensus, which he blamed on Vietnam's "primitive," "backward" condition and the absence of unity during the colonial era. In an editorial in *Chi-Dao*, the journal of the defense ministry, Nguyen Van Chau called disunity the "most damaging enemy of all." Without "group solidarity," he argued, there would be no basis on which to build a strong and effective state.[54]

To defeat this trio of "enemies," the Ngos sought to fashion their own nation-building strategy—one that promised the rapid development of the country and met the palace's ideological concerns. From the outset, they pointedly rejected the idea of copying the Western models of development. Nhu argued that each country's circumstances were unique, so the slavish imitation of foreign examples was inappropriate. "The history of mankind offers us two alternatives," Diem stated, "the capitalist solution through freedom and the Communist solution through coercion." Both had paved the way for the development of the state, he noted, but neither was suitable for Vietnam.[55]

Liberal capitalism fell short as a model on several counts. Politically, the Ngos regarded it as a recipe for chaos and confusion because it placed individual freedom above collective discipline. For newly independent countries in particular, commented Diem, this kind of free-for-all could only end in disaster; he pointed to the early abandonment of parliamentary democracy in several Third World states to bolster his case.[56] Nor did the Ngos much like liberalism as an economic model. They exhibited a barely concealed distaste for money-making materialism, which manifested itself in the regime's efforts to restrict free enterprise and its emphasis on joint, government-private economic ventures. Like other Third World leaders, moreover, the Ngos wanted economic, in addition to political, independence, to which end they sought to direct and accelerate the state's development, rather than leave the job to the predatory instincts of private/foreign capital or the slow workings of the free market. "If you want to emerge rapidly from this humiliating condition, and not in a few centuries," Diem remarked during a visit to Malaya in 1960, "you are led to adopt some sort of forced march."[57]

Communism was not the answer either, although the palace did acknowledge that it held a certain appeal. "We must not forget," Diem informed an audience in Seoul in September 1957, "that the technical effectiveness represented by Communism exercises a great temptation to the Asian masses, impatient to catch up with their technical backwardness and thirsty for social justice." However, this model of development came at a heavy price, he warned; the communists' obsession with materialism turned people into cogs in a machine and threatened to extinguish the national soul. Marxism represented a "universal tyranny of the mind," which relegated national cultures "to the domain of folklore, little capable of modifying the vision of the external world, once and for all set by historical and materialistic dialectics." During a visit to India, Diem told Prime Minister Jawaharlal Nehru that communism's "atheistic materialism" ran counter to "all the lofty tenets of Asian religions, particularly the dignity of man."[58]

Saigon's solution to its nation-building conundrum was to find an alternative path to development, a "third way" between capitalism and communism. South Vietnam needed a model, Diem believed, "capable of quickly achieving the industrial revolution without the evil consequences of the two solutions mentioned above."[59] In particular, the Ngos sought a blueprint for modernization that was somehow authentically Vietnamese. As conservative nationalists, they wanted to take a route to modernity that would not only meet the needs of an underdeveloped state but also combine change with tradition.

At a national cultural convention held in January 1957, Nhu argued that any country without "an authentic culture" would be "eliminated sooner or later from the concert of nations." To succeed, nation building had to be an organic process, firmly rooted in the cultural soil of Vietnam; the country's traditions had to be adapted selectively rather than abandoned wholesale. "Should one make a 'tabula rasa' of the past, as is advocated by Communism?" Nhu asked. "Or should one, on the contrary, only eliminate the practices which hamper progress while preserving the quintessence of national culture?"[60] Diem answered the question in the same interview in which he spoke of his pride in being a mandarin. "We are not going to go back to a sterile copy of the mandarin past," he stated. "But we are going to adapt the best of our heritage to the modern situation."[61]

The Ngos viewed the process of cultural revision as a prerequisite for nation building. It was clear, Diem remarked, "that intellectual and moral factors" must "play a great part in our national recovery." South Vietnam's trio of "enemies" had to be confronted ideologically as well as physically. Hence, the regime sought a new national credo to guide its efforts, in much the same way as its Southeast Asian neighbors who proclaimed *Panca Sila, Rukunegara,* or "The Burmese Way to Socialism." The need to find a suitable formula for nation building also seemed imperative in view of the ideological challenge presented by the Vietnamese communists. Ever since the 1920s, noncommunist nationalists had lacked an effective doctrinal counter to Marxism-Leninism; they had merely been practicing "political handicrafts," Nhu warned. Given communism's "definite appeal to the masses," Ngo Dinh Thuc told one U.S. official, "purely anti-communist propaganda is not effective"; the regime needed a positive program that would rally popular support.[62]

Central to the palace's search for a new credo or formula were its efforts to draw on Western ideas in order to revitalize certain aspects of Asian culture. While they rejected the slavish imitation of foreign models, the Ngos did look to borrow from them. Attempts at this kind of synthesis had a long pedigree in Vietnam and the rest of East Asia, ever since the first encounters with the West had demonstrated the latter's technological superiority. The adaptation or domestication of Western ideas proved challenging, however, especially to those who were keenest on preserving the "quintessence of national culture." Conservatives found it difficult to combine, in any sort of convincing fashion, traditional ethical principles with Western science and materialism, or to make Confucianism appear synonymous with modern nationalism. Thus, an updated "Confucian nationalism," promoted in the decades before the Second World War by writers such as Tran Trong Kim and Pham Quynh, failed to generate much enthusiasm.[63]

The Ngos were well aware of this history of cultural revision and, as devotees of an occidental religion, perhaps naturally inclined to seek a bridge between East and West. Nhu described efforts to synthesize the values of the two traditions as "a basis for all the national revolutionary movements among the peoples of Asia."[64] At the same time, the palace was conscious of some of the problems involved in the process of cultural borrowing. Diem expressed doubts, for example, about the oft-repeated contrast made between Western "technique" and Eastern "spirit," a distinction that had attracted traditionalists who hoped to acquire the former without prejudicing the latter. "Does not the force of western technique, which some of us despise, while others admire without reservation, contain a creative spirit which justifies it?" he asked. "Likewise, does not our spiritualism, of which we are so proud, simply conceal a narrow conservatism or a form of escapism from concrete historical responsibilities?" Asians must tap into this Western spirit, he argued, in order to enrich their own cultural heritage, especially to orient their thinking "toward the exploitation of nature for the service of Man, and no longer toward the identification of Man with nature."[65]

According to the Ngos, the challenge for Asian states lay neither in the wholesale abandonment nor dogged defense of traditional ideas, but in reevaluating their contemporary relevance. Diem explored the potential for updating aspects of Vietnamese culture in an article penned before his appointment as premier in 1954. He claimed that there were certain basic principles inherent in the country's traditions, such as the reciprocal obligations that bound the sovereign and the people, which could provide the foundations for a modern and cohesive state.[66] Once in power, the Ngos supported a number of initiatives designed to encourage critical interest in Asian philosophies and religions: they revived the celebration of the anniversary of Confucius; sponsored the establishment of a number of associations for the study of Confucianism, Buddhism, and popular culture; and made the issue of cultural revision the theme of the weeklong convention in January 1957 that Nhu had addressed.[67] Diem also talked extensively about the need to revitalize Asian culture during a series of visits to neighboring states in 1957, where he called on intellectuals to provide policy makers with "the guiding principles which should motivate them in solving the great problems of Asia."[68]

The Ngos proposed to develop a cultural synthesis for Vietnam by drawing upon a doctrinal import from Europe called Personalism. Although by now a somewhat obscure political philosophy, Personalism had once been a major intellectual force, especially in the 1930s. It was most closely associated with the Frenchman Emmanuel Mounier and the journal *Esprit*, which he founded in 1932. Personalism drew upon Catholic humanism and the Church's long-standing concern with the ills of modern industrialism; more specifically, it reflected the Catholic Left's search for a new order amid the disintegrating social fabric of prewar Europe. "It mirrored," wrote John Hellman, "the desperate effort of intellectuals in the early nineteen-thirties to navigate a 'third way' between capitalism and communism."[69]

Personalism emphasized spiritual and humanist values, including the belief in a supreme being, the creative potential of man, the importance of personal struggle and responsibility, and the need to provide people with the basic material requirements for existence. Its exponents believed that the threat to these values came from the two extremes of bourgeois individualism/ liberal capitalism and fascist/communist collectivism. According to Mounier, liberalism promoted a selfish anarchism by making the individual "sovereign lord of a liberty unlimited and undirected"; it encouraged people to pursue their interests at the expense of others, leaving the majority "in material conditions of slavery—social, economic and, before long, political." Collectivism, meanwhile, impugned the dignity and worth of individuals by inducting them into "a régime of industrial armies and their leaders, in which persons are less than pawns"; it dehumanized people, denying their "corporal and moral immunity" from oppression and reducing them to a state of "material and vegetative existence."[70]

To counter these excesses, Personalists advocated a middle way that would secure the common good as well as the rights of the person. Their central preoccupation was to find the correct balance in the relationship between man and the state; their ideal was a communal society, in which people possessed the ability to develop as individuals but also bore a responsibility to promote the well-being of the group. It was for this reason that Personalists drew a distinction between the idea of the "individual" and the "person." The "individual" was the atomized man, pursuing his selfish goals in a liberal society, or standing helpless and alone before the power of a totalitarian state. The "person" possessed certain inalienable rights but was also an inherently social animal, oriented toward the life of the community and part of a larger organism whose aim should be to secure the common good of all its constituent elements.[71]

Personalists viewed ideologies as inherently oppressive, so they shied away from developing a systematic political program based upon these insights. Their writings, however, do offer some prescriptions for the good society. They advocated a kind of communitarian socialism—with worker control and ownership of industry—that would guarantee people's basic material needs while simultaneously purging society of "the tyranny of production for profit." Only on the basis of this kind of economic decentralization, Mounier suggested, could real political democracy be established. In addition, they favored a pluralist society composed of a diverse collection of autonomous groups. Such associations would serve to curb the excesses of individualism by integrating people into a network of social relationships; at the same time, they would check the authority of the state by creating a series of countervailing powers. The essential point, argued the philosopher Jacques Maritain, was that a "personalist democracy" must promote the active participation of the people in the political as well as economic life of society.[72]

As the self-appointed intellectual of the Ngo family, Nhu led the way in promoting a version of these ideas in South Vietnam. He probably first encountered Personalism while studying in France in the 1930s, although he denied ever meeting Emmanuel Mounier. He had certainly become familiar with the philosophy by 1949, when he assisted a French priest in delivering a series of lectures on the rights of the human person. Personalist themes, and the use of the Vietnamese term *Nhan vi* ("Personalism" or "Humanism"), later appeared in the journal *Xa Hoi* that Nhu published from 1953 until his brother's return to Vietnam as premier.[73] After Diem's accession, the Ngos adopted the philosophy as the regime's official ideology, sometimes referring to the state as the "Personalist Republic" and even enshrining Personalist themes in the preamble to the RVN's constitution.[74]

Personalism proved attractive to the Ngos on several levels. Given their interest in cultural borrowing, it enjoyed, as a Western political philosophy, the appropriate cachet, while its Catholic origins no doubt made its ideas more familiar and palatable. It also spoke directly not only to their hatred of communism but also to their distrust of capitalism; its emphasis on the value of community, rather than individualism, complemented the traditional focus of Vietnamese culture on social relationships as well as the concerns of modern nationalism with group solidarity. Hence, the palace believed that a Vietnamese version of Personalism, transposing the basic tenets of the European original, could serve as a framework for the modernization of South Vietnam.

The philosophy would provide a vehicle for the rejuvenation of certain indigenous traditions and the elaboration of a new formula for nation building, an authentic "third way" to modernity. "Personalism is not only a way to emerge from a state of underdevelopment but also a means of preserving our ancestral traditions," declared Diem, "for it liberates without abolishing, perfects without destroying, preserves as well as completes and enriches."[75]

The Ngos claimed that Personalism was compatible with a number of Asian traditions. Hinduism, Buddhism, Taoism, and Confucianism—all expressed, they suggested, certain universal values that mirrored the spiritual and humanist concerns of Personalism.[76] In an interview with John C. Donnell, a former official with the U.S. Information Service (USIS), Nhu placed particular emphasis on the similarities between Personalism and Confucianism. Both focused, he explained, on man's philosophical location between "heaven and earth." On the one hand, man was a spiritual being, who possessed an inner life directed toward his own self-cultivation and self-improvement. At the same time, he was a social being, bound by a series of relationships to others and toward whom he was also responsible.[77] From this perspective, Personalism appeared to affirm the Confucian view of the individual as someone possessing both rights and responsibilities.

Given Confucianism's centrality to Vietnamese culture, Nhu's interest in a philosophical comparison with Personalism was perhaps no surprise. Indeed, noncommunists were not the only Vietnamese whose outlook was strongly influenced by Confucian thought. According to the historian Nguyen Khac Vien, Confucianism's stress on communal relationships and collective discipline facilitated the acceptance of Marxism in Vietnam; the revolutionary morality emphasized by communist cadres also bore a strong resemblance to Confucian ethics.[78] Of course, to the extent that they drew consciously on them, the communists probably treated Confucian principles as more of a tactical convenience, whereas Saigon viewed the same ideas in a far more positive light. Yet the Ngos were also engaged in a process of conscious manipulation, for they were seeking to promote the cultural synthesis that they considered critical to nation building.

Nhu's comparison of Personalism and Confucianism aimed at revitalizing elements of the country's heritage, not repackaging damaged goods. Conscious, perhaps, of the failure of previous efforts to revive Confucianism, the Ngos were suitably selective in their treatment of the great sage's teachings. Government pronouncements focused on Confucius's broadly humanist values, contrasting them with communist ideology; they devoted little attention to the more parochial aspects of his doctrine, namely his obsession with familial obligations. As a conservative, strongly influenced by tradition, Diem did refer to the family as a vital pillar of society, yet the Ngos evidently rejected the notion that patriotic citizens and a modern state could be created by "family morality written large." This aspect of Confucianism, observed the Personalist scholar Nguyen Huy Bao, was all too closely associated with the perils of "family individualism" and the sentiment of "perish the nation so long as my family prospers." Personalism, by contrast, offered a more expansive conception of social relations, in which the individual was also a citizen with ties to the rest of society.[79] For the palace, these were the kind of bonds that would help to foster group solidarity, national loyalty, and a popular commitment to the task of nation building.

In particular, new social attachments would facilitate the mobilization of the population, which the Diem regime saw as the key to pursuing its "third way" and defeating its three "enemies." "In Viet Nam, as in other newly developed countries," Vu Van Mau informed delegates to the 1960 Colombo Plan Conference, "technological backwardness cannot be overcome, nor can general welfare be attained in a short time without the collective and active participation of the masses."[80] The Ngos envisaged this mass mobilization as a popular struggle, in which individuals freely submitted to "national discipline" and willingly joined a "forced march" toward a better future. Their thinking was enshrined in the idea of "Community Development," the supposedly voluntary contribution of people's labor and money for the construction of roads, bridges, canals, schools, hospitals, and the like. How else could the regime transform the country, unless it chose to rely on foreign backing and capital, or resort to the kind of coercive methods for which it routinely condemned the communists? "In order to avoid borrowing and achieve economic independence," stated Diem, "we must mobilize the most precious and abundant capital at our disposal—the labor of all classes of the nation."[81]

Not only would this collective effort contribute to the physical transformation of the country; the Ngos also believed that the process itself would serve to temper and ennoble those engaged in it. Nhu referred to an existentialist element in Personalism—the individual discovering him- or herself by confronting difficult realities—which, he argued, applied to the task of nation building as well. "The personalist conception holds that freedom in an underdeveloped society is not something that is simply given or bestowed. It can only be achieved through militancy and vigilance," he told Robert Shaplen. "Human rights and human dignity are not static phenomenons. They are only possibilities which men must actively seek and deserve, not just beg for." In this view, struggle in adversity "liberated" individuals, in the sense that it would purge them of selfish concerns and create strong, civic-minded "persons." For the Ngos, South Vietnam's struggle would serve as the handmaiden for personal as well as collective advancement, helping to create both modern citizens and a modern state.[82]

The emphasis on the virtues of "struggle" *(dau tranh)* had been a prominent feature of Vietnamese nationalist thought from the late 1920s onward, and it ran like a thread through the palace's thinking.[83] The big question was how to generate and harness a collective effort of this kind. One answer was to induct individuals into government-sponsored groups and organizations, such as the National Revolutionary Movement and the later Republican Youth Movement. These "intermediate social structures" sought to muster the population by bridging the gap that traditionally separated the center and the periphery.[84] In addition, the regime established a variety of economic cooperatives, the largest and most ambitious of which were the farmers' associations that integrated peasants into organizational networks stretching from the village to the national level. According to Tran Ngoc Lien, the commissioner general for Cooperatives and Agricultural Credit, such "cooperative action undertaken by and for the people not only provides [economic and social] benefits to everyone, but creates better individuals and a healthier citizenry."[85]

The success and vitality of these government-sponsored organizations, however, ultimately depended on a degree of popular commitment to them. The palace's concept of struggle would only work in practice if people were willing to do of their own volition what the Ngos deemed necessary for the common good. To develop the requisite enthusiasm for nation building, Saigon planned to create a so-called "infrastructure of democracy" by "rearming" the Vietnamese people, "morally" and "materially."[86] In this context, the use of the term "democracy" did not refer primarily, or even necessarily, to the granting of Western-style freedoms, for the Ngos echoed the arguments made by European Personalists that such formal political liberties lacked meaning without a socially engaged and economically secure population.[87] What the Ngos sought to do was to create a set of conditions—through the moral and material rearmament of the population—which would encourage popular participation in national affairs, albeit a narrow form of involvement that fell within their definition of the common good.

In view of his classical training, Diem's interest in a moral revival was no surprise. One of the first international groups that the new premier received in South Vietnam was a delegation from Frank Buchman's Moral Re-Armament, the group dedicated to developing an ethical counter to communism.[88] Diem saw moral rearmament in terms of restoring traditional virtues—discipline, responsibility, honesty, and sacrifice—that would help create civic-minded citizens. To this end, the regime launched various morality campaigns, such as the effort to eliminate "feudal" hangovers like the "four vices of society" (prostitution, alcoholism, opium smoking, and gambling); it also sought to propagate Personalism through programs of education and indoctrination. During a presentation at the Department of Information in 1957, Nhu told officials that the aim was "to make each citizen aware of his own great value, his rights and his duties toward himself and his society."[89]

Moral rearmament was not deemed sufficient, however. Asia's traditional concern with ethical principles negated man's material needs, Diem's brother warned, whereas Personalism addressed both; people could not devote themselves to their civic responsibilities on an empty stomach. "The citizen's potentially democratic spirit would be troubled if he had to live in unduly straitened economic circumstances, so the government has striven to provide him with material weapons, in addition to spiritual ones," the counselor explained. The regime proposed to rearm people materially by furnishing them with a "basic piece of property" and the wherewithal to develop it, such as a system of agricultural credit. Nhu argued that, by providing people with a measure of economic independence, the regime could create a politically engaged and communally oriented population that was committed to the task of nation building. "We know that the citizen will realize his rights and responsibilities when he possesses housing and food," he stated.[90]

With this appropriately "rearmed" citizenry, the Ngos believed that they could build the country economically and solidify it politically. They could follow their "third way" to modernity, avoiding what they regarded as the pitfalls of both capitalism and communism. In place of the anarchic freedom of the one and the suffocating collectivism of the other, they would embark on a "forced march" under conditions of "national discipline," in which an organized and energized populace would contribute actively and enthusiastically to the business of nation building. In the process, they would create a modern state, one that was independent, prosperous, and united. "Communism, Underdevelopment, and Disunity" would be overcome by the Diem regime's own trinity of "Personalism, Community, and Collective Advancement," a slogan that beamed from neon signs in towns and cities across South Vietnam.[91]

Success in the south, moreover, would reverberate beyond its borders, reasoned the Ngos. By turning the Republic of Vietnam into a "model zone" or "show case," they hoped to provoke the progressive disintegration of Ho's regime in the north. Diem told U.S. officials in May 1957 that the communists had expected the Saigon government to crumble shortly after partition, but they now faced the prospect of an extended period of competition, for which they would have to maintain heavy controls over their supposedly disgruntled subjects. If this burden eventually proved too much, he argued, and the communist regime felt compelled to loosen its hold over the people, there would follow an "influx toward the South of a new and much more important exodus of population than that of 1954 after Geneva." This movement would either precipitate the collapse of the Hanoi regime or leave it desperately weakened, thus paving the way for the peaceful reunification of the country.[92] The Ngos evidently envisaged a chain of events similar to those that culminated in the collapse of communist East Germany in 1989–1990.

These, then, were Diem's plans for nation building. They made sense in a general sort of way, although the regime's often rambling expositions did little to further public understanding. In fact, many observers, foreign and Vietnamese, were mystified by the palace's philosophical ruminations, while some of them suspected its motives, not least because of the troubling gap that seemed to separate the regime's rhetoric from its actual conduct. Particular confusion surrounded the espousal of Personalism. Not only did the Ngos fail to publish a formal treatise on the subject; they also appeared to violate most of the philosophy's basic tenets. They spoke of "human dignity" and "democracy," but ran an authoritarian regime that governed with a heavy hand and brooked no opposition. Jean-Marie Domenach, editor of *Esprit,* the spiritual home of European Personalism, described the RVN's version of the doctrine as a "usurpation and travesty."[93] Such comments naturally beg the question: did the palace's publicly expressed views truly reflect its thinking and guide its policies, or did they merely represent empty rhetoric?

Lack of doctrinal clarity nourished many of these doubts. European Personalists, who feared the tyranny of theory, had for the most part preferred to contemplate the human condition rather than elaborate a program of political action. Similarly, the Ngos, with their vague pronouncements and passion for metaphysical abstraction, did little to overcome this doctrinal fuzziness. Although they contended otherwise, the regime's ideology was not easy to comprehend, even for those RVN officials who had attended the special course of study at the Personalism Training Center in Vinh Long. Personalism was "a confusing counterideology to Communism," commented David Halberstam, "which no one else in Vietnam ever understood."[94]

Confusion over the meaning of the regime's philosophy in turn encouraged misgivings about the palace's intentions. Robert Shaplen took Nhu's "semi-practical, semi-mystical talk" with a large dose of salt because, whatever Personalism was, "it was only a theory, while in practice it was what Nhu wanted it to be." Like Shaplen, many of the regime's critics suspected that Personalism's call for a "collective advance" was merely a thinly veiled cover for the Ngo family's dictatorship.[95] U.S. officials expressed similar concerns. The Saigon embassy's first detailed analysis of the philosophy, sent to Washington in December 1958, described it as a "somewhat cryptic statement of good intentions" that "may also be suspected of being used at times to cloak crasser motives."[96] In the briefest of reports to Washington in October 1963, Henry Cabot Lodge pointed to a case of the regime's use of torture in order to cut through such ambiguity and dispense with the palace's ideological pretensions.

"This is apparently what is involved by what [Nhu] calls the 'revolution,'" the ambassador remarked.[97]

Yet however reprehensible some of the palace's behavior, Lodge's casual dismissal of its ideas lacked perspective. It was not a "power-mad regime," observed John Mecklin, who was certainly no fan of the Ngos, and its concentration of power was "never an end in itself."[98] In addition, the process that led the palace's incumbents to adopt Personalism suggests that their publicly articulated views genuinely mirrored their thinking. Their search for a guiding philosophy was characteristic of the "progressive" concerns of Vietnamese nationalism, and consistent with the intellectual and political milieu in which they found themselves: conservative Vietnamese, seeking to reconcile change with tradition and facing a serious ideological challenge from their communist compatriots. The efforts of the Ngos to elaborate "a new national 'formula,'" noted John Donnell, one of the keenest students of Personalism, "stand out clearly as attempts to answer ideological needs of the Vietnamese which are far more fundamental than mere propaganda devices."[99]

Their chosen formula, of course, paled in comparison to the theoretical rigor of Marxism–Leninism. Communist ideology offered a clear conception of the good society and the class "enemies" that stood in its way; the Ngos subscribed to a much hazier vision of progress as a "collective advance" against "enemies" that were altogether more intangible and elusive ("Communism, Underdevelopment, and Disunity"). While the palace did loosely identify potential opponents—"wicked landlords," "men of influence," and "Saigon plutocrats"[100]—its Personalist revolution was to be open to all those willing to sacrifice for the "just cause"; it was to be a national rather than a social one, more in the spirit of the Meiji Restoration than the French Revolution. The problem of formulating a political program on such an amorphous basis was neatly illustrated by the experiences of Vu Van Thai, the director-general of Budget and Foreign Aid. When Thai asked the palace for guidance on applying Personalism to matters such as tax rates and income distribution, Nhu, who felt more at home with existentialism than economics, told him that he obviously lacked the imagination to understand the regime's doctrine.[101]

However, the fact that the palace's ideas proved hazy, and difficult to apply, does not necessarily mean that they were also a sham. One of the reasons why critics tended to view Personalism as merely a public relations exercise was that they often imputed a meaning to the language used by the palace that was not intended by the Ngos. When the latter spoke of "human dignity," for example, the phrase referred more to the inner life of the person— the development of character—than it did to the enjoyment of political freedoms. The Ngos tended to define character development, moreover, in distinctly social, as opposed to individual, terms. Thus, in the emphasis that they placed on popular struggle, they argued that individuals would find their greatest fulfillment in submitting to group discipline and meeting their communal obligations. Society's needs, in this view, seemed to be indistinguishable from, and to subsume, those of the person. Similarly, the Ngos defined "democracy" in terms of a politically engaged and united population, rather than individual rights and representative government. Diem sought to "rearm" the people and build the "infrastructure of democracy," which was not necessarily synonymous with the promotion of Western-style liberties.

This loose definition of "democracy" is an important key to understanding Saigon's ideas about the nature of political participation in South Vietnam. The Ngos genuinely sought to galvanize the populace for the task of nation building, but they intended to keep a firm hand on the tiller as they guided this process. They looked to build the state from the bottom up, by exercising strong leadership from the top down, a point that was made most explicitly at the time of the Strategic Hamlet program. Like the leaders of other newly independent states, they expressed faith in the democratic potential of the peasant masses but argued that the present situation required effective controls at the top.[102]

On the one hand, the Ngos romanticized the peasantry, especially when they compared the rural population with the urban elite. While the latter was a self-interested and privileged clique, they noted, the former was a source of nationalism and primeval democracy. Before colonialism, observed Diem, the villages had governed themselves, generating a spirit of unity among ordinary people that had played a critical role in shaping the nation. Historically, rural Vietnam had spawned the pioneers, who had extended the frontiers of the country, and the fighters, who had maintained its independence against more powerful enemies. Diem argued that there was a communal energy in the villages, which the regime could exploit in order to mobilize the population and that would ultimately help forge a new state built upon these robust local foundations.[103]

Yet, at the same time as romanticizing peasants, the Ngos also regarded them as ignorant and backward. "You have seen the Montagnards, with their spears and their superstitions. The Chams. The Cao Dai. The Hoa Hao. The primitive villages where the ancestors rule—as they do most places in Vietnam," Diem told Marguerite Higgins. "Tell me, Miss Higgins, what can parliamentary democracy mean to a Montagnard when his language does not even have a term to express it." Given the country's backwardness, the legacies of colonialism, and the depredations of the communists, the Ngos believed that it would take time before they could loosen the reins of power and let the population assume the responsibilities of modern citizenship.[104] The rural masses needed tutelage and guidance; and, if necessary, people would have to be forced to do what was in their, and everybody else's, best interest and learn how to be good citizens. Thus, Nhu defended the regimented character of the regime's mass organizations by arguing that since the Vietnamese were "not used to the idea of voluntary association," they had to be compelled to participate "in order to teach the people solidarity."[105]

For the foreseeable future at least, the Ngos regarded the formal apparatus of Western-style democracy as a dangerous distraction from the real business of nation building: mobilizing the population by creating an "infrastructure of democracy." In this view, the kind of "bourgeois" political freedoms advocated by Washington merely provided a platform for their critics among the urban elite to oppose the regime; hence, their neglect of institutions like the National Assembly. The palace wanted the assembly to be a source of political solidarity, a place where the people's representatives met to express support for the "just cause"; it was not meant to be a forum for substantive debate.[106] For the Ngos, a U.S. embassy report concluded in August 1956, there "could be no real difference of opinion among true patriots on the basic tasks facing the government at this critical period of the country's history, and these tasks are of such transcending importance that all energies must be bent toward their accomplishment."[107]

To the extent, then, that there was a gap between the regime's rhetoric and practice, it was not one separating promises of democracy from the realities of "Diemocracy," for the Ngos were plainly not talking about Western-style freedoms; or, rather, as their attitude toward the National Assembly reveals, they were only interested in attenuated versions of such freedoms that fitted with their own ideas about popular political participation. The real disparity in Diem's Vietnam was between the goals of the Personalist revolution and their practical fulfillment. The Ngos possessed no hidden agenda; it just proved difficult to carry out their publicly articulated one. Ultimately, it was this gap between theory and practice that would prove to be their undoing, as we shall see by examining the palace's attempts to put its plans into effect.

3

Land Reform,
Land Development,
and Agrovilles

"Each time that I visited President Diem in his office," Edward Lansdale re-called of his days in Saigon in the mid-1950s, "I would find him deep in the study of some new program, often of vast dimensions."[1] Grandiose nation-building projects fascinated the Vietnamese premier. According to a mini-biography, composed by Lansdale for the Pentagon, Diem first exhibited this interest in public works in the 1920s when, as a young province chief, he encouraged population resettlement on open land.[2] As the leader of a new re-public, he had the opportunity to put such designs into practice on an un-precedented scale. The progress or otherwise of the Saigon regime can be charted by a series of vast rural schemes, which would culminate in the Strategic Hamlet program.

The palace initiated three major projects in the period of the mid- to late 1950s: land reform, and the Land Development and Agroville programs. Their origins and evolution shed light on several key facets of the history of the Diem regime. First, these schemes illustrate the palace's modus operandi, the manner in which it sought to put its nation-building ideas into practice. Second, U.S.–Vietnamese differences over nation building became quite evi-dent in the implementation of such projects, especially in the case of the Land Development and Agroville programs; they served as lightning rods for allied disagreements and colored the attitude of each partner toward cooperation with the other. Finally, the three programs demonstrate the weaknesses of the Diem government, and the exposure of these problems would, in turn, encourage the palace to develop strategic hamlets.

We start with land reform, arguably the most important program but one that, for a number of reasons, the regime pursued with least vigor. Despite prodding from the Americans, who had championed agrarian reform ever since their deepening support for the French in the early 1950s, Diem was slow to get started in this field, in large part because of the enormous difficulties he faced in consolidating his authority in the period 1954–1955.[3] The premier's attention was "riveted to the immediate day-to-day internal political developments," complained Wolf Ladejinsky, the veteran agricultural expert who served with USOM in Saigon before becoming a personal assistant to Diem. "While such issues continue to dominate the scene, he is inclined to look upon most other problems as essentially peripheral."[4]

Although still preoccupied with its immediate survival, the government introduced its first agrarian reforms—Ordinances 2 and 7—in January and February 1955. Ordinance 2 sought to ameliorate the condition of tenant farmers by ensuring security of tenure and limiting rent payments to between 15 and 25 percent of the main crop. Ordinance 7 provided tenants with the right to farm abandoned or uncultivated land. These decrees, however, suffered from the aforementioned lack of high-level attention during Diem's difficult first year in office. It was not until October 1956, moreover, that the regime augmented them with the more important and radical measure of land redistribution. This step, promulgated as Ordinance 57, aimed principally at expropriating land in the Mekong Delta, which ranked as one of the worst spots in the world in terms of the concentration of ownership. Here, some twenty-five hundred landowners, 0.025 percent of the rural population, possessed about 40 percent of the rice land.[5]

In spite of his slow start, Diem was a supporter of land reform, albeit of a conservative hue. In a memorandum handed to Richard Nixon during a visit by the U.S. vice-president in July 1956, Diem described changes in the rural milieu "as *the* pre-condition of meeting the threat of Communism, of broadening the base of our political power, and of increasing the productivity of the land."[6] Politically, agrarian reform promised to win people over to the side of the Personalist revolution by "rearming" them morally and materially. "[Personalism] finds a first application in the effort of the Government to provide each landless family, directly or indirectly, with a house and sufficient land for its subsistence," the president informed the National Assembly, since "this basic property is a real guarantee of individual freedom."[7] Diem told U.S. officials that landless farmers constituted a rural "proletariat" and that the attitude of certain landowners in the Mekong Delta was "almost feudal." Rural exploitation had reduced poor farmers to a state of listlessness and passivity, the regime contended; they had lost their "humanity/personality." Furnishing them with the means to be self-sufficient would generate a new spirit of energy and enthusiasm, which could then be harnessed in the service of the "just cause."[8]

Reforms, especially land redistribution, would simultaneously "take the political wind out of the Communist sails," Diem observed, since rural conditions made poor peasants "easy prey to Communist propaganda." The party did indeed make the land issue a central theme of its appeal to the rural population. As one former communist cadre noted, it told farmers that "they will become masters of the countryside and owners of their land, and that scratches the peasants right where they itch." Since Vietnam was an agrarian country, Diem explained to Nixon, "I am convinced that, if we are to secure the lasting support of an overwhelming majority of the people, the individual farmer must own the land he cultivates. In accomplishing this," he added, "we will at the same time meet, by tangible deeds, the false Communist claim that they are the authentic spokesmen of the hopes and aspirations of the peasantry."[9]

Owner cultivation promised economic as well as political benefits. Providing the landless with land, and opening up abandoned or uncultivated areas, was a way to develop the country's untapped resources and improve agricultural production. Agrarian reform would also lay the basis for industrialization by converting "feudal" landowners into budding industrialists; the compensation package for individuals whose property was to be expropriated under Ordinance 57 offered some money in cash and the rest in government bonds that could be invested in state-run industrial enterprises. Diem told General O'Daniel that his aim was "to create an economic base out of our own resources that in time will raise the standard of living of all our people. If achieved, our dependence upon American aid would eventually be eliminated." Successful development in the south, he informed Nixon, would also prove that "our methods are superior to those of our enemies," thus undermining the legitimacy of the communist regime in North Vietnam.[10]

The palace's reforms, however, failed to achieve all these promising goals. Research carried out in the late 1960s, under the auspices of U.S. AID (Agency for International Development), suggested that Diem had "missed the chance to carry out a competitive democratic land reform." Not only did Saigon fail to stop abuses in landlord-tenant relations; land redistribution, the jewel in the crown of any meaningful reform program, also benefited few farmers. Ordinance 57 was a conservative piece of legislation, which allowed owners to retain about one hundred hectares of land, a ceiling thirty times higher than the limits set for similar schemes in Japan, South Korea, and Taiwan. Thus, the ordinance made available about seven hundred thousand hectares for distribution, which only constituted a third of the tenanted land in South Vietnam. Wolf Ladejinsky had advised the palace of this problem, although, as he later observed, there had been a reasonable assumption at that time that, after their unpleasant experiences in the First Indochina War, "landlords would be inclined to dispose of a good deal of the remainder of their land." To make matters worse, the government only managed to transfer to new owners about 40 percent of the land that Ordinance 57 did make available. Consequently, some areas of the countryside were hardly touched at all by Saigon's efforts.[11] In the strategically critical province of Long An, for example, probably about 90 percent of farm families worked on land wholly or partly rented. Less than 5 percent of these people ultimately profited from the regime's program.[12]

What had gone wrong? To some extent, the palace's dismal record on land reform was self-inflicted. First of all, the Ngos believed it advisable to avoid too radical a set of reforms in order to preserve the fragile base of support that they had inherited in 1954.[13] After all, when Diem returned to Vietnam as premier, he was like a man arriving from Mars; he possessed little organization of his own, apart from a few close associates and members of his family. Instead, he had to take over the ramshackle remnants of the State of Vietnam, with its self-interested coterie of officials and landowners. This is not to say that the Ngos were creatures of the existing elite; in fact, they generally despised their new "supporters," whom they regarded as insufficiently imbued with a sense of patriotic pride and Personalist principles. These groups were not particularly enamored with the Ngos either; Ladejinsky met many unreconstructed landowners who deeply resented the government's agrarian reforms.[14] Still, given the alternative, each side was stuck with the other, at least for the moment. From the palace's point of view, it could ill afford to alienate such people until it had developed an alternative base of support.

Nor, for ideological reasons, were the Ngos prepared to carry out the kind of clean sweep of the social order that had taken place in North Vietnam. Personalism sought to promote a "collective advance," argued Diem, not to excite class conflict. Hence, the regime proposed to harmonize the interests of tenants and landlords. This approach also provided Saigon with an opportunity to contrast the RVN's land reform efforts with the coercion and bloodshed that had accompanied the DRVN's recent program, in which between three thousand and fifteen thousand "enemies" of the revolution had been executed. "We have rejected the ruthless methods the Communists use," Diem told Nixon in his 1956 memo, "and are determined to achieve our goal without confiscation, hatred, violence or execution." Saigon believed, in any case, that it offered southern peasants a far better deal than the communists, particularly since Hanoi's policy aimed ultimately at the collectivization of agriculture.[15]

Besides the self-imposed limitations that followed from these political and ideological concerns, the other main shortcoming of the regime's policies was the problem of implementation. For a start, poor peasants, the supposed beneficiaries of agrarian reform, generally treated the regime's efforts with indifference, in large part because earlier Viet Minh land policies had already stolen Saigon's thunder. Government reforms actually antagonized some farmers since they sought to restore a version of the ancien regime, albeit an ameliorated one, in formerly remote and/or communist-dominated areas of the countryside. During the war years, many peasants had paid no rent to their landlords in such areas, while others moved onto abandoned land without much concern for the niceties of legal ownership. Restoration of government control, however, spelled the return of rents, or repayments for land ownership, which a more politically aware and assertive peasantry refused to take lying down.[16] The events of the last decade had evidently wrought significant changes in the outlook of ordinary farmers. During field trips in the spring and summer of 1955, Ladejinsky witnessed bitter wrangling between tenants and landlords over fixing the 15–25 percent rental rate under Ordinance 2. "In the old days," one tenant remarked, "what the landlord said the land produced was law and I paid accordingly. Now I know what it produces and I don't accept his estimate any longer."[17]

Landowners may have understood from such encounters that times had changed, but they showed no more enthusiasm for the regime's policies than their tenants. In March 1955, Ladejinsky met representatives from a group of big southern proprietors who were opposed to any real agrarian reform, an attitude that spread as the shadow of the Viet Minh receded.[18] Given such sentiments, the reaction to Saigon's policies, especially the land-redistributing Ordinance 57, was predictably hostile. The Federation of Vietnamese Landowners submitted a series of proposed amendments to the ordinance that would have drastically watered down an already moderate piece of legislation. "Life will have no charm," the federation asserted, "if the land is divided into small parcels just to let people have a minimum to live on."[19] The regime's policies clearly disturbed and angered many proprietors. "We have been robbed by the Viet Minh over the years," a landowner in the Delta's Soc Trang province told Ladejinsky, "and we resent similar treatment from the national government."[20]

Ladejinsky's interlocutor also happened to be the chief of the province, which pointed to another problem in implementing policy. For a number of reasons, Saigon's provincial administrations were just not up to the job of carrying out the reforms, a failing that would plague all of the palace's rural initiatives. Lassitude and indifference characterized the approach of many local officials. Others, such as the chief of Soc Trang, deliberately set out, with the connivance of local landowners, to sabotage the regime's efforts. Even well-intentioned officials found it difficult to get anything done because they lacked the wherewithal to do so. "In Japan, in conditions of a well-functioning government and a host of capable technicians," reported Ladejinsky, "the land reform program was carried out with the assistance of nearly 400,000 paid and volunteer workers. In all of Vietnam there are not 400 people directly and actively engaged in this task."

Nguyen Tran, who served as a province chief during this period, described the administrative apparatus that Diem inherited as an inverted pyramid, with the personnel and resources concentrated in the central, rather than local, government. This "huge head and small buttocks" problem, as Nguyen Van Thieu later called it, severely hampered the work of local authorities. So too did the security situation in the countryside. In 1955, large parts of the southern provinces still remained under the jurisdiction of the Hoa Hao and the Cao Dai, and were off-limits to officials. Soon, the resurgence of the communist-led resistance would similarly impede the operation of local government. "They are not authorities in the real sense of the word," Ladejinsky concluded of the regime's provincial administrations, "for their power to govern is so limited as to be almost non-existent; and the sects, the Communists, and the farmers behave accordingly."[21]

In short, Diem's agrarian reforms not only were a wary compromise but also proved difficult to enforce. Progress was slow, too slow to make the kind of impact on the peasantry that might have prevented the outbreak of a new insurgency in the late 1950s. Occasional crackdowns on corruption, or the well-publicized expropriation of land belonging to high-ranking officials, could not cure the program's administrative shortcomings. Indeed, inefficiency, and perhaps foot-dragging, in Saigon only served to exacerbate them; the performance of at least one minister of agrarian reform, Nguyen Van Thoi, left much to be desired.[22] As the program stuttered, moreover, the palace neglected to provide the drive that might have given it some further impetus. In fact, Diem's attention was on the wane as the regime embarked in 1957 on another rural scheme, the Land Development program.

Land Development was a large-scale resettlement program. It aimed at relocating thousands of Vietnamese—inhabitants of the overcrowded central lowlands, demobilized soldiers, and refugees who had fled south after the country's partition in 1954—in new centers on uncultivated or abandoned tracts of land in highland areas and in the Mekong Delta. At the same time, it sought to encourage the indigenous population of the highlands—often referred to in the West by the French term "Montagnards"—to give up their "uncivilized" and seminomadic existence by moving into permanent settlements. It thus complemented efforts that had been under way since 1955 to resettle and assimilate the Montagnards in new "model villages."[23]

Diem promoted Land Development with a passion that was missing from his earlier advocacy of agrarian reform. Recent experiences in resettling northern refugees, such as the Cai San project, the giant scheme of land reclamation and reconstruction to the southwest of Saigon, had no doubt whetted his appetite for a program of this kind.[24] There was also a dramatic and patriotic quality to the settlement of new land that strongly appealed to him; in an interview with *Le Figaro,* Diem described Land Development as "rough, healthful and virile," a "typically Vietnamese operation." The more mundane business of land redistribution seemed to pale before the vision of hardy pioneers engaged in the physical transformation of the country. After all, the carving out of new territory was how the Vietnamese had come to occupy the present boundaries of the nation, migrating southward and settling the land. "Our history tells that a man could seek no greater honor than to be the founder of a new village," Diem explained during a state visit to Australia in September 1957.[25]

Saigon was particularly keen to settle and develop the sparsely populated Central Highlands, in order to incorporate it fully into the national patrimony. After 1945, the French had effectively kept the area under their direct control and out of the hands of colonial-backed Vietnamese governments; they also encouraged an anti-Vietnamese, ethno-nationalism among the Montagnards. When Cao Van Luan first met Diem in 1948, the future premier described French policy, in a region of such strategic and economic importance to Vietnam, as intolerable.[26] A decade later, then, Land Development provided a means to reclaim the Central Highlands by "Vietnamizing" them; ethnic Vietnamese would be brought in to settle land, while the indigenous population would be incorporated into the body politic and granted the benefits of Vietnamese civilization.[27] Perhaps it was no coincidence that the program's title, *Dinh Dien,* had also been one of the terms used historically to describe the settlement and cultivation of new land by the Vietnamese.[28]

Planning for Land Development began in the autumn of 1956 following a long period of gestation. U.S. officials participated in the process and Washington agreed to provide more than $10 million for the project. The program officially got under way in April 1957, headed by Bui Van Luong, who had been responsible for the earlier resettlement of northern refugees.[29] Luong's commissariat general for Land Development surveyed and prepared the sites, and then transported people to the new centers. Here, the authorities provided the settlers with various forms of assistance to restart their lives: subsidies for the cost of constructing houses, grants of food, and the provision of farm implements, seeds, and so on. The settlements themselves contained a number of public facilities, such as a dispensary, maternity hospital, school, and marketplace. They ranged in size from one hundred to five hundred families, each family receiving between one and three hectares of cleared land within a central residential area as well as being free to clear further ground, farther afield, at their own expense.[30]

By mid-1959, according to government figures, eighty-four new centers had been established, with a population of 125,000. The majority of these settlers, over 70,000, came from the provinces of the central lowlands. In addition, there were 17,000 former northern refugees, who had originally been settled in other areas of South Vietnam. Six of the centers, with a population of 6,000, were reserved for Montagnards. By the end of 1962, the regime reported the establishment of 173 settlements, with a population of over 230,000 people, by which time the regime had begun to integrate the centers into the expanding Strategic Hamlet program.[31]

Like their other big nation-building programs, the Ngos viewed Land Development as a way of tackling simultaneously all of the RVN's "enemies"— "Communism, Underdevelopment, and Disunity." Nhu told U.S. officials in April 1957 that the regime "took a broad view of its problems and tried to link them together when possible." For the Ngos, the issues of modernization and pacification were intimately related; South Vietnam had to overcome its societal weaknesses in order to counter the communists, while the latter had to be quashed to stop them undermining the regime's efforts to strengthen the country.[32] The palace's sense of urgency also dictated a multidimensional approach to the south's problems. On a number of occasions during this period, Diem argued that he only had a couple of years in which to establish a secure and stable South Vietnam, before communist pressures increased and American aid dried up.[33] Consequently, the palace saw Land Development as a recipe for short-order nation building, which would deliver, in rapid fashion, an array of strategic, economic, and political benefits.

First, Diem wanted to build a "human wall" for security purposes in the Delta's Plain of Reeds and in the Central Highlands by settling land in these critical frontier areas. At the same time, regrouping the Montagnards into resettlement centers would deny the communists a potential source of support in the vulnerable borderlands. Diem warned U.S. officials that, even though the Geneva deadline for nationwide elections had passed, he was under pressure from communist propaganda, as well as the Indian representatives on the International Control Commission (ICC), to open up communications between north and south. Before he could take that risk, he argued, the regime had to move quickly to fill vacant territory with a contented population, in order to prevent the enemy from successfully infiltrating the country through the leaking sieve that constituted South Vietnam's frontiers with Laos and Cambodia.[34] According to the U.S. embassy in Saigon, an attempt on Diem's life in February 1957—at a fair in Ban Me Thuot, ironically held to promote Land Development—had exacerbated this concern about the vulnerability of the RVN's borders.[35]

Land Development promised various economic benefits as well. Resettlement would relieve population pressures, especially in the crowded coastal provinces of central Vietnam, by offering land to the landless and underemployed; Diem also envisaged wilderness areas as a perfect place to resettle more northern Vietnamese, should there be a further influx of refugees. In turn, the redistribution of the population would complement the regime's existing efforts at land redistribution by providing people with the basic piece of property that the regime saw as critical to their moral and material "rearmament." The regime's *News from Viet-Nam* even suggested that the Central Highlands could support a population of almost thirty million.[36] Resettlement would also contribute to the national economy, of course. Opening up new territory would boost agricultural production as well as facilitate a measure of economic diversification; in favorable areas, Saigon hoped to grow new cash and industrial crops, such as coffee, rubber, kenaf, and ramie.[37]

Finally, Land Development was shaped by the palace's interest in some of the less tangible aspects of nation building. Diem envisaged resettlement in terms of a popular struggle, a collective effort that would not only help strengthen the country physically but also nurture a socially engaged and civic-minded population. During frequent inspection tours of the new centers, he exhorted his audiences to work hard and emulate the pioneering traditions of their ancestors, who had earlier carved settlements out of the wilderness.[38] Historically, he noted, settling new lands had "called for qualities of initiative, a communal sense, ability to organize, mutual assistance, discipline, recognition of merit, self-policing and defense against robbers and brigands." The process had also contributed to the "homogeneity and binding of the country." What was needed, in Diem's view, was a program that would foster a new generation of pioneers with similar nation-building qualities. "National Reconstruction is the task of every citizen, and each of us must do his utmost for it," he told a crowd of settlers during a visit to the Central Highlands at Christmastime 1957.[39]

To help foster this spirit of collective endeavor, the Land Development program was based on the principle of "Community Development." Thus, inhabitants contributed to the establishment of the new centers by constructing buildings, roads, and canals, and by participating in civic associations and self-defense units; they also cultivated, on a community rather than an individual basis, those parts of their land devoted to cash crops. The centers themselves, noted Vu Van Thai, were intentionally larger than traditional villages in order to create more scope for such projects, thereby encouraging a greater communal spirit among their residents. In short, besides the physical act of settling new land, the program was designed to serve as a giant act of civic education. The shared hardships required to carve out new lands would promote the Personalist ideals of self-sacrifice and civic responsibility.[40]

The palace believed that all of these strategic, economic, and political benefits would significantly strengthen South Vietnam and so improve its position in the competition with the north. In a meeting with Ambassador Durbrow and Senator John Sparkman in September 1957, Diem stated that, if he could make solid progress in the next few years, the emergence of a strong and flourishing south would put great pressure on the regime in Hanoi. Diem "expressed the opinion," Durbrow reported, "that, with such firmness and solid development, he expected the situation in North Viet Nam to deteriorate sufficiently in the next three years or so to bring about an enforced liberalization of the Viet Minh regime which would eventually make unification possible."[41]

Fueled by such visions, and a great sense of urgency, Diem set a blistering pace in implementing Land Development. He devoted a good deal of personal attention to the program, even choosing many of the settlement sites himself.[42] As with the later Agroville and Strategic Hamlet schemes, Saigon sought to get things done with the utmost dispatch, ignoring impediments as well as the hardships confronting settlers. The aim was to fill up empty land, with large numbers of people, as quickly as possible. Land Development was an urgent task of national reconstruction in which settlers were expected to do their bit and bravely shoulder their burdens. Indeed, the palace regarded such hardships as part and parcel of the exercise.

This approach led to a number of problems, however, as well as generating tensions between the palace and the Americans. First, Diem's demand for speed and sacrifice encouraged RVN officials to employ coercion in dealing with the population because many of the prospective beneficiaries of Land Development evidently did not share the palace's enthusiasm for the scheme. Montagnards resented Diem's heavy-handed attempts at assimilation and the regime's failure to recognize their land claims. Ethnic Vietnamese, meanwhile, tended to regard the highlands as desolate, inhospitable, and malaria-ridden, and some people simply did not want to move there.[43] The regime's use of coercion was particularly evident in its efforts to corral the Montagnards, but it extended to would-be Vietnamese settlers as well. If their attempts to publicize the program failed to recruit enough settlers, local officials sometimes tricked or forced people into moving. The U.S. consulate in Hue also reported that the government cut off aid to villages of northern refugees, so as to put their inhabitants "into the proper frame of mind" when considering the benefits of resettlement.[44]

The reluctance of northern refugees to play the role of nation-building pioneers particularly disappointed the palace, which had viewed its coreligionists as perfect settler material. They were bred of hardy stock, Diem believed, in comparison to the "lazy" southern Vietnamese, and their anticommunism would help to establish a loyal population in border areas. Yet, rather than face the travails of life in the Central Highlands, many northerners still clung to the hope that Vietnam's partition would be short-lived and their next move would be an early return to their original homes above the Seventeenth Parallel. Their attitude further damaged relations between Saigon and the Catholic community, already strained as a result of the government's efforts to curb the temporal authority exercised by priests in refugee villages. In a speech in March 1957, Madame Nhu lambasted people whose "cowardice or laziness" was stymieing the regime's attempt to open virgin lands; it was generally understood that Catholic refugees were the principal targets of this invective.[45]

It is unclear whether coercive practices pervaded the implementation of the program and, if so, whether the orders for such actions came from the top. Official descriptions of Land Development emphasized that relocation was by choice, a point that Diem reiterated in private as well. Gilbert Jonas, the RVN's public relations counsel in the United States, noted after a conversation with the president that Diem was "particularly proud of the voluntary nature of the resettlement program" and wished to avoid the use of force "as far as possible." But coercion was also a vital element in bringing about social change, Diem informed Jonas, citing the Enclosure Movement in British history.[46] At the very least, this sentiment—that some people might have to be compelled to do what was in everybody's best interest—created a climate conducive to the use of force by lower-level officials.

Although the Americans expressed some concern about instances of forced relocation, their response to the problem was generally muted; they seemed willing to turn a blind eye because of their support for the broad objectives of Land Development. In any case, information about the regime's coercive practices was patchy, and RVN officials kept things that way by restricting the access of U.S. reporting officers to certain settlements.[47] However, a number of other aspects of the program did lead to serious disagreements between the Vietnamese and Americans. These clashes, particularly over questions of the choice and development of the resettlement sites, reflected the two partners' differing conceptions of nation building. While U.S. officials paid close attention to technical issues concerning the viability of new settlements and the economic well-being of their inhabitants, Diem wanted rapid progress and demanded the appropriate sacrifices from his people.

The original U.S.–Vietnamese project agreement on Land Development had called for careful examination of new sites, in order to establish their potential in terms of soil fertility, access to water, and transportation links. Yet the palace rode roughshod over these procedural safeguards in its headlong rush to complete the program. U.S. agricultural experts also clashed with the regime over the question of the acreage necessary for subsistence in the new centers, arguing that settlers would need more land than the government envisaged, especially in the less fertile areas of the highlands. Saigon's decision to concentrate its resettlement efforts on the tougher terrain of the highlands, rather than the more accommodating southern plains, only served to exacerbate this problem. Other U.S. concerns—about RVN administrative procedures, the use of some centers as political detention camps, and the displacement of the indigenous Montagnards—added to the mounting ill will that soon came to characterize U.S.–Vietnamese collaboration on Land Development. By the end of 1957, working-level relations had reached rock bottom, with USOM technicians deeply critical of the palace's implementation of the program.[48]

Top-level U.S. officials also expressed misgivings. Ambassador Durbrow remained generally supportive of Land Development. He thought the scheme had "considerable merit" and sympathized with the Vietnamese complaint that the Americans only appeared willing to help them "on our own perfectionist terms." At the same time, Durbrow criticized Diem's single-minded obsession with resettlement—one of the president's "pet ideas and schemes"—which, he argued, left languishing other pressing matters such as land reform and industrial development. He also worried about the impact of allied disputes on U.S. relations with Saigon. In a February 1958 telegram to Washington, Durbrow advised that the United States withdraw from the program in order to get out of "many controversial Land Development questions which have caused serious friction to develop during [the] past year."[49]

After 1957, the Vietnamese and Americans found a way of agreeing to disagree. The United States largely withdrew from the program, limiting itself to technical advice and minor assistance. It transferred the 1958 funds already assigned to Land Development into the RVN's military budget and, in turn, the Diem regime was able to use money that it would otherwise have contributed to that budget in order to finance its resettlement scheme. Thus, Saigon could carry out its version of Land Development, while the United States was absolved of any direct responsibility for the program's implementation. Working-level collaboration on the project actually improved after this change, in part because the Vietnamese found U.S. advice and support more palatable when it came without strings attached.[50]

The disagreements over Land Development, however, highlighted the conflicting perspectives of patron and client. They heightened Saigon's concern about the issue of sovereignty and strengthened its determination to limit the embarrassing presence, and potentially meddlesome activities, of its foreign backers. They also reinforced the palace's conviction that American guidelines for the dispensation of aid simply hamstrung the recipient and failed to meet the urgent requirements of a newly developing country, especially one in a virtual state of siege. This criticism, of course, was aimed at more than just the "red tape" associated with the delivery of aid, since the procedural checks employed by the Americans also reflected certain U.S. conceptions of what constituted appropriate development policies. The Ngos, on the other hand, wanted aid without preconditions and the freedom to fashion their own nation-building programs. The fact that Land Development proved to be a moderate success, in spite of USOM's Cassandra-like warnings, only served to fuel their belief that they knew what was best for South Vietnam.[51]

Even before the dispute over Land Development, the palace had expressed a desire to hire and pay U.S. technicians in order to "Vietnamize" aid programs, rather than running joint projects with the Americans.[52] In the aftermath of the clashes of 1957, it moved to keep the U.S. role in South Vietnam within acceptable limits, vetoing an aid program proposed by USOM's Field Service Division, restricting the movement of U.S. personnel in the countryside, and forbidding provincial officials to provide Americans with information unless expressly authorized.[53] Saigon's desire to run its own show was also clearly demonstrated in mid-1959 when the regime initiated a major new rural project—the Agroville program—without notifying, or seeking the support of, its superpower patron.

While Land Development concentrated on the settlement of new lands, especially in the Central Highlands, the Agroville program focused on the regroupment of the existing population in the Mekong Delta. In April 1959, Diem ordered a committee of technical experts to choose sites for the construction of a number of new model settlements, or mini-towns, that would provide their inhabitants with security, offer peasants the amenities of a modern life, and stimulate regional development. Early designs called for twenty-four of these agrovilles, with the expectation that this figure would rise, perhaps to as many as eighty new settlements. Each agroville would contain about four hundred families (two thousand to three thousand people), who would purchase, at a low price and on credit, small plots of land for residences and gardens as well as retaining their old property outside the settlement. Every agroville would provide its inhabitants with a range of public facilities, such as a school, hospital, and market. In June 1960, Diem also proposed the construction of a number of smaller agro-hamlets that would serve as satellites for the larger agrovilles. Together, these schemes represented another major nation-building program, with as many as five hundred thousand peasants likely to have been affected if the most ambitious of these plans had ever been fully implemented.[54]

This sort of population regroupment, and the creation of rural showplaces, already had established pedigrees in Vietnam as well as in the folklore of counterinsurgency. The Franco–Bao Dai regime constructed several show-piece settlements in the early 1950s, such as the "new-life village" of Dong Quan.[55] British resettlement in Malaya was also a fashionable example of how to beat guerrillas; Diem later told U.S. officials that he patterned much of the Agroville program on Malaya's "New Villages."[56] Given the complex way in which ideas develop, it is difficult to pin down the precise influence of these precursors on the regime's new scheme, particularly in light of the overlapping jumble of theories and clichés that made up the newly emerging doctrine of counterinsurgency. However, it is not especially important to trace the distant inspirations for the Agroville program, which can be better understood by examining the particular circumstances of its emergence and the special brand that the palace stamped on any imported models that it did seek to copy.

The original stimulus for the new scheme was the deteriorating security situation. There was a perceptible increase in antiregime activity from early 1958 onward, much of it a matter of self-defense on the part of hard-pressed communist cadres and other victims of government repression. The southern branch of the communist party had almost ceased to exist in some areas, its members arrested or liquidated as the Diem regime dealt ruthlessly with real, and perceived, signs of opposition. As one cadre noted, this was "the darkest period for the Party in the South, when if you did not have a gun you could not keep your head on your shoulders."[57] Previously loath to sanction armed action in the south, the leadership in Hanoi decided in the spring of 1959 to endorse the incipient revolt, approving the formation of "self-defense and armed propaganda forces in order to support the political struggle." It also issued instructions to establish Group 559, which would organize the infiltration of people and supplies from north to south.[58]

Saigon was slow to appreciate that while government repression had seemingly quashed its opponents, it had also generated widespread discontent and created conditions ripe for a backlash. In particular, local officials charged with maintaining security had liberally interpreted their orders, targeting, for example, ex–Viet Minh, even if they were no longer politically active. Most officials that dealt with security in the provinces had served under the colonial power, observed Tran Ngoc Chau, a former anticolonial guerrilla who had later joined the RVN's forces. As a result, they viewed the old Viet Minh as enemies and peasants as potential enemies. Chau recalls lunching one day at a village restaurant with the local police chief, who informed him that their waitress was under surveillance. Her husband, the chief confided, had been one of "them" during the First Indochina War and had killed many of "us." Chau thought it very strange that an official should describe those who fought for independence as "them" and the Vietnamese who sided with the French as "us." What would have happened, he mused, if he was not an RVN officer and the police chief knew that he had spent four years with the Viet Minh?[59]

In places, local officials presided over a virtual reign of terror. In effect, they defined who constituted a threat and fed higher echelons on a diet of their suspicions. In addition, some of them used their police powers for the purposes of bribery and extortion. If people attempted to resist the authorities, local officials often clamped down even harder, thus encouraging a vicious action-reaction cycle between the government and the rural populace.[60] Under the circumstances, it is not hard to understand why, in addition to its other failings, the Diem regime generated an enormous amount of bad blood among the peasantry, or why the communists, so badly hit by government repression, could rise phoenixlike in the period 1959–1960. However much Saigon had hurt its opponents, it had created thousands more by its repressive tactics. "I'm only afraid that once Ben Tre turns to military action we won't be able to restrain them," commented one party official about cadres and peasants in the Delta province of Kien Hoa.[61]

Amid signs of this impending storm, Saigon instituted a new security program based on an experiment in Phong Dinh province, where Lieutenant Tran Cuu Thien had resettled isolated peasants into nearby villages. According to Thien, Diem had visited his district and left impressed with these efforts.[62] In February 1959, the regime started to compulsorily regroup people in insecure areas into two types of "agglomeration" centers. Those suspected of communist sympathies, because of family connections or past loyalties, were to be resettled in "regrouping zones," where they could be watched, while loyal citizens were to be removed to "regrouping hamlets" to secure them against communist intimidation. The program was an arbitrary and entirely security-oriented operation, which ran into rapid and bitter opposition from both sets of people.[63]

Problems with this new campaign coincided with, and stimulated, a palace debate over the best way to deal with the security situation. Wolf Ladejinsky noted that Vice-President Nguyen Ngoc Tho and Minister of Agriculture Le Van Dong had both voiced their concern over the regime's emphasis on suppressing its enemies, rather than more positive efforts to win peasant support. The U.S. embassy also reported that Ngo Dinh Can wanted provincial authorities to show more interest in the welfare of peasants, and to distinguish between hard-core communists and those intimidated into assisting the insurgents.[64] These expressions of concern suggested that the palace was becoming aware of the extent to which its policy of repressing opposition, especially in the hands of zealous local officials, was actually fostering discontent.

For example, in promulgating the notoriously tough Law 10/59, Saigon emphasized to its subordinates that the legislation sought to address "current" threats to security, not to take "revenge" against old Viet Minh activists.[65]

By the spring of 1959, those within the regime advocating "win over peasants" seemed to be gaining the upper hand, commented Ladejinsky.[66] In March, the palace appointed Major Pham Ngoc Thao to reexamine the agglomeration scheme. His report supported the idea of regroupment but criticized the attempt to categorize families on the basis of political loyalty. He also recommended combining the security aspects of resettlement with an effort to improve economic and social conditions in the countryside. Thao's report, according to its author, encouraged Diem to flesh out the Agroville program.[67] At the end of June 1959, a few days before officially launching the new scheme, Diem informed Ambassador Durbrow that the regime was now turning its attention to the Delta and that it was essential to win the confidence of the peasantry in order to quell the insurgency. Saigon gave Tran Cuu Thien, promoted to the rank of major and chief of province, the task of converting some agglomeration settlements into the regime's first showpiece agroville at Vi Thanh-Hoa Luu.[68]

Like Land Development, the Agroville program sought to turn necessity into a virtue. Concerns about security provided the catalyst for the elaboration of another multidimensional scheme for Ngo-style nation building. First, the program aimed at reasserting government authority in the Mekong Delta. Vast, and inaccessible in places, this part of the country had long been a haven for dissident elements. The region's dispersed pattern of settlement exacerbated the problem of security, with villages being strung out for miles along canals and waterways.[69] The palace assumed that these features of the Delta enabled the insurgents to dupe or intimidate isolated peasants into supporting them, since, naturally, no right-minded person would voluntarily wish to cast his or her lot with the communists. Regroupment, therefore, would free villagers from the clutches of the enemy, an assumption that may explain why the authorities do not appear to have placed a premium on physical defenses for the new program. As a guide at the Vi Thanh agroville told one American visitor, the "people's common sense" was the settlement's "first line of defense."[70]

Agrovilles sought to promote social and economic development as well. Saigon stressed repeatedly, in both its internal and public explanations of the program, that the new scheme was not simply a copy of the security-oriented "New Villages" of Malaya; it sought to promote the regime's Personalist revolution. "Higher Authority" wanted to make it clear to provincial officials, the government delegate for the eastern region informed his subordinates in a June 1960 memorandum, that the program aimed at not only solving the security problem but also creating a new society. Agrovilles, the regime contended, would raise people's standards of living by providing them with new homes and gardens as well as access to public facilities; they would thus bring benefits to the rural population hitherto enjoyed only by city dwellers and the wealthy.[71] In addition, they would end the physical and spiritual isolation of peasants, integrate them into thriving new communities, and make them aware of the larger national entity to which they belonged. This process would help to bridge the traditional gulf that separated town and country in Vietnam. Each center would serve as a focus for the development of the surrounding area, helping to knit together the local economy and the broader fabric of the national polity.[72]

Such communal and national cohesion, so central to the palace's concerns, would also be fostered, the Ngos believed, by popular participation in the Agroville program. For practical and ideological reasons, Saigon emphasized the importance of "Community Development" in the implementation of the scheme. In drawing on the manpower of the population in this fashion, Diem made a point of contrasting the French use of corvée labor, which merely represented foreign exploitation, with the regime's program of "Community Development," which benefited the country materially and schooled people in their civic responsibilities. The government could not afford to undertake such a large project any other way, he stated. At the same time, popular participation in a collective endeavor of this kind promoted group solidarity, by helping people to realize what the individual could achieve through united action, and served to nurture a new generation of rural leaders to replace the parochial and backward-looking ancien regime.[73] Nguyen Dinh Thuan, secretary of state for the presidency, even told U.S. officials that the lack of mechanical equipment for the construction of agrovilles was a blessing in disguise because the palace believed that "the people should feel that this was something they had done themselves."[74]

Diem stressed that the Vietnamese had to rely on their own resources in constructing agrovilles; the only alternative was a debilitating, will-sapping dependence on foreign aid.[75] This emphasis on self-help, of course, also meant the convenient sidelining of the regime's superpower patron, for Saigon had decided to fashion the Agroville program without involving the meddlesome Americans. According to Ambassador Durbrow, the palace avoided discussing its plans with the U.S. embassy in order to avoid a repetition of the Land Development experience. Nor did the regime invite the United States to contribute directly to the program. Saigon planned to finance the agrovilles from sources it controlled and with the assistance of thousands of Delta peasants. This was, as Bui Van Luong later described it, a "specifically Vietnamese effort."[76]

Although reduced to the role of spectators, U.S. officials expressed many of the same concerns about the progress of the regime's new program that they had voiced in the case of Land Development. They worried about the uprooting of peasants, the economic viability of the new centers, and, in particular, the manner of the program's implementation.[77] In a conversation with Diem in March 1960, shortly before the president's trip to inaugurate the showpiece settlement at Vi Thanh-Hoa Luu, Durbrow reported that provincial officials had conscripted thousands of peasants for construction work, far more than were needed, without pay, and during the harvest time. He also noted that the regime had made no attempt to explain to the people the reasons for these sacrifices.[78] Durbrow's visit to Vi Thanh at the end of April confirmed many U.S. concerns about the program. The ambassador described Major Thien, the Phong Dinh province chief, as "one of the most egotistical men I have ever met." Besides bragging about his rapid promotions, Thien boasted about how he had completed the agroville in just fifty days by keeping an average of twenty thousand disgruntled peasants working on the project.[79]

Diem did not welcome such criticism from the Americans, but neither did he approve of the mass coercion practiced by his provincial officials. The palace conceived of the Agroville program in terms of a popular struggle that would mobilize an enthusiastic peasantry, not as an exercise of raw power by the government. Since Diem assumed that his cause was just, and the agrovilles in everybody's best interest, he did not see why peasants should not see things in the same way. In an October 1959 directive, Saigon had instructed its province chiefs to make sure that they explained these facts carefully to the population so that the people would willingly participate in the program. Less than six months later, however, the palace had to reissue these instructions because of the actions of its local officials.[80] Almost inevitably, there had emerged a significant gap between the ideas that circulated in the rarefied atmosphere of the palace and their practical application by the regime's cash-strapped and understaffed provincial administrations.

As with Land Development, Diem set a fast pace for the new scheme's implementation, which sorely tested the capacity of local government. Moreover, Saigon provided the provinces with only one million piasters (about thirteen thousand dollars) for each settlement, around a third of the estimated costs of some of the centers.[81] Consequently, local officials began a panicked effort to cobble together the resources needed to satisfy their superiors and, in the rush, the fine-sounding rhetoric of "Community Development" dissolved in many places into the large-scale coercion of the peasantry. Because of the lack of funds and the pressure to achieve results, Khuu Van Ba, the chief of the Delta's Vinh Long, felt he had no choice except to conscript labor from the entire province in order to construct two agrovilles. Nor did he have sufficient time or personnel to explain the regime's policy to the centers' prospective inhabitants, who thus lost the opportunity to "volunteer" for resettlement. "Sometimes," Ba lamented of his efforts to put flesh on the palace's policies, "the distance between Saigon and Vinh Long is much, much greater than 175 kilometers."[82]

Even had local officials not resorted to coercion, it seems unlikely that the Agroville program would have sparked much popular enthusiasm; it uprooted some peasants from their homes and severely disrupted the lives of many others. As a result of the way in which the program was actually carried out, agrovilles quite clearly generated discontent and active opposition. Peasants disliked the costs and burdens of regroupment as well as those of forced labor. They were sullen, resentful, and sometimes boldly disobedient.[83] The insurgents, for whom Saigon's scheme provided ideal propaganda, encouraged popular resistance and hampered the program's implementation. They targeted agrovilles, telling peasants not to labor on the program and warning officials not to carry out their duties; they also harassed the construction work and even attacked some settlements.[84]

In Kien Hoa (Ben Tre), according to Nguyen Thi Dinh, a local party cadre at the time, villagers slated to move into the Thanh Thoi agroville joined with the insurgents in a campaign of passive resistance. People refused to move until compelled, and then held protests against the program. When Diem came to inspect the agroville in early 1960, they organized a rather innovative demonstration. Feigning to be loyal and enthusiastic citizens, the villagers lined up along the roadside, dutifully waiting for Diem's car to arrive. Then, they tore off their outer garments to reveal "ragged and filthy clothes" and poured onto the road. "It was complete chaos," recalled Dinh. "The policemen blew their whistles, tried to hold the people back with their rifle butts, and fired madly into the air, but could not prevent the ring of people from closing around Ngo Dinh Diem's car." Diem, "greatly embarrassed, stood up to make a few promises and then fled from the scene."[85] Other forms of resistance were less peaceful. The insurgents assassinated officials closely associated with the program, including Vinh Long's Khuu Van Ba, and attacked and destroyed agrovilles in several other provinces.[86]

Agroville construction in early 1960 coincided with a marked upsurge in antigovernment resistance, a reflection of the guerrilla buildup in 1959 and Hanoi's formal approval of armed activity. In January 1960, the communists launched a general uprising and the government's authority crumbled in some areas. In Kien Hoa, the insurgents succeeded in taking military posts, neutralizing the regime's local apparatus, and liberating a number of villages.[87] They killed twenty-six officials in nearby Long An during the week of Tet. Only three individuals in the province had met such a fate in the whole of

1959. The tally would have been far higher, except that many officials had already fled in anticipation of the uprising. In one of Long An's districts, 90 out of 117 hamlet chiefs had resigned before Tet.[88] These events struck a devastating psychological, as well as physical, blow to the regime's position, badly exposing its fragile hold over the countryside. The RVN's provincial apparatus soon began to resemble a series of scattered armed camps rather than a regular network of administration.[89]

In a cabinet meeting in early February 1960, Diem attributed the increase in insurgent activity to the guerrillas' fear of the Agroville program. In spite of the evidence of peasant discontent, he also remained convinced that the population would come to appreciate the value of the new centers once the benefits became clear.[90] Nonetheless, the palace recognized that its scheme was in trouble. The U.S. embassy reported in March that Saigon had sent inspectors to the provinces to gather information about popular dissatisfaction with the actions of local officials. Nhu told CIA sources that, all too often, provincial officials neglected the political and psychological aspects of the situation because they sought to please the president with impressive physical results.[91] As a result of these mounting concerns, Saigon issued instructions to the provinces at the end of March, warning officials that arbitrary actions alienated the people and played straight into the enemy's hands. Diem also told Ambassador Durbrow that he had decided to slow down the program in order to overcome the problems associated with its implementation.[92]

This deceleration soon turned into a terminal decline. In April, Secretary Thuan stated that sixteen agrovilles would be completed by June, out of a planned total of fifty. By the end of August, however, the regime had still only inaugurated thirteen agrovilles, many of them not yet complete, and it announced that none of the satellite agro-hamlets would be built.[93] Finally, at the end of September, Diem informed Durbrow that the program would be temporarily suspended after the construction of about twenty centers. The president cited the financial costs of the program as the reason for this early termination, but monetary difficulties were only part of the far more substantial obstacles that the regime had encountered in attempting to implement the scheme. "Perhaps he has finally been convinced," the U.S. ambassador concluded after meeting with Diem, "that the 'real cost' is loss of popular support for his regime."[94] While the palace never formally terminated the agroville scheme, it had effectively ground to a halt.

This turn of events was a serious blow to the palace's nation-building plans; it also left the regime bereft of a strategy for quelling the growing insurgency. The dimensions of the war had changed dramatically in the course of 1959–1960, confronting Saigon with a new and dangerous situation. Perhaps if the regime had pursued its land reform efforts with more vigor in the mid-1950s, it might not have had to face this problem, but security conditions now precluded further progress in this field. Nor was the palace's Land Development program a match for the new guerrilla menace. Land Development could be considered quite successful in economic terms, but the scheme addressed security matters only in a very broad sense, notably in its concern to populate empty land, and was largely limited to highland areas. To counter increased rural resistance, particularly in the critical Mekong Delta, the regime had initiated the Agroville program, another scheme aimed at combining pacification with the palace's broader nation-building agenda. Yet the agrovilles failed to stem the rising tide of the insurgency and even appeared to have contributed to the communists' mounting success.

With the Agroville program at a standstill, the regime began to rethink its strategy and search for a new formula for defeating its three "enemies." The palace also factored into this reassessment its concerns about relations with the Americans. The Land Development and Agroville programs had highlighted the potential for conflict between Saigon and Washington, at the root of which lay their differing ideas about nation building. U.S. officials were critical of the regime's approach and, in turn, their behavior had confirmed the palace's view of the Americans as unreliable and meddlesome. By 1960, a pattern of disagreement had clearly emerged in the patron–client relationship, which the intensifying guerrilla war only served to exacerbate. The burgeoning insurgency, and the rising tension in U.S.–Vietnamese relations that it helped to generate, set the scene for a change of administration in Washington and the arrival of the New Frontiersmen.

4

Origins of
the Strategic Hamlet
Program

Exercising a pervasive influence over U.S.–Vietnamese relations in 1961 was the specter of the expanding insurgency, which set alarm bells ringing in both Saigon and Washington. Diem faced a threat to his regime's survival, while the Americans had to contemplate the collapse of their strategic position in Southeast Asia. Consequently, each side looked to the other to make the appropriate changes in policy that would help turn the situation around. These reciprocal demands inevitably fueled tensions within the alliance because they exposed the two partners' differing conceptions of the best way forward.

The ensuing disagreements, set against the background of the deteriorating security situation, established the critical context in which the Diem regime attempted to respond to the failure of the Agroville program. With that scheme now in abeyance, the Ngos sought to develop a new strategic formula to defeat the guerrillas and promote their Personalist revolution. They also needed to devise a response to the south's problems that would counter the increased pressure coming from the Americans to accept U.S. policy prescriptions. Indeed, as the Americans pressed, with ever more insistence, to reform the regime along lines prescribed by Washington, the Ngos looked to free themselves from what they perceived to be an increasingly troublesome relationship. In the course of 1961, they found an answer to all of these concerns in the shape of the Strategic Hamlet program.

Guerrilla activity had mushroomed in the course of 1960. The insurgents showed most strength in the Mekong Delta, as demonstrated in their campaign against the Agroville program. Their activities in central Vietnam also increased significantly. In October 1960, for example, guerrilla units launched a series of coordinated assaults against government installations and outposts in the highland province of Kontum. Equally disturbing for the authorities was the information extracted from prisoners captured during these attacks; the units involved were led by local people, who had gone north in 1954 and had now infiltrated back into the south across the porous border with Laos. By December 1960, as a result of infiltration and local recruitment, RVN military sources put the number of guerrillas operating in organized units at ten thousand, a two- to threefold increase on the figures for March. This growth occurred in spite of the heavy losses that Saigon claimed to have inflicted on the insurgents.[1]

To provide an organizational focus for this heightened activity, Hanoi directed the southern branch of the communist party to establish what became the National Front for the Liberation of South Vietnam (NLF). On December 20, 1960, at a secret inaugural meeting near the Cambodian border, the NLF issued a call to arms for the overthrow of the "U.S. imperialists and their stooges—the Ngo Dinh Diem clique." The "front" strategy, designed to appeal to as many opponents of the government as possible, sought to fracture the Diem regime politically. At the same time, the NLF expanded its control over the countryside, mobilizing support in the villages by publicizing the goals of the revolution, highlighting the injustices of the Saigon regime, and engaging in selective acts of violence.[2] This extension of NLF influence appeared to be proceeding at a rapid pace. In April 1961, General Lionel C. McGarr, chief of the MAAG, stated that less than half of South Vietnam remained firmly in government hands.[3]

The security situation continued to deteriorate during the summer and autumn of 1961. The Mekong Delta remained the most insecure part of the country, many of its provincial seats resembling islands in a sea of hostile territory. In October, Major Nguyen Viet Thanh, the newly appointed chief of Long An, discovered that, Route 4 apart, he could not drive more than two kilometers in any direction from his headquarters without coming under fire or running into an enemy roadblock.[4] Outside the Delta, there was a series of unexpectedly aggressive guerrilla operations. In mid-September, the insurgents seized the provincial capital of Phuoc Thanh, staging a "people's trial" in the marketplace and publicly beheading the province chief.[5] They also launched a large attack in September against military posts north of Kontum, shortly followed by a rash of smaller raids. The I and II Corps regions experienced the biggest increases in insurgent activity during this period, especially in highland areas where the evident disaffection among the Montagnards was a particularly ominous portent.[6]

The specter of increased infiltration from North Vietnam heightened concern in Saigon and Washington about the security situation. The U.S. embassy and MAAG attributed much of the NLF's enhanced capability to border crossings, as did Diem.[7] US/RVN intelligence estimates suggested that about 70 percent of the guerrillas were recruited and trained in the south, 25 percent were southerners, trained in the north and reintroduced into the south, and the remaining 5 percent were northern cadres.[8] "While it is clear that most VC [Viet Cong] have not been infiltrated from the north," observed Chalmers Wood of Washington's Vietnam Task Force, "it is also apparent that both the rate of infiltration and the percentage of infiltrees in the VC forces have increased." In addition, he argued, "it has always been true that this element provides the leadership and the backbone of VC forces."[9]

Guerrilla units were certainly becoming larger and better organized. In February 1961, the party had formed the People's Liberation Armed Forces (PLAF) in order to unify armed groups in the south. The insurgents proceeded to expand and revamp their military wing, "organizing a regular force structure from numerous platoon and skeleton-type units." By late 1961, US/RVN estimates put the number of PLAF troops at sixteen thousand to eighteen thousand, half of these being regular or main-force soldiers.[10] Such units, moreover, represented only the tip of an iceberg that drew its real strength from extensive organization at the village level. Briefing U.S. officials in October, a CIA officer, just returned from Vietnam, warned that the communist infrastructure was "much more effective than anything Diem has been able to create."[11] The RVN's local military infrastructure, which was composed of the weak and overstretched Civil Guard and Self-Defense Corps, seemed in danger of collapsing under the strain of increased guerrilla action. Morale among the Self-Defense Corps was particularly bad, with desertion rates rising to alarming levels.[12]

The exponential growth of the insurgency forced Washington and Saigon to reassess their efforts to maintain the south's security. On the U.S. side, this review initially took the form of the Counterinsurgency Plan, completed by the country team in Saigon shortly before the arrival of the new administration in Washington. Billed as a comprehensive answer to the insurgency, the plan was essentially a souped-up amalgam of the various proposals previously advocated by different U.S. agencies. At its heart lay an implicit quid pro quo. In return for increased American assistance, principally U.S. support for an expansion of the Army of the Republic of Vietnam (ARVN) from 150,000 to 170,000, the Diem regime was expected to institute the kind of military and political reforms long cherished by U.S. officials: improved control and coordination in the security and intelligence fields; more effective mobilization of the RVN's economic resources; and efforts to galvanize popular support among all sectors of society. At the present time, the study argued, "the Diem Government offers the best hope for defeating the Viet Cong threat," as long as "necessary corrective measures are taken and adequate forces are provided."[13]

The key question, of course, was whether Diem was willing to take the "necessary corrective measures." On the eve of the Kennedy presidency, U.S.

opinion was divided, roughly along civilian-military lines, over American policy and Diem's prospects. The State Department's Seymour Weiss outlined the two positions in a January memorandum. The first, essentially civilian point of view, he noted, held that "Vietnam is on a rapid downhill toboggan." Unless it introduced reforms, the present government would be overthrown. Thus, the United States should compel Diem to "accommodate himself to our proposals" and, if he refused, "we find an alternative, i.e. permit his overthrow." Proponents of the second point of view, Weiss stated, "acknowledge that Diem is not doing nearly enough but are not completely prepared to write off the possibility of his making a few concessions in time." They also contended that the RVN president had sometimes been right in the past about what needed to be done and, in any case, there was simply "no one better to whom we could throw our support." "You bets your money and you takes your choice," Weiss opined. Yet, while inclined toward the first position, he saw little likelihood of its adoption. "The responsibility for rocking even as leaky a boat as Vietnam currently represents," he concluded, "is too great and the stakes too high."[14]

Weiss's prediction proved to be accurate. Among incumbent officials, and the incoming New Frontiersmen, the inclination was to press ahead and hope for the best, rather than initiate a dramatic change in course. This approach had already begun to attract adherents among working-level officials as a result of the precipitous decline in U.S.–Vietnamese relations in late 1960. In October, Ambassador Durbrow had strained relations with the palace by delivering a démarche, proposing measures to broaden the regime's political support and suggesting that Diem's brother Nhu be transferred abroad because of his "adverse public image."[15] Less than a month later, relations plumbed new depths as a result of an abortive coup attempt by South Vietnamese paratroopers, during which the U.S. embassy played the role of an "honest broker" instead of squarely backing the palace's incumbents.[16] After further sparring between Durbrow and Diem in December, the State Department decided to rein in its ambassador, arguing that any more pressure on the Ngos to liberalize the regime was "likely to be counterproductive." While Diem should be encouraged to adopt reforms, an interagency meeting concluded in early January 1961, the first priority was to concentrate on the worsening security situation.[17]

The hubris and impatience of the New Frontiersmen overrode any residual opposition to this emerging consensus, although the problems in Vietnam actually came as something of a shock to the incoming administration. Despite candidate Kennedy's emphasis on the Third World, Vietnam hardly figured in the campaign of 1960. In a preinaugural briefing, moreover, Eisenhower had directed the president-elect's attention to communist advances in neighboring Laos as the main concern in Southeast Asia.[18] The gravity of the situation in Vietnam was only brought home to the White House in a report written by Edward Lansdale, who had just returned from a trip to his old stamping ground. "This is the worst one we've got, isn't it?" JFK reportedly said after reading Lansdale's memorandum. "You know, Eisenhower never uttered the word Vietnam."[19]

The new president moved quickly to try to remedy this oversight, holding a Saturday morning meeting at the White House in late January to discuss the new Counterinsurgency Plan. There is very little to suggest from the record, however, that the president and his advisers explored seriously the linkage between RVN reforms and increased U.S. assistance, or appreciated the problem of getting Diem to accept the former in exchange for the latter. Kennedy's overriding concern, in South Vietnam and elsewhere, was to get moving, not to engage in a strategic review of U.S. policy. Referring to the crisis areas of Vietnam, the Congo, Laos, and Cuba, he declared that the United States would have to change course in these places and be better off in three months' time than at present. Although he endorsed the Counterinsurgency Plan, JFK's approach suggested that, in the event of opposition from Diem, the insistence on a quid pro quo was likely to give way before the new president's desire to demonstrate America's determination to quash communist "wars of national liberation."[20]

Washington's instructions to Ambassador Durbrow anticipated that the palace would accept the Counterinsurgency Plan within two weeks, but the initial negotiating phase alone dragged on inconclusively for several months. By the time the ambassador left Vietnam in early May, the regime had made no concessions on the most important proposals for political liberalization, and was following its own timetable and format for reforms in the fields of military operations and intelligence.[21] Durbrow appeared increasingly isolated during this period, attempting to maintain pressure on Diem while other U.S. officials preferred to put a brave face on Saigon's limited concessions and get on with the conflict.[22] Kennedy was also impatient to proceed and anxious to prove his mettle, especially after the Bay of Pigs fiasco and in the face of a mounting crisis in Laos. Trying to make the best of a bad job in the case of Laos, and avoid the lurid scenarios for intervention favored by his advisers, JFK refocused attention on Vietnam as the place to take a stand in Southeast Asia.[23]

The upshot of the imperative to get moving was a new "Presidential Program" for Vietnam, thrashed out in Washington by an interagency task force. The program, issued on May 11 as National Security Action Memorandum No. 52, sought primarily to build on existing efforts, providing for a cautious increase in U.S. technical and logistical support for South Vietnam.[24] It also

abandoned the Counterinsurgency Plan's demand for a strict quid pro quo
from Saigon. While "we must not relax in our efforts to persuade Diem of
the need for political, social and economic, progress," the task force warned,
the "primary emphasis must be placed on providing a solution to the internal security problem." Diem was also given a clear, albeit grudging, pledge
of support. "We must continue to work through and support the present Vietnamese government despite its acknowledged weaknesses," the task force
noted. "No other even remotely feasible alternative exists at this point in time
which does not involve an unacceptable degree of risk."[25]

Instead of demanding a quid pro quo, the Americans would seek to influence Diem's behavior by winning his confidence, an approach originally recommended in Lansdale's report to Kennedy. Friendly persuasion would
replace ultimatums as a way of encouraging the palace to accept U.S. advice.
This was the "first commandment" that Frederick Nolting, Durbrow's successor as ambassador, carried with him to Saigon in early May.[26] Winning
Diem's confidence was also the aim of Lyndon Johnson's cheerleading visit
to Vietnam in mid-May. The vice-president spent three days in the country,
during which time he engaged in some morale-boosting hyperbole for the
benefit of his hosts, describing Diem as the Vietnamese Churchill as well as
comparing him to George Washington, Andrew Jackson, Woodrow Wilson,
and Franklin Roosevelt. He also delivered a letter from Kennedy that pledged
increased U.S. support.[27]

The new "Presidential Program" thus codified an emerging consensus
on the need to get behind the Ngos and get on with the war. It represented a
fragile consensus, however, one that could not hide the uneasiness that many
U.S. officials felt about their Vietnamese ally. Johnson, for example, was considerably less flattering about Diem in private than in his public comments.
"Did you really mean it?" the journalist Stanley Karnow asked him about his
comparison of the Vietnamese premier with Winston Churchill. "Shit," the
vice-president drawled, "Diem's the only boy we got out there."[28] While the
first few months of 1961 had witnessed increased U.S. concern about the situation in South Vietnam, JFK had offered only a modest increase in American
assistance and there remained serious doubts about the ability of the incumbent regime to turn things around. The official consensus about the direction of U.S. policy was a brittle one, very reminiscent of the ambivalence that
had characterized American attitudes toward Diem in the period 1954–1955.

Naturally, such ambivalence did not escape the attention of America's
watchful ally. Ever sensitive to the mood of its powerful patron, the Diem
regime eyed the Kennedy administration with considerable concern. LBJ's
buttery rhetoric could not overcome the palace's own long-standing reservations about its partner, nor its jaundiced view of U.S. advice. Recent events,

moreover, had only served to exacerbate its doubts about the Americans. Notwithstanding the disagreements over Land Development and the like in the late 1950s, the Ngos had grown accustomed to dealing with a fairly tolerant and indulgent ally. The deteriorating security situation, however, had generated new American demands, with Durbrow's démarche of October 1960 ushering in a period of heightened tension in U.S.–Vietnamese relations.

U.S. policy during the November 1960 coup came as a particularly nasty shock to the Ngos. Instead of swinging loyally into support of their ally, the Americans had adopted a neutral stance, maintaining contact with both the rebels and the palace in an effort to promote a peaceful resolution of the crisis and avoid ending up on the losing side. General McGarr had even argued that the rebellion might fortuitously compel Diem to make the kind of reforms that the United States had been urging on him for some time.[29] For the Ngos, the U.S. position demonstrated that they could no longer count on unconditional American support; they also knew that many U.S. officials sympathized with the rebels' cause. Diem compared the situation to recent events in South Korea, where the United States had acquiesced in the overthrow of another old ally, Syngman Rhee. In his eyes, U.S. policy represented not only a betrayal but also a bid to control South Vietnam's destiny. As an editorial in the *Times of Viet Nam Magazine* declared, the rebel soldiers "had given foreigners the opportunity of interfering in our internal affairs, and if the 'putsch' had succeeded, our country would have been run by foreigners through their control over the colonels." The "threat to our independence," the paper concluded, "does not come from our (communist) enemies alone, but also from a number of foreign people who claim to be our friends."[30]

The poisonous atmosphere generated by the coup was hardly conducive to an agreement over the Counterinsurgency Plan. Diem resented and resisted the proposed quid pro quo. U.S. advice was "narrowly rigid and really too foreign" for Vietnamese tastes, he informed Lansdale during the latter's January visit to Vietnam.[31] Implacably opposed to a number of the American proposals, especially those dealing with political liberalization, Diem did not even bother to show the U.S. plan to most of his top officials. Instead, Saigon announced its own set of administrative changes in early February 1961, a sort of counter to the Counterinsurgency Plan that would keep reforms within acceptable limits.[32]

America's "meager" offer of extra assistance added to Saigon's dismay. For all the sound and fury in Washington, the cautious increase in U.S. aid in the first half of 1961 hardly overwhelmed the embattled Ngos. The regime had been badgering the Americans since 1956 to support a twenty-thousand-man increase in the ARVN, yet, only now, when the need seemed so much greater to Diem, was Washington receptive to his pleas. Even so, the United

States initially tied its support for the proposed increase to the RVN's acceptance of the Counterinsurgency Plan, and despite Kennedy's gradual abandonment of this quid pro quo, the allies continued to haggle over the share
of the costs through the summer of 1961.[33] The palace's testy reply to JFK's
letter, delivered by Johnson during his May visit, expressed the regime's sense
of exasperation. Kennedy's dispatch, remarked Diem, contained "wise and
far-sighted proposals, many of which I myself have advocated for four years
or more." LBJ's solicitous interest in the RVN's requirements, he added
sourly, had been most welcome, "particularly as we have not become accustomed to being asked for our own views as to our needs."[34]

Haggling over the Counterinsurgency Plan appeared to the Ngos as a case
of fiddling while Rome burns, especially given the situation in neighboring
Laos. *Cach Mang Quoc Gia*, the daily newspaper of the National Revolutionary Movement, had greeted the new U.S. administration with a barrage of
editorials on the Laotian crisis and the need for the Americans to stand up to
the Russians in the divided kingdom. Since communist advances there threatened to lay bare the RVN's borders, Diem told the Americans that the Southeast Asia Treaty Organization (SEATO) should intervene militarily in order
to secure control of the southern half of Laos.[35] Kennedy was very dubious
about the option of armed intervention, however, and instead sought an international settlement of the crisis. Despite communist violations of a cease-fire,
as well as evidence of increased infiltration across the frontier with South
Vietnam, he stuck by negotiations that had begun in Geneva in May 1961.
W. Averell Harriman led the U.S. negotiating team, seeking to secure a neutral Laos with a coalition government that would embrace the country's warring factions.[36]

Saigon regarded this approach as deeply flawed. After returning in July
from the talks in Geneva, Vu Van Mau stated that the perfidy of the communists cast considerable doubt on the value of a negotiated settlement in Laos,
which would merely be a step toward the country's communization.[37] Diem
described neutralization as a "Munich-type" agreement, while Nhu told
Lansdale that the West did not seem to understand the psychological shock
to Asian anticommunists of its approach in Laos. The policy of neutralization, the counselor argued, had destroyed the credibility of SEATO and
fatally undermined faith in America's strategic reliability. If the United States
was prepared to negotiate with the communist bloc over Laos, Nhu suggested
to Harry Hohler, the British ambassador, might Washington not one day try
to do the same thing in Vietnam?[38]

With Kennedy bent on securing a negotiated settlement, the palace sought
other ways to shore up the south's position. In a June letter to JFK, Diem cited
the problem of infiltration to support his request for a substantial increase in

aid. He wanted the United States to assist in putting one hundred thousand more RVN soldiers in the field and to expand the U.S. advisory presence. The latter move would serve "the dual purpose of providing an expression of the United States' determination to halt the tide of communist aggression and of preparing our forces in the minimum of time." Without immediate assistance, Diem warned, he would be forced to retreat from his northern borders, ceding "progressively greater areas of our country to the communists."[39] Washington approved an expansion of only thirty thousand men, however, and evidently expected certain changes in RVN practices as the price of this, and other measures, of increased U.S. backing.[40] Diem was not happy with what he regarded as an equivocal and halfhearted display of support, soon compounded by Washington's failure to follow through on the aid package recommended in July by the Staley-Thuc group, a joint commission of U.S.–Vietnamese economic experts.[41]

Following the further decline in security conditions in the autumn of 1961, Saigon made fresh demands for additional support, hoping that the situation might have fostered a more receptive mood in Washington. At a meeting on September 29, Diem told Admiral Harry Felt, commander-in-chief Pacific (CINCPAC), that he needed more soldiers, a large increase in the number of advisers, and improved air and naval capabilities. He also asked for a bilateral defense treaty with the United States as a formal expression of U.S. support. Two weeks later, Diem coupled the treaty idea with a request that the United States send "Combat-Trainer Units" to Vietnam. He proposed that these troops be deployed near the Seventeenth Parallel and in the highlands, thus freeing ARVN units for operations elsewhere, serving as a deterrent to a communist invasion, and offering proof of America's strategic commitment to the south's defense.[42]

These requests in the summer and autumn for substantially increased U.S. support triggered renewed debate in Washington about Diem's performance. Walt Rostow, JFK's chief adviser on Southeast Asia, suggested that, before the United States committed more resources to help Saigon, the administration should look beneath the surface of the requests and examine whether Diem was doing enough to remedy his own shortcomings. Rostow noted the palace's reluctance to delegate authority, problems with the chain of command in the military and intelligence fields, and the lack of a national plan for defeating the insurgents.[43] These were the same issues that the United States had pressed the regime to resolve in early 1961, before the administration abandoned hard bargaining in favor of trying to woo Diem into accepting American advice. If Saigon failed to address such shortcomings, the State Department's Bureau of Intelligence and Research now warned, the result would not only be more communist successes in the countryside but also the increased likelihood of another military coup, with all its attendant uncertainties.[44]

To coordinate his administration's response to this mounting crisis, Kennedy decided to send a fact-finding group to Vietnam. General Maxwell Taylor, the "Military Representative of the President," led the mission, which arrived in Saigon on October 18. The group spent a week engaged in an exhausting round of briefings and field trips before repairing to the Philippine summer capital of Baguio to compile a report. Taylor's findings, formally presented to JFK on November 3, identified a "double crisis in confidence" in Vietnam: concern about America's guarantee to defend Southeast Asia and doubts about Diem's ability to deal with the insurgency. Nonetheless, the situation could be turned around, Taylor concluded, for "the atmosphere in South Vietnam is, on balance, one of frustrated energy rather than passive acceptance of inevitable defeat."[45]

To achieve victory, Taylor proposed a "massive joint effort" by Washington and Saigon. First of all, the Americans should significantly increase the number of U.S. personnel in South Vietnam as well as offer the regime further material and technical assistance. This increase should include the deployment of eight thousand U.S. troops in the recently flooded Mekong Delta, ostensibly as a "flood reconstruction force." Second, Taylor recommended a major change in allied relations. The United States should stick with Diem, he argued, a man of "extraordinary ability, stubbornness, and guts." The present advisory relationship, however, should be replaced by a "limited partnership," with Americans working closely at every level and in all fields with their Vietnamese counterparts. Taylor suggested placing U.S. advisers in key RVN ministries, instituting combined operational planning, and creating joint survey teams that could recommend improvements in such areas as intelligence gathering and command arrangements. "The present character and scale of the war in South Vietnam," his report stated, "decree that only the Vietnamese can defeat the Viet-Cong; but at all levels Americans must, as friends and partners—not as arms-length advisors—show them how the job might be done." Previous attempts to modify Saigon's policies by applying pressure and advice at "arms-length" had clearly failed; "limited partnership" would enable U.S. officials to reform the Diem regime from the inside out.[46]

Kennedy endorsed the essentials of the Taylor report, minus the proposal for a "flood relief" task force. He evidently viewed the deployment of U.S. combat troops as the first step on a slippery slope and expressed concern about his ability to control the process of escalation once it had begun. "It's like taking a drink," he told Arthur Schlesinger, Jr. "The effect wears off, and you have to take another." JFK's decision mirrored the one that he had taken in early 1961 and those he would make throughout his presidency when it came to Vietnam. He was willing to increase the U.S. commitment, but also concerned, at each juncture, to avoid overly committing the United States. Kennedy "took the minimum steps he judged necessary to stabilize the situation," recalled Rostow, "leaving its resolution for the longer future, but quite conscious that harder decisions might lie ahead."[47]

With the debate settled in Washington, attention now turned to presenting the U.S. proposals in Saigon. Secretary of State Dean Rusk instructed Nolting to discuss with the palace the recommendations for a "sharply increased joint effort" to combat the insurgency. To fulfill the terms of this "limited partnership," Rusk observed, "the concept of the joint undertaking envisages a much closer relationship than the present one of acting in an advisory capacity only. We would expect to share in the decision-making processes in the political, economic and military fields as they affected the security situation." Washington's instructions also included an additional quid pro quo that was not specifically contained in the Taylor report. "You should bear in mind," Rusk told Nolting, "that a crucial element in [the] U.S. Government's willingness to move forward is [a] concrete demonstration by Diem that he is now prepared to work in an orderly way with his subordinates and broaden the political base of his regime."[48]

Together, these proposals constituted a significant set of demands, which was not likely to be well received in Saigon. Washington had not even consulted its ally about the purpose of Taylor's visit to Vietnam.[49] Nor, in the course of his discussions with the general, did Diem apparently appreciate the import of some of the issues raised by the Americans. Taylor talked only in very broad terms about his findings and suggestions, while Diem treated the discussions as an opportunity to explain the situation as he saw it, not the prelude to a U.S. démarche.[50] Thus, the proposals that Nolting subsequently delivered to the palace on November 17 came as a profound shock to the Ngos. As in the case of the earlier Counterinsurgency Plan, Diem regarded them as a demand for substantial concessions in return for a disappointingly modest increase in U.S. assistance.

In the first place, Diem was not impressed by the amount of extra U.S. aid on offer, especially the absence of Taylor's "flood-relief" task force. Tran Kim Tuyen told a CIA source that the president had only reluctantly assented to this idea, and other measures to increase the U.S. presence in South Vietnam, after pressure from several of his closest advisers. Diem faced a dilemma over the issue of a U.S. troop deployment, even a token one. To rely on the help of foreign forces laid him open to the charge of being an American puppet; it also threatened to increase Washington's leverage over the regime and expand U.S. contacts with disgruntled Vietnamese, particularly in the ARVN. At the same time, the palace wanted a demonstration of American backing, in order to bolster the south's security, allay Vietnamese fears of being abandoned, and silence the regime's domestic critics.[51] Thus, Diem had endorsed the "flood-relief" force suggestion, which Taylor had outlined in a discussion at the palace on October 24. To the president's chagrin, this proposal was the notable casualty of the subsequent debate in Washington.[52]

To make matters worse, the Americans expected significant concessions in return for the support on offer. Not surprisingly, the palace dug in its heels. To the U.S. demands to reform his government, Diem responded that he was always seeking to make changes but did not want to do so in ways that would jeopardize order and stability. He likened the Taylor mission to George Marshall's trip to China, an ill-conceived attempt to impose reforms on Chiang Kai-shek that had only played into the hands of the communists. As for the idea of a "limited partnership," he stated that Vietnam "did not want to be a protectorate" and such an infringement of sovereignty threatened to give the communists a "monopoly on nationalism."[53] Diem spent the next several days brooding over the U.S. démarche. In the meantime, Nhu orchestrated a campaign in the Saigon press that lambasted the United States for treating small countries as pawns and attaching meddlesome conditions to the provision of aid. Given the character of U.S. policy, several newspapers suggested, the Vietnamese might have to rely on themselves in order to defeat their enemies.[54]

On November 27, Rusk instructed Nolting to correct Diem's "apparent misinterpretation" of Washington's proposals, for the United States had no intention of dictating changes or "taking over his government."[55] Such denials, however, reflected a measure of self-deception on the part of U.S. officials. Taylor had seen fit to state in his report, for example, that the United States was not seeking to "recreate a colonial system" in Vietnam, as if that might now be in some doubt. U.S. policy makers also expressed views that fully justified Diem's fears for Vietnamese sovereignty. Rusk talked loosely of assuming "de facto direction" of RVN affairs, while Diem's hostile response to the U.S. proposals stimulated analyses of likely coup scenarios in Vietnam, including suggestions for a range of roles that the United States might play in these circumstances.[56] U.S. officials, it seemed, had entered a diplomatic no-man's-land in their attempt to fashion a relationship going beyond friendly advice but stopping short of colonial control.

In Saigon, Nolting sought to find a compromise to prevent a breakdown of relations. After a bruising four-hour session with Diem on December 1, the ambassador informed Washington that he thought an agreement was within reach. In fact, Diem had stood his ground on the most contentious issues, but Nolting was sympathetic to the palace's position. He had never believed that Diem would accept U.S. proposals as a package deal and preferred to solicit the regime's cooperation by quiet diplomacy. "I believe that the tide can be turned with the limited concessions which Diem is prepared to make now," he reported, "and other[s] that we can obtain on [a] piece meal basis."[57] In response, the Kennedy administration admitted that Diem had "not gone as far as we would like" and that constant pressure would be required to get the palace to follow through on its promises. Nevertheless, Washington accepted Nolting's formula, effectively capitulating in the face of Diem's intransigence.[58]

It was a surprisingly tame ending to the dispute, which exposed the perennial weakness of America's bargaining position vis-à-vis its Vietnamese client. Despite the massive power imbalance between Washington and Saigon, the Americans found it difficult to translate raw strength into effective influence. The problem was that they needed Diem as much as he needed them; the palace knew it, moreover, and this gave Diem a good deal of leverage in allied disputes. Thus, the choice confronting the Americans, noted the Pentagon's William Bundy, "lay between taking what one could get or dissociating the U.S. from Diem—a drastic step involving publicity and unforeseen problems." Under the circumstances, Washington decided to follow the path of least resistance. The Kennedy administration remained wedded to its uneasy consensus on supporting the incumbent regime, despite recognizing that America might now be backing a "losing horse," as Rusk described the Saigon government.[59]

This capitulation was little cause for celebration in the palace, however. Taylor's visit and its aftermath was a stark reminder to the Ngos of why they found the relationship with the United States such a troubling one. U.S. proposals infringed on Vietnamese sovereignty and weakened South Vietnam's claim to the mantle of Vietnamese nationalism. They also encouraged noncommunist critics of the regime, reminding the palace of the dangerous connection between the American presence and internal dissent, notably within the U.S.–sponsored ARVN. General Duong Van Minh, for example, took the opportunity of discussions with Taylor to launch an outspoken attack on Diem, accusing him of favoring Catholics and stymieing military operations.[60] Coup rumors also abounded following Taylor's departure, especially when Nhu's anti-U.S. press campaign suggested that Saigon and Washington might be headed for a showdown. U.S. officials got the impression that the regime's critics were probing their position, trying to determine whether the United States might sanction Diem's overthrow.[61] The events surrounding the Taylor visit thus exacerbated the palace's suspicious nature and encouraged Diem to fall back on those he believed he could most trust, particularly his brother Nhu.[62]

Nhu led the way in shaping the regime's response to the U.S. proposals, taking the results of the Taylor mission as the cue to articulate a broad critique of American policy. The key problem in the U.S.–Vietnamese relationship, he

told a CIA source in late November, was that the West simply did not understand the problems of newly developing countries, expecting them to "move
from the stage of underdevelopment to full-blooming democracy in one
jump." Because of this blind spot, he argued, the United States had consis-
tently failed to provide the right kind of support for South Vietnam. The Taylor mission, which had raised such great expectations, was another page in this
catalog of failure. Once again, Nhu complained, the palace's domestic critics
had seduced American visitors into recommending unsuitable remedies for
the country's difficulties.[63]

None of Nhu's criticisms were particularly novel. Yet, taken together like
this, they constituted a significant attack on U.S. policy and evidence of a
hardening of the palace's attitude toward the Americans. By the end of 1961,
the Ngos, and Nhu in particular, had begun to view the United States as part
of the problem, rather than solution, to their country's difficulties. In meetings with province chiefs in December, Nhu stated that the Vietnamese
needed to rely on themselves and promote their own revolution. They must
plan their defense without depending on the United States, he argued; the
Americans could no longer be trusted over the long haul and actually represented an obstacle to the revolutionary transformation of Vietnamese society.[64] This conclusion set the stage for Saigon's vigorous promotion of the
Strategic Hamlet program. The burgeoning insurgency, and the ensuing crisis in U.S.–Vietnamese relations, convinced the Ngos that they needed a new
nation-building program—one that would not only tackle the NLF and
advance the regime's ideological agenda but also free South Vietnam from the
clutches of its increasingly overbearing superpower patron.

Long before the crisis of 1960–1961, Saigon was aware that its position in the
southern countryside was a tenuous one. From the very outset of his government, Diem had faced a major problem in asserting his authority in rural areas,
which were in the hands of the sects or the Viet Minh. The latter were also
bent on ensuring that his new regime would be unable to put down any solid
roots there. The U.S. embassy reported in June 1954 that the communists were
seeking to hamstring Diem's government by intimidating local notables and
village councils. Over a year later, Tran Van Lam, a regional delegate, noted
that, where they existed at all, most local councils were very susceptible to
clandestine control by communist agents.[65] The palace regarded this situation
as intolerable. "The entire country is no freer than the individual villages,"
Diem informed Michigan State University's Ed Weidner and Howard Hoyt
in September 1955. "They are the key to the success of a free Viet Nam."[66]

To establish the government's writ at the village level, the regime had created the system of "mutual-aid family groups," expanded the activities of its

mass organizations, replaced locally elected councils with appointed ones, and sought to root out suspected opponents. In the autumn of 1955, the palace also pressed the Americans to finance the creation of a Self-Defense Corps, a rural militia of ten-man units that would provide a permanent police presence in every village in the country. Although some U.S. officials were distinctly lukewarm about the proposal, Diem argued that the regime must counter communist activities at the village level and that conventional armed forces were not a suitable instrument for flushing out enemy agents from populated areas. "We should start Guerrilla Warfare of our own," he told General Williams in December 1955. "The Army does not understand, as it sees only the classic military solution." Local security could only be assured by local militiamen, who knew the area and its people, and could prevent the communists from terrorizing the population when regular forces were operating elsewhere. Diem believed that, without this kind of security presence, the enemy could paralyze rural administration and sever Saigon's ties with the peasantry.[67]

In the latter half of the 1950s, the palace's continued preoccupation with this concern led it to seek to recruit peasants as part-time village militia, in order to reinforce the Self-Defense Corps.[68] This effort met with only mixed success; some province chiefs reported that people were too afraid of the communists or too tired after a day's work to mount patrols at night. The dramatic upsurge in insurgent activity in 1960 certainly exposed the fragility of the RVN's provincial apparatus, putting pay to the Agroville program. In response, Saigon redoubled its efforts to bolster the government's position in the countryside. In the summer of 1960, for example, the regime launched a "Rural Consolidation" campaign in the provinces surrounding Saigon, dispatching teams of cadres to revive village-level administration, establish intelligence networks, and "win the hearts of the people" through propaganda and the provision of aid.[69]

The Ngos devoted particular attention to the task of mobilizing rural youth, which constituted the "backbone of the country" according to Diem. During the course of 1960, the Republican Youth Movement emerged as the regime's chief organizational vehicle for enlisting popular support; it soon numbered some 1.6 million members, although this feat required a somewhat expansive definition of "youth." The palace expected the Republican Youth to assist in community development projects, provide a fresh infusion of rural leadership, and, in particular, help protect villages. In March 1960, Colonel Paul Burns, a MAAG senior adviser, reported that the ARVN Seventh Division had begun training thousands of young civilians to serve as paramilitary forces in their home villages. A program of indoctrination accompanied the training, including a lecture from the divisional commander on "The Role of the Young Man and His Duties to the Country." Diem told General Williams that he wanted to have 480 of these youth guards in every village to replace the ten-man-strong units of the Self-Defense Corps.[70]

To encourage the enthusiastic participation of the peasantry in these efforts, Diem reemphasized the importance of developing the "democratic infrastructure" and building the country from the bottom up. He told U.S. officials in October 1960 that the government would have to provide rural inhabitants with better administration, as well as improved security, if it was to win their support. Consequently, he noted, the palace wanted to increase the number and quality of officials sent to the provinces. At the same time, the regime began a vigorous effort to root out corrupt and abusive administrators. In June 1961, the U.S. embassy noted that the Vietnamese press contained "almost daily reports of provincial or lower level officials discharged, suspended or punished for various offenses."[71]

Saigon also sought to engage the peasantry by the selective revival of local elections. In December 1960, the government issued instructions to enable Republican Youth groups to elect one of their members to sit on village councils. "Diem believes this will be well-received by youth, whose loyalty it [is] essential [to] retain in [the] VC fight," commented Ambassador Durbrow. As the official *News from Viet-Nam* explained, "The participation of these young, enthusiastic delegates with a will to work and a solid understanding of their responsibilities will be helpful in guiding the people in this vital fight against Communism."[72] Following this innovation, Diem expressed an interest in extending the electoral process further, in effect proposing to restore a measure of the local democracy that he had felt compelled to limit in 1956. If people did not choose those responsible for organizing local activities, he argued at a cabinet meeting in May 1961, they simply would not participate in them.[73]

Diem's stress on mobilizing the rural populace to defend itself represented an important change in his conception of the RVN's security problems. Until now, he had viewed the issue primarily in terms of the government's ability to protect peasants from communist coercion and propaganda. Since he believed that most supporters of the insurgency must have been terrorized or duped into standing against the regime, it followed that the key to promoting security was to prevent communist agents from being able to exercise their baleful influence over villagers. The necessity of providing the populace with this kind of protection was the original reason for establishing the Self-Defense Corps and underlay Diem's increasingly plaintive appeals to the Americans for additional support. The expanding insurgency, however, forced the palace to confront the limits of this numbers-game approach to the problem because it was evident that the regime just did not have enough troops to maintain security everywhere. Nor, as the events of 1961 demonstrated, could the Ngos rely on their ally to finance suitably large increases in the size of the RVN's forces. The logic of the situation was inescapable; if there were not enough soldiers available to protect the population, then people must be organized to defend themselves.[74]

In grappling with this problem, it was evident that the Ngos were thinking not only about the immediate demands of the security situation but also the way in which the requirements of the war might serve to promote the regime's broader political agenda. This holistic approach to the south's troubles had been evident in the earlier Land Development and Agroville programs, where schemes with an obvious security dimension sought to achieve a variety of social and economic goals as well. Similarly, the heightened insurgency appeared to the Ngos as an opportunity to use the exigencies of the conflict to reorganize the regime at the grass roots and advance their Personalist revolution. By mobilizing peasants to defend themselves, the palace hoped to generate the kind of collective spirit and social solidarity that it deemed essential for the larger process of nation building.

In an October 1960 address to the National Assembly, Diem described South Vietnam's situation as "grim but promising," pointing, in particular, to the new role that the nation's youth was playing "in the development and defense of the country." Their sense of duty and ardor, the palace argued, would help to revitalize and rejuvenate society.[75] *Cach Mang Quoc Gia* also lauded the long-term benefits of mobilizing youth to defend the country. Combating the insurgents, a series of editorials declared in November 1960, provided a unique opportunity to reorganize society from the bottom up, thereby removing "rotten officials," "cruel men of influence," "political speculators," and "communist dictators." "If you want to build a healthy new society," the paper exhorted, "then you must have new cadres, a new class of people and a new generation to settle once and for all with the old system, ideology and life." The Republican Youth Movement would serve as "a true nursery of cadres trained eventually to replace their elders in various public services," noted *News from Viet-Nam.*[76]

Nhu, the principal patron of the Republican Youth, took the lead in fashioning the regime's response to the crisis of 1960–1961, emerging in the process from the political shadows and eclipsing the influence of other advisers, including his brother Can. While Diem tended to focus on the more concrete manifestations of nation building, such as land resettlement or economic development, Nhu's fascination was with the problem of political organization. Like many Vietnamese, drawn from all shades of the political spectrum, the counselor had long been impressed by the systematic and methodical character of Marxist-Leninist thinking, and by the communist techniques of manipulation and mass organization. Much of the regime's political apparatus—its government-sponsored organizations and the semisecret Can Lao—reflected these influences. The growing insurgency, however, had clearly exposed the failure of this existing apparatus to provide a political base to match that of the communists, especially in the countryside. Thus, Nhu began casting around for a new strategy, one that would simultaneously advance the palace's nation-building goals and tackle the insurgency.[77]

One person who was particularly well placed to chart the progress of Nhu's efforts was William Colby, the CIA station chief in Saigon from 1960 to 1962. As the counselor's intelligence counterpart, he met every week with Nhu in the latter's cramped office in the presidential palace. The two men succeeded in establishing a close working relationship, which contrasted with the tension that often characterized relations between the regime and the rest of the U.S. diplomatic community. Like Edward Lansdale, an earlier CIA confidant of the Ngos, Colby sympathized with many of the palace's concerns, including the idea of mobilizing peasants in their own defense. He was convinced that the answer to the insurgency "would be found only in the villages, not in political circles in Saigon or in General Staff Headquarters." Indeed, the palace and the CIA would collaborate on a number of projects that emphasized a community-based approach to security, notably the Buon Enao experiment that began in October 1961 among Rhade tribesmen in Darlac province.[78]

As the war in the south intensified, observed Colby, his weekly encounters with Nhu frequently turned to a discussion of the communist concept of "people's war." The two men also examined case studies of guerrilla conflicts, including the First Indochina War, the Malayan Emergency, and the Algerian insurrection. "As these conversations proceeded," Colby recalled, "Nhu gradually moved from his initial fascination with the Leninist technique of the controlling party apparatus (his own Can Lao) to an acceptance of the necessity that the ordinary citizen not only be directed but also be motivated to resist the incursions of the enemy and be confident that in doing so he would be supported and protected in his choice." Nhu's thinking was moving toward the idea of mobilizing the population by enlisting peasants to defend their communities, in much the same way as the insurgents who were busy attempting to create their own "combat villages" in the south. Thus, just as the communists sought to use the country's rural settlements as a framework for organizing their own revolution, the regime would do the same thing in order to promote its Personalist revolution.[79]

To put these ideas into practice, Nhu began to formulate strategic plans for countering the guerrillas. In October 1960, he outlined to an unnamed U.S. official, perhaps Colby, a strategy of "strength lines," which envisaged establishing circles of government-controlled villages, "the rims of which would be strengthened militarily and politically on a priority basis." Like the proverbial "oil spot," the edges of the secure zones would gradually push outward, intersecting with one another and expanding the territory under the regime's control.[80] At the beginning of 1961, Nhu also asked Tran Kim Tuyen, head of the presidency's Service for Political and Social Research, to examine various counterinsurgency strategies. Tuyen, who had compiled a number of reports on the problems with the Agroville program, put together an in-house brain trust to look at the security situation as well as foreign experiences that might be relevant to Vietnam.[81] Several of the latter illustrated the role that strategic communities could play as a framework for pacification. In a later discussion with Britain's Harry Hohler, Nhu singled out the Israeli kibbutz and Malaya's "New Villages" as particularly valuable case studies.[82]

The Strategic Hamlet program itself seems to have developed as an outgrowth of local experiments in several provinces, notably Tay Ninh, Quang Ngai, and Vinh Long. In Tay Ninh, the border province to the northwest of Saigon, local Catholic priests, with the help of the provincial authorities, started to organize "combat hamlets" in June 1961. These efforts included the building of watchtowers, the training of local youth, and the creation of hamlet management committees.[83] In Quang Ngai, meanwhile, an old Viet Minh stronghold and one of the most insecure provinces in central Vietnam, the local authorities began to fortify "combat villages" in preparation for a renewed communist offensive. Nguyen Van Tat, the chief of the province, told his district subordinates that the goal was to raise morale and the spirit of resistance. In August, John Helble, the U.S. consul in Hue, reported that this program was in evidence throughout Quang Ngai, with bamboo fences surrounding settlements as well as large cultivated areas.[84]

By far the most influential of these local experiments was the one initiated in the Delta's Vinh Long by Major Le Van Phuoc. Phuoc had become the province chief in 1960 following Khuu Van Ba's assassination. According to one of his former classmates at the Da Lat military academy, the new chief was smart, ambitious, and a brilliant salesman; he was famous for having named a main street in the province capital after Ngo Dinh Thuc, the president's eldest brother and long-serving bishop of Vinh Long.[85] In mid-1961, Phuoc established three model "strategic hamlets" in the village of Tan An, which became showplaces for officials from Saigon and other provinces. In addition, he compiled a series of instructional manuals on the creation of strategic hamlets for distribution to local officials and cadre teams, copies of which he also dispatched to the palace.[86]

Phuoc stressed that the hamlet, a number of which made up the larger village, was the place to start if the regime wanted to organize the country from the bottom up. If Saigon sought to develop its rural infrastructure, and simultaneously strangle the NLF, it should begin at this lowest level of community life. His program included the training of youth militia, the strengthening of local organizations, and the creation of new hamlet committees. Phuoc emphasized that the political aspects of his program were more important than the military ones. Thus, Vinh Long's settlements did not possess elaborate fortifications, relying instead on a central defense post, stronger hamlet-level organization, and youth militia.[87] By the end of July 1961, Phuoc claimed that the experiment had already proved its worth, and he intended to gradually extend the strategic hamlet scheme to all the settlements in the province.[88]

Although the experiments in Tay Ninh, Quang Ngai, and Vinh Long seem to have sprung from local initiative, they matched the palace's growing interest in a community-centered approach to security. No doubt they also reflected the pressure that provincial subordinates felt emanating from the capital as the crisis in the countryside worsened. As the U.S. embassy noted, visits to the provinces by high-ranking officials started to increase in early 1961. Bui Van Luong, now the minister of the interior, was particularly active in this regard, spearheading the palace's efforts to stimulate local action and improve the coordination of government policy. He held numerous meetings with lower-level officials and solicited suggestions about how to strengthen the regime's presence in the villages; in the summer of 1961, he also instructed province chiefs to submit plans for the pacification of their territory.[89] The trail blazed in places like Vinh Long thus fitted squarely into the government's attempts to promote provincial activity; these experiments also provided the palace with useful models to help flesh out its own ideas and hold up as examples for other provinces to follow.

Vinh Long was a particularly popular destination for RVN officials during the summer of 1961. Ngo Trong Hieu, the secretary of state for civic action, and Bui Van Luong both visited the new hamlets there. The ubiquitous Luong also examined Quang Ngai's "combat village" program.[90] By August, the regime's interest in promoting a new effort in the countryside started to take more concrete forms, Secretary Hieu announcing that the government would allocate two billion piasters for the creation of "strategic" villages as well as the construction of more agrovilles.[91] Hieu also held a press conference on August 21 at which he suggested that Saigon saw "strategic hamlets" as a new national strategy. "There must be as many 'strategic hamlets' as there are hamlets," the U.S. embassy reported Hieu as stating, "and as many anti-communist combatants as citizens."[92]

With Saigon's encouragement, provincial authorities began to construct strategic hamlets throughout the country in the final months of 1961. Luong told province chiefs in a memorandum of October 5 that this new formula would be the means of overcoming the country's three "enemies" and should be their number one priority; he cited the experiments in Tay Ninh, Quang Ngai, and Vinh Long as examples of how to proceed. At the beginning of 1962, the palace noted that over five hundred strategic hamlets had been established during the course of the previous year.[93] The regime even began to extend the strategic hamlet concept to its urban, as well as rural, population, with the establishment of so-called strategic quarters in Saigon and other cities. The idea was to group people in urban neighborhoods into various associations, in the same way that the regime was seeking to organize and mobilize the peasantry.[94]

One notable feature of this increasingly active promotion of strategic hamlets was the palace's waning interest in other alternatives, not least the stalled Agroville/Agro-hamlet program. Although the U.S. embassy reported in late 1960 that Saigon had put this program on hold, the provinces continued through the first half of 1961 to regroup elements of the rural population and submit requests to establish agro-hamlets.[95] Even as the authorities in some provinces began to experiment with prototype strategic hamlets, Saigon showed some interest in constructing more agro-hamlets as well as reviving the dormant Agroville program. In a July 1961 letter to Ben Wood of the Vietnam Task Force, Nguyen Dinh Thuan emphasized the importance of regrouping peasants and "expanding as much as we can the agrovilles network."[96] Such plans, however, either failed to materialize, or the palace fitted them into the broader framework of the hamlet program. Agrovilles and agro-hamlets suffered from certain disadvantages when compared to the emerging strategic hamlets, as the regime's review of these earlier efforts made clear.

First, agrovilles and agro-hamlets were specially constructed settlements and involved regrouping large numbers of peasants. This represented a heavy and unpopular undertaking, especially in the case of the larger agrovilles. Resettlement and new construction had caused considerable peasant unrest, both among people forced to move into the new centers and those drafted to build them. Official corruption had also flourished because the size of the projects provided ample opportunity for graft. Meanwhile, the NLF had taken advantage of popular discontent and found the settlements, especially the big agrovilles, easy targets to infiltrate or attack. These kind of large-scale public projects were also expensive, which exacerbated all of the foregoing problems because the lack of resources encouraged the use of coercion and forced labor. In contrast, strategic hamlets proposed to focus on the development of existing settlements rather than mass regroupment. Moreover, their inhabitants would carry out any construction work necessary, so the costs would be borne by those who were expected to benefit from them. Thus, strategic hamlets appeared to be more viable politically as well as less of a financial burden.[97]

For the Ngos, agrovilles and agro-hamlets also suffered from the disadvantage of being favored by the Americans, who seemed interested in supporting an expansion of the existing program. The U.S. Counterinsurgency Plan had called for increased efforts to improve the economic life of the countryside in order to win over the rural population; its recommendations included government payment for labor on agrovilles, if the regime resumed the program, and subsidies for resettlement.[98] Kennedy's "Presidential Program" also advocated measures such as "rural development–civic action" and the establishment of "agricultural pilot-projects," for which JFK pledged increased U.S. backing in the letter that his vice-president delivered to Diem in May.[99] All these proposals found more concrete expression in the recommendations of the joint financial commission led by Eugene Staley of the Stanford Research Institute and Vu Quoc Thuc of the Saigon University Law School. In mid-July, the Staley-Thuc report proposed U.S. support for the construction of one hundred new agrovilles, describing these settlements as "one of the more promising counter-guerrilla methods."[100]

Yet, if the Diem regime chose to tie its plans to American support in this way, it would be depending on an ally that the palace viewed with increasing distrust. For example, Kennedy accepted the recommendations of the Staley-Thuc report but, faced with uncertainty about the exact costs of the program and continued internal divisions over U.S. policy, he did so "without a present commitment of precise amounts of money over a precise period of time."[101] A letter from JFK to the palace along these lines brought the blunt response from Diem that he could find no "figures about the amount of U.S. aid." Kennedy's letter, and Nolting's presentation to Diem of the U.S. proposals, also contained thinly veiled references to changes that Washington expected Saigon to make in return for the offer of expanded assistance, including fiscal and political reforms, joint planning, and the creation of a national strategic plan.[102]

The palace knew from past and more recent experience that American support came with a variety of strings attached. U.S. officials were often skeptical or dismissive of Vietnamese plans and preferred to pressure the regime into accepting their own formulations. They had been quite critical, for example, of Nhu's idea of "strength lines," which General McGarr described as an overly defensive, Maginot Line, or Dien Bien Phu–style strategy. Instead, MAAG had developed its own tactical treatise for securing rural areas, which U.S. officials wanted the palace to adopt instead of Vietnamese plans. Throughout the spring and summer of 1961, McGarr, backed by Nolting, lobbied the regime furiously to accept the MAAG blueprint. Kennedy's letter to Diem in early August also appeared to condition U.S. support for a further increase in the size of the ARVN on the drawing up of an American-backed plan of action.[103]

Not only did the Ngos dislike being subjected to such pressure but they also found the content of the American plans unappealing. U.S. officials repeatedly stressed, for example, that a single military chain of command was a prerequisite for the effective coordination of military-civil operations. Otherwise, McGarr warned, the result would be "37 miniature campaigns—each one proceeding at its own pace and intensity, rather than a national campaign against the Viet Cong in accordance with a cohesive, coordinated plan."[104] Yet, to embrace such logic, the Ngos would have to accept changes that would weaken their stranglehold over the levers of power, with serious implications for their own authority and safety. In particular, MAAG's promotion of its ARVN protégé, an organization that the palace neither favored nor trusted, was not likely to endear McGarr's proposals to the wary Ngos. In addition, the emphasis that U.S. counterinsurgency plans placed on conventional military operations no longer conformed to the regime's interest in mobilizing ordinary peasants to defend themselves.

In short, accepting a U.S.–backed program threatened to draw the palace into a whole series of unwelcome arrangements with its superpower patron. American support meant American advice on a range of military, political, and economic matters. If the regime entered into a joint effort on these terms, it would no longer be certain exactly who was running things in South Vietnam; the implications of the Taylor report's "limited partnership" made that fact abundantly clear. This concern helps to explain why talk about an expanded Agroville program in mid-1961 remained just that. Besides the many problems with the original scheme, its proposed revival was too closely associated with the Americans, with all that this implied for Vietnamese sovereignty and the regime's freedom of action. Evidently these drawbacks significantly reduced its appeal to key figures in the regime, as the journalist Theodore White noted after a visit to Vietnam in July. U.S. officials thought that the palace wanted more agrovilles, commented White, but Nhu had told him that they would not work and that the Americans were trying to force them on Saigon.[105]

Strategic hamlets provided the Ngos with the opportunity to make a fresh start, to channel the regime's energy into promoting a new program rather than reviving a tarnished one.[106] By focusing on existing settlements, rather than attempting to construct new ones, the hamlet program appeared to be a more suitable vehicle for fulfilling the palace's aims than agrovilles and agro-hamlets. By concentrating specifically on the hamlet, moreover, the lowest level of communal life in Vietnam, it offered the Ngos the enticing prospect of establishing their "infrastructure of democracy" and carrying out a grassroots

revolution in South Vietnam. Last but not least, the adoption of strategic hamlets would allow the Ngos to fashion their own response to the insurgency,
deftly sidestepping their ally's demands for changes in the regime's modus
operandi.

Not surprisingly, the Ngos chose not to involve the Americans in their
evolving plans. Certain U.S. officials, of course, were aware of the palace's
budding interest in strategic hamlets. MAAG knew something of the regime's
rural experiments, as General McGarr noted in a report to CINCPAC at the
beginning of September 1961.[107] So too did the CIA station, which enjoyed
an unusual degree of intimacy with the palace. Yet, as in the case of the
Agroville program, the Ngos did not seek the active participation of Washington or its Saigon embassy in planning this most important of efforts. The
embassy's report of Ngo Trong Hieu's August press conference nicely captures the Americans' sense of surprise at the sudden attention being devoted
to this new scheme. "We are seeking further information re [the] nature and
results [of] this program," Ambassador Nolting informed Washington,
"which [is] evidently being attempted on [a] limited basis [in] several
provinces."[108] While U.S. officials had been busy developing a series of American proposals to counter the insurgency, the palace had come up with its own
homegrown solution to South Vietnam's problems.

The Americans were not the only foreigners to find themselves sidelined
in this way by the palace's penchant for independent action. A similar fate
befell the advice of Robert Thompson, the head of a small British Advisory
Mission (BRIAM) composed of veterans of the Malayan Emergency. Thompson had already visited South Vietnam in the spring of 1960. When he
returned in the autumn of 1961, he began to put together a pacification plan,
based on the successful British experience in Malaya. In November, Thompson presented the palace with the "Delta Plan," which called for the creation
of a network of "defended" and "strategic" hamlets on the pattern of the
"New Village" program.[109] This proposal is often credited with exerting a
formative influence on the emergence of strategic hamlets,[110] but the latter
owed much more to the evolution of the regime's own thinking than to any
imported blueprints.

While the Malayan experience was a fashionable object of study in the
palace, the Ngos were not starry-eyed about it. Diem told U.S. officials in
June 1960 that the insurgencies in the two countries were not comparable
because Malaya was an isolated peninsula, food was not so easily available,
and the guerrillas, all of whom were ethnic Chinese, were more readily iden-
tifiable.[111] Thompson's "Delta Plan" also arrived rather late in the day, when
the palace's own thinking about strategic hamlets was reasonably well formed
and a program already under way in the countryside. BRIAM's approach,

moreover, clashed in certain important respects with the regime's conception of strategic hamlets. Thompson wanted to use the existing apparatus of the state and establish the kind of administrative controls over the population that had been the hallmark of the British success in Malaya; Nhu wanted to mobilize, not corral, the peasantry, with a view to transforming the South Vietnamese state. British officials would report with increasing concern this yawning gap between their advice and the palace's policies.[112] They suspected, as did U.S. officials, that the Ngos flirted with BRIAM's proposals in order to stymie U.S. attempts to promote an American plan of action and provide moral support for their own ideas.[113]

By late 1961, those ideas were far enough advanced for Saigon to take a more active role in managing the various efforts of its provincial subordinates. At Ban Me Thuot, in mid-October, Nhu told a conference of senior and provincial officials that the regime needed an overarching concept that would address all of its military, political, and economic problems. It was clear, he observed, that officials had lots of ideas but lacked focus; strategic hamlets could provide that focal point. Nhu instructed the attendees to collect all the documents relating to strategic hamlets, file them in a special folder, and give those materials first priority in the daily order of business.[114] Walt Rostow, who accompanied the Taylor mission to Vietnam later that month, spent three hours with the president's brother on the day before the U.S. group's departure. He found the counselor eager to develop a political system to "hold the country together, reaching from Saigon down to the villages."[115] The American proposals that followed the Taylor report only served to reinforce this concern and, as the U.S. embassy reported in December, encouraged Nhu's conviction that South Vietnam must push ahead with its own plans because of the problems with the American alliance.[116]

Saigon finally moved at the start of 1962 to direct and coordinate the expanding program of hamlet construction in the provinces. Bui Van Luong drafted a study document for discussion of the hamlet scheme at a security council conference on January 8, 1962. The meeting decided to establish strategic hamlets as a national policy and the regime's number one priority; it also agreed to organize a body responsible for formulating plans and coordinating construction throughout the country.[117] The Interministerial Committee for Strategic Hamlets officially came into being on February 3 and met weekly to discuss the program's progress. Nhu, who later described himself as "both the originator and the prime mover" of the hamlet scheme, ran the meetings.[118] The Strategic Hamlet program was now officially launched.

At this point, Saigon began to develop the plans and the machinery to guide the program in the provinces. As it did so, it also began to articulate more fully the ideas behind the hamlet scheme. Like the earlier Land Development and Agroville programs, the Ngos saw strategic hamlets as a multidimensional endeavor that would address a variety of military, political, and economic concerns. Also figuring prominently in the palace's explanations of the program was the need for the Vietnamese to rely on themselves, rather than their wealthy patron, in defeating the NLF and building the country. The events of 1961 had served to reinforce the palace's doubts about its U.S. ally and convinced the Ngos that South Vietnam's independence was threatened not only by a communist takeover but also a de facto American one.

All of this, of course, was long on theory and short on detail. There remained several crucial question marks hanging over the palace's initiative. Whatever its desires, the Diem regime remained dependent on U.S. support for its survival, at least in the short term, and the ambitious scope of the hamlet program would necessitate a degree of American assistance. But would U.S. officials find the palace's plans palatable, and how would the two allies reconcile any differences in their conceptions of the program? In addition, the regime faced the perennial problem of actually implementing its plans, something that had plagued its previous rural projects. Could the government's apparatus digest a program that would stretch its capacities to the limit? And how would the peasantry, not to mention the NLF, react to strategic hamlets? Once again, fine-sounding theories were about to be tried and tested in the world beyond the confines of the corridors of the palace.

Members of the Ngo family: Diem, Nhu, Madame Nhu, and Thuc (Michigan
State University Archives and Historical Collections).

Above: Diem revels in the role of South Vietnam's savior (Michigan State University Archives and Historical Collections). *Facing page, top:* President Eisenhower greets his South Vietnamese counterpart at the start of Diem's visit to the United States, May 8, 1957 (National Archives). *Facing page, bottom:* Eisenhower's successor, John F. Kennedy, with Secretary of State Dean Rusk and Secretary of Defense Robert McNamara (Photographer, White House, John F. Kennedy Library).

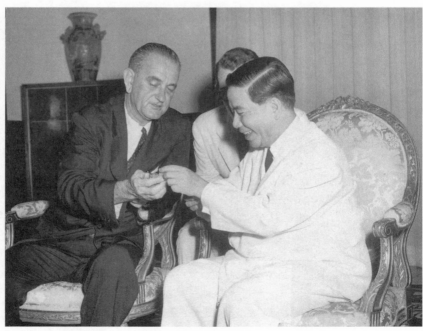

Facing page, top: Lyndon Johnson describes Diem as the Churchill of Asia at a luncheon hosted by Vice-President Nguyen Ngoc Tho (seated opposite), Hotel Caravelle, Saigon, May 12, 1961 (LBJ Library, photo by USIA). *Facing page, bottom:* Johnson and Diem, Independence Palace, May 13, 1961. Behind the rhetoric and the smiles, there were growing tensions in the U.S.–Vietnamese relationship (LBJ Library, photo by USIA). *Below:* Secretary Nguyen Dinh Thuan, Senator Hubert Humphrey, and Vice-President Johnson on board the navy yacht *Sequoia*, Washington, D.C., June 14, 1961. Thuan had just delivered a letter from Diem requesting another increase in the RVN's armed forces (LBJ Library, photo by unknown).

Nhu visits the new strategic hamlets at Cu Chi, March 31, 1962 (Getty Images).

Rounding up the population for resettlement, Operation Sunrise, 1962 (Corbis Bettmann).

Above and facing page: The inauguration of a strategic hamlet, central Vietnam, 1963 (VA 0003521 and 0003523, Folder 1, Box 15, Douglas Pike Collection, the Vietnam Archive).

Strategic hamlet defenses and defenders (VA 003501 and 0004925, Folders 1 and 4, Boxes 15 and 20, Douglas Pike Collection, the Vietnam Archive).

Thich Quang Duc's fiery suicide, June 11, 1963, the most potent symbol of the Buddhist crisis, which precipitated the collapse of the Diem regime (Getty Images).

The new U.S. ambassador, Henry Cabot Lodge, presents his diplomatic credentials, August 26, 1963; he was already engaged in plotting against the Diem government (Corbis Bettmann).

President Kennedy's interview with Walter Cronkite, Hyannis Port, September 2, 1963: "In the final analysis, it is their war . . . but I don't agree with those who say we should withdraw" (Photographer, White House, John F. Kennedy Library).

General Maxwell Taylor and Secretary of Defense Robert McNamara with President Kennedy. Their report of October 2, 1963, attempted to paper over the cracks in the administration's Vietnam policy (Photographer, White House, John F. Kennedy Library).

Soldiers outside the bullet-scarred presidential palace in the aftermath of the coup of November 1, 1963 (VA 0000590, Folder 2, Box 3, Douglas Pike Collection, the Vietnam Archive).

Celebrations in Saigon at the overthrow of the Diem regime (VA 0000609, Folder 3, Box 3, Douglas Pike Collection, the Vietnam Archive).

Peasants tear up the defenses of a strategic hamlet, Cu Chi district, November 2, 1963 (VA 0005072, Folder 2, Box 21, Douglas Pike Collection, the Vietnam Archive).

5

Theory and Practice

At a cocktail party at the U.S. ambassador's residence in the autumn of 1963, Robert Thompson, disgruntled head of the British Advisory Mission, engaged in a terse exchange about strategic hamlets with Political Counselor Nhu. "He referred to me as the father of the programme," Thompson noted sourly, "to which I replied that I did not recognize these children." At the time and in later postmortems, Thompson highlighted the differences that separated his ideas about strategic hamlets from Saigon's version of the program, especially in terms of the pace and scale of the construction undertaken by the Diem regime. Similarly, the State Department's Roger Hilsman, an early U.S. proponent of strategic hamlets, criticized the regime's approach and blamed the Ngos for the problems experienced by the program. With Diem and Nhu directing affairs, he lamented, "the strategic concept was never given a fair trial."[1]

Although such critiques correctly identify certain flaws in the hamlet program's execution, they tend to misconceive the issue. Thompson and Hilsman suggest that there was a soundly conceived concept, British and/or American in design, which the Diem regime proceeded to misinterpret and mismanage. They imply that proper implementation of this concept, especially careful and rational planning, could have defeated the NLF. Quite apart from the question of whether such an idealized scheme could have succeeded, this line of argument ignores the whole context in which the hamlet program actually developed. Conceived in the corridors of the palace, and implemented by the RVN's administration, strategic hamlets inevitably reflected Vietnamese goals and methods, not the preferred policies of the Americans or the British. The advisory relationship, moreover, severely circumscribed the ability of the regime's allies to influence the program's direction. Thus, to understand its theory and practice, we must set the hamlet scheme within its Vietnamese context by examining the ambitious designs of the Ngos and the actual shape that the program assumed in the process of implementation. What did the palace hope to achieve by constructing strategic hamlets, and what happened in practice?

117

* * *

As with its previous rural projects, the palace conceived of the hamlet scheme as a solution, in fact the ultimate solution, to its trio of enemies, "Communism, Underdevelopment, and Disunity." Thus, the regime chose to use the term "strategic hamlet" *(ap chien luoc)*, rather than other appellations that official documents had employed when the program was still in its infancy, such as "combat hamlet" *(ap chien dau)*. In a December 1961 memorandum to the president's office, Bui Van Luong explained that the word "combat" implied a narrow focus on the security situation, whereas "strategic" captured the palace's concern to address multiple problems: military, social, political, and economic.[2] Strategic hamlets aimed not only at defeating the NLF but also building a new society. "This program was to create a true revolution," recalled Lieutenant Colonel Hoang Van Lac, the permanent commissioner of Nhu's interministerial committee, "not the sort of temporary and superficial reforms that were done in the past."[3]

Nhu spearheaded the program, confiding to the U.S. embassy's John Mecklin that strategic hamlets had become a personal raison d'être. "Until this task," he observed, "I had been drifting, never sure how best to use my energies."[4] The counselor chaired the weekly sessions of the regime's coordinating committee; he was also the principal exponent of the program's purpose. Consequently, the palace's articulation of the scheme's goals, as well as its instructions to subordinates, reflected Nhu's penchant for philosophical rumination and were heavily laden with metaphysical ideas drawn from the theory of Personalism. Although the program suffered as a result from a certain amount of confusing verbiage, the regime's expositions on the subject of strategic hamlets represented the most elaborate articulation of its vision of a modern Vietnam.

The counselor, who once said that he would rather be an "archivist-paleographer" than a policy maker,[5] sought to set strategic hamlets within a panoramic vision of the nation's historical development—one that reflected the interest of the Ngos in an authentically Vietnamese route to modernity. "Behind us, behind our people is a heritage of struggle and of march toward progress," he proclaimed to a class of strategic-hamlet trainees in April 1963. "In front of us, in front of our people opens a long road which calls us forth." Strategic hamlets, he explained, were the next frontier in this story of struggle, the third stage of Vietnamese history. The first stage was the "march to the North of the 'One Hundred Viets' tribes' of prehistory"; the second, the "march to the South of our people in the Middle Ages, during modern times and in our contemporary epoch." These historical phases, argued Nhu, had "unfolded with the village as the framework," the essential unit of national vitality and cohesion. So too with the third stage, centered on strategic hamlets, which would achieve the equally monumental feat of overcoming "Communism, Underdevelopment, and Disunity." Indeed, the counselor suggested that this new movement had begun another "march to the North" that would culminate in the reunification of the country.[6]

These excursions into the past, to which Nhu also subjected individual visitors to the palace, did not seek to satisfy a "few intellectual bourgeois whims," he was at pains to point out; they reflected the fact that a grassroots mobilization of the people was the key to overcoming the regime's "enemies," just as a series of mass communal movements in the past had shaped the development of the nation. "The national policy of Strategic Hamlets is the quintessence of our truest traditions," Diem declared. "It is the pure out-growth of our ancestral virtues." To meet the current crisis in all its forms, the people in the villages had to be roused to emulate the exploits of their forefathers; they must become part of a popular struggle.[7] The Ngos constantly emphasized the importance of "struggle" *(dau tranh)* if the nation's enemies were to be overcome, just as the Vietnamese communists used the same term to describe their own efforts to promote change. In a 1961 study document for government cadres, Nguyen Van Chau, the RVN's director of psychological warfare, explained that only by confronting obstacles could a nation develop the moral and material strength necessary to prosper. The past demonstrates, he warned, that a people that did not struggle could not expect the history of their country to last much longer.[8]

The emphasis on the value of "struggle" manifested itself in one of the central themes of the hamlet program: the need for popular self-sufficiency. Government pronouncements repeatedly stressed that the people must take the initiative and carry the burden of defeating the nation's enemies; the role of the authorities was only to provide the stimulus to action and the minimum of support necessary to kick start the program.[9] The Ngos considered such self-reliance to be both a virtue and a necessity. It was a virtue, they believed, because people forced back upon their own resources would develop the inner strength and common bonds of unity necessary to build a new society. "Being personalist," as one official explanation of the hamlet program put it, "requires a militant democratic spirit which conceives liberty as a conquest over oneself and exterior obstacles."[10] Self-sufficiency was also deemed a necessity because of the government's limited resources; the only alternative was continued dependence on foreign aid. Why was it, Nhu complained at an interministerial meeting in July 1962, that, when the Vietnamese discussed the problem of finances, they could only think about U.S. support? That kind of childlike reliance on others, he asserted, was humiliating and dangerous; it was not characteristic of a truly independent country.[11]

As an organizational framework for promoting a popular struggle, the hamlet program sought to generate a revolution in four areas: military, social, political, and economic. Militarily, strategic hamlets hoped to reverse the deteriorating situation on the battlefield, where the RVN's forces had proved incapable of maintaining security. On the one hand, when dispersed in isolated camps and forts, they lacked the numbers, and also apparently the will, to protect surrounding villages.[12] On the other hand, when the ARVN concentrated its big battalions and ventured into the countryside, the insurgents usually evaded battle or melted away into the population. These big sweeps reminded Lieutenant Colonel John Paul Vann of a ship moving through the ocean, temporarily displacing water that flowed right back into place as soon as the vessel sailed on.[13] Besides yielding few results, they could also be positively self-defeating. "Since we did not know where the enemy was," stated Nhu, "ten times we launched a military operation, nine times we missed the Viet-Cong, and the tenth time, we struck right on the head of the population." The result was popular hostility toward the military as well as frustration within the ranks of the armed forces.[14]

Strategic hamlets, however, promised to establish a new front line in the contest between the government and the guerrillas. Rather than giving the insurgents unrestricted access to the population, they would erect physical and psychological barriers between the NLF and the peasantry. This approach assumed, of course, that most villagers agreed to NLF demands for support only because they were terrified or tricked into doing so; and, once caught up in the ranks of the insurgents, people would not dare to desert for fear of retribution. Inside strategic hamlets, however, peasants would be able to stand up to the NLF and press-ganged guerrillas find safe havens. Consequently, the insurgents would be compelled to attack hamlets in order to maintain access to their bases of support and, in the process, would reveal themselves as the true enemies of the people. Physically and morally isolated, Diem argued, the guerrillas would gradually be reduced to the status of "a foreign expeditionary corps facing a hostile population." With the enemy forced out into the open, moreover, the ARVN would be free to finish off a cornered quarry, instead of chasing shadows.[15]

In this scheme of things, the primary responsibility for the defense of the country would be assumed by a hamlet-based, citizen militia, with the regular army and provincial forces reduced to a supporting role, providing initial protection for fledgling hamlets, and hunting down the remnants of the PLAF. According to Nhu, this arrangement represented a fundamental change in the spirit of the war, in line with the regime's call for popular struggle and self-sufficiency. The country could not afford to fight a conventional or counterguerrilla conflict against the insurgents, he argued, for that style of warfare was not only tactically bankrupt but also kept Saigon dependent on the United States for the support of the RVN's lavishly equipped forces. National pride, and real independence, demanded that South Vietnam develop an alternative approach, one better suited to the conditions of a poor and underdeveloped country. Nhu envisaged a defense posture eventually founded on a smaller regular army, a variety of special forces units, and, at the core, a guerrilla substructure of seven hundred thousand hamlet militia. Thus, just as strategic hamlets would flush out the NLF and compel it to adopt more conventional military tactics, they would also allow the Diem regime to wage an anticommunist version of a "people's war," based on a militarily and politically mobilized population.[16]

The advantages that the Ngos hoped to derive from this strategy also tied in with the hamlet program's second main area of concern: social change. By making ordinary people responsible for the nation's defense, the palace sought to overcome peasant parochialism and engage the rural populace in national affairs. There was no point trying to interest villagers by lecturing them about world politics or ideological theory, Nhu warned an interministerial meeting in March 1962, but if peasants saw that their own interests coincided with those of the community and nation, then strategic hamlets might start to change social attitudes.[17] In protecting their homes, the Ngos reasoned, hamlet residents would be defending not only themselves and their families but also their communities and country. Hence, the anticommunist struggle would kindle a new sense of communal solidarity and national consciousness among the peasantry, gradually overcoming the isolated and atomized nature of rural life. Backward attitudes, mired in a narrow concern for individual and family interests, would slowly give way to broader commitments. Indeed, the belief that shared hardship could foster social cohesion suffused all aspects of the establishment of strategic hamlets, from the building of their fortifications to plans for their economic development. "Using difficulty as a springboard," Diem declared in October 1962, "the soul of the nation is forging its unity in the trials of war."[18]

Nowhere were these expectations better illustrated than in Nhu's ambitious conception of hamlet defense, for the counselor expected peasants to wage their own guerrilla struggle against the NLF. He argued that a hamlet militia, usually known as the "combat youth," was capable of defending its settlement against a small band of insurgents. In the event of an attack by a larger unit, however, its role was only to retard and harass the enemy's advance. During this delaying action, the hamlet's other inhabitants would hide food and money; the young people would also disappear into secret cellars, so the guerrillas would enter a hamlet composed only of old people and children. Meanwhile, the combat youth would continue to harass the enemy from concealed positions; and, if the intruders tried to remain in the hamlet, secret cells would conduct sabotage operations and contact nearby posts or settlements.[19] In effect, the NLF would find itself in the same kind of hostile environment that the ARVN encountered in its sweeps through the country-side. To emphasize further the active role that the regime expected ordinary people to play in the nation's defense, the palace proposed to lend weapons to hamlet defenders only for a period of six months, during which time they had to capture their own guns from the insurgents.[20]

Naturally, such sterling service could only be expected if peasants believed that their strategic hamlet deserved protecting in the first place. The regime's program "is valid only if the life on the inside of the hamlet is worth living, and therefore worth being protected and defended," Madame Nhu observed, "for it must be remembered that it is always the population of the hamlet itself which closes the hamlet gates and no one else."[21] To secure this commit-ment, and give meaning to its social revolution, the palace planned to create a new set of social classes, based on contributions to the "defense and welfare of the nation." The three-tier system comprised, first, combatants and their families; second, hamlet leaders and locally elected officials; and, third, poor peasants and workers. Rank in this social order would entitle holders to cer-tain privileges, such as priority in the distribution of rice land, and better ac-cess to education and medical treatment.[22] Everybody would be given equal opportunity to benefit materially from the new scale of values depending on their contribution to defeating "Communism, Underdevelopment, and Dis-unity." The new system thus sought to embody Personalism's concern to com-bine individual rights with collective responsibility.

There would be "losers" as well as "winners" in this reshuffling of the social order. The "losers," Nhu explained at an interministerial meeting, would be those whose status derived from the traditional advantages of wealth and education. The well-off, who concerned themselves only with their own private affairs, were "parasites," he stated, and must be replaced by those will-ing to sacrifice enthusiastically for the "just cause."[23] Thus, the first duty of government cadres, Nhu told a class of strategic-hamlet trainees, was not to defend the current order but to overthrow it. "The traditional system," he noted, "product of a backward, political, economic and social structure . . . would give place to a more progressive, revolutionary one." Clearly, the regime's social revolution represented not only an attempt to promote service to the nation but also an assault on the established social structure. Far from seeking to bolster the existing order, as its critics generally alleged, the palace intended to replace it.[24]

This goal was more fully expressed in the third element of the hamlet scheme: political revolution. If the government was to succeed in generating social change, reasoned the palace, then this also had to be accompanied by political change. The people, clearly unwilling to fight for the ancien regime, would only rally to the government's side if the rewards of the new social system were backed by political developments that served to promote that new order. "If fortifications were built around the hamlets while injustice prevailed inside," Bui Van Luong observed, "the people would believe that they were [being] imprisoned." Government officials had to understand, Nhu told a group of them in March 1962, that strategic hamlets were not designed to corral peasants but to provide a framework to improve their lives.[25] The hamlet program sought to furnish an appropriate political structure in two ways: through the holding of local elections and by establishing the rule of law in the countryside.

Although Vietnam had a long history of local democracy, when the Diem regime first came into power it preferred to appoint officials directly because of the dire security situation. The proposed new system of elections represented a reversal of this policy and also extended the electoral principle down to the hamlet level. The most important elected bodies were to be the hamlet management committee and the village council. The former would consist of a chief and three or four commissioners; the youth delegate was to be chosen by members of the Republican Youth Movement, while the other commissioners were to be elected by a secret ballot of all residents over the age of eighteen. The village council would comprise five officials, who were to be elected indirectly by members of each village's hamlet committees and the leaders of hamlet organizations.[26]

The purpose of these elections was to cut out the deadwood and plant new shoots in the villages. Existing officials were usually cronies of the district chiefs, Nhu complained; they had little or no connection to the villages they ran, commanded no respect or support among the population, and drove peasants into the arms of the insurgents. Elections, he argued, would promote local self-government, encourage political participation, generate support for elected authorities, and nurture a new generation of rural leaders.[27] The counselor dismissed the concerns of provincial officials that it was too dangerous in a time of war to introduce such changes and depend on a new batch of inexperienced local leaders. Popular elections, particularly the speedy establishment of hamlet committees, were essential in order to demonstrate to the people the government's intentions.[28]

The regime did not intend to allow known communists to stand for office, of course; moreover, it effectively invited electoral abuse by advising local officials to endorse informally the candidacies of those residents who demonstrated the most enthusiasm during the building of strategic hamlets.[29] Foreign observers often took such measures to mean that elections were merely a sham and evidence of the government's real intent, which was simply to control villagers.[30] In fact, the palace was being simultaneously naïve and manipulative, rather than disingenuous. Its instructions to subordinates carried the conviction that rural inhabitants would freely embrace the hamlet scheme, and naturally wish to elect the "right" candidates for office, as long as they understood the program's purpose. Provided local officials explained the scheme's benefits properly, villagers would do everything they could to make strategic hamlets a success and eagerly accept advice about which of their number would make the best leaders.

Peasants, in this view, were enthusiastic pupils but desperately in need of tutelage. Electoral advice, then, would help steer them in the right direction. Nhu criticized those officials who suggested that elections were only for form's sake and the idea was to rig the vote so that the right people won. Strategic hamlets were a revolutionary concept, he insisted, not simply a policy for restoring security; if peasants believed that elections were a sham, they would ignore the decrees of the locally "elected" bodies. "We are not establishing Strategic Hamlets as a trick but because we genuinely want to carry out a structural revolution," he emphasized at an interministerial meeting in October 1962.[31]

A similar concern, both to embody and demonstrate political change, underlay the establishment of new legal codes, called "Communal Rules." Based upon a government model, but adaptable to the customs and concerns of different localities, these regulations were to be drawn up and voted into effect by local residents. Each set of rules enshrined the regime's call for "democratic law," "collective development," and "social justice" in the countryside, and represented the new scale of social values in action. The regulations outlined the responsibilities of hamlet residents—the defense and development of their communities—as well as their rights.[32] One point emphasized in regard to residents' rights was the need to stop local abuses of power, especially the arbitrary arrest and imprisonment of political suspects. As with his support for elections, Nhu rejected criticism from the provinces that introducing such safeguards might be dangerous in the present emergency. Communal rules sought to guarantee a democratic regime at the grassroots level, he argued, not to chain the people. "In time of war people think you must suppress democracy to win," he told USOM's Rufus Phillips, but "we shall use the war against communism as a means to introduce democracy and we shall use democracy to win the war."[33]

In addition to energizing the population, Saigon also expected these laws and elections to help eliminate the influence of those groups that it viewed as obstacles to revolutionary change, starting with the existing rural elite. In a discussion with a British official in January 1962, Nhu explained that he wanted to create a new rural leadership from the Republican Youth Movement in order to replace the current village elders and local notables, whose anticommunism stemmed only from a desire to maintain their power and privileges.[34] At a meeting of RVN officials at Phan Thiet in March, the counselor stated that the present rural leadership looked backward, not forward, and had pushed peasants into the arms of the communists. With hindsight, he admitted, the government had made a mistake in preserving the position of this rural elite merely because it possessed administrative experience. The regime should have followed the example of the communists, who had created a new class of cadres after 1945, free of old feudal and colonial attitudes.[35] Strategic hamlets would now seek to remedy the oversight.

This housecleaning promised to lay the foundations for the fourth and final pillar of the regime's revolution: economic development. At the start of the hamlet program, this issue received much less attention than the scheme's military, social, and political aspects. Although there were certain elements within the regime that hoped from the outset to incorporate the provision of schools, hospitals, and other amenities into the program,[36] the palace took the position that this was putting the cart before the horse. In its view, there could be no economic development without first establishing security in the countryside; indeed, by restoring security, strategic hamlets would finally allow the government to implement its existing economic policies properly.[37] Nhu argued, moreover, that, until the hamlet scheme's social and political revolutions gathered momentum, local amenities would principally benefit the rich, who were the only ones who had time to take advantage of schools, hospitals, and the like.[38] Thus, the regime put economic concerns on the back burner until late 1962, when the hamlet program was well under way.[39]

For Nhu, economic development was intimately related to the social and political transformation of Vietnamese society. In addresses to trainee cadres in mid-1963, he referred to Walt Rostow's stages of economic growth, emphasizing the need to put an end to "traditional society" before proceeding to the point of economic "takeoff." Government officials, he observed, must help to free people from the bonds of the ancien regime and instill in them a revolutionary spirit. Without a change in the nature of the regime—a new administrative base, laws, educational system, and class structure—South Vietnam would not have the strength to build an industrial society; it would remain a terminally ill patient, kept alive only by the drip feed of foreign aid.[40]

This concept strongly influenced Nhu's approach to the economic aspects of the hamlet program. He was particularly concerned about the implications of providing large amounts of government or foreign aid to strategic hamlets. Lavishing support on the peasantry, in his view, threatened to undermine the spirit of self-reliance that was the basis for economic progress in an underdeveloped country; hamlet residents must bear the primary responsibility for developing their economic life, just as they bore the major burden for the defense of their homes. The U.S. embassy's Douglas Pike recalled attending an inaugural ceremony for a new strategic hamlet at which a delegation of village elders asked Nhu for assistance in building a school. He refused: "The government's means are stretched now to their limit. Do not rely on outside aid. First build a revolution within yourself. Then build the school with your own hands." Nhu parried the protests of the Americans in attendance, who tended to see the hamlet program as a way for the government to extend a helping hand to peasants. "You do not understand these villagers," he countered. "Satisfy one demand and they would return with ten more."[41]

Nhu preferred small economic projects, such as the development of cottage industries—endeavors that required minimal outside support, could be sustained without continued government backing, and might generate income to pay for hamlet and village administration. Such considerations underlay the palace's agreement with the Americans to provide hamlets with twenty thousand piasters (about three hundred dollars) for small-scale local initiatives.[42] Besides encouraging self-sufficiency, the palace believed that such enterprises would help to school peasants in their rights and responsibilities. Saigon intended residents to choose, debate, and then vote on these "self-help" projects before they could be undertaken. This program, a government publication explained, "not only permits the rural population to raise its voice in matters affecting the local welfare, but it also draws the people into the processes of self-government, and gives them a personal stake in the future of their country."[43]

What was "the future of their country" that this multifaceted revolution—military, social, political, and economic—was to bring about? For the Ngos, the hamlet program represented an authentic national revolution, which drew upon the vitality of the village in Vietnamese life. The villages, as Nhu argued in his excursions into history, were the source of the country's strength, the guardians of its national spirit. That vitality, in turn, was the product of their unique place in the traditional administrative system. In the past, an official pamphlet explained, Vietnamese society was composed of two ostensibly opposing systems: a centralized monarchy and "a popular, autonomous and representative democracy" in the countryside. The two coexisted because of the limits of imperial power embodied in the adage "The laws of the emperor bow before the customs of the village." Thus, "the Vietnamese nation was like a federation composed of numerous and small communal states in a super-state."[44] The Ngos believed that the hamlet program could harness the latent energy that supposedly existed in these robust corporate communities and, through the development of local self-rule and self-sufficiency, create a modern version of this traditional democracy. "There is a tradition of democracy and autonomy in the village," Diem told Marguerite Higgins. "And we want to tap these deep roots of our Confucian traditions in rebuilding our society."[45]

While they focused very much on immediate events in the countryside, the Ngos evidently viewed this grassroots revitalization as the first step in the transformation of South Vietnamese society as a whole. Nhu informed newspaper reporters in September 1963 that the scale of the changes under way in the nation's strategic hamlets also "necessarily entails a revision of the state's superstructure." The revolution in the countryside would advance toward the urban areas, Diem told the National Assembly in October 1963. "The strategic hamlet policy has in effect already set in motion a vast movement of study and full revision of the institutions of the present government," he observed.[46] Thus, the old order in the villages was not the only target of the Ngos; they also envisaged that the effects of the hamlet program would cleanse the rest of the body politic as well, especially the French-trained urban elite for whom the Ngos held particular contempt.[47]

There was a significant drawback in targeting members of this elite, of course. After all, these were the same people that staffed the government's offices and implemented its policies, a problem that Nhu identified in discussions with U.S. officials.[48] Perhaps this situation helps account for the difficulty experienced by RVN officials in fully comprehending the counselor's turgid explanations of the hamlet program. "They couldn't figure [out] what the hell he was talking about," William Colby recalled of meetings between Nhu and the program's administrators. "He wasn't that clear—let's face it—because what he was really saying underneath is, 'We're going to replace all you guys.'"[49] Nhu also included the present leadership among the eventual victims of this renovation of the state, noting that, in promoting the hamlet program, he was effectively "working for [the] destruction of my family."[50]

The Ngos never spelled out in detail how this revision of society would occur, or exactly what form the new state would eventually take. Their sporadic commentary on the subject suggests that they envisaged a ripple effect based on the electoral initiatives begun in the period 1960–1963. On a number of occasions, Nhu stated that local elections would gradually be extended to progressively higher administrative levels. He told John Donnell in an interview in August 1961 that members of the Republican Youth who were elected to village councils might later be chosen to sit on district and then provincial councils; in time, they might even become national political figures.[51] If extrapolated from the type of elections instituted as part of the hamlet program, this process would amount to a vertical system of indirect democracy; hamlet inhabitants would elect hamlet committees as well as the leaders of hamlet organizations, then these representatives would elect village councils and the leaders of village-level organizations, and so on. The regime had instituted a similar procedure for its network of farmers' associations that it founded in 1958, and Nhu was familiar with this system from his work in trade union organization; it was also reminiscent of the Leninist organizational framework adopted by the Vietnamese communists, whose techniques were so admired by the president's brother.[52]

This vision of a state organized from the bottom up matched the palace's oft-repeated claim that it was not interested in centralizing power for its own sake. From the outset of his regime, Diem had spoken of his desire to develop a decentralized system of government, based on the traditional autonomy of the village, and he had always justified his concentration of power as a temporary expedient. These themes were also evident in the palace's explanation of the ultimate goal of the hamlet program. Nhu stated in an interminister-ial meeting that the regime only sought to use its authority in order to direct a process of decentralization; to retain power indefinitely would constitute a dictatorship.[53] He told the British ambassador that he saw the country's villages eventually forming a network of semi-independent republics, a vision he returned to in a meeting in September 1963 with Mieczyslaw Maneli, the Polish delegate to the International Control Commission. "I am temporarily curtailing freedom to offer it in unlimited form. I am strengthening discipline to do away with its external bonds. I am centralizing the state in order to democratize and decentralize it," Nhu explained to the Pole. "The strategic hamlets are the basic institutions of direct democracy. When they develop and flourish, they will become the real nucleus of national organization, and then the state itself—as Marx said—will wither away."[54]

Such comments sound quite surreal, and it would be easy to dismiss them as a political smoke screen. Yet they fit with the palace's long-standing concern to find an authentically Vietnamese route to modernity as well as a third way between liberalism and communism. On the one hand, the Ngos proposed to create a state more disciplined and ordered than the liberal one, based on a series of interlocking associations and bound by a strong sense of civic responsibility. At the same time, they spoke of the need for society to be founded on the principle of decentralization, in order to avoid the excesses of a state-centered totalitarianism. What the palace seemed to be outlining was something akin to the self-regulating communitarianism envisaged by European Personalists, or the kind of collective harmony advocated by various theorists of the corporate state.[55] The Ngos wanted to establish a "new Vietnamese social and political community, built up from the rural areas to replace the elites left over from French colonial times," observed William Colby. From this foundation "could develop the leadership of a free and authentic Vietnam, neither Communist nor Western in culture or character."[56]

Given their imminent demise, the willingness of the Ngos to relinquish power as part of this process was never put to the test. No doubt they would have found it difficult to do so, for political reality is a lot messier than political theory. Reducing state power after it has succeeded in establishing a new, self-governing order is a nice idea that seems to have eluded most of its twentieth-century exponents. It is particularly hard to imagine leaders as uncompromising as the Ngos being prepared to tolerate the diffusion of power for very long if it encouraged the emergence of political forces that they considered objectionable.[57] Nevertheless, this new order was their avowed goal, and they were sufficiently convinced of their infallibility to have believed in its fulfillment; Diem's sense of destiny and Nhu's intellectual arrogance made for a potent combination.

Indeed, so impressed was the palace with its concept of nation building that it argued the approach could serve as a model for the rest of the Third World. According to the Ngos, newly independent states faced two, equally unappetizing routes to modernity: Western-style democracy or dictatorship. The former initially attracted many nationalist leaders but proved a recipe for chaos and disorder, given the social divisions bequeathed by colonialism; the latter brought order but at the expense of freedom. "Taken in their extremes," noted the *Times of Viet Nam Magazine*, "these trends would lead to anarchy on the one hand and to a monolithic totalitarianism on the other." By simultaneously promoting democratic decentralization while building a strong and united nation-state, strategic hamlets seemed to solve this dilemma. This approach provided the underdeveloped world with a strategy for development, Nhu contended, and the Free World a solution to the problem of communist guerrilla warfare.[58]

Needless to say, these grand plans failed to materialize, and the hamlet program that actually took shape in the countryside did not look much like the one that the Ngos waxed lyrically about in Saigon. Communist tracts frequently described strategic hamlets as disguised prisons or concentration camps, which, while suitably overblown for propaganda purposes, was closer to reality than the palace's description of budding village democracies.[59] Tran Van Giau, the historian and veteran party activist, even argued that the publicly articulated objectives of the hamlet scheme were merely a cover for a much narrower military goal: the elimination of the NLF's armed forces.[60] A similar charge appears in many Western accounts of the conflict, which interpret the palace's program primarily as a security measure aimed at controlling the peasantry.[61]

Such interpretations are misleading, however. Although there was a yawning chasm between the theory and practice of the hamlet program, this was not the result of some hidden agenda. The Ngos, in fact, appear to have been quite obsessed with their concept of nation building. "Practically the first words out of his mouth anytime I saw him were 'Hameaux Stratégiques,' " Frederick Nolting recalled of Counselor Nhu. Cao Van Luan, who spoke privately with both Diem and Nhu about strategic hamlets, described them as intoxicated with the idea of building the country from the bottom up. For the Ngos, remarked the State Department's William H. Sullivan, the Strategic Hamlet program was a means of inculcating "a sense of national identity and purpose" among a "hitherto passive peasantry"; it was "something far more significant than merely a counter-insurgency measure."[62] The problem for the palace was that while material signs of the hamlet scheme sprang up all over the countryside, it proved far more difficult to generate the popular struggle needed to breathe life into these physical forms.

One of the initial obstacles in turning theory into practice was the lack of proper guidance and direction from Saigon. With government encouragement, local authorities had been busy building strategic hamlets for months prior to the creation of Nhu's interministerial committee; and construction continued apace even as the committee sought to grapple with such basic issues as determining exactly what constituted a "strategic hamlet." In addition, Saigon experienced some difficulty at first in persuading Ngo Dinh Can, the regional boss of central Vietnam, to throw his weight behind the program. Can evidently preferred his own concept of the *Force Populaire,* roving groups of cadres modeled on the NLF's agit-prop teams.[63] In light of these problems, internal reviews of the program concluded that the government had failed to establish a clear concept of its goals and methods, and many strategic hamlets were of dubious value, if not a complete waste of time and effort.[64] At an interministerial meeting on April 6, 1962, General Tran Tu Oai reported that there was still not a single settlement in the entire country that conformed to the palace's ideas.[65]

Nhu's committee served as the chief forum to develop national guidelines and discuss the problems with the program's implementation. In July 1962, a full year after the first provincial experiments with hamlet defense, the regime finally promulgated a list of the six criteria that determined a strategic hamlet's progress toward completion: clear the communists from the locality; organize the inhabitants into groups according to age and by neighborhood; assign residents their roles and responsibilities in case of enemy attack; complete the settlement's fortifications, including a fence surround, trenches, and house cellars; establish two secret cells in case the hamlet is occupied by the insurgents; hold elections and draw up a set of communal rules.[66]

Even with the dissemination of such guidelines, the palace remained very critical of the scheme's progress. Nhu complained that the provinces devoted too much attention to the physical aspects of strategic hamlets—the digging of trenches and the construction of fences—and not enough to the social and political revolution that the regime wanted to promote inside them. He blamed the problem on the "feudal" and "colonial" mentality of RVN officials; they lacked the requisite revolutionary spirit, he commented, preferring to "command" and "administer" the people in traditional fashion rather than encourage peasants to help themselves.[67] Frequently, even the physical aspects of strategic hamlets lacked substance. In August 1962, the central committee of the National Revolutionary Movement reported that, apart from a few model settlements to which local officials invariably steered visiting delegations, most strategic hamlets were flimsily defended as well as badly organized; officials also resorted to coercive methods reminiscent of the Agroville program, paying little attention to the winning of people's hearts.[68] In March 1963, more than a year after his committee's creation, the counselor stated that, of the approximately five thousand hamlets reportedly completed, perhaps only a third really satisfied the government's six criteria.[69]

The triumph of form over substance, and coercion over consent, characterized all aspects of strategic hamlets, from their initial establishment through to their internal organization. For example, one of the original attractions of the program was that it would forego the need for the kind of large-scale, forced resettlement of the population that had characterized the agroville scheme. Saigon did envisage the need for some relocation, especially in guerrilla strongholds where the intention was to regroup peasants, by force if necessary, in "combat hamlets." As the name suggested, this type of settlement would require greater military support and emphasis on its defensive qualities; once firmly established, a combat hamlet could then be converted into a strategic hamlet, with its inhabitants assuming responsibility for its security. The palace also anticipated that, in places where a hamlet's population was scattered over a wide area, there would be the need for some concentration of outlying homes within a manageable perimeter. In this case, however, Nhu argued that regroupment would be minimal and voluntary.[70]

These guidelines were extremely vague and, in the hands of lower-level officials, became a recipe for mass, forcible regroupment. Since much of the countryside lacked security—50 percent of it according to the regime's own estimates—the hamlet program was likely to entail considerably more movement of the population than Nhu seemed to imagine.[71] In addition, the dispersed pattern of settlement in the Mekong Delta, where hamlets often stretched for miles along roads or waterways, meant that large numbers of people would probably have to be regrouped in order to create more secure and defendable positions. In fact, provincial officials forcibly moved thousands of families. In the Delta's Long An alone, about eighty thousand of the province's four hundred thousand people were relocated, with more than 80

percent of the inhabitants of some areas experiencing a degree of resettlement. Nhu evidently underestimated exactly what minimal regroupment
might entail, and the extent to which local officials would resort to massive
and compulsory relocation, especially among the widely scattered population
of the Delta and in the thinly inhabited Central Highlands.[72]

Government expectations about the process of hamlet construction suffered a similar fate. To prevent the provinces placing excessive demands on
the peasantry, and keep corruption in check, Saigon fixed popular contributions to the building of strategic hamlets at five to ten days of labor and fifty
to one hundred piasters in money. As a result of provincial violations of these
limits, the palace subsequently forbade compulsory financial contributions,
and established complaints procedures to deter and punish abuses.[73] Yet, in
many places, officials continued to ignore restrictions, placing a heavy burden on the populace to provide the manpower, money, and materials necessary to complete strategic hamlets. The U.S. consulate in Hue reported that,
in parts of central Vietnam, peasants contributed the equivalent of more than
three hundred piasters each for bamboo to construct hamlet defenses.[74] In the
Delta's Vinh Long, some peasants ended up working as many as sixty days on
what appeared to be a local version of the Great Wall of China.[75]

Local reinterpretation plagued the internal organization, as well as physical construction, of strategic hamlets. One of the scheme's central tenets was
the training and arming of the inhabitants. Nhu pressured the provinces to
do so, although he warned against distributing weapons too liberally because
that would violate the principle of self-sufficiency. Wary officials, however,
were slow to comply, preferring to rely on their own regular forces, which
they deemed more reliable than ordinary peasants.[76] They also sabotaged the
process of local elections, simply rigging the vote, appointing committees, or
establishing shadow administrations. "Democracy here cannot come before
security," a province chief bluntly informed Theodore Heavner of the Vietnam Working Group. Consequently, newly "elected" leaders often turned out
to be the old leaders.[77] Not surprisingly, the regime's new communal rules fell
by the wayside as well; district authorities usually drew them up without even
the pretense of popular participation and presumably treated their provisions
with equal contempt.[78] Saigon's wishes notwithstanding, it was business as
usual in the countryside.

In short, the implementation of the hamlet scheme differed significantly
from the palace's blueprint. While a physically imposing program began to
develop in the countryside, the anticipated rural revolution did not. This gap
between theory and practice transcended the growing pains of the first half
of 1962 and reflected a series of more fundamental problems. These difficulties were, first, the unrealistic pace set by Saigon for the program's imple-

mentation; second, the impact of this demanding schedule on provincial government; and, third, the reaction of peasants and the NLF to strategic hamlets. The combination of these three factors accounts for the hamlet program's mutation as it went from the palace's drawing board to rural reality.

First, the Ngos set a blistering pace for hamlet construction, which inevitably sacrificed quality for quantity. At the outset, Nhu proposed to "strategize" all sixteen thousand of the country's hamlets within twelve months. High-ranking officials were aghast, noting the terrible burden this would place on the RVN's resources, especially financial. The national budget could initially provide only one hundred million piasters ($1.4 million) for the program, almost forty times less than one early estimate of the costs. With limited resources, senior officials pointed out in a meeting at the interior ministry in January 1962, the resulting burden would have to be borne by a disgruntled populace.[79] Nhu argued, however, that strategic hamlets would not prove overly taxing because they did not require large-scale regroupment or the construction of new settlements. Indeed, the counselor estimated that the average settlement could be established in only three weeks, with more difficult places perhaps taking four or five weeks.[80] The program's progress in 1962 exposed this wild optimism, with only four thousand strategic hamlets completed by the year's end. In response, the palace set a new and equally unrealistic target of eleven thousand by the end of June 1963.[81]

What lay behind this call for speed? One possible answer is the advice of Lieutenant Colonel Pham Ngoc Thao, an inspector of the hamlet program and probably an undercover enemy agent. Years later, Stanley Karnow was told by "communist sources" that Thao had "deliberately propelled the program ahead at breakneck speed in order to estrange South Vietnam's peasants and drive them into the arms of the Vietcong." Truong Nhu Tang, a longtime friend of Thao's and a founding member of the NLF, also believed that the mercurial colonel had probably helped sow confusion in the program.[82] If Thao was a communist agent, he was in good company; two other operatives, Pham Xuan An and Vu Ngoc Nha, had also penetrated the palace's inner circle.[83] However, his influence on the direction of the hamlet program is unclear. From the available documentation, he does not appear to have featured prominently in high-level deliberations; in fact, David Halberstam suggests that he was in some political disfavor and his job was a "relatively unimportant" one.[84] In addition, if he did encourage the Ngos to push ahead rapidly with strategic hamlets, his advice only confirmed their own predilections, for they had expressed this sentiment long before the scheme's official launch, when Thao was still the chief of Kien Hoa province.

Behind the palace's sense of urgency lay its fears about the growing strength of the NLF. At Ban Me Thuot in October 1961, Nhu told officials that they must build strategic hamlets as quickly as possible so that the rate of construction would outpace the insurgents' efforts to destroy the scheme. To go slowly would only allow the guerrillas to overwhelm the program, a rationale he repeated in an interministerial meeting one year later.[85] Rapid construction would also forestall communist efforts to consolidate a liberated zone in the south. The palace feared that, if the insurgency continued to expand at its present rate, the NLF would not only overpower the hamlet program but also be in a position to declare a provisional government. Consequently, the building of hamlets must continue apace in order to "keep the enemy on the run," Diem stated in September 1963.[86]

From the start, the Ngos sought to establish strategic hamlets all over South Vietnam, as rapidly as possible, showing little interest in the kind of measured progress that so concerned the Americans and the British. The palace initially delegated to the localities much of the authority for deciding where to begin operations and recommended only the vaguest of criteria, such as securing axes of communication and population centers. This expansive approach really did not constitute a set of priorities at all.[87] Even when the regime came up with more detailed plans in the summer of 1962, these rapidly fell by the wayside. Trying to target certain areas was simply incompatible with the palace's stress on speed and advancing simultaneously throughout the country. "We must control territory and defend everything under the sun," Diem told Karnow in late 1963. "We must suffocate the Communists. This job can't be done drop by drop."[88]

On the receiving end of the resulting flood of demands were the provinces. Saigon put intense pressure on its subordinates to meet its impossible schedules, compiling a weekly league table to chart the progress of each province's efforts. Nhu told a group of USOM officials that deadlines helped "to stimulate cadres."[89] RVN officials, however, simply found them unrealistic and intimidating. With Long An firmly rooted to the foot of the hamlet league table, Nguyen Viet Thanh had to endure frequent criticism during visits to the capital. Nearby Kien Hoa shared Long An's lowly position, and its chief, Tran Ngoc Chau, recalls similarly unwanted attention directed at the progress of his province's program.[90] Yet Thanh and Chau were both dedicated officials, whose provinces were not the only ones experiencing difficulties. The fact that Long An and Kien Hoa were in poor standing was less the result of their peculiar problems than the tendency of officials elsewhere to cut corners in order to meet Saigon's demands, even reporting nonexistent hamlets as complete.[91]

The palace's rapid implementation of the program thus had important negative consequences. Few officials dared to resist the pressure coming from Saigon, particularly since they had been appointed first and foremost on the basis of their political loyalty to the Ngos.[92] In seeking to comply with the palace's demands, however, they developed hamlets very different from the original copy. Prodded mercilessly by the Ngos, most officials sought to placate their superiors by creating passable physical imitations of strategic hamlets, neglecting the political aspects that were so central to Saigon's scheme. Indeed, the palace's sense of urgency exacerbated certain features of provincial administration that proved most damaging to the prospects of actually mobilizing the population politically, for the stress on speedy execution exposed the perennial lack of resources at the province level and encouraged the authoritarian tendencies of local officials.

Provincial administrations did not have the means to establish strategic hamlets at the pace set by the palace. As with previous rural projects, the grand plans drawn up in the comfortable and well-staffed offices of the capital overwhelmed the limited capabilities of local government. Province chiefs protested about the lack of personnel and materials to build fortifications; they worried about how their hard-pressed forces could maintain security for the construction work; and they scoured their offices, drafting education and finance officials, to fill out the hamlet cadre groups that were to go into the villages. As a U.S. report of April 1962 succinctly observed: "There are not enough S[elf] D[efense] C[orpsmen], not enough barbed wire, not enough cement, not enough weapons, not enough administrators, not enough cadre, not enough piasters."[93]

Lack of means meant more than just thinly stretched resources; it also affected the modus operandi of administrators. Officials could not interpret and respond properly to the welter of instructions and demands coming from Saigon, especially if these orders failed to provide clear practical guidance; after Nhu's weekly interministerial meetings, recalled Hoang Van Lac, he had to recompose the counselor's rambling philosophical expositions into sets of minutes that made some sense.[94] Under the circumstances, harassed provincial officials fastened like limpet mines to the most easily grasped and executed aspects of the program. William Colby witnessed this process at work during Nhu's lectures to subordinates, one of his methods of policy transmission: "The quivering officials, well aware that their careers could depend on pleasing the brother of the President, anxiously tried to ascertain from Nhu's convoluted discourses what exactly it was that they were expected to do to carry out the program. Their bewilderment at everything beyond a few practical steps like digging a protective ditch, throwing up a fence, conducting an accurate community census, and asserting control over the inhabitants was often evident."[95]

In this way, the information that descended the chain of command progressively filtered out the palace's concepts of popular mobilization, boiling down the hamlet program to its more understandable physical residue. Nhu complained at an interministerial meeting in July 1962 that district officials attending the Thi Nghe training center confessed to know nothing about strategic hamlets except the building of fences.[96] Local authorities also resorted to the time-honored tradition of imposing policy from above in order to construct these Potemkin villages. Starved of resources and unclear about the palace's purposes, officials paid scant attention to explaining the program to hamlet residents, let alone trying to generate their enthusiastic participation. Instead, they proceeded to coerce the population into providing the money and manpower to complete the physical requirements of strategic hamlets. Consequently, peasants became passive instruments in the mere fortification of settlements, rather than active participants in a popular revolution.[97]

No doubt the biases and prejudices of local officials assisted in this process of filtration. Jeffrey Race described RVN officials as possessing "blank areas of consciousness" when it came to understanding what was really going on in the countryside. They were the products of urban, educated backgrounds, and many of them had learned their trade under the colonial power; they failed to identify with the peasantry, understand the sources of rural unrest, or appreciate that to counter the insurgency they might have to do more than just control the population. They tended to treat peasants "as *les administrés* rather than as the served," noted Robert Scigliano. In a time of war, moreover, most RVN officials saw no reason to change their ways or pander to the population; indeed, quite the opposite was the case. As General Van Thanh Cao told a group of officials in Tay Ninh province in June 1962: "Many people are obliged to support the VC and we must give them good reason to refuse by shooting some of them."[98]

Not everyone subscribed to such studied brutality. There were exceptions, such as Tran Ngoc Chau, who had gained an insight into guerrilla warfare from four years of fighting with the Viet Minh; he paid careful attention to local concerns and interests in fashioning Kien Hoa's hamlet program.[99] Nor did General Cao's sentiment represent the sum total of most officials' thinking, for there was a strong streak of paternalism that mixed with their authoritarian inclinations. Thus, after advocating a ruthless, get-tough policy, Cao could, in almost the same breath, talk of offering peasants a helping hand. "We must realize that we are training a weak man to climb a mountain," he noted, "and we must not demand more from him than he has the capacity to supply."[100] Yet such paternalism easily degenerated into a supposedly benevolent despotism. Strategic hamlets sought to bring the population security and a better life, officials reasoned, and so, if people did not recognize that fact, they must be made to appreciate it. As Le Van Phuoc told one journalist in reply to a question about corvée labor: "Well, how can you call it forced when it is in the people's own interests?"[101]

Unfortunately, the peasantry never quite came around to this point of view. Strategic hamlets, in fact, ran headlong into rural resistance, which only served to encourage the provinces' penchant for employing coercion. If Saigon inadvertently reinforced the attitudes of local officials by its peremptory demands from above, so too did peasants, and the insurgents, by their stubborn opposition from below. Villagers evidently did not share the palace's enthusiasm for "struggle," which brought with it significant costs. Thousands of peasants suffered the wrenching experience of relocation, often moved considerable distances from their original homes. Some fled at the first opportunity;[102] others received little or none of the promised compensation because of local corruption or lack of funds.[103] In addition, peasants had to provide the materials and manpower for the construction of strategic hamlets. These contributions represented an enormous burden, argued General Oai, the director of the hamlet training center at Thi Nghe, because, in many places, people were just too poor to devote time and money to the program.[104]

Guerrilla activities also increased the burden on the populace. Contrary to the palace's expectations, the insurgents did not usually launch frontal assaults against strategic hamlets.[105] Instead, the NLF adopted tactics that delayed, and increased the costs of, the program, such as enlisting peasants to destroy the hamlet fortifications that they had just built. In turn, the failure to complete hamlets on schedule threatened to expose RVN officials to the glare of the palace's spotlight, so they proceeded to force peasants to repair the damage, frequently without informing Saigon of the bad news, or daring to request additional aid to lighten the new load they were about to heap on the population. "When the government told them to build the strategic hamlet, they did; and when the Viet Cong told them to destroy it, they destroyed it," commented a former guerrilla. "To speak from the point of view of the villagers, they were fed up; they had to build and they had to destroy things they had built."[106]

The costs of the program extended beyond the task of construction and maintenance. People found themselves roped into new organizations or defending their hamlet as members of the combat youth. Such activities were not only time-consuming but also thrust many reluctant villagers into the front line of the contest between the government and the guerrillas. In addition, peasants chafed under the new controls that came with the construction of strategic hamlets. Gates and fences restricted freedom of movement, and blocked shortcuts into and out of settlements. Some fields now lay too far away to cultivate, especially if hamlets strictly observed a curfew that prevented peasants leaving their homes before daybreak or returning after dusk.[107] These controls, in fact, rarely matched the exacting standards demanded by the likes of Robert Thompson, or the lurid pictures painted in communist propaganda.

U.S. officials noticed in many hamlets that gates remained unguarded during the day and peasants cut small exits through fences for their own private use.[108] Nonetheless, restrictions, together with the new duties imposed on residents, brought inconveniences and added to peasant discontent.

Some sense of that discontent can be gauged by the virulent propaganda campaign waged against strategic hamlets by the NLF. To some extent, this was a necessary response because, for all its shortcomings, the program caused the insurgents considerable problems. Yet the guerrillas also viewed it as an incredible opportunity to rally support for their cause. "When the masses are oppressed and exploited," stated a NLF study document, "they hate the enemy and they are ready for, and they are waiting for, the leadership of the Party."[109] NLF propaganda made the hardships incurred by strategic hamlets its principal theme, and used this message to great effect in mobilizing peasants to harass and retard the program. The RVN's central intelligence organization compiled a forty-page report in June 1962 that examined the insurgents' reaction to the hamlet program, including their efforts to organize popular resistance. It noted that the NLF encouraged peasants to plead poverty, sham illness, draft petitions, get government troops drunk, and drag their feet in any other way imaginable, a campaign that no doubt helps explain the enormous difficulties that provincial officials faced in meeting Saigon's schedule for completing the program.[110]

Peasant antipathy toward strategic hamlets went beyond their obvious costs and inconvenience; there were deeper forces at play as well. Why, for example, if the palace was correct in assuming a basic antagonism between the guerrillas and the populace, did peasants not look beyond the initial costs of the program to its potential benefits? Or why did many residents seem to blame the authorities as much as the insurgents when the latter tore down hamlet defenses? One reason, as Nhu feared, was that the program's implementation focused primarily on physical construction rather than efforts to mobilize the population politically. The much-touted "revolution" in the hamlets appeared to most peasants as more of a case of "meet the new boss, same as the old boss." As a result, residents showed little interest in making sacrifices for this "new" hamlet regime.

People exhibited a marked reluctance to participate in those activities essential to the defense and organization of settlements, notably the combat youth and the hamlet committees. RVN reports noted that these tasks were unpopular because they took inhabitants away from their own work, with little or no recompense,[111] but peasants viewed them with a jaundiced eye for other reasons as well. Several villagers from Long An recalled the lack of morale and motivation of the combat youth in their area; all the members were from poor families, the well-off having evaded service through bribery.

"When the communists come in, they never bother us—they go to the homes of those who got rich by taking from others," the villagers observed. "Are we so stupid as to protect them?"[112] Service on, and support for, hamlet committees engendered a similar lack of enthusiasm. Residents tended to view them, a U.S. embassy report noted, as "something imposed from above rather than as deriving from themselves and created for their own benefit."[113]

Even if the authorities had tried to carry out Saigon's instructions to the letter, it is still open to question whether the rural population would have reacted much differently to strategic hamlets. Notwithstanding the coercion and political inertia that came to characterize the program, there was an air of unreality about the palace's plans. Possessing an unshakeable faith in the justness of their cause, and the communal spirit that supposedly resided in the countryside, the Ngos failed to appreciate the impediments to mobilizing popular support. They believed that RVN cadres could march into the villages, raise the banner of the republic, and, in the several weeks it would take to establish a strategic hamlet, plant the seeds of a rural revolution. Practically overnight, the regime hoped to create its "infrastructure of democracy," the sort of popular base of support that it had taken the insurgents years to construct.

Peasants needed to be coaxed and encouraged into collective action, however; they were not itching to man the barricades. For a start, the palace's image of the corporate peasant community—that "myth of the village," which beguiled many postcolonial Asian leaders—had little basis in reality.[114] Communal spirit was in particularly short supply in the vital Mekong Delta. As studies sponsored by Michigan State University discovered, the dispersed settlements of the Delta lacked the corporate character still evident in the more compact communities of central and northern Vietnam. While their inhabitants maintained many of the traditional rituals that bound them together, they tended to observe these more loosely than their compatriots elsewhere. People's concerns focused on affairs below or beyond those of the village. On the one hand, the individual and the family took precedence over the community; on the other hand, communal affairs competed with interests beyond the confines of the village, particularly given the intellectual and commercial pull of Saigon. "The net effect of all these factors," James Hendry concluded, "is to cast considerable doubt on the validity of the view that rural communities in South Viet Nam are essentially village-centered and strongly receptive to anything with a communal or cooperative orientation."[115]

The Ngos were not entirely unaware of this problem, since it had influenced their decision to focus on the hamlet, rather than the village, as the basis for popular mobilization. Nhu noted in an interministerial meeting in April 1962 that people were more willing to organize at this lower level because they could envisage the undertaking, whereas the prospect of constructing "strategic villages" would overwhelm them.[116] Nevertheless, the Ngos placed altogether too much faith in their ability to generate peasant support, a conviction that reflected their ivory-towered view of the situation in the countryside. Not that mobilizing villagers was impossible. They could be organized, and a degree of group solidarity fostered, but it was the Vietnamese communists that proved most adept at doing so.

The communists had mastered the art of channeling local concerns into support for their larger goals. As early as the 1920s, one scholar notes, they had "engaged in a pertinacious search for existing personal ties, primordial social attachments, and existing corporate bodies" that they could harness in this way. Their genius was to appreciate the "rather simple sociological truth" that they could derive enormous strength by harmonizing a series of parochial attachments with the broader purposes of a national movement.[117] Jeffrey Race examined the communists' modus operandi in his study of the war in Long An: "The Party's approach was to develop bonds of loyalty between individuals and the local community leadership on the basis of the latter's ability to resolve concrete local issues of importance in the peasant's life: land, taxation, protection from impressment into the national army, or a personally satisfying role in the activities of the community. That such communities would then behave in conformity with the demands of the national communist leadership was assured by the previously secured loyalty of the community leadership itself to the revolutionary movement through the continuous vertical career structure from hamlet to Central Committee on which Party organization was founded."[118]

In looking to build the state from the bottom up, the Ngos sought to achieve a similar goal, but their approach suffered by comparison. The insurgents' strength was founded on extensive organization at the village level; they devoted careful attention to local concerns; and they offered peasants tangible changes in their social and economic status.[119] The Ngos proposed to establish a new base of support where none had really existed before; they appealed to generalities—anticommunism, nationalism, and Personalism; and their promises of a new life in strategic hamlets lacked substance, especially given the approach to the program adopted by the RVN's local officials. In any case, the NLF's rural infrastructure was already well entrenched, so it could nip in the bud any nascent signs of support for the regime's cause. The long arm of the NLF confronted rural residents with the ultimate question: was the regime's cause one for which they were prepared to risk dying? Most answered in the negative, and that response was going to make it very difficult for the palace to fulfill its goal of mobilizing the population.

6

Competitive Cooperation

The program may have been taking quite a different shape in the country-side to the one desired by the palace, but strategic hamlets still caused the NLF many problems. Although there were precious few signs of the popular struggle envisaged by the Ngos, the scale of the regime's efforts did serve to beef up Saigon's physical presence in rural areas and so threaten the guerrillas' access to the peasantry. As we shall see, this would prove to be only a temporary fillip. Nevertheless, strategic hamlets, together with the new U.S. support that began to arrive in the wake of the Taylor mission, put the insurgents on the defensive for the first time since the war had expanded in 1960.

As the threat of an imminent communist victory receded, there was a corresponding improvement in U.S.–Vietnamese relations. The tensions of 1961 gave way to a period of enhanced cooperation that lasted until the Buddhist crisis of May 1963. This collaboration centered on strategic hamlets, which Robert McNamara, the U.S. secretary of defense, described as the "backbone of President Diem's program for countering subversion directed against his state."[1] The belief that the hamlet scheme represented a winning formula enabled the two partners to temper their disagreements in pursuit of a common cause. Yet there remained strains in the alliance, for Saigon and Washington held conflicting conceptions of the program, even as they collaborated on its implementation. As a result, its execution became something of a case of competitive cooperation, with each side attempting to carry out its version of strategic hamlets. Submerged differences frequently resurfaced and contributed to the crisis that finally overtook the alliance in 1963.

What, first of all, was the American reaction to a program whose emergence caught many U.S. officials by surprise? According to William Colby, "the Americans were somewhat bewildered by the sudden appearance of a major activity that had not been processed through their complex coordinating staffs," but "they subordinated their injured pride and swung into support" of strategic hamlets.[2] One reason for this willingness to entertain the scheme was that it met the Kennedy administration's desire to get moving and stem

the rising tide of the insurgency. In addition, the hamlet program complemented the increasing emphasis that U.S. officials placed on improving security at the village level. Following his appointment as MAAG chief in August
1960, General McGarr proved a particularly strong proponent of combined
civil-military operations that sought to clear and hold rural areas.[3]

U.S. interest in this approach took on added urgency in the summer of
1961 as the war threatened to spiral out of control. In September, MAAG
brought out its "Geographically Phased, National Level Operation Plan for
Counterinsurgency," which envisaged a series of phases to clear and hold
parts of the countryside and the gradual expansion of these secure areas on
the oil spot or "amoeba principle."[4] The country team in Saigon also drew up
an "Outline Plan for Counterinsurgency Operations," incorporating
MAAG's ideas, which sought to "provide a systematic, coordinated approach
to counterinsurgency operations in all fields (military, political, economic and
psychological) throughout all of South Vietnam." While it did not make a
strategic hamlet concept its centerpiece, the "Outline Plan" did incorporate
a number of features that characterized the Diem regime's own program: fortifying settlements, arming local defenders, and beefing up village and hamlet administration.[5]

With U.S. plans proceeding along these lines, the Diem regime's new
scheme received a reasonably warm reception from American officials. "The
results of this program are still to be assessed," the U.S. embassy reported in
November 1961, "but the idea of the GVN [Government of Vietnam] match-
ing the VC's efforts at the basic rural administrative level is an encouraging
one."[6] Robert Thompson also helped to crystallize support in Washington
with his "Delta Plan" proposal for a network of "defended" and "strategic"
hamlets. When the State Department's Roger Hilsman visited Vietnam in
January 1962, he found Thompson's ideas persuasive and compatible with
some of the thinking in the nation's capital. On his return there, Hilsman presented his findings to the president, who "agreed that this was the direction
we should go in developing a strategic concept for Vietnam." Hilsman spent
the next several weeks briefing agency chiefs about the virtues of a village-
level strategy, and Kennedy also asked him to write a formal report.[7]

Hilsman's report, entitled "A Strategic Concept for South Vietnam," was
unusually explicit in addressing the reasons for the growth and persistence
of the insurgency. The author argued that infiltration from North Vietnam
was not the main cause of the war in the south, nor did the guerrillas flourish merely because of their ability to intimidate peasants into providing support. "Instead, they seek to win the cooperation of the villagers, and use
terror mainly in retaliation against unpopular government officials or villagers
who communicate with or aid the Vietnam forces." Consequently, the key to

the war was to cut off the NLF from the population and win the peasantry's allegiance. "The struggle for South Vietnam," Hilsman concluded, "is essentially a battle for control of the villages." He built his plan to win this fight around the creation of "strategic" and "defended" villages, which would form a "security framework and a solid socio-political base" to deprive the insurgents of their means of support.[8]

Strategic hamlets thus made sense to many U.S. officials as building blocks for pacification. At the same time, most recognized that, with the palace pushing full steam ahead with its own program, there was little choice except to climb aboard, unless the United States chose to change trains and abandon the Ngos. To be sure, the conflict over the Taylor report had given skeptics renewed cause to question the U.S.–Vietnamese relationship, especially since Diem showed little inclination to carry out the promises he had made at that time.[9] Ambassadors John Kenneth Galbraith and W. Averell Harriman, longstanding critics of Diem, duly took the opportunity to reaffirm their opposition to the incumbent regime. Galbraith told Kennedy in April 1962 that "almost any non-Communist change would probably be beneficial and this should be the guiding rule for our diplomatic representation in the area."[10] Most U.S. officials, however, remained reluctant to risk a change in leadership. Given his emerging role as the driving force behind the hamlet program, even Nhu now appeared a sacrosanct figure. As Hilsman noted in March 1962, the chief U.S. representatives in Saigon all "want Harriman to lay off trying to get rid of Brother Nhu at just this time."[11]

Perhaps McNamara was the key figure in focusing attention on the war effort, rather than the perennial problems of the Diem regime. With the expansion in U.S. military assistance that followed the Taylor mission, the secretary of defense seized the reins of policy in Washington and injected a new sense of urgency into American planning.[12] McNamara wanted to reinvigorate the war effort rather than talk about coups or long-term political reforms, a message that came across loud and clear at the first secretary of defense's conference (SECDEF) held in Honolulu in mid-December 1961. As one of the participants recorded: "The Secretary commented that Diem was the only man we had, that he had some basis for being suspicious because of all the coup talk, and that if we concentrated on fundamental military specifics he thought we could get Diem to cooperate."[13] McNamara also came out in favor of strategic hamlets. "It would appear, at this early moment," stated a Pentagon report on McNamara's May 1962 visit to Vietnam, "that the strategic hamlet program promises solid benefits, and may well be the vital key to success of the pacification program."[14]

With an emerging consensus in support of strategic hamlets, and McNamara cracking the whip, U.S. agencies wheeled into action. From the spring of 1962, the Americans began to reorient their programs and develop the institutional machinery necessary to bolster the RVN's scheme. The newly formed Military Assistance Command, Vietnam (MACV) set up a strategic hamlets division, headed by Colonel Carl W. Schaad, to oversee military assistance, especially much-needed material aid. This support eventually took the form of hamlet "kits" composed of barbed wire, telephones, trip flares, and weapons.[15] USOM/AID, meanwhile, engaged in a major overhaul of its own operations, including the establishment of a new Office of Rural Affairs led by Rufus Phillips, an old Lansdale hand. Bert Fraleigh, Phillips's deputy, described USOM at this time as "pretty much a comfortable, business-as-usual AID operation," with only 3 out of its 110 American employees stationed outside of Saigon. The new goal was to shift the emphasis of operations from supporting big development projects managed by the RVN central government to assisting locally administered programs that would contribute directly to the counterinsurgency campaign and win the backing of the rural populace.[16]

In addition to changing the focus of its operations, the U.S. side also sought to improve interagency coordination, which had come to be regarded as a sine qua non for successful pacification. To promote integration, and serve as the liaison with Nhu's interministerial committee, the country team formed the Interagency Committee for Province Rehabilitation in March 1962, under the chairmanship of William C. Trueheart, the deputy chief of mission.[17] Bureaucratic parochialism persisted, of course, in spite of this effort to coordinate policy. For example, the U.S. military endorsed strategic hamlets, but tended to view them through the prism of its own particular concerns. In this case, the program's main appeal was that it promised to free the ARVN from static security duties and make troops available for conventional operations against the insurgents.[18]

Differences within the U.S. establishment, however, paled in comparison with those separating the American and Vietnamese views of strategic hamlets. Although Washington and Saigon agreed that the aim was to win the hearts and minds of the rural population, they disagreed about the way in which the program would achieve this goal. On the one hand, the Ngos sought to mobilize peasants in strategic hamlets through an emphasis on popular struggle, self-sufficiency, and revolutionary change. In this scheme of things, they assigned a strictly limited role to government and foreign support of the population because they believed that excessive assistance would weaken the popular will and imperil the country's transformation. On the other hand, U.S. officials believed that peasant support could only be won by providing hamlet residents with extensive assistance. They viewed their role, moreover, as a major source of this support and of the technical expertise that would facilitate its use; they would serve as the managers of change, assisting a struggling client to overcome its backwardness.[19]

Such imperial assumptions offered a comforting measure of certainty amid the unfamiliar terrain of Vietnam, for U.S. policy makers knew very little about the peasantry, the new focus of their attention. Several members of the administration recognized this shortcoming. Robert Johnson of the State Department's Policy Planning Staff was active in addressing, and attempting to generate interest in, peasant politics.[20] So too was the National Security Council's Michael Forrestal. "I don't find this either particularly informative or encouraging," Forrestal wrote in September 1962 of a rather flimsy paper analyzing rural opinion. "We are trying to improve our specific information on peasant attitudes and then step up some action on such information." The NSC staffer was still none the wiser several months later when he reported on a trip to Vietnam with Roger Hilsman. The thinking of rural inhabitants was the key to the "whole war," the two officials opined, but "it is difficult, if not impossible, to assess how the villagers really feel and the only straws in the wind point in different directions."[21]

Nonetheless, U.S. officials did not allow this uncertainty to deter them from making generalizations about the needs of the people. Two assumptions served as their guide. The first was that the NLF's strength lay in its ability to manipulate an isolated and neglected peasantry. According to Hilsman, "Villagers in Southeast Asia are turned inward on themselves and have little or no sense of identification with either the national government or Communist ideology." They were "isolated physically, politically and psychologically," he observed, and in "such circumstances, it is not at all difficult to develop a guerrilla movement." This assessment underlay the second assumption and proposed solution to the problem. "Measures must be taken," Hilsman stated, "to tie the villages into the network of government administration and control. Channels must be established through which information of the villages' needs and problems can flow upward and government services can flow downward."[22] In short, the more South Vietnam developed into a cohesive and responsive state, the less that peasants would be attracted or intimidated into supporting the guerrillas. After all, as the modernization theorists argued, civil unrest was a symptom of the growing pains that accompanied the development process, and it would presumably subside as the modern state reached maturity.[23]

In broad terms, this emphasis on overcoming rural isolation, and building a cohesive state, corresponded perfectly with the concerns of the Ngos. In other respects, the views of Saigon and Washington differed significantly. The Americans did not share the regime's vision of the social and political revolution that strategic hamlets would supposedly bring to the countryside.

Indeed, both American and British officials had serious misgivings about the palace's interest in creating new social classes and promoting organizations like the Republican Youth. Britain's Ambassador Hohler suggested in a telegram to London that the regime's plans would prove administratively counterproductive because they would cut across, rather than consolidate, the RVN's existing rural apparatus. William Trueheart argued that Nhu's desire to promote "a 'revolutionary change of society' at the hamlet level could lead to further division among the population at [a] time when the aim should be to establish unity."[24]

U.S. officials also disagreed with the palace's notion that strategic hamlets should serve as an arena for popular struggle and sacrifice. As Trueheart stated, "The theme needs to be what the Government can do to help the people (together with their own efforts) and not what the people should do for the government."[25] Peasants had "needs and aspirations," noted a USOM/ Rural Affairs booklet, that must be met if the government was to solicit their support and bring them into the national fold. Those requirements included a reasonable degree of safety, prosperity, elementary justice, social status, and opportunity. "The crucial requirement, which some in authority seem not adequately to appreciate, is insuring support for the government by the people now in hamlets," stated the booklet's authors. "This can be accomplished only by providing these people with continuing concrete evidence of government concern for their welfare; with convincing evidence that the government is *their* government."[26]

In place of the palace's Personalist revolution, the Americans argued that the key to the conflict was the rational application of resources that would provide peasants with security and socioeconomic benefits, and so win their support. U.S. officials also emphasized that this process required an effective organizational framework if Saigon and Washington were going to apply their combined efforts successfully. There must be a campaign plan to clear and hold territory and careful coordination of civil-military operations. Without this kind of approach, the Americans contended, the regime's efforts would be confused and piecemeal. The Vietnamese authorities would fail to provide peasants with adequate security, and so the latter would not dare to resist the insurgents; the government would also be unable to follow up military operations with the socioeconomic programs needed to attract popular support and guarantee lasting security.[27]

In sum, U.S. officials had their own agenda in backing the hamlet scheme. They hoped to shape the program to their specifications and use American aid as a way of injecting their concerns into its implementation. Although the palace's new scheme appeared to make redundant the U.S. plans put together during late 1961 and early 1962, the Americans intended to use these as points of reference for their own version of strategic hamlets.[28] They believed that U.S. material assistance, together with the sound management and application of that support, could overcome some of the problems they perceived with the regime's approach to the program. In its role as the manager of modernization, the United States would turn strategic hamlets into a successful tool of nation building. The trick was to convince the Ngos of the soundness of the American approach, or seek to bypass the palace in the process of implementation.

The first concern of U.S. policy makers was to establish an overall plan, in order to carry out hamlet construction effectively and at a manageable pace. The Americans viewed with dismay the palace's intention to build strategic hamlets everywhere, as quickly as possible, which seemed wholly unrealistic given the enormity of the task and the regime's limited resources. Although Nhu initially hoped to complete the program within a year, George Tanham, an associate with the RAND Corporation, had only recently argued that it would take ten years to make South Vietnam "secure and prosperous." "The manpower and financial requirements for successful actions are so great and the native skills so limited at present," he suggested, "that only one province or so could be covered at a time."[29] In addition, U.S. officials in Saigon needed a campaign blueprint in order to plot how best to supplement the regime's inadequate means. The country team came under considerable pressure from Washington in the spring of 1962 to get on with the war effort, but it was difficult to do so in the absence of an overall plan and a set of geographical priorities from which to work.[30]

U.S. officials encouraged the regime to adopt a modified version of Thompson's "Delta Plan" as an appropriate guide. The British proposal designated parts of eleven provinces near Saigon as a priority and laid out operational procedures for pacifying them. Although the Americans had clashed with Thompson over the submission of his original plan, the new recommendations met with their approval.[31] Securing the palace's support, however, proved difficult. Diem signed a decree in mid-March that was based on the British proposal and appointed Hoang Van Lac as the executive officer. Nevertheless, the regime took no further steps to implement the plan, and Lac "remained singularly elusive" whenever members of BRIAM sought to contact him.[32] In fact, the palace was in the process of trimming the "Delta Plan" to fit its grander scheme, rather than vice versa. Bui Van Luong told Trueheart at a meeting in mid-April that the "Delta Plan" provinces were indeed a priority, but the regime intended to go on building strategic hamlets in the rest of the country at the same time.[33]

The palace's approach frustrated U.S. officials, but they were not prepared to sit idly by and wait for the regime to get its act together. With no sensible master plan in sight, it made sense, they reasoned, to carve out a role for themselves in the hamlet program as best they could. U.S. agencies might provide, on an ad hoc basis, assistance for specific operations that would enable them to get in on the war effort. This approach might also allow the Americans to circumvent the central government by working directly with the local authorities carrying out such operations. Thus, they could channel aid directly to the provinces concerned, which not only would be more efficient but also would provide an opportunity to influence the character of these local efforts.[34] There was a precedent for this kind of approach, with the country team already participating in regroupment efforts that had begun in March in Binh Duong province. With this example in mind, the United States lent support to Operation Sea Swallow II, a campaign of strategic hamlet construction that began in the coastal lowland province of Phu Yen in May.

Sea Swallow II originated with a plea from Major Duong Thai Dong, the chief of Phu Yen, for outside aid. Although his province was not of vital strategic importance, Dong's request offered the Americans a chance to demonstrate the value of a coordinated civil-military campaign as well as the effectiveness of direct U.S. backing for local operations. "With quiet U.S. assistance," noted Rufus Phillips, "an operational plan was prepared for the province and presented to Saigon for approval." The palace proved amenable, if only to placate its enthusiastic partner. "It makes the Americans happy," Diem told Robert Thompson, "and it does not worry either me or the Viet Cong!"[35]

The operation did, indeed, make the Americans happy because it conformed to their view of the way the hamlet program ought to work. Sea Swallow II represented a carefully orchestrated clear-and-hold campaign, which sought to secure areas on the principle of the expanding oil spot. USOM/AID was also able to provide extensive assistance for the province's newly established strategic hamlets, such as supporting families relocated from guerrilla-controlled areas and equipping hamlet schools. In addition, U.S. officials welcomed the decentralized nature of the operation, in which a joint Vietnamese-American province committee organized support for the campaign and authorized expenditures without recourse to Saigon. Working directly with the local authorities in this way, reported the U.S. embassy, proved "faster and more efficient" than going through the capital, where requests for assistance could languish for months; the embassy also noted that the U.S. side successfully played the role of "an intra-GVN coordinating body" by prodding the central ministries to fulfill their part in the campaign. All in all, the operation demonstrated that "when there is a well-planned rehabilitation campaign our response can be effective and dramatic; this is to encourage others to come up with new 'Sea Swallows.' "[36]

To the embassy's delight, Saigon subsequently agreed to American involvement in several other clear-and-hold operations in the autumn of 1962: Royal Phoenix in Quang Ngai and Forward Together in Binh Dinh. Thus, the Phu Yen model held out the prospect that the country team's ad hoc involvement in the provinces might prove to be more than just a useful expedient in the absence of an overall RVN plan; it might also serve to encourage general planning for the hamlet program along U.S. lines, with the Americans substituting their own priorities for those of the palace in a growing number of provinces.[37]

In effect, this amounted to an attempt to reform the regime's working practices from the inside out. Phillips described it as "a revival of the Lansdale approach," with Americans able to "act as a catalyst to get things done" and "help the Vietnamese channel their efforts in constructive directions."[38] U.S. policy makers had already approved this kind of "limited partnership" approach at the time of the Taylor report. Diem had reacted angrily to that earlier proposal, but the new and gradual extension of American influence had the advantage of avoiding another full-frontal and probably fruitless confrontation with the palace. Instead, the regime could be reformed by stealth.

The palace took some persuading before it accepted this kind of expansion of the American role because it had no desire to plant a shadow U.S. administration in the provinces. Diem was reluctant to sanction an increase in the number of U.S. advisers stationed in the countryside; he also resisted giving blanket approval to allow MAAG and AID to provide direct assistance to the provinces without having to go through Saigon. Nonetheless, the regime recognized the value of U.S. support, so the Americans found Diem far from intractable on the issue of extending the advisory effort. Saigon agreed to the permanent assignment of military advisers to the province chiefs. Their number increased from just two at the beginning of 1962 to over one hundred by the year's end, a figure that did not include the rising number of U.S. intelligence and battalion advisers serving with the ARVN. The regime also accepted the establishment of U.S. Information Service subposts in a number of provincial capitals. Most important, in terms of American involvement with strategic hamlets, the palace approved direct U.S. support to the provinces on a case-by-case basis, as with the operation in Phu Yen.[39] Phillips, whom Diem had known in the mid-1950s and treated "somewhat like a lost son," met with the president to explain the value of this approach and seek the president's approval. Diem's fond memories of the Lansdale era helped carry the day.[40]

Saigon also agreed to several other changes in the summer of 1962 that deepened the U.S. role in the hamlet program. The first was a U.S.–Vietnamese agreement to allow AID to stockpile commodities for general use, rather than having to procure material support for specific operations before their launch. This procurement authorization (PA/PR) procedure promised to make the delivery of aid more flexible and responsive.[41] In addition, the Americans purchased 730 million piasters from the RVN government, in exchange for an equivalent cash grant of $10 million, in order to create a special U.S. fund that would allow them to offer prompt and effective support for counterinsurgency operations. To a large extent, this was an expedient forced on the Americans by the regime's reluctance to provide more money for pacification if this further increased its budget deficit. Without sufficient local currency, U.S. officials feared that operations might grind to a halt or the regime would pass the extra costs onto the populace. In seeking to plug this financial gap, however, the Americans also recognized the potential leverage that this new fund gave them. Control over local currency, together with the new procurement procedures, would allow them to channel aid more efficiently and exert influence over the conduct of operations. "With [the] establishment [of a] U.S. owned piaster fund and [the] PA/PR for dollar procurement," reported Ambassador Nolting, "we should have [the] carrot with which to induce [the] GVN to come up with coordinated clear and hold operations in those areas which we regard as having highest priority."[42]

The U.S. part in the hamlet program began to assume its final, formal shape in the latter half of 1962, thanks in part to the RVN's long-awaited introduction of an organizational blueprint. In July, Saigon created special committees on strategic hamlets in each tactical (division) area, chaired by the divisional commander and including the relevant province chiefs. These committees were responsible for carrying out central directives, coordinating civil-military operations, and working out timetables for hamlet construction.[43] One month later, the regime published a geographical plan for hamlet construction. While the plan proposed to build strategic hamlets simultaneously throughout the country, it did at least rank regions and provinces in order of priority.[44] Together, these new arrangements went some way to meeting U.S. concerns and also made it possible for the Americans to integrate their own activities into the RVN's new framework.

The emerging system of planning and implementation enabled the Americans to carve out a significant role for themselves in the hamlet program. The process worked as follows. A so-called province rehabilitation committee, composed of the province chief, a USOM/Rural Affairs representative, and a MAAG sector adviser, drew up an operational plan for its area. This was submitted, via the relevant tactical area committee, to the Nhu and Trueheart committees in Saigon. Once approved at the national level, the three-member province committee oversaw the plan's execution, trying to resolve any problems without recourse to Saigon. In the course of implementation, the province team agreed upon any minor changes to the plan and all expenditures of reha-bilitation funds. This system of decentralizing authority not only provided the speed and flexibility desired by the Americans but also gave them a say in the uses to which funds were put.[45]

"In view of the many administrative difficulties normally encountered in Viet-Nam," the U.S. embassy reported at the beginning of 1963, "the devel-opment of this agreed and workable U.S.–GVN procedure from the provin-cial to the national level represents a major accomplishment."[46] U.S. support for strategic hamlets seemed, in the view of many American officials, to be on the right track at last. The country team had reoriented its programs to focus on the village-level war, the appropriate planning for new funding cycles was in hand, and significant quantities of materials were scheduled to arrive from the beginning of 1963. Moreover, the hamlet program now possessed some sort of organizational framework that might make proper use of that Ameri-can support. As one U.S. report of late 1962 argued, "The Taylor recommen-dation that de facto administrative changes be accomplished by persuasion at high levels, by cooperation with Diem's aides who want improved adminis-tration, and by a U.S. operating presence, has been largely effected."[47]

Growing satisfaction with the development of the advisory effort reflected and encouraged more optimistic U.S. assessments of the general state of the conflict. From the summer of 1962, high-level reports began to suggest that the hamlet program, as well as the expansion of the U.S. war effort, had halted the downward spiral in the security situation. Officials called upon a whole slew of indicators to make a case for guarded optimism about the future. Saigon's forces were now larger and better equipped, assisted by a siz-able U.S. military contingent providing both advice and combat support; meanwhile, the level of NLF activity had dropped, insurgent casualties had risen, and there was evidence of declining morale in the enemy's ranks. In addition, MACV estimated that the number of people in RVN-controlled areas was on the increase, thanks in part to the thousands of Montagnards that were streaming into government-held territory in an attempt to escape the fighting in the Central Highlands. Surveying all of these developments, a State Department paper concluded that "as in 1862 and 1942, no one clearly has the initiative. However, [the] VC are clearly further from their objective than they were in October, 1961." This was a cautious but comforting anal-ogy; tough times lay ahead, but victory would be won in the end.[48]

Not all U.S. officials subscribed to this line of argument. In August 1962, Joseph Mendenhall, who had recently returned from serving in the Saigon embassy, delivered a damning swan song. "To win against the Communists," he stated, "the Government of Viet-Nam should be either *efficient* or *popular*, but the Diem Government is neither." He predicted a "gradual deterioration" unless the United States got "rid of Diem, Mr. and Mrs. Nhu and the rest of the Ngo family."[49] Senator Mike Mansfield, an old friend and supporter of Diem, wrote a less inflammatory but still sobering assessment following a trip to Southeast Asia in December. "It was distressing on this visit," he commented in a report to the White House, "to hear the situation described in much the same terms as on my last visit although it is seven years and billions of dollars later."[50] As a general rule, a spirit of optimism tended to prevail among high-level U.S. officials in Washington and Saigon, while those in the field remained more circumspect. On a visit to Vietnam in January 1963, General William B. Rosson found most personnel in the provinces notably more pessimistic than their superiors. At higher levels, Rosson recalled, optimism had become institutionalized and "seemed to be almost the party line."[51]

Rank, institutional affiliation, and personal perspective all shaped these differing views of the state of the war. There was also plenty of scope for conflicting interpretations because, in spite of the expansion of the American advisory presence, U.S. officials still remained dependent on the regime for the execution of policy as well as much of the data about the progress of the conflict. RVN figures on guerrilla casualties, for example, were notoriously inaccurate, as Vice-President Tho warned Mendenhall. "[Tho] said many of these casualties were not VC at all but members of the population killed by the GVN forces," Mendenhall recorded. "If all these casualties were VC, [Tho] said, the war would be over."[52] Often, it was difficult for U.S. officials to check on RVN activities and information because this might stray into the sensitive area of "internal administration."[53] Moreover, there were simply not enough Americans in South Vietnam to oversee the regime's work. As Rufus Phillips observed of the hamlet program: "The provincial representatives of USOM, and the sector advisors of MAAG, get around as much as they can, and visit as many hamlets as possible, but to the best of my knowledge it is probable that a majority of the hamlets which are listed as existing have never been visited by personnel on whom the U.S. can rely for accurate first-hand observation and factual reporting."[54]

The frustration of advising, rather than directing, the war effort, especially the problem of prodding the Diem regime to move in desired directions, was a shared complaint of nearly all Americans, optimistic or otherwise. If only the Vietnamese would accept U.S. advice and get their act together, reasoned Diem's allies, the war could be won. As an exasperated John Paul Vann declared after the defeat at Ap Bac in January 1963: "These people won't listen. They make the same goddam mistakes over and over again in the same way."[55] The only remedy for this failing, U.S. officials believed, was for the United States to keep up and even intensify its efforts to get the Vietnamese to conduct the war along U.S. lines. They admitted that the Diem regime was displaying a newfound energy in its prosecution of the counterinsurgency campaign, especially in carrying out the hamlet program. "The problem," an embassy report stated in August 1962, "is to maintain that momentum and to channel it in the most effective direction."[56]

The call for added American vigor was a key theme of the Hilsman-Forrestal report of January 1963. Reviewing the state of the war at the year's turn, the two officials were neither starry-eyed nor unduly pessimistic. "Our overall judgement," they commented, "is that we are probably winning, but certainly more slowly than we had hoped." The main problem was not the current village-level concept of the war but the persistent difficulties in carrying it out, especially in the case of the Strategic Hamlet program. They pointed out that there was still "no single countrywide plan worthy of the name but only a variety of regional and provincial plans, some good and some not so good." Consequently, the hamlet scheme continued to lack the organizational framework necessary to assure its success. We must "increase our leverage in the face of Diem's biases and general resistance to advice," Hilsman and Forrestal concluded. Given the expansion of the advisory system, "the time has probably come when we can press our views on Diem more vigorously and occasionally even publicly."[57]

The Americans were about to discover that this was much easier said than done, however. The palace had its own ideas about the parameters of the advisory relationship and, like its ally, was also prepared to press these views with vigor and occasionally in public. Although the regime had agreed to the expansion of the U.S. presence in 1962, it did so with a good deal of trepidation. Desire for American support competed with the palace's concern to preserve national sovereignty, its own authority, and the ideological agenda of the Ngos. Given their conflicting visions of strategic hamlets, and of each other's role in the scheme, the stage was set for another serious crisis in the patron–client relationship.

In early 1962, the Diem regime had taken stock of the scarce resources available for implementing its ambitious new project, but, in assessing the potential for U.S. support, the Ngos had some doubts about their ally's ability to offer effective assistance. They argued that U.S. regulations governing the delivery of imported goods had reduced South Vietnam's ability to consume the amount of aid programmed for 1962. If the economy could not absorb the aid assigned to the Commodity Import Program, then it could not generate the piasters needed to pay for the government's operations. Thus, as Nhu commented in an interministerial meeting on April 6, a lot of American support existed only on paper and was not immediately available. The palace regarded U.S. aid procedures as too slow and cumbersome to be of much benefit, at least in the short term. In turn, procedural problems tended to reinforce its conviction that South Vietnam would have to rely on its own resources to push the hamlet program forward.[58]

The regime did want U.S. support, however, especially if this fell within Saigon's definition of effective assistance. Nhu spoke of his preference for some kind of direct aid; he also expressed immediate interest in the sort of material help—barbed wire, radios, and guns—that would get the hamlet program off the ground.[59] Perhaps more surprisingly, the palace agreed to various changes in the advisory relationship that would facilitate U.S. support for strategic hamlets. To some extent, these were concessions made to maintain American goodwill. Yet, at the same time, the palace recognized that the United States could play a useful role beyond that of a mere cash cow. Direct U.S. support to the provinces could circumvent the hidebound central ministries and their French-trained functionaries, which both the Ngos and U.S. officials saw as obstacles to the program's implementation. Nhu also told a meeting of USOM/Rural Affairs personnel that Americans working in the provinces could report on problems with local incompetence or corruption. It was a measure of the palace's low regard for many of its own officials that Nhu hoped the Americans might ride shotgun on the RVN's provincial administrations.[60]

On several occasions in the latter part of 1962, the palace expressed satisfaction with such developments in the advisory relationship.[61] Since the Ngos were not renowned for hiding their feelings, especially negative ones, they appeared to be sincerely appreciative of their ally's efforts. Still, the palace was deeply concerned about the increasing number of Americans operating in the provinces and the implications of some of the new advisory arrangements. As Nhu told Nolting in May 1963, the palace would like the Americans to act as diagnosticians, helping to size up the hamlet program's problems, but did not want them to turn into physicians trying to fix everything in sight. The Ngos feared that U.S. advice and support had the potential to turn into something quite different to an arm's-length advisory relationship. Diem thought that American aid "was the most generously motivated thing in history," the U.S. ambassador reported after a discussion with the RVN president, "but that somehow we had not yet found the key for its most effective use, particularly in highly sensitive, excolonial, underdeveloped countries."[62]

The palace was afraid that increased U.S. support might subvert its plans to transform Vietnamese society. Nhu complained repeatedly, for example, about the American policy of issuing large numbers of weapons to hamlet defenders. The liberal distribution of guns, he argued, would undermine the self-sufficient guerrilla spirit that the regime wanted to inculcate in the population. As the counselor told Australian officials, U.S. generosity—"You lost your rifle? Why, sure, take two more!"—was self-defeating.[63] This complaint was only part of a much broader critique of the U.S. approach of using strategic hamlets to assist the peasantry. The Americans always wanted to build schools, hospitals, and the like, Nhu commented in several interministerial meetings, but the first task was to restore security, organize the population, and lay the basis for a new society. Lavish support and expensive amenities might come later, he noted; in the meantime, the profligate distribution of aid undermined the development of a spirit of self-sufficiency, without which there could be no real progress.[64]

The seductive dangers of foreign aid constituted a key theme of the palace's critique of American support. Indeed, the Ngos suggested that U.S. assistance not only sapped the popular will but also threatened the nation's political cohesion. Diem talked of a slavish "colonial mentality" among the Vietnamese that the advisory presence served to encourage. On one occasion, Nolting sought to calm such fears by noting how rural people usually greeted Americans with "a friendly signal and grin." "Yes, that is often the case," Diem replied with unexpected regret. "That is what I meant by the colonial mentality of the Vietnamese people. I have complaints from my own officials in those areas to the effect that the people believe that the Americans are now the government and disregard the authority of my local officials." The impatience and arrogance that many U.S. advisers displayed toward their Vietnamese counterparts—"Get out of the way, I'd rather do it myself"—reinforced the president's fears.[65]

The activities of the CIA and U.S. Special Forces in the Central Highlands provided the palace with a particularly graphic illustration of the threat to national unity posed by the growing American involvement in South Vietnam. Although Nhu had accepted U.S. assistance for the Buon Enao experiment among Montagnards in Darlac province, the regime was wary of American activities in the area. The chief of Darlac warned the palace in March 1962 that the U.S. presence, and the distribution of weapons to tribesmen, would inevitably fuel demands for self-rule among the Montagnards. Nhu reiterated this concern at an interministerial meeting several days later, stressing that the U.S. role must be phased out as soon as possible.[66] By the end of 1962, however, the program had been extended to hundreds of villages; moreover, there were nineteen thousand armed tribesmen defending them, a figure that, according to the CIA's Lucius Conein, had not been divulged to the palace. In a gathering at Buon Enao in the autumn of 1962, General Ton That Dinh, the corps commander, told a visibly shaken Nhu that "the Americans have put an army at my back."[67] Given its long-standing interest in restoring Vietnamese sovereignty over the Central Highlands, the palace could not have failed to see the disturbing parallels with the past; the Americans, albeit inadvertently, were playing the same role as the French in succoring the secessionist sentiments of the Montagnards.

In surveying the dangers of U.S. aid, the palace appeared to reserve the greatest concern for the susceptibility of its own officials to the blandishments of powerful foreigners. In a telegram to Washington in June 1962, the U.S. embassy reported a number of instances of high-level RVN disapproval of close contact between Vietnamese and American officials.[68] Again, the Ngos framed their concerns in terms of a lingering "colonial mentality" among their fellow countrymen. According to Nhu, this characteristic could be traced to the south's recent catalog of foreign interventions: French colonialism, the Japanese occupation, the British arrival in 1945, and the First Indochina War. The presence of outside powers, he observed, encouraged divisions and shifting allegiances among officeholders, which hindered the growth of national loyalty. Consequently, the growing U.S. involvement in South Vietnam would appeal to those lacking a well-developed sense of nationalism, further undermining the nation's solidarity and sense of purpose.[69]

The palace regarded the problem as twofold. First, there was the threat of another coup attempt. Antiregime Vietnamese might seize on American expressions of dissatisfaction with the Ngos and try to overthrow the government. The expanded advisory relationship offered plenty of scope for this kind of scenario since it led to far greater contact between Americans and Vietnamese. While there were less than one thousand U.S. military personnel in Vietnam in 1960, there were more than eleven thousand of them by the end of 1962. Some advisers, moreover, were less than discreet in their criticism of the Diem regime, freely airing their views in front of their Vietnamese counterparts as well as the American press.[70]

In addition, the Ngos believed that the U.S. presence presented a less drastic but equally insidious threat. By working directly at the local level and bypassing Saigon, the Americans might impose their view of the war on provincial officials. This circumvention of the palace's authority would not only cause confusion but also lead some administrators astray and distort the government's plans to generate an authentic Vietnamese revolution. The more assistance the Americans proffered, the less inclined the regime's officials would be to rely on Vietnamese ideas and resources to carry out policy.[71] Nhu argued that dependence on U.S. support stymied the development of the self-sufficient, revolutionary spirit that a poor and underdeveloped country needed in order to progress. He contrasted this reliance on outside aid with the strength and creativity displayed by communist cadres. The insurgents were suffering crushing losses because of the arrival of American helicopters, he told a class of trainee hamlet officials, but they did not ask Ho Chi Minh for more assistance; they looked to themselves to solve the problem.[72]

Given all of the palace's fears and concerns, the deepening advisory relationship raised troubling questions for the Ngos about just how far they could permit the process to go. Nhu's position, expressed in the first formal meeting of his interministerial committee, was that any Vietnamese contact with U.S. agencies must have the palace's approval.[73] Even after granting permission for a U.S. role in operations like Sea Swallow II, the regime remained leery of such American involvement.[74] In September 1962, Nhu reiterated his opposition to direct liaison and planning between the Americans and the province chiefs, which, he argued, resulted in myriad local plans that lacked a broad conceptual framework. Only the center could take cognizance of the national, as opposed to the local, picture. A province chief "cannot see beyond the end of his nose," the counselor complained, nor could U.S. advisers understand the needs of an underdeveloped country at war. Contrary to American hopes of extending their involvement in the provinces further, Nhu was inclined to restrict U.S. activities and reassert the regime's control over the counterinsurgency campaign.[75]

The issue that brought these simmering concerns to a boil was the funding of the counterinsurgency program. At the start of 1963, the Americans began to press the regime to finalize details for financing "civil" operations, notably strategic hamlets, because the special fund of 730 million piasters, purchased by the United States the previous August, would be exhausted within a few months. For fiscal reasons, U.S. officials considered this kind of dollars-for-piasters purchase to be a "one-shot affair" and did not intend to repeat it for 1963. However, they did regard the counterinsurgency fund as indispensable; it provided local currency for strategic hamlet operations and underpinned the U.S. role in the provinces. Thus, the country team proposed that the two sides establish a new and larger fund of 2.3 billion piasters (about $33 million) to carry out a set of projects mostly related to strategic hamlets. This fund would be composed of the remnants of the old one, counterpart revenue, and up to 1.4 billion piasters from RVN sources. In the case of province-administered projects, the Americans suggested that money from the new fund be expended under the current arrangements, with U.S. representatives signing off on any expenditure.[76]

Rufus Phillips acknowledged that the existing disbursement procedures had represented a "considerable abrogation of Vietnamese sovereignty,"[77] so their renewal might not be a formality. There were also several novel aspects to the new U.S. proposal. One was that the regime would contribute to the new fund from its own coffers; the other was that the Americans would be allowed a say in the spending of this RVN money because of the continuation of the current arrangements for disbursement. Diem objected, especially to the latter provision, which appeared to give the Americans control over RVN money and thus could be seen as an infringement of national sovereignty. In

early March, after a little more prodding, he accepted the new plan in principle, but negotiations over the details broke down several weeks later. The U.S.
proposal served to focus the palace's fears about developments in the advisory
relationship, and these concerns suddenly came to the fore in March 1963.[78]

The catalyst for the regime's about-face was the release in late February
of Mike Mansfield's report on his trip to Vietnam. The senator's pessimistic
assessment, magnified by its coverage in the U.S. press, shocked Saigon. At
first glance, it is difficult to see why Mansfield's views would encourage the
regime to seek to curb U.S. activities in Vietnam. After all, the palace's interpretation of the report was not that it heralded a U.S. attempt to take over the
running of the war; rather, it kindled long-standing suspicions, fueled by U.S.
policy in Laos, that America might cut and run in Vietnam.[79] Yet, although
apparently separate concerns, the issues of a deepening advisory relationship
on the one hand, and a wavering ally on the other, were linked, at least in
Nhu's eyes. In his view, the prospect of a possible U.S. withdrawal only added
to the problem of an expanded advisory presence. The danger was that South
Vietnam would grow hopelessly dependent on increased levels of U.S. support at the same time as the Americans became increasingly disenchanted
with their adventure in Southeast Asia. If the United States then suddenly
pulled the plug on its operation, the South Vietnamese would slip rapidly
down the drain. Nhu would not live to see it, but this was a remarkably accurate prediction of what would happen in the course of the next decade.[80]

Nhu told Australian officials that although he initially viewed the Mansfield report as a disaster, it was, on reflection, a timely reminder of the realities of allied relations. South Vietnam, he argued, must organize itself for the
day when the Americans departed. Not only did Nhu oppose the proposal to
extend and institutionalize the advisory relationship; he also argued, in public and private, that there were too many Americans in Vietnam and as many
as half of the twelve-thousand-odd U.S. personnel could be withdrawn.[81] In
the meantime, Diem, who had seemed prepared to accept the U.S. funding
proposal, now echoed his brother's criticisms. Nolting reported that the president "felt the real trouble was that we had too many people here, advising in
too much detail on too many matters, and that the remedy was to gradually
cut back the number of people, thus 'restoring control at the top.' " Diem believed that to agree to American control over RVN finances "would be considered by the Vietnamese people, both in form and execution, as proof of the
establishment of a U.S. 'protectorate.' " Instead, as the president told a cabinet
meeting in mid-March, the regime must start to plan to increase its own resources in order to reduce its dependence on U.S. aid.[82]

In a telegram to Washington, Nolting described the palace's position as
"another perplexing turn in GVN policy with far reaching implications for

American policy." How could the Ngos balk at an American say in the use of a relatively small amount of RVN money when the regime had exercised the same prerogative for years over much greater amounts of U.S. aid? In a marathon session with Diem on the evening of April 4, the ambassador used all of his "ammunition and personal persuasion" to attempt to reverse Saigon's decision. He informed Diem that his stance struck "at the root of our joint cooperative effort" and that he did not see how the U.S. government could justify its Vietnam policy domestically under these circumstances; he also threatened Diem with a reduction in aid to the counterinsurgency program. As Nolting told his superiors several days later, the country team "gravely doubt that [the] momentum of [the] strategic hamlet program can be maintained and, especially, gains already made consolidated without [a] piastre fund of roughly [the] size we have proposed and procedures for its use as effective as those we have had for purchased piastres."[83]

This was a strong and swift response to what U.S. officials saw as a major crisis, particularly when combined with the palace's negative comments about the number of U.S. personnel in the country. Ironically, the Americans had already begun internal planning aimed at phasing out most of their advisory effort by the end of 1965, based on the assumption that South Vietnam would be able to handle the insurgency by that date.[84] Nevertheless, warned Nolting, "we don't think [the] GVN can win without U.S. advisors in roughly [the] present density for the next year at least." The palace's approach, on both the number of U.S. personnel and the funding issue, represented a "repudiation of [the] concept of [an] expanded and deepened U.S. advisory effort, civil and military." With so much at stake, the ambassador argued, the United States must "convince Diem that we mean business." Yet he ruled out the idea that a change of leadership might be the solution to the problem; indeed, beneath all the tough talk, the accent was very much on reaching a compromise.[85]

Ostensibly, the palace was the first to crack. There were figures in the Saigon government much less suspicious of the U.S. presence than the Ngos, such as Vice-President Tho and Secretary Thuan. The president also seemed more disposed than his brother to settle the dispute amicably.[86] Still, the resulting agreement was a compromise, not a capitulation. The regime dropped its talk of reducing the number of U.S. advisers and agreed to contribute RVN money to a new counterinsurgency fund. Disbursement from the fund, however, would be under the sole control of the province chiefs and no longer needed to be countersigned by the USOM/AID and MAAG representatives on the three-member province committee.[87] In addition, Saigon sent a memorandum in May to all its senior regional and provincial officials prohibiting the receipt of direct aid from foreign agencies. Although the message made particular reference to "secret funds," perhaps suggesting that some RVN officials had received under-the-table support from the CIA, the general tenor was clear: the center intended to restore control over the allocation of resources.[88]

Nolting described the agreement as the "best compromise obtainable in present circumstances,"[89] but some U.S. officials regarded it as a bitter blow. Rufus Phillips and several members of his staff even threatened to resign over the issue. "We are winning the war at the only place where a counterinsurgency can be won—in the minds and hearts of the people," Phillips argued. "It is my profound conviction, which is shared by my staff, that the proposed changes, and their inevitable consequences, would seriously jeopardize the continued success of the Strategic Hamlet Program." In this view, the regime was unlikely to make adequate funds available to the provinces on a timely basis. Without U.S. supervision, moreover, province chiefs would use money for window dressing and to satisfy the "understood desires of Mr. Nhu," rather than projects designed to win popular support. "If we accept full GVN control of financing, and give up the right of approval of proposed expenditures at the province level," stated Phillips, "we virtually eliminate the U.S. from any significant voice in provincial affairs. This will be tantamount to giving up any appreciable influence over the conduct of the most important part of the war, at its most crucial phase." Twelve months into its support for the hamlet program, the United States appeared to be back to square one—searching for the means to influence its recalcitrant ally.[90]

In the course of the summer of 1963, U.S. officials were pleasantly surprised by the efficacy of the new funding procedures, although an even greater crisis in U.S.–Vietnamese relations soon overshadowed such concerns.[91] Phillips used his entrée with the palace to smooth relations, organizing a meeting with Nhu on May 29 that helped preserve the basic elements of the decentralized, province committee system.[92] Nonetheless, the funding issue highlighted certain salient features of the patron–client relationship that could not be papered over so easily.

First, the crisis illustrated the two partners' conflicting conceptions of the hamlet program, which also went to the very heart of each side's view of how best to overcome the insurgents and the problems of nation building. As Nolting observed, the regime, "under Ngo Dinh Nhu's theory, seemed to expect the Vietnamese peasants to pull themselves up by their own bootstraps when they have no shoes; we, to [the] contrary, felt that they must be given, either in money or in kind, some inducement to work for the government's cause."[93] Second, the funding debate demonstrated the practical limits of American influence. From the beginning of 1962, the United States vastly increased the amount of material aid and the number of personnel sent to

South Vietnam. On the strength of this effort, U.S. officials sought to alter the approach and practices of the Diem regime. Yet it took nearly a year to establish procedures that they deemed reasonably effective, while the brief crisis from March to May 1963 showed that it might be difficult to preserve these arrangements, let alone extend them. Indeed, in October 1963, the regime began to plan another shake-up in the distribution of aid to the provinces, unilaterally ordering the ARVN and Republican Youth to take over the system of supply used for delivering American assistance.[94]

Given their ideological precepts and nationalist convictions, the Ngos would not permit the advisory relationship to progress beyond a certain point, thus exposing a central dilemma in America's Vietnam policy. The United States believed that there were certain things that South Vietnam must do to survive and prosper, but it did not want to play the role of a colonial power in order to get them done. As long as the conflict in Vietnam appeared to be under control, U.S. officials could avoid having to choose between their sense of what actions needed to be taken to win the war and their reluctance to act, and be seen to act, as more than mere advisers. Would the turn of events, however, including the progress of the hamlet program, allow the United States to continue to fudge this issue?

7

Binh Duong Province:
Case Study of
a Program in Trouble

Recalling his trip to Vietnam with the McNamara-Taylor mission in the autumn of 1963, William Bundy wrote that he "became aware for the first time of how immensely diverse the war was in itself—how different from one province to another." This image of the insurgency made a strong impression on the Pentagon official. "I was left," Bundy observed, "as I think McNamara was, with a lasting skepticism of the ability of any man, however honest, to interpret accurately what was going on. It was just too diffuse, and too much that was critical took place below the surface."[1] Vietnam was, indeed, a complex, often subterranean war; the state of the insurgency differed from region to region, from province to province, and even between neighboring villages. Factors such as geography, the ethnic or religious composition of the population, local history, and provincial leadership could all affect the dynamics of the war in any particular area. Bundy's comments thus provide a useful caveat when considering the representative value of a case study of the hamlet program in a single province, which cannot hope to capture the full picture of the conflict in the rest of South Vietnam.

Nevertheless, a well-chosen case study may offer one of the few ways of overcoming the doubt and confusion expressed in these observations about the nature of the war. Since so much of the conflict took place "below the surface," perhaps we need to focus on a detailed example in order to shed some light on the general character of the murky, village-level struggle. In this case, Binh Duong fits the bill for a number of reasons. First, the province's geography led local officials to build a variety of types of strategic hamlets, which reflects some of the diversity of the national scheme. Binh Duong was located in an area of transition between the populous plains of the Mekong Delta and the less populous, and more rugged, lands to the east of Saigon, so provincial officials adapted the program accordingly, both fortifying existing hamlets

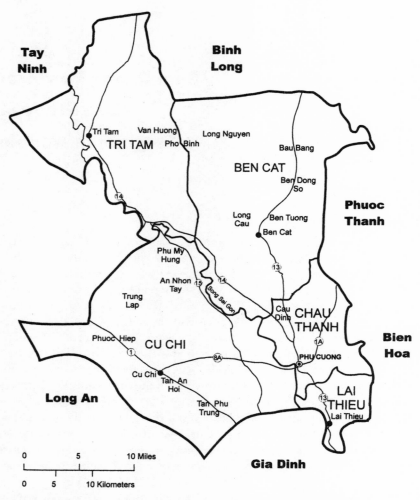

Binh Duong province, 1961–1963 (adapted from maps contained in South
Vietnam Provincial Maps 9/67, Doc. 1, Country File—Vietnam, Box 180/181,
National Security File, Lyndon B. Johnson Library). Binh Duong maintained
these boundaries until October 1963, when the Diem government detached six
villages from the lower half of Cu Chi district to form part of the new province of
Hau Nghia.

and regrouping the population in new settlements. Second, Binh Duong was a strategically important province; it lay just to the north of the capital and sat astride the insurgents' lines of communication between War Zones C and D. Consequently, both sides strongly contested control of the region, conducting a series of campaigns and counteroffensives that help illuminate the dynamics of the wider struggle. By paying so much attention to the war in Binh Duong, moreover, the government and guerrillas bequeathed a rich documentary record, which enables us to piece together enough of the story there to make informed generalizations about the progress of strategic hamlets in the rest of South Vietnam.[2]

Binh Duong first emerged as a center of RVN operational activity in mid-1961, at a time when Saigon was desperately seeking ways to respond to the expanding insurgency. In May, the palace gave General Van Thanh Cao, the government delegate for the eastern region, the responsibility for pacifying the provinces of Binh Duong, Tay Ninh, and Phuoc Tuy.[3] As the regional delegate, Cao was in charge of administrative liaison between Saigon and the block of ten provinces that separated the Mekong Delta from the central and northern parts of South Vietnam. The new grant of authority made the general responsible for security, as well as administration, in these three particular provinces. The interest in Binh Duong, Tay Ninh, and Phuoc Tuy reflected their strategic location; they formed a critical and roughly unbroken line, stretching from the Cambodian border to the capital and thence to the South China Sea. Soon christened the Rural Reconstruction Campaign, operational planning for the pacification of the three provinces commenced in the summer of 1961, and several hundred cadres underwent training at the port city and beach resort of Vung Tau.[4]

Operations started in early August, focusing, in the case of Binh Duong, on the southwestern district of Cu Chi. This was the province's largest district, straddling National Route 1 that connected Saigon with the city of Tay Ninh to the northwest. During the First Indochina War, the French nicknamed Cu Chi the "Red Capital." The area emerged as a formidable center of resistance during the Second Indochina War as well; its northeastern edge bordered what the Americans later called the "Iron Triangle." The insurgents, who constructed a vast tunnel network in the district, gave it the titles "Steel Land" and "Brass Citadel."[5] Cu Chi certainly deserved its reputation in 1961. The guerrillas had racked up an impressive record of subversive activities, including assassinations and abductions, while the PLAF conducted sizable military operations in the area. The NLF had crippled village-level administration, the local authorities admitted, and RVN-sponsored organizations had ceased to exist except on paper. The government controlled little more than a narrow strip of land on either side of the main highway and rated half of the district's fourteen villages as totally lacking in security.[6]

The rural reconstruction campaign concentrated initially on the villages of Tan Phu Trung, Tan An Hoi, and Phuoc Hiep, all of which lay along Route 1. RVN soldiers and teams of cadres moved into the villages to clear out the NLF, revive the district's paralyzed administration, and reestablish local organizations; the authorities also sponsored a variety of social and economic projects, such as providing sanitary facilities and improving roads. Provincial officials expressed satisfaction with the operation's progress, attributing much of its success to the enthusiastic participation of the population. By the spring of 1962, the campaign had been extended into neighboring areas, leaving untouched only five villages in the northeastern part of the district, which remained NLF strongholds.[7]

Strategic hamlets do not seem to have formed part of the original planning or initial operations. However, at the end of August and beginning of September 1961, General Cao instructed his province chiefs to incorporate the concept of defended communities into their plans, reflecting the Diem regime's quickening interest in this strategy.[8] Strategic hamlets soon became an integral part of rural reconstruction, providing a framework for the local authorities' efforts to organize the population and restore the government's presence in the countryside. By early 1962, there were three completed strategic hamlets in Cu Chi and another thirty-two under construction. One of the completed settlements was really a series of interconnected strategic hamlets, which surrounded the district capital of Tan An Hoi with eleven kilometers of ditches, walls, bamboo, and barbed wire. Nhu inaugurated this complex at a ceremony at the end of March.[9]

Behind this image of progress lay a rather different tale, however—one that reflected the gap that separated Saigon's grand ideas from provincial practice. Cu Chi's strategic hamlets evidently did not impress Nhu when he visited the district, although this was not entirely surprising since their construction had been under way long before the palace began to provide its subordinates with proper guidance about the nature of the program. The British embassy, which described their fortifications as "quite inadequate," suggested that Nhu had only attended the inauguration ceremony at Tan An Hoi as a "political gesture."[10] Shortly after his trip, the counselor criticized the district's strategic hamlets in an interministerial meeting. He argued that local officials needed to get their priorities right, not waste time on big projects like building schools and hospitals, and that forcing the population to contribute too much to the creation of strategic hamlets was a mistake. He also stressed that what really mattered was not physical accomplishments but the mobilization of the people inside the settlements.[11]

The counselor's criticisms reflected his concern at the tendency of provincial officials to focus on form rather than substance in their implementation of the hamlet program. This characteristic of Cu Chi's strategic hamlets could be glimpsed during Nhu's inauguration of the complex at Tan An Hoi. The ceremony was a formal and tightly orchestrated event, more reminiscent of a well-drilled state occasion than the launch of a popular struggle. Tanks guarded the main highway, and there appeared to be more soldiers than civilians in the audience. Local officials had instructed most residents to keep to their homes, or to water down a dusty road expected to be used by the visiting dignitaries; those villagers in attendance had to stand in the sweltering heat for several hours, while the VIPs sat in easy chairs on a canopied grandstand. The entire proceedings seemed to be at odds with an event supposedly celebrating the mobilization of the populace in defense of their homes. Perhaps the occasional bursts of gunfire that the visitors could hear in the distance offered a better clue to the real state of affairs in Cu Chi.[12]

Despite the optimistic tenor of provincial reports, strategic hamlets in Cu Chi, as elsewhere in South Vietnam, created neither popular enthusiasm nor effective security. Peasant support, a crucial prerequisite for long-term security, was hardly likely to flourish in light of the local authorities' heavy-handed approach toward the population. General Cao set the tone with his comment in neighboring Tay Ninh province about shooting some of the local inhabitants in order to deter others from supporting the guerrillas. Notwithstanding the palace's desire to promote the active involvement of peasants in the program, officials in Cu Chi built the district's strategic hamlets with minimal attention to the matter of popular participation and consent.

Cu Chi's residents did not receive much advance notice of the hamlet program's commencement, nor did local officials subsequently appear too concerned with explaining the scheme's goals to them. The chief of one of the new strategic hamlets along Route 1 noted that government cadres conducted only two brief sessions of political training in the two months following the start of his settlement's establishment.[13] Moreover, much of the official propaganda employed in Cu Chi seems to have dealt with issues far removed from the hamlet program or the concerns of ordinary peasants. Many civic action and information cadres were northern refugees, and their propaganda attacks on Russian/Chinese support for Hanoi, or oppression in North Vietnam, meant little to southern farmers. Such themes also clashed with most peasants' experience of the communists, especially during the war against the French when the Viet Minh were clearly regarded as liberators.[14] To the extent that residents did hear more specifically about the goals of strategic hamlets, it is doubtful that they learned much from RVN cadres, who were, in fact, little better informed about the program's purpose. One peasant involved in constructing a strategic hamlet told a team of American visitors that she was helping "to build a fence around 'Mr. Communist.' "[15]

Popular discontent accompanied such bewilderment. Resettlement did not initially occur on a large scale in Cu Chi, so this was not a major source of dissatisfaction; for example, at Xom-Hue hamlet, in Tan An Hoi village, only ten families were regrouped out of a total population of 1,768. The local authorities did impose severe demands on the people in other ways, however, as was observed by John Donnell and Gerald Hickey, RAND consultants who visited Cu Chi in early 1962. They noted that Captain Nguyen Van Binh, the district chief, seemed intent on employing many of the same heavy-handed methods used during the Agroville program. Contributions toward the building of hamlets included "obligatory communal labor, the use of local resources (such as bamboo and other woods), cash for the purchase of such materials as barbed wire and concrete for fence posts, and the sacrifice of paddy land to the construction of earthworks." To compound peasants' misery, forced labor schedules prevented them from tending their crops, some people working almost on a full-time basis for up to ninety days on labor projects; sometimes, the work was not even in their own communities, with people drafted to help construct neighboring hamlets. Hickey and Donnell encountered suitably sullen and discontented peasants. For many of those "willing to tolerate or even support local Viet Cong activities," they concluded, "the strategic hamlet presents no visible advantages and may indeed, in view of the hardships and sacrifices it entails, appear to them as having distinct disadvantages."[16]

Without popular sympathy or support, the district's efforts merely constituted the beefing up of physical and administrative controls over the population, not the creation of the kind of political environment that would turn hearts and minds against the insurgents.[17] That said, stronger controls did increase the danger for guerrillas operating in many parts of Cu Chi, as communist accounts of the struggle attest. Not long after the start of the rural reconstruction campaign, improved intelligence enabled the local authorities to surprise an NLF meeting in Phuoc Hiep village, killing seven insurgents and taking a larger number prisoner.[18] Such successes, however, masked a basic problem with the regime's position in Cu Chi. One of the compelling practical reasons for the palace's adoption of the hamlet program was the realization that the government lacked the resources to protect the entire population; hence, the people must be mobilized to defend and police themselves. Yet how could this occur if peasants remained so obviously disenchanted with the current regime?

Events in Cu Chi badly exposed this underlying weakness. Like John Paul Vann's metaphor of the ship moving through the ocean, the government only really controlled territory while its forces occupied a particular location. Once they left, the insurgents slipped right back into place. The village structures organized by RVN officials in Cu Chi lapsed once government forces moved on to other places. Areas declared clear and safe remained embarrassingly insecure, subject to regular NLF propaganda activities and acts of sabotage. In mid-1962, the guerrillas even succeeded in breaking into the showpiece hamlet complex around the district capital, kidnapping twenty members of the Republican Youth.[19] Such incidents suggested a significant degree of popular collusion with the insurgents or, at the very least, a fatal lack of commitment to the government's cause. By late 1962, some observers questioned whether the yearlong campaign in Cu Chi had made any real progress at all. A "little digging below the smooth and artificial surface," reported Colonel Francis P. Serong, the Australian counterinsurgency expert, "reveals complete disintegration of the established security procedures."[20]

If supposedly secure areas were still dangerous, traditionally insecure zones remained firmly under guerrilla control. Government forces in Binh Duong never succeeded in establishing their presence in villages like Phu My Hung and An Nhon Tay, located on the wooded northeastern edge of Cu Chi; district reports simply described these settlements as VC war zones.[21] In turn, this failure to extend the regime's reach exacerbated security problems in supposedly "safe" areas, since the insurgents could launch attacks from their strongholds in order to menace the regime's fragile hold over other villages. Only a few days after Nhu's visit to Cu Chi, RAND's Donnell and Hickey drove to Trung Lap, a village sandwiched between the RVN-controlled settlements along Route 1 and the guerrilla zones to the northeast. It was "very scary and strange," Hickey recalled. "A teacher we were talking to suddenly leaned forward and said that we should not be there. She said that a hamlet chief had been found dead in a well the night before." The two Americans left along a road that had "an eerie air about it," where the next day approximately two hundred insurgents ambushed an ARVN platoon.[22] Despite the regime's claims that substantial areas were now clear and safe, the entire district remained, to some extent, insecure.

The stock response of local officials to this persistent insecurity was to complain that they lacked the personnel required to pacify areas thoroughly. Shortly after the start of the rural reconstruction campaign, Captain Binh stated that he did not have enough local forces to carry out current operations safely, let alone advance into less secure areas of his district.[23] Yet this argument merely papered over the underlying weakness of the district's position. Without popular support, the local authorities could only hold areas by keeping officials and forces there in strength, because the villagers could not, or would not, administer and protect their own communities. Consequently,

Binh Duong's officials found their hands full trying to maintain control in one area, and were unable to transfer personnel and resources elsewhere in order to extend government control. Nor did Cu Chi receive the extra support requested by Captain Binh because, in the spring of 1962, the locus of campaigning in Binh Duong shifted to other parts of the province. The pacification effort languished, until the NLF smashed the district's hamlet program in the wake of the November 1963 coup.[24]

In early 1962, the priority in Binh Duong switched from Cu Chi to the districts of Ben Cat and Tri Tam, which made up the northern half of the province. Sparsely populated and heavily forested, this area had witnessed one of the biggest battles in the south during the First Indochina War.[25] A decade later, it remained a region of critical importance. One reason was economic; Ben Cat and Tri Tam contained sizable rubber plantations that helped bring in much of the RVN's foreign earnings. Of more immediate concern was the strategic value of the two districts. Heading due north through Ben Cat ran National Route 13, connecting Saigon with the border province of Binh Long and linking up there with a main highway into the Central Highlands. Running from east to west was the communications route that joined the guerrillas' War Zone D to the provinces of the Mekong Delta. Lying between Ben Cat and Tri Tam, moreover, was the Long Nguyen forest, which not only formed part of the PLAF's east-west line of supply but also provided a base for guerrilla operations, including armed forays into southern districts of the province.[26]

The importance of northern Binh Duong generated the first, and best-publicized, joint U.S.–Vietnamese operation of the hamlet program, code named Sunrise I.[27] The road that led to U.S. involvement in this scheme began with plans drawn up by CINCPAC and MAAG for an assault on War Zone D, which lay to the east of Binh Duong. They proposed to deploy substantial ARVN forces in Binh Duong as part of this attack, in order to sever supply lines and help to encircle the insurgent stronghold. However, at the first SECDEF conference in December 1961, McNamara expressed doubts about the utility and feasibility of the offensive, advocating instead an attempt to clear and secure a "test" area that would serve as a symbol of progress in the war. "I'll guarantee it (the money and equipment)," McNamara told the conferees, "provided you have a plan based on one province. Take one place, sweep it and hold it in a plan." With an eye to keeping the Zone D operation alive, General McGarr nudged the palace to choose Binh Duong as the "test" area.[28]

Diem needed little encouragement. He had already indicated in early December that he wanted to regroup the population in NLF base areas, beginning in Binh Duong. He shared McGarr's view of the region's strategic value and argued that current operations in the province needed to be extended in order to prevent the NLF from sabotaging existing efforts. In addition, McNamara's offer of support would increase the resources available for activities in northern Binh Duong, an important consideration given the area's difficult terrain, scattered population, and large guerrilla presence. "If the Americans wish to concentrate in one province and if they are willing to underwrite the effort with resources," wrote the authors of the *Pentagon Papers*, neatly capturing the palace's train of thought, "why not begin in an important strategic area where work is already underway?"[29]

Planning for Operation Sunrise began in earnest in January 1962, with General Cao acting as the liaison between the province and Saigon on the one hand, and the Vietnamese and the Americans on the other.[30] In its final form, the plan aimed at establishing twelve "secure villages" or "combat hamlets" in Ben Cat and Tri Tam districts by resettling about 13,500 people. "Combat hamlet" was the regime's term for a heavily defended settlement in an insecure area, created by regrouping the surrounding population in a new location. The idea, as outlined by Nhu in interministerial meetings, was that such settlements would require extra protection and assistance from the authorities and then, once firmly established, revert to the status of regular, self-sustaining strategic hamlets. Since the Sunrise campaign envisaged the creation of a substantial number of combat hamlets, in very insecure areas, Cao expected the operation to last about six months.[31]

Binh Duong's officials approached Sunrise with a notable absence of that "revolutionary spirit" that Nhu wanted Saigon's subordinates to display. They tended to regard the solution to South Vietnam's problems in terms of the government bringing security to the people rather than actively soliciting the latter's support—in short, old-fashioned pacification rather than popular mobilization. The reports of Captain Ho Van Hung, the district chief of Ben Cat, expressed the view that most villagers already believed in the regime and hated the communists, although those in insecure areas necessarily bowed to NLF pressures. The key to securing his district, argued Hung, was to construct strategic hamlets as rapidly as possible and swamp areas of operation with military forces, so that the guerrillas could not infiltrate or destroy newly established hamlets. Hung seemed to regard peasants as passive objects in this scheme of things, which also enabled him to rationalize a tough approach to any pockets of resistance. In NLF-controlled areas, he observed, the only way to bring about security was to create free-fire zones and compel people to seek safety inside strategic hamlets.[32]

The dire situation in the Sunrise area only served to encourage this emphasis on corralling peasants rather than attracting their support. RVN officials viewed northern Binh Duong, perhaps with some justification, as "Indian country." The population was sunk in darkness as a result of twenty years of communist control, stated a government pamphlet; villagers still believed that the French were in Saigon.[33] Consequently, reasoned the provincial authorities, stern measures were justified in order to overcome such ignorance as well as the hostile response expected from the insurgents; the government would have to be cruel to be kind, in order to bring people back to the "just cause." Diem told General Cao as much, permitting him to employ "severe methods" where necessary in regrouping the population.[34]

Some Americans sensed danger in the regime's plans. Large-scale population regroupment in NLF-infested territory threatened to be a public relations nightmare and a military fiasco. Several days before Sunrise was scheduled to start, Roger Hilsman, General Harkins, and Ambassador Nolting met at Saigon's Tan Son Nhut airport, where they all expressed concern about the forthcoming operation. The palace seemed intent on proceeding, however, and the doubters felt constrained by the existing U.S. pledge of support.[35] Last-minute reservations proved no bar to the irresistible momentum of operational planning.

At 7:30 on the morning of March 22, 1962, Cao's task force began operations, fanning out over a large area about four miles to the north of the town of Ben Cat. The initial objective was to establish the first of four settlements in this region by concentrating the surrounding population. RVN forces, including two battalions of regular infantry as well as provincial troops and civilian officials, moved to encircle nearly a dozen small, scattered settlements that lay next to a series of natural springs. About one hundred people, either guerrillas or frightened farmers, succeeded in slipping through the government cordon as it tightened around the area. Soldiers gathered the remaining inhabitants for relocation to Ben Tuong, another small settlement earmarked as the point of population concentration. Over the course of several days, the task force moved over two hundred families, nearly one thousand people, to Ben Tuong.[36]

According to Major R. M. Rhotenberry, a U.S. adviser who accompanied the operation, the process of removal was "chaotic." Fear of guerrilla attack spurred RVN officials to hurry the roundup of the population, while moving peasants from the area proved difficult because the insurgents had dug up or blocked local roads and the surrounding terrain precluded cross-country movement. As a result, officials forced peasants to abandon many of their belongings, and soldiers burned some homes as soon as their inhabitants left them.[37] Homer Bigart of the *New York Times* reported that 70 families agreed to move voluntarily, but troops needed to herd 135 others from their homes by force. By design or default, the most recalcitrant peasants were only able to bring about a third of their property with them, according to General Cao's report to the palace. Even this figure may have erred on the side of optimism, for Bigart observed that some peasants arrived at Ben Tuong with "almost nothing but the clothes on their backs." To add insult to injury, banners strung between trees welcomed them to their new home with the promise that "we will root out all the Viet Cong who destroy our villages."[38]

The confusion that accompanied the removal process evidently characterized the reaction of peasants to the whole experience as well. Did he prefer Ben Tuong to his old home, *Time* correspondent Jerry Rose asked one of the evacuees. "I had a nice home with a garden before," the farmer replied. What about the Viet Cong? "I saw them, but they never bothered me." Why had he come here? "We were told to come by the chief of the province." Why had he been moved, Rose persisted. "I don't know," the peasant admitted.[39] It was not a surprising response, for, in an attempt to maintain operational secrecy, the local authorities had avoided actions that might alert the target population and the guerrillas to the impending campaign.[40] No doubt officials also spent precious little time in the chaos of the relocation process trying to explain the nature of the Strategic Hamlet program. Like the peasants of Cu Chi, Ben Tuong's new inhabitants possessed little, if any, sense of the program in which they were supposed to be the key participants and principal beneficiaries.

Local officials attempted to remedy this omission with a number of propaganda initiatives. Loudspeakers bombarded Ben Tuong's residents with information about the benefits of their new life, secure from the depredations of the enemy. Aircraft dropped safe-conduct passes outside the settlement, encouraging those who had fled into the forest to return to their families. The U.S. Information Service also published a free weekly paper for the inhabitants, *Kien Quoc,* which carried government news, propaganda, and even the latest soccer results.[41] It is unlikely these efforts won over Jerry Rose's peasant interviewee, however, although he might have taken quiet satisfaction in Peru's three-to-zero victory against the Vietnamese General Staff, as reported in the first issue of *Kien Quoc.* Even Douglas Pike, the USIS representative assigned to Sunrise, was skeptical of the value of such mass communication techniques, which lacked the close attention to local concerns and grievances that characterized NLF propaganda.[42]

Promises of a brave new world, moreover, contended with the wretched reality of life in the new hamlet, at least in the initial stages of resettlement. March and April are usually the hottest months of the year in southern Vietnam, and Ben Tuong was an especially desolate site, lacking shade and vegetation. In addition, Sunrise's planners had not taken any concrete steps to prepare the area prior to the arrival of the refugees, in a vain attempt to preserve operational secrecy.[43] Most people spent the first week or so living in hastily erected communal barracks, while bulldozers cleared land for homes, and dug a defensive ditch and mud wall. Forced labor demands compounded their misery, with local officials immediately impressing the population to assist in the construction of new houses and hamlet defenses. As Hilsman and others feared, this was not the most auspicious of starts with which to mark U.S. support for the hamlet program, especially with the American press on hand to expose the attendant hardships. "It's no happy hollow," conceded Major Marvin Price, surveying the settlement after a week of the operation's commencement.[44]

To alleviate the burden of resettlement, peasants received rice, money and assistance for the building of new homes, agricultural implements, and livestock; the large number of families whose original fields now lay too far away to cultivate were also given land.[45] Still, these measures would not dispel the effects of a traumatic and disorientating experience as well as justified peasant concerns that their new home put them squarely in the front line of the contest between the government and the guerrillas. "The relocated people, apathetic and even sullen in some cases," commented General Rosson on an April 1962 visit to Ben Tuong, "appeared to be going through the motions of participation instead of manifesting enthusiasm at the prospect of making the hamlet a bastion of freedom."[46] Such discontent portended an uncertain future for Sunrise and raised troubling questions about the burdens borne by peasants elsewhere in South Vietnam. Given the aid and attention lavished on the operation, the people within its embrace received far more support than others in constructing strategic hamlets, yet they showed few signs of rallying to the regime's cause.

Peasant discontent notwithstanding, General Cao proceeded with further regroupment efforts near Ben Cat. Operations began to establish hamlets at Ben Dong So on April 17, Bau Bang on April 30 and Long Cau on July 17, eventually bringing the total number of people resettled in the area to over thirty-five hundred.[47] Because of guerrilla resistance, relocation at these sites was, if anything, more chaotic than the experience at Ben Tuong. PLAF interference with the Ben Tuong operation was negligible, with RVN intelligence reports indicating that insurgent forces were away on operations in War Zone D at the time.[48] Sunrise either took the guerrillas by surprise, or they underestimated its importance. Once in motion, however, the NLF's regional command recognized the potential danger posed by the campaign. Strategic hamlets might not generate popular enthusiasm, but they did threaten the insurgents' physical access to the population. Instructions immediately went out to cadres to organize popular resistance to further regroupment efforts, and in April, several PLAF units, including a main-force battalion, moved into an area fifteen miles east of Ben Cat in order to harass RVN operations.[49]

Consequently, the guerrillas played havoc with the new relocation efforts. Rhotenberry noted that, in the course of assembling people at Ben Dong So and Bau Bang, RVN forces encountered "booby traps," "moderate sniper fire," and "several small ambushes." The resettlement at Long Cau in July experienced the worst problems. In this case, General Cao had tried to ease the problems for both the authorities and the local population through a preliminary propaganda campaign, which sought to encourage people to abandon their old homes and thereby reduce the chaos that had accompanied previous relocations. Instead, this approach merely appeared to assist the NLF in planning their opposition to the resettlement effort. Before the operation opened, the insurgents took away all the local males of military age, and, when RVN troops subsequently sought to assemble the remaining population, they came under continuous fire. Peasants, hurriedly corralled by soldiers, succeeded in removing few belongings. As the British military attaché concluded: "The previous regroupements as already reported were extremely badly conducted and there is little doubt that the regroupement at Long Cau must have been considerably worse, with little or no consideration being given to the people or their wants."[50]

Guerrilla activity also exposed the continued costs and vulnerability of the newly established settlements. By the summer of 1962, it was no longer clear whether the Sunrise hamlets were the vanguard of a government advance or hostages of the PLAF. Each settlement required a Civil Guard company to maintain security, while a reinforced battalion of the ARVN's Eighth Regiment defended the general area. In effect, Binh Duong had committed about one-fifth of its five thousand regular and provincial troops to maintain control of only four hamlets and several thousand people.[51] The insurgents increased the strain on resources further by ambushing the military traffic that regularly traveled up and down Route 13 in support of Sunrise. On the morning of June 16, for example, several hundred guerrillas destroyed a seven-vehicle convoy only a mile or so south of the district capital of Ben Cat, killing at least fifteen Vietnamese troops and two U.S. advisers. In spite of the scale of the ambush, and the elaborate preparations that preceded it, no one warned the authorities. In a telling illustration of the government's tenuous position in the countryside, local people either collaborated or acquiesced in the attack.[52]

Tied down north of Ben Cat, and vulnerable everywhere else, Sunrise's planners now faced the same dilemma as their colleagues in Cu Chi: lack of forces to push on into new territory without exposing those areas currently under control. Sunrise's command put the strength of the PLAF's regular and local forces in Binh Duong at eighteen hundred.[53] Thus, government troops possessed less than a three-to-one advantage over the guerrillas, a far cry from the fifteen to one usually touted as a manageable ratio. In theory, the hamlet program's solution to this problem was to arm the local people to defend themselves, but many male inhabitants had fled the original roundup operations or were already with the resistance; at Ben Tuong, women in the age range eighteen to thirty-five outnumbered men by almost two to one. The local authorities, moreover, were very reluctant to risk arming the populace because they just did not trust the villagers in the area.[54]

Outside Saigon, the palace's neat distinction between "the people" and "the guerrillas" rapidly broke down. Most local inhabitants possessed few, if any, incentives to take up arms against the insurgents, especially after their recent experiences with resettlement; moreover, many of them had family members serving in the ranks of the PLAF. The presence of NLF agents in the hamlets also served to remind any residents who needed it of the dangers of collaborating with the authorities. In short, the calculus of interests, loyalties, and pressures that determined local attitudes toward the conflict did not conform to the palace's pat assumptions about mobilizing the populace in defense of their homes. If anything, the distinction in the Sunrise settlements was between the people and the government, rather than the people and the guerrillas.

The problem was evident during a visit to Ben Tuong by Robert McNamara. He spent several hours ranging around the settlement on May 9, 1962, firing questions at anxious officials and puzzled peasants, and scribbling comments in a notebook. The secretary of defense saw everything, except those things that really mattered in a people's war. Just before departing, he spotted a series of fortified pillboxes. These were not big enough to hold all the inhabitants, he noted to his entourage. "They aren't for the people," an American colonel explained. "They are for the hamlet officials in case the hamlet is overrun." "But what about the people?" asked a worried McNamara. "The Viet Cong don't want to hurt the people, Mr. Secretary," the colonel replied. "They're all related to them. The last thing most of the people would want to do would be to get in those pillboxes." An awkward silence ensued, but McNamara failed to draw the logical conclusion about where the loyalties of Ben Tuong's residents might lie.[55]

In the absence of a popular commitment to the new hamlets, the local authorities lacked the support necessary for their long-term defense. Without hamlet militia, General Cao did not have sufficient personnel to both protect the settlements and carry the campaign into other areas. Thus, Sunrise bogged down with only four hamlets completed out of the twelve originally planned. To push on, Cao required additional outside assistance, especially military support from the army. The problem of securing adequate military backing had dogged the operation from the outset, however. The ARVN high command evinced little interest in strategic hamlets, particularly if they threatened to tie down large numbers of troops in static security missions. Military commanders argued that the army did not possess sufficient forces to be everywhere at once, nor did they see this as the ARVN's role in the war. Like their American sponsors, they preferred the beat of the big battalions.[56]

Lacking the sympathy of the generals, Cao needed the palace's backing to get the requisite cooperation from the ARVN, but Saigon's goodwill was also in short supply by the autumn of 1962. As in the case of Cu Chi, the palace was not overly impressed by the performance of its subordinates. Diem criticized Sunrise's costs in terms of personnel and resources.[57] Nhu was especially critical of the operation's shortcomings, arguing in interministerial meetings that the regime's "combat hamlets" had turned into Malayan-style defended settlements: too much forcible relocation had replaced the ideal of voluntary regroupment; control and regulation of the populace had supplanted the promotion of popular self-sufficiency and self-defense. The type of settlements established in the Sunrise campaign, he complained, were "counterguerrilla" in character, which made them very costly, financially and politically; if South Vietnam was going to overcome its problems, they had to be converted into the kind of "guerrilla" strategic hamlets that would mobilize the people to defend themselves.[58] In the light of the Sunrise experience, Nhu was toying with new ideas for operations in enemy-held territory, such as creating settlements populated by youthful volunteers, which would supposedly serve as a magnet for the surrounding population.[59]

Without the patronage of the Ngos, Sunrise faltered. "After a big press write-up of the announcement of this operation," the British military attaché wrote at the end of September 1962, "interest, drive and initiative, now seems to have completely died out."[60] If anything, the situation only went from bad to worse. In February 1963, Cao recommended that Captain Hung, the chief of Ben Cat, be dismissed for incompetence and corruption in his administration of the district's affairs. The general noted that Hung had made no effort to organize a people's militia in the Sunrise hamlets; in fact, he rarely bothered to visit the settlements, leaving them to the tender mercies of corrupt and incapable village councilors, whom he had chosen from among the residents of the district capital. Not only had the situation in Ben Cat failed to improve, noted Cao; it had actually deteriorated.[61]

Poor administration only served to exacerbate existing weaknesses. Without some dramatic improvement in conditions in the Sunrise area, the principal experience most inhabitants were likely to associate with the operation was the misery and hardships of resettlement. Herein lay the fundamental problem, which Binh Duong's officials never fully appreciated or proved able to solve. The local authorities could create new settlements, but these physical structures could not stand alone without the pillars of popular support. In the final analysis, as Nhu observed of the Sunrise hamlets, such support was the key to the conflict. The weakness of the Sunrise settlements was graphically illustrated in August 1963, when the insurgents overran Ben Tuong, the campaign's first hamlet. According to the *New York Times,* the guerrillas "apparently met no resistance"; a later communist history noted that party cadres had already cleared the way by leading the people in eliminating several individuals and rendering ineffective the settlement's Self-Defense Corps unit. The neighboring Sunrise settlements would soon follow suit, collapsing like a house of cards.[62]

In the summer of 1962, Saigon brought out its new nationwide plan for hamlet construction, dividing the country into four priority regions and creating a series of tactical areas corresponding to ARVN divisional boundaries. Binh Duong was one of eleven provinces near Saigon or in the Delta assigned first priority. Although General Cao retained responsibility for the province's security, the ARVN Fifth Division assumed control over operations for the rest of the eastern region. The U.S. embassy described the new plan as "a most welcome step forward in the GVN's effort to organize the Strategic Hamlet Program in a more effective manner."[63]

The problems that had plagued the province's activities could not be solved by the stroke of a planner's pen, however. From mid-1962 onward, the authorities responsible for Binh Duong came under relentless pressure, which overwhelmed their ability to plan and execute operations properly. On the one side, there was the palace with its insatiable demands for progress; on the other, the indifference and hostility of the local population, and the increasingly fierce resistance of the insurgents. Squeezed between the two, the province's hamlet program began to lose even the semblance of planning and organization that had characterized the earlier efforts in Cu Chi and Ben Cat.

By the end of July 1962, Binh Duong had completed 30 strategic hamlets, with another 27 under construction, but its planned total stood at a daunting 319.[64] Thus, local officials faced an uphill climb, with their advance monitored unerringly by Saigon's weekly statistical update of the hamlet program's progress. Nhu had already given the province a sharp prod, complaining that the emphasis on Sunrise had distracted attention from Binh Duong's southern districts. Concentrating too much on one place merely gave the insurgents a free hand in other areas, the counselor informed an interministerial meeting on June 29. General Cao duly informed Major Tran Van Minh, the province chief, to take remedial action.[65]

One of Cao's original arguments for focusing on northern Binh Duong was that operations there would alleviate security problems in the south of the province as well. The southeastern districts of Chau Thanh and Lai Thieu appeared far from secure, however, despite the fact that the tip of the latter was only a dozen or so miles from Saigon. On April 19, 1962, two PLAF platoons ambushed a squad of Self-Defense Corpsmen in Lai Thieu, which the province chief described as just one of a number of regular skirmishes with the enemy. The insurgents were also active in neighboring Chau Thanh, where efforts to construct strategic hamlets in outlying villages had been hampered by a lack of personnel and the sabotage of fortifications.[66]

Turning their attention southward from the Sunrise area, the province's officials decided that the most pressing problem was the security of Route 13, south of the town of Ben Cat, where the guerrillas regularly ambushed passing traffic. To improve security, Major Minh proposed to establish five combat hamlets along a stretch of Route 13 in northern Chau Thanh and southern Ben Cat districts, which required the regrouping of more than seven thousand people from the surrounding area. Operations began in mid-November and received glowing praise from the U.S. embassy in a January 1963 progress report. Ambassador Nolting contrasted this relocation effort with that of Sunrise, pointing out that peasants could move their belongings at leisure because an intensive propaganda campaign had preceded resettlement and troops had completely secured the area. "In [the] new hamlets [the] houses [are] better, [and] people seem to have been glad about moving," noted the ambassador. "They were either friendly or indifferent to 'visitors in uniform,' and there was industrious activity throughout."[67]

The embassy appears to have based its rosy report on outdated or suspect information, at least in the case of one of the new combat hamlets. Colonel Wilbur Wilson, the senior U.S. adviser to the ARVN III Corps, painted a very different picture in the course of explaining an ambush that took place at Cau Dinh hamlet in May 1963. According to Wilson, work stopped on Cau Dinh not long after its establishment, with only a "crude moat" to serve as a defensive perimeter. Without even adequate physical defenses, the hamlet proved highly vulnerable, the NLF murdering its chief in March. By May, the incomplete settlement contained only 50 of the 138 families reportedly regrouped there. On May 14, ten days after an ARVN company had established a base in Cau Dinh, PLAF forces wiped out one of the company's platoons, using the hamlet's houses as cover.[68]

One month later, General Victor Krulak, the joint chiefs of staff's special assistant for counterinsurgency and special activities, visited Cau Dinh during a trip to South Vietnam. Since his subsequent report failed to mention the ambush, and described a flourishing settlement with a contented population, there had either been a remarkably rapid improvement in the situation or the general was wearing rose-colored glasses.[69] The latter seems the more likely explanation. At the time of Krulak's trip, the U.S. III Corps advisory team reported that the guerrillas still disrupted traffic on the way to Ben Cat, more than six months after the resettlement operations aimed at securing the road.[70]

Wilson's account of events at Cau Dinh suggested that the reason for the dismal situation in the hamlet was that the province chief had virtually abandoned the area, in order to meet "higher priority requirements elsewhere."[71] More likely than not, this reference was to additional operational demands made by Saigon. Even as the overtaxed local authorities sought to parcel out their limited resources, the palace piled on new burdens, such as Operation Ben San, an attempt to clear guerrillas from the borders of Binh Duong and Phuoc Thanh provinces. This was an NLF-infested area, and the insurgents subjected the strategic hamlets established there to a good deal of harassment.[72] Saigon also demanded that local officials secure Binh Duong's rubber plantations. This latter order resulted in another major campaign that not only diverted attention and resources from elsewhere but also demonstrated, once again, how difficult it was to make any headway in the more insecure parts of the province.

The palace's concern for Binh Duong's rubber estates reflected their value to both the government and the guerrillas. According to Nhu, the country's plantations brought in 80 percent of South Vietnam's foreign exchange earnings, so the large rubber holdings in Binh Duong represented a significant economic asset.[73] At the same time, the guerrillas gained much needed supplies for their armed forces by extorting food and money from the estates, so securing the plantations would badly hurt the enemy as well. As the insurgents stepped up efforts to increase their supplies in the autumn of 1962, government interest in the security of the plantations quickened accordingly.[74] The French owner of the Michelin holdings added his voice to the rising chorus of concern, telling Diem that increased guerrilla pressure on the rubber estates presented a serious threat to the economy.[75]

In January 1963, the minister for rural improvement presented the palace with a plan to protect the Michelin plantations in Binh Duong's northwestern district of Tri Tam. He proposed to establish three new settlements along the southern border of the rubber estates, regroup plantation workers into strategic hamlets, and turn nearby Vang Huong and Pho Binh into combat hamlets. The latter two settlements appeared to be the keys to the security of the area because the guerrillas used them as bases from which to menace the Michelin workers and destroy equipment belonging to the plantations.[76]

The provincial authorities began concentrating people at Vang Huong in February. There was little response from the insurgents, although the number of people resettled—386—fell short of official estimates and there were only 71 adult males among them. The operation at Pho Binh in May proved to be a complete fiasco, however. Government forces fought a running battle with the PLAF, losing 16 dead and 52 wounded. The fighting was so intense that it was not possible to regroup all of the target population, nor could those moved bring their possessions with them. The troops managed to resettle 155 people, of whom only 4 were adult males; the rest were with the enemy, admitted Major Minh. To keep the new hamlet supplied, the authorities carved out a six-kilometer road through dense forest, but, with the onset of the rainy season, this lifeline soon became impassable; supplies had to be dropped by plane. Life was grim inside the hamlet as well. Lack of equipment and able-bodied manpower meant that the construction of houses was slow, while the inhabitants could not make a living in their new home and had to be supplied with food. Under the circumstances, commented Minh, people would abandon Pho Binh at the first opportunity. Like the Sunrise hamlets, Vang Huong and Pho Binh turned into liabilities rather than assets, and the campaign of which they were a part seems to have petered out.[77]

Severe problems in widely separated parts of the province, from Pho Binh to Cau Dinh, pointed to the general failure of Binh Duong's hamlet program. In the summer of 1963, after almost two years of intensified RVN operations, a U.S. advisory report noted that the insurgents "still control or are in the ascendancy over the greater portion of the province."[78] Binh Duong had finished only around 100 strategic hamlets out of a revised total of 216. Each hamlet took a minimum of six months to establish, reported the Americans, so the planned program could not be completed before July 1964, and only then with additional troops.[79] The perennial problem of limited means continued to plague provincial officials as the hamlet program moved into the second half of 1963. In July, Major Minh asked Saigon to spare a further five companies of Civil Guards, in order to protect a number of exposed hamlets. Even this request paled beside the estimate of U.S. advisers that Binh Duong required a minimum of six ARVN battalions to be deployed in the province on a permanent basis.[80]

Once again, the key problem was the failure of the local authorities to create a viable popular infrastructure in the hamlets that would free regular forces from static guard duty to participate in operations elsewhere.[81] During the summer of 1963, the province began a special effort to speed up the training and arming of combat youth units, in order to address this problem. Yet, in some places, such as the Sunrise settlements and Vang Huong/Pho Binh, there were simply not enough eligible people among the inhabitants to form hamlet militia. From the sizable number of "young, healthy soldiers in VC ranks," noted U.S. advisers, it appeared that many of them were already with the enemy. Progress was also slow because local officials remained wary of arming the population and feared that the insurgents would infiltrate hamlet militia.[82] Even the RVN's provincial forces proved less than reliable. In June,

for example, eleven members of Cu Chi's Self-Defense Corps went over to
the NLF, taking their weapons with them.[83]

U.S.–RVN figures of September 1963 put the PLAF's strength in Binh
Duong at twenty-five hundred to thirty-five hundred troops, a significant
increase on 1962 estimates. Guerrilla activity also rose steadily from the
spring of 1963 onward, earning the province the dubious distinction of having the highest incident rate of any area in III Corps.[84] Under increasing pressure, Binh Duong's forces abandoned outlying strategic hamlets, leaving
behind a few, generally unmotivated, local militiamen to hold off the NLF.
"Security forces were withdrawn from the countryside to defend vital installations and routes of communications," recalled Major Rhotenberry. "More
and more troops were deployed to garrison the provincial capital and district
towns. All of these troop deployments were at the expense of providing security for the strategic hamlets which had been constructed since 1962."[85]

Trying to explain the growing security problem, Vietnamese and American reports attributed it to the insurgents' violent reaction to strategic hamlets, something that was expected and even welcomed as a sign of the NLF's
concern about the scheme. Neither provincial officials nor U.S. advisers gave
the impression that they believed the war might be lost in Binh Duong. RVN
assessments, in particular, lacked perspective and seemed devoid of a real
appreciation of the situation. Although they did record the extensive NLF
activity in the region, Binh Duong's province and district chiefs concluded
their reports with glib assertions of the people's love for the government and
confident predictions about the eventual outcome of the conflict.[86]

One might be tempted to regard such reporting as an attempt to pull the
proverbial wool over the eyes of their superiors in Saigon. While this kind of
game undoubtedly did occur, most RVN officials, like most U.S. advisers,
probably genuinely believed that the war could be won. As Jeffrey Race noted
in his study of Long An, provincial officials had much less understanding of
what was really happening in the countryside than members of the local militia or the hamlet and village councils.[87] They filtered events, moreover,
through a prism that viewed the province's difficulties essentially as a matter
of restoring security, rather than the more deep-rooted problem of winning
peasant support. What they failed to appreciate, or admit, was that the guerrillas had not only stymied the province's program but were also poised to
tear it apart. Local authorities lacked personnel and had lost the initiative,
while PLAF strength was growing and its units were increasingly taking the
war to the government.

The evolution of the hamlet program in Binh Duong illustrates the extent of
the gap that separated the palace's concept of the scheme from its actual

implementation by provincial officials. While Saigon wanted to mobilize the peasantry politically, its subordinates viewed the program primarily in terms of restoring security by reasserting physical control over the population. This more limited vision of strategic hamlets reflected not only the local officials' attitudes toward the insurgency but also the difficult position in which they found themselves. From above, they felt the pressure coming from Saigon to push ahead with the hamlet program as quickly as possible; from below, they faced a recalcitrant peasantry and armed resistance. They tailored the province's strategic hamlets accordingly, establishing physical structures that they could point to as signs of progress and that they hoped would keep the population pacified; they lacked the interest and the resources to attempt to promote the palace's ideas about a popular revolution.

Although the palace's vision of the hamlet program would have been difficult to fulfill even if provincial officials had really tried to do so, it did recognize the folly of attempting merely to corral peasants. As Nhu had pointed out in his criticisms of the hamlets in Cu Chi and Ben Cat, what went on inside the settlements was ultimately much more important than the surrounding fortifications. The course of events in Binh Duong illustrated the truth of this proposition; the province's tendency to treat the program as a glorified control measure failed because the local authorities did not have the resources to secure the region in the absence of popular support. As Rufus Phillips concluded: "Control cannot be imposed from without if it is to be effective, particularly in Vietnam (witness the failure of the initial four hamlets in Operation Sunrise) but must be essentially self-imposed, resting upon the will of the population."[88] The events of 1963 would prove just how vulnerable was a program built on such weak foundations.

8

The Reckoning

While an examination of events in Binh Duong clearly exposes the failings of the Strategic Hamlet program, hindsight obviously provides us with an advantage that was not available to the protagonists. For many observers at the time, the outcome of the conflict in South Vietnam was not so clear. Initially at least, a combination of strategic hamlets and increased U.S. military support seemed to herald a change for the better in the Diem regime's fortunes. As we have seen, this perception of progress led to an improvement in allied relations in 1962; it also served to mask some of the underlying weaknesses of Saigon's position in the countryside. In an oft-quoted judgment, Wilfred Burchett, the Australian journalist and communist sympathizer, concluded that the turn of events had set back the NLF's cause and bolstered Diem's. "If 1961 was a 'Front year' in terms of territory and population gained, 1962 however must be largely credited to Saigon," he conceded.[1] The palace concurred, with notably more enthusiasm, devoting an entire issue of the *Times of Viet Nam Magazine* to "1962: The Year of Strategic Hamlets."[2] Many U.S. officials expressed similar optimism. "In the whole long decade," William Bundy recalled, "this was perhaps the time of greatest hope."[3]

Not that there was any sign of an imminent NLF collapse. From mid-1962 through to the spring of the following year, U.S. assessments frequently described the situation as a "standoff" or an "escalating stalemate." Drawing liberally on the statistical indicators that became the conflict's trademark, reports noted that both the government and the guerrillas had strengthened their hands.[4] Nevertheless, while American officials acknowledged the resilience of the insurgents, most believed that U.S.–RVN forces were making progress, especially when compared with the desperate situation of late 1961. In what would emerge as an embarrassingly familiar refrain, a string of high-level reports proclaimed that a hard slog lay ahead but there was light at the end of the proverbial tunnel.[5]

These same reports did stress, however, that the struggle could quite easily go against the allies unless they maintained the momentum generated by the hamlet program and expanded U.S. aid. American officials thought that the war had entered a critical phase, in which gains had to be consolidated in order to turn the current stalemate into eventual victory. Ambassador Nolting warned in August 1962 that "several GVN, U.S.-supported, programs have made commitments and raised hopes, which could boomerang disastrously if not followed through"; the present situation contained "great risks" as well as a "great opportunity." Roger Hilsman and Michael Forrestal repeated the warning in their January 1963 assessment of the war. Although the allies were probably winning, they stated, "a sudden and dramatic event would upset the gains already made." Similarly, a National Intelligence Estimate of April 1963 concluded that, in spite of the evident improvements in the war effort, fresh PLAF successes or the RVN's perennial weaknesses could still imperil the Diem regime; in sum, the situation in South Vietnam "remains fragile."[6]

Events from the spring of 1963 onward demonstrated just how fragile. Two distinct, but mutually reinforcing, developments dealt a series of mortal blows to strategic hamlets and the Diem regime. First, the insurgents began to reassert their control on the battlefield, launching a vigorous assault on the hamlet program that lay bare its weaknesses. Thus, the increasing tempo of PLAF operations that was evident in Binh Duong was mirrored in much of the rest of the country as the guerrillas moved to smash the entire counterinsurgency effort. Second, there was the Buddhist crisis and the rapid deterioration in U.S.–Vietnamese relations. This political debacle, culminating in the coup of November 1963, exacerbated Saigon's security problems and delivered the coup de grâce to the hamlet program. Together, these military and political events constituted one of the most dramatic and decisive turning points of the Vietnam conflict.

Perhaps even true believers in the communist revolution would have been hardpressed to predict the rapid shift in the war's fortunes that occurred in 1963 after the difficulties experienced by the insurgents the preceding year. These problems do not receive much attention in most Western accounts, where the guerrillas appear only fleetingly—a mysterious but irresistible foe, absorbing punishment unflinchingly and brushing aside every attempt to quash them. Like an "organizational steamroller," they advance slowly but inexorably to victory.[7] In reality, the insurgents were not "ten feet tall," and the road to victory was an uphill climb, even before the arrival of five hundred thousand American GIs. The party leadership in Hanoi recognized as much when it became apparent that Washington intended to make a stand in South Vietnam. In February 1962, the politburo warned that increased U.S. involvement presented new obstacles to the progress of the revolution in the south, which would necessitate a change in tactics and organization.[8]

Two factors served to check the momentum of the insurgency: the development of strategic hamlets and new U.S. assistance to the Diem regime. First, there was the hamlet program, which, despite its many defects, still presented a problem for the insurgents. Although strategic hamlets did not generate popular support for the government, they did represent a physical obstacle that threatened to deprive the guerrillas of their access to the peasantry. As Nguyen Chi Thanh, a member of the DRVN's politburo, observed, the scheme was a "relatively 'clear-headed' " strategy for "taking a firm hold of the population, isolating the adversary and eventually winning victory."[9] In some areas, population regroupment disturbed existing communist networks and threw their organization into chaos.[10] In general, NLF cadres found their freedom to operate limited by the beefing up of the regime's presence in the countryside and the introduction of new control measures, such as the issuing of identity cards. In June 1962, the State Department's Bureau of Intelligence and Research reported that the ID card scheme had already netted fifty-two communist agents as well as two thousand RVN military deserters. Even in guerrilla strongholds like the Delta's Kien Hoa and Long An, these sorts of measures forced cadres to curtail their activities and even to abandon settlements altogether.[11]

As strategic hamlets struck at the ties between the insurgents and the population, they also began to affect the PLAF's military capabilities. In central Vietnam, for example, especially in highland areas, the guerrillas lacked food and medical supplies to maintain the expansion of their armed forces, with the U.S. embassy reporting that their daily rice rations were almost half the levels of 1960.[12] Because the guerrillas then resorted to coercion in order to secure supplies from villagers, such shortages also served to poison relations with the local populace. Caught between NLF exactions on the one hand, and RVN military operations on the other, thousands of highlanders proceeded to flee contested areas to seek sanctuary in government-controlled territory. As a result of this hemorrhaging of the population, the insurgents suffered further supply problems, while U.S.–RVN forces experienced some success in organizing Montagnards against the insurgents.[13]

Increased RVN control over the peasantry also threatened to sever the vital connections between the PLAF's local guerrilla and main-force units. The former constituted the base of an organizational pyramid, providing the latter with auxiliary support and a source from which to draw seasoned recruits. In many areas, this base began to erode as a result of the hamlet program, yet the increased tempo of the war demanded more troops to replace losses and counter the enemy. High casualties in the Delta's Dinh Tuong, for example, compelled the PLAF to assign raw levies to regular units, rather than employing the usual recruiting process. The insurgents also turned to coercion in order to enlist peasants, resorting at times, in the words of a later study, to "methods of conscription reminiscent of the press gangs in eighteenth-century England." In one village, they made an example of the first two people to protest against these practices by shooting them in front of their neighbors. Clearly, the war was starting to test the NLF's ability to maintain its forces.[14]

New levels of U.S. assistance to the Diem regime compounded the problem. The number of American advisers tripled in 1962, accompanied by a rise in U.S. military aid. There was a corresponding increase in the size of the RVN's regular armed forces from around 180,000 to over 214,000, while the number of Civil Guard and Self-Defense Corps troops rose from 123,000 to nearly 172,000. In addition, there was a burgeoning collection of irregular units, most of them trained by the U.S. Special Forces. The Americans delivered new equipment as well—including helicopters, aircraft, and armored personnel carriers—that transformed the nature of the battlefield in South Vietnam.[15] General Le Quoc San, in charge of one of the NLF's Delta zones, described the state of his command in late 1962 as shell-shocked from the impact of new allied tactics and technology. Whereas it had taken the French several days to reach the scene of a battle, he commented, the enemy could now be there in a matter of hours. Consequently, his command suffered heavy casualties, including the loss of veteran cadres like San's deputy, Colonel Do Van Giong, killed in Dinh Tuong in December 1962.[16]

Not surprisingly, the hardships and costs imposed by strategic hamlets and the intensified fighting started to take their toll on NLF morale. PLAF troops were often hungry, continually harassed by the enemy, and in much greater danger of being killed than a year earlier. RVN reports, as well as information from prisoners and deserters, began to note a variety of tensions within the resistance movement: between local cadres and infiltrators from the north; nonparty and party members; cadres and conscripts; territorial and regular troops; and members of religious sects and other personnel. Previous expectations of an early victory, now dashed by the war's transformation, only served to exacerbate these tensions.[17] Declining morale also led to a notable increase in desertions, which the Diem regime belatedly sought to encourage with the introduction in April 1963 of its "Open Arms" amnesty program. Saigon's figures for the success of the program were open to question, but, according to Tran Van Giau, the "Open Arms" scheme did add to the revolution's mounting list of problems.[18]

Perhaps the most troubling aspect of these changes in the fortunes of war was the popular response to them. The NLF no longer found it so easy to convince communities to participate in sabotaging roads and other labor tasks. Hamlet youths, who previously joined enthusiastically in local guerrilla activities, now sought to lie low, especially if cadres wanted to send them far from their homes to fight with main-force units.[19] Communist assessments of the situation in mid- to late 1962 concluded that the population seemed to be losing faith in the insurgents. "Our people are generally good, and do not like the U.S. and Diem," an NLF study document commented, "but when they are under oppression, they will unintentionally stand against the revolution."[20]

The counterinsurgents interpreted these signs rather differently, of course, arguing that allied successes encouraged the anticommunist impulses of the population. In general, this belief betrayed a misplaced faith in the peasantry's political convictions, although there were indications that some people were now prepared to assist the authorities, especially by providing intelligence information. Counterinsurgency experts like Robert Thompson and Francis Serong viewed this kind of support as one of the keys to the struggle. As a BRIAM assessment explained: "SUCCESS leads to KILLS, KILLS to CONFIDENCE, CONFIDENCE to better INTELLIGENCE and INTELLIGENCE to greater SUCCESSES and more KILLS."[21] One well-publicized example of popular support for the authorities occurred during a series of heavy clashes between PLAF units and the ARVN's Twenty-fifth Division in Quang Ngai in April 1963. Peasants provided intelligence on guerrilla movements, supplied RVN troops with food and water, and even helped to fight off a series of insurgent attacks. "This is the first time a local populace has cooperated fully with the Vietnamese Army," proclaimed a triumphant General Harkins.[22]

Faced with these kinds of developments, the insurgents engaged in a soul-searching analysis in mid-1962. They concluded that the optimism of late 1961 had led the leadership and cadres to relax their efforts in anticipation of an easy victory. Thus, they had not expanded the movement vigorously enough, nor responded properly to the enemy's new tricks, especially strategic hamlets.[23] The U.S. embassy noted that one high-ranking communist captive told his interrogators that the guerrillas had reacted slowly to the hamlet scheme because "they initially thought that it was merely a propaganda ploy which [the] GVN would not be able [to] fulfill."[24] Similarly, a communist case study on combating strategic hamlets explained that while local cadres had understood the potential danger, they did not consider the regime capable of implementing its plans; some of them had not even bothered to oppose government activities, or report them to higher authority, because they expected to use the newly constructed defenses to turn RVN strategic hamlets into NLF combat hamlets. To compound this original sin of complacency, the study commented, the cadres and local populace had now developed an equally debilitating overestimation of the enemy.[25]

To lift flagging spirits and combat the enemy's efforts, the guerrillas revamped their strategy in mid-1962. The new policy, repeated endlessly in

NLF documents, reaffirmed and elaborated upon the politburo's February 1962 assessment of the war. Given the increase in enemy capabilities, there could be no immediate seizure of power; nor, the revolutionaries pointed out, did they wish to precipitate a further U.S. escalation of the war. Still, they emphasized, the struggle would eventually be won. U.S.–RVN forces might have achieved a temporary tactical success, but the strategic initiative remained with the revolution because it represented the will and strength of the people. The new policy line concluded that the NLF needed to dig in for a protracted war, intensify politico–military efforts to generate support, and beef up its armed forces in order to counter the increased pressure being exerted by the enemy.[26]

Consequently, the insurgents continued to flesh out their military infrastructure, in spite of their difficulties.[27] Estimates put PLAF casualties in 1962 at over 30,000, yet registered an increase in the number of its main-force troops from 17,600 in June to 22,000 to 24,000 by the year's end. "This suggests either that the casualty figures are exaggerated or that the Viet Cong have a remarkable replacement capability—or both," concluded a CIA intelligence memorandum.[28] Substantial infiltration from North Vietnam, as well as local recruitment, helped to bolster the NLF's forces. A later U.S. report estimated that almost 13,000 personnel came south in 1962, among them leading cadres and military specialists; the infiltrators also brought with them heavier weapons to improve the PLAF's arsenal.[29]

The NLF leadership stressed that the key to the struggle was the defeat of the hamlet program, which was Diem's "last card." If the resistance could "oppose and destroy the strategic hamlets," one assessment argued, "then we shall have smashed up the entire program of the enemy's plots of aggression, and advanced forward the movement of the revolution."[30] The leadership disseminated broad guidelines on how to deal with strategic hamlets. First, the insurgents must orchestrate a "three-front attack" strategy, combining the three principal weapons in their arsenal: political struggle, armed struggle, and proselytization among RVN troops. Second, they should adopt a different mix of these tactics, depending on the balance of forces in any particular area and the extent of hamlet construction. Third, they must coordinate armed pressure from outside settlements with political mobilization of the population from the inside. Overall, the goal was to block new construction, sabotage the enemy's existing efforts, and gradually move toward the program's complete destruction.[31] Nguyen Van Vinh, the DRVN theoretician, claimed that, in the course of 1962, the NLF succeeded in destroying 320 strategic hamlets and preventing the Diem regime from repairing hundreds of others.[32]

At the end of 1962, the politburo in Hanoi argued that events had confirmed the underlying strength of the revolutionary movement, but the nature of the war demanded that even more attention be given to the armed struggle.[33] The revolution's leadership in the south proceeded to put flesh on these theoretical bones and devise an appropriate set of tactics. It was at this level of the struggle that the NLF proved why it held a decided edge over the Diem regime. The RVN's bureaucracy proved incapable of carrying out the demands of the Ngos, but the revolutionaries possessed an ideological and organizational framework that could translate broad directives into effective action. General Le Quoc San's account of the war in the Delta neatly illustrates the point.

San's command in the provinces to the west of Saigon had taken serious losses in 1962. The general concluded that the principal danger when engaged with the enemy was attempting to scatter and disperse, since this left PLAF troops vulnerable to their more mobile and well-armed foe. Instead, the guerrillas needed to stand their ground, adopting defensive techniques that would counter new allied tactics and equipment. San organized and trained his forces accordingly, and they rewarded his efforts with a spectacular victory in January 1963. At Ap Bac, about a dozen miles from the Dinh Tuong capital of My Tho, two PLAF battalions used entrenched positions in order to fight off a heavy assault, downing five helicopters in the process. MACV and the U.S. embassy downplayed the battle's broader significance. "Like any engagements in war," remarked General Harkins, "there are days—and there are days." The NLF regarded Ap Bac as a crucial event, however, for its forces had shown that they could win a pitched battle, in spite of their enemy's material advantages.[34]

General San believed that this proof of military success could have wider application, not only in defeating Saigon's forces but also destroying the hamlet program. Although strategic hamlets proved vulnerable, the guerrillas had still not found a formula for overcoming the entire scheme. They could penetrate many hamlets, often without firing a shot and frequently with the connivance of the local defenders; they could destroy fences and fortifications.[35] RVN reports also admitted that the authorities found it difficult to uncover communist cell structures inside settlements.[36] Yet strategic hamlets continued to impede the insurgents' access to the population, and Saigon continued to build them faster than the NLF could take them apart. Under the circumstances, San concluded, trying to defeat the program by destroying one hamlet at a time was futile. What the insurgents needed to do was to develop a more comprehensive strategy, based on the demonstrated effectiveness of their forces at Ap Bac. Defensive tactics designed to nullify the enemy's firepower could be used as the basis for a strategic counteroffensive against the hamlet program.

The PLAF, he argued, should fight back against RVN operations that supported strategic hamlet construction and seek to destroy the security framework that protected completed settlements. The guerrillas must strike at one location, draw out and defeat the enemy's reinforcing troops, and then pick off the isolated posts in an area. Then, as the RVN's local security structure collapsed, the population could be successfully mobilized to tear the hamlets apart from the inside. In sum, the hamlet system could be destroyed by the kind of coordinated effort and expanded armed struggle that Hanoi and the NLF leadership had called for in their assessments of the war. San's command launched the first major operation of this kind in three districts of Dinh Tuong in mid-July 1963. Over the course of several days, the guerrillas proceeded to paralyze local RVN forces and overran the military posts in the area. The campaign succeeded in liberating twelve villages and destroyed all of their strategic hamlets. The results and experiences of the operation were shared with other provinces, an example of the impressive learning process that characterized the NLF's organization.[37]

By early 1963, the NLF had begun to take the measure of strategic hamlets. After dipping in the second half of 1962, guerrilla activity started to rise in the spring of 1963, with the hamlet program singled out for special attention. In April, the insurgents launched a nationwide drive to emulate the victory at Ap Bac. They also expanded their main-force contingents as well as creating specialized support units that were equipped with heavy weapons like mortars, recoilless rifles, and antiaircraft guns. By the summer, their preparations had reached the point where they could make ambitious strikes against RVN security forces and belts of strategic hamlets. After mid-July, the insurgent incident rate increased by a third in comparison to the first half of the year and exceeded the average for 1962. Consequently, the PLAF hit the hamlet program even harder and with increasing success.[38] This counteroffensive coincided, moreover, with the political crisis that gripped South Vietnam in the second half of 1963. The ensuing turmoil badly damaged the RVN's war effort just at the moment when the guerrillas had begun to put it to its sternest test.

The events in Hue on May 8, 1963, when the regime's policing of a Buddhist demonstration left eight people dead, triggered a full-blown political crisis in South Vietnam. On the one hand, the incident brought to a boil the long-simmering tension between the Buddhist Church and the Ngo family over what many Vietnamese saw as the sectarian character of the Diem regime;[39] it also served as a lightning rod for all those discontented with the palace's incumbents. At the same time, the political unrest in South Vietnam led to a showdown between Saigon and Washington because the Americans demanded that the palace compromise with its domestic critics, which the Ngos steadfastly refused to do.[40]

Diem established the basic position that he took throughout the Buddhist crisis just a few days after the incident in Hue. In a cabinet meeting on May

13, he denied charges of sectarianism and argued that the NLF had a hand in the recent events.[41] In one fell swoop, he brushed aside Buddhist grievances and turned their protests into a communist assault on his government. This position was not one best suited to resolving the crisis peacefully. Nor, as the CIA reported, were some of the more militant Buddhist monks, such as Thich Tri Quang, interested in a peaceful resolution.[42] Their challenge to the regime's authority only served to encourage the Ngos' penchant for stubborn intransigence, especially that of Nhu and his wife, who opposed any compromise.[43]

U.S. demands to placate the Buddhists raised the palace's patriotic hackles and stiffened its resistance to compromise, although the Ngos recognized the dangers of defying their powerful patron. They knew that their domestic opponents would find succor from U.S. criticism of the regime and any signs of a weakening in Washington's support. In addition, they suspected that the Americans might not be averse to seeing a change of government in Saigon. Nguyen Dinh Thuan told the U.S. embassy on June 25 that Diem feared the Americans were trying to undermine him by insisting on concessions to the Buddhists and that the appointment of Henry Cabot Lodge as the new ambassador presaged a change in U.S. policy. "They can send ten Lodges," Thuan reported the president as saying, "but I will not permit myself or my country to be humiliated, not if they train their artillery on this Palace."[44]

Saigon's siege mentality deepened as the crisis unfolded. Diem charged "American services" with orchestrating the attacks against his regime by the Western press and simultaneously accused reporters of fomenting the Buddhist protests.[45] The palace fretted about U.S. contacts with the Buddhist opposition and deeply resented the Americans for giving sanctuary in their embassy to Thich Tri Quang.[46] In the meantime, U.S. pressure on the regime mounted, including demands that the Nhus withdraw from public life. The palace also knew that the Americans were in touch with coup groups plotting its downfall. In a meeting on August 29, Truong Cong Cuu, the RVN's acting foreign secretary, asked Ambassador Lodge to "cease the efforts of your CIA to make us a nation of 'boys.' " Four days later, an article in the *Times of Viet Nam,* probably written by Madame Nhu, publicly charged the CIA with trying to organize the government's overthrow.[47]

In response to these challenges, the palace stood its ground and looked for ways to maximize its room for maneuver. Nhu added a new twist to the old dispute over the issue of U.S. assistance, raising the possibility of an aid-without-strings policy "along the lines of the wartime Lend Lease program." This approach, he told U.S. officials, would not only give the recipient control over the use of aid but also absolve the United States of any moral responsibility for the uses to which it was put.[48] At the same time, Saigon initiated a belt-tightening campaign in case of a unilateral reduction in U.S. support. According to a CIA report, Nhu told an assembly of high-ranking ARVN officers in mid-August that American support for South Vietnam might soon come to an end because Washington had adopted a policy of appeasing the Soviet Union; he cited the Partial Test Ban Treaty as proof of this policy shift. Consequently, observed the counselor, the country needed to economize and conserve resources in order to be able to stand alone if necessary, something it was now in a better position to do as a result of the success of the Strategic Hamlet program.[49]

The Ngos may have entertained the even more radical possibility of reducing their dependence on the United States by seeking a rapprochement with Hanoi. This flirtation with the Vietnamese communists remains one of the most intriguing and murky episodes of this period. According to Frederick Nolting, the Americans had known for some time that Nhu was in contact with members of the NLF. In a meeting in the counselor's office in the spring of 1963, Nhu surprised the U.S. ambassador by stating that he met frequently with senior NLF cadres, with a view to encouraging their defection.[50] In the summer of 1963, however, Saigon was buzzing with rumors about contacts of an altogether more momentous nature: direct talks between North and South Vietnam aimed at settling the burgeoning conflict. The French president, Charles de Gaulle, fueled the speculation with a call in late August for the neutralization and eventual reunification of the two Vietnams.[51]

The substance and seriousness of these North-South contacts remains unclear. We do know that, from the spring of 1963, several foreign diplomats embarked on an earnest attempt to promote negotiations between Saigon and Hanoi. At the forefront of these efforts were Ramchundur Goburdhun, the Indian chair of the International Control Commission, and Roger Lalouette, the French ambassador to South Vietnam. They represented countries with a special interest in reconciling the two Vietnams, and both believed that the current situation presented an opportunity for an indigenous solution of the conflict. In their view, Saigon and Hanoi shared a mutual interest in seeking a diplomatic settlement: the Ngos chafed at the growing American presence in South Vietnam, while the Vietnamese communists naturally wanted to limit U.S. involvement there as well.[52]

To explore these mutual concerns, Goburdhun and Lalouette found a go-between in the figure of Mieczyslaw Maneli, the Polish delegate to the ICC, who met with DRVN leaders during visits to Hanoi in the spring and summer of 1963. During these encounters, the North Vietnamese informed the Pole that they were ready to institute trade and cultural exchanges across the Seventeenth Parallel. They also expressed a willingness to negotiate a political settlement with the Ngos, as long as this included the removal of the Americans; they even agreed that this could take the form of a federation rather than a coalition government, thus allowing Diem to remain at the helm in Saigon. "Everything is negotiable on the basis of the independence and sovereignty of Vietnam," Pham Van Dong told Maneli. "We have a sincere desire to end hostilities, to establish peace and unification on a completely realistic basis."[53]

It is not clear whether these tentative overtures blossomed into anything more substantive, and the available evidence tends to point in different directions. When Maneli met Nhu on September 2, the latter seemed amenable to contacts. "I am not against negotiations and cooperation with the North," Nhu explained. "Even during the most ferocious battle, the Vietnamese never forget who is a Vietnamese and who is a foreigner." Yet he denied that there were any direct talks already under way.[54] Indeed, Diem and Nhu seemed more interested in mending their fences with the Americans than abandoning the alliance, making several overtures to Ambassador Lodge in late October.[55] Still, rumors of peace talks persisted and, according to the testimony of Tran Van Dinh, the start of formal negotiations may have been imminent. Dinh, who was about to transfer from the RVN's embassy in Washington to its mission in India, met with Diem on October 29. The president stated that "new developments" required that Dinh proceed to New Delhi immediately in order to meet "the highest person" that Hanoi decided to send there for talks. This person was apparently Le Duc Tho, Henry Kissinger's nemesis during the later Paris peace negotiations, and talks were scheduled to begin on November 15. "While Hanoi wants a period of real nonalignment," Dinh recalled Diem as saying, "we can profit from it, too."[56]

If the extent of the palace's contacts with the communists remains shrouded in mystery, so too do the motives of the Ngos. Were they serious about some kind of rapprochement with the enemy, or just attempting to blackmail Washington into reaffirming its support for them? Given their anticommunist convictions, one might be skeptical of the notion that the Ngos seriously contemplated making a deal with Hanoi. They must also have realized that the communists would treat any agreement as a work in progress, not a lasting settlement. How, then, could Saigon afford to dispense with the help of its U.S. ally, which would be the price demanded by Hanoi for a deal? Whatever their long-term aspirations, the Ngos were not yet in a position to stand alone. Logic would suggest, therefore, that the palace was using the rumors of a peace agreement in order to encourage the Americans to reduce their pressure on the regime.[57] No doubt the Ngos also got some emotional satisfaction from threatening to ditch their ally, which was one of the few ways left to them of striking back at the Americans and asserting their independence.[58]

Blackmail may not have been their only motivation, however. Given the state of U.S.–Vietnamese relations in the second half of 1963, it is not beyond the bounds of possibility that the Ngos saw little alternative except to come to terms with Hanoi. Several historians have suggested that U.S. pressure and the threat of an American-backed coup might have convinced them that they had no choice but to wind up their alliance with Washington.[59] The summer and autumn crisis, moreover, came on the heels of the spring dispute over the U.S. advisory presence, which had revealed Saigon's dismay about developments in the patron–client relationship. With the Americans now pressuring the palace over the Buddhist issue, there seems little doubt that the Ngos feared they could no longer contain their ally's growing influence in South Vietnam. Diem expressed his exasperation in a conversation with Cao Van Luan in June. The Americans made incessant demands and would not listen to his requests, he complained; their only interest was in swamping South Vietnam with U.S. troops.[60] Hence, might the Ngos have preferred a compromise peace with Hanoi, however distasteful and transient, to what they deemed to be a bid by the Americans to take over the running of their country's affairs?

There is also a third possibility—namely that the Ngos were flirting with the communists not out of a sense of desperation but because they actually believed they were winning the war. In other words, they were not interested in any *compromise* settlement with Hanoi; they were looking toward a victor's peace and all the political benefits that would accrue from such a triumph. Although such reasoning seems far-fetched in the light of the NLF's advances in the countryside, the Ngos gave every indication of believing that, beyond the turbulent confines of the cities, the war for South Vietnam was going well. On August 30, Secretary Thuan, who was a reliable source of information on palace matters, told one U.S. official that Nhu thought the NLF had been "practically defeated" by strategic hamlets and this put South Vietnam "in a good bargaining position vis-à-vis the DRV." The counselor also expressed confidence about the progress of the war at a meeting with Ambassador Lodge several days later. He informed Lodge that insurgent forces were now "extremely discouraged and ready to give up"; they also felt that they "had been used and let down by North Vietnam." South Vietnam, Nhu concluded, was "now three months away from the end of the long and oppressive war against the Viet Cong."[61]

Nhu had long been convinced that there were fissures within the guerrilla movement, and between the NLF and Hanoi.[62] While the palace issued mixed signals regarding North-South contacts, he was forthright in claiming to be in touch with members of the NLF, with a view to exploiting these divisions. In an interview with a CIA source, probably John Richardson, the Saigon station chief, Nhu stated that his contacts were with the southern guerrillas, not North Vietnam. The regime's objective was to wean the NLF away from Hanoi and win the war, he argued; only from such a position of strength could there be realistic negotiations with the north.[63] According to Ambassador Lalouette, Diem also opposed a compromise settlement, preferring that any modus vivendi with the communists come about informally without the need for official talks.[64] In any case, the Ngos did not seem to believe that there would be a need for a compromise peace because they argued, as they had done at other times since 1954, that the emergence of a strong south would lead to the disintegration and peaceful absorption of the north. By defeating the NLF, Saigon would inflict a mortal wound on Hanoi, so that any accommodation would take place on the south's terms. As Nhu told his CIA contact, a peace settlement would be "within [the] framework of [a] strong [South Vietnam] seeking to incorporate North Vietnam within [the] free world order."[65]

Without further evidence, the precise purpose of the palace's flirtation with the communists is unclear. The Ngos "were carrying on such a complicated and many-sided game that one could not be certain about the direction in which they were heading," remarked Mieczyslaw Maneli. Given the volatile nature of the situation in the autumn of 1963, they were probably trying to keep their options open, simultaneously blackmailing their ally and enticing their enemy, playing for time and watching to see the turn of events.[66] What does seem clear from this otherwise murky episode is that, as a result of their conviction about the state of the conflict in the countryside, the Ngos believed they still held a strong political hand. Rather than recognize that the gathering guerrilla storm might be a prelude to disaster, they thought that victory was within sight, especially as a result of the Strategic Hamlet program. We will never know whether a more realistic view of events would have altered their behavior toward friends and enemies, but they were seemingly making policy during this period on the basis of a fundamentally flawed assessment of the state of the conflict.

In arriving at this view of the situation, the palace was well aware of some of the hamlet scheme's shortcomings, as was evident from Nhu's inquisitions at interministerial meetings; it was also well-informed about the NLF's vigorous response to the program. Yet the Ngos interpreted this information in the light of their stubbornly held beliefs about the nature of the conflict. Hence, they argued that NLF activity was a reaction to the regime's successes; the enemy was on the run, not running rampant. In this view, the insurgents were forming larger units and launching bigger operations because that was the only way they could survive, as strategic hamlets cut off their access to the population and RVN forces proceeded to hunt them down.[67] This was a pattern of events that the palace had predicted in its original conception of the hamlet program and one that others had anticipated as well.

For example, Robert Thompson argued in a series of generally upbeat analyses during the course of 1963 that increased NLF activity represented an entirely predictable response to the extension of government authority into areas that had once been guerrilla preserves.[68] In short, the Ngos expected, even welcomed, the intensification of the war in the countryside; they just did not understand that the NLF was actually taking the hamlet program apart.

Perhaps they had also invested too many hopes in the scheme to entertain doubts about its effectiveness; after all, this was their solution to the insurgency, the problems of nation building, and their troublesome relationship with the United States. Thus, there were powerful emotional and political incentives for the palace to view the state of the war through rose-colored glasses. Those who spoke with the Ngos in this period, both foreigners and Vietnamese, found them obsessed by the hamlet program and convinced of its success; they were, in fact, almost insensible on the subject. They were like hard-line communists who had come to believe that "the world was described by their slogans and clichés," Maneli observed. "When I listened to Diem's and Nhu's monologues about 'nationalist revolution,' the program of 'strategic hamlets,' a new national unity, it was as if I were reliving experiences in the Polish party."[69]

By this time, many U.S. officials shared the Pole's belief that the palace was out of touch with reality. For the Americans, it was bad enough that the Ngos never listened to good advice, let alone that they might start negotiating with the communists. A CIA memorandum of September 26 judged "the chances less than even that the GVN is now seriously interested in some form of rapprochement of lesser dimensions than reunification." Still, the memo noted, that calculation could change since the residents of the palace "may no longer be rational."[70] Ambassador Lodge certainly gave the impression that he considered the Ngos to be unbalanced. He put credence in rumors that Nhu was an opium addict and even that the regime planned to assassinate him as well as other senior U.S. personnel.[71] When the new ambassador presented his diplomatic credentials to the palace, he approached the event as if he were about to meet with a Mafia don rather than a friendly head of state. "Paul," he told General Harkins, "perhaps you better not come. If they try any funny business, it might be better if one of us were on the outside."[72]

Not only had some Americans lost faith in the sanity of the Ngos; they no longer even put credence in their own official claims about the war's progress. The embassy's John Mecklin told Lodge, shortly after the new ambassador's arrival, that "you will hear indignant contrary views, but my observation is that not only the newsmen here but also a good many Americans in relatively senior official positions believe very nearly nothing that any official U.S. Agency says about the situation in Vietnam."[73] Similarly, in Washington, the statistical drumbeat coming from the field—number of enemy dead, weapons captured, ARVN operations launched, etc.—could not hide the fact that the NLF appeared far from beaten. Colonel Francis Serong made a particularly strong impression on several officials, including Averell Harriman and William Bundy, during a trip to the United States in May. He argued that the hamlet program was badly overextended in places, advancing rapidly along communication axes but leaving crucial pockets of resistance in between. In other words, more—in this case, the increasing number of strategic hamlets— might not always be better.[74]

Two views of the conflict began to emerge in the second half of 1963, roughly dividing Americans in Saigon and Washington along civilian-military lines. For military officials, the statistical indicators for the hamlet program and the shooting war pointed to continued progress. On the civilian side, judgments about the political situation in urban areas and the lack of popular support in the countryside suggested that all, in fact, was not well.[75] This division brought about an important change in the tenor of policy debates in the autumn of 1963. For nearly eighteen months, the Pentagon had dominated policy making, and in the hustle and bustle that accompanied its efforts, the United States pushed to one side many of its long-standing political concerns about the Diem government. As a result, civilian critics of the regime had to bite their tongues, particularly since Secretary of State Rusk chose to defer to the new all-action agenda. Evidence that this military effort might be failing, however, loosened the Pentagon's stranglehold on policy and revitalized debate about the merits of the incumbent regime. The Buddhist crisis, moreover, injected overtly political concerns into that debate.

Civilian officials, such as Harriman, who had not been happy with Rusk's abdication of responsibility for Vietnam, took this opportunity to reassert their views.[76] The situation reawakened the dormant issue of Diem's leadership, which, in the period 1954–1955 and again in 1960–1961, had loomed large on the U.S. policy-making agenda. Indeed, the crisis did more than just cast renewed doubt on Diem's ability to pull the nation together over the long term; it also appeared to imperil the short-term prospects of holding off the insurgents. U.S. officials noted the widespread hostility toward the government that was evident in the size and frequency of public protests. If Diem continued to try to resolve the crisis by repressive methods, Roger Hilsman warned in early August, "it is quite possible that his popular support will be so reduced that he could no longer hope to defeat the Viet Cong."[77] In particular, officials worried that the regime's handling of the crisis would alienate the RVN's civilian bureaucracy and officer corps, upon which the prosecution of the war depended.[78]

At the same time, the crisis threatened to upset domestic support for Washington's foreign policy. While Vietnam was no longer back-page news by 1963, the Buddhist-led protests and their suppression turned the Diem regime's failings into a matter for widespread public debate.[79] The Buddhists were also much smarter at public relations than the palace, which became evident at the time of Thich Quang Duc's self-immolation on June 11. Malcolm Browne of the Associated Press received a tip-off from a prominent monk to attend the protest that culminated in the fiery suicide. Browne's photographs of the grisly affair became the most potent and lasting image of the crisis, even appearing in full-page advertisements in American newspapers condemning the Diem regime.[80] The Ngos fatally weakened their own cause with their response to events, notably Madame Nhu's callous dismissal of the suicides as "barbecues" and the regime's raids on Buddhist pagodas on the night of August 20–21. "The United States can get along with corrupt dictators who manage to stay out of the newspapers," Lodge later concluded of the regime's behavior. "But an inefficient Hitlerism, the leaders of which make fantastic statements to the press is the hardest thing on earth for the U.S. Government to support."[81]

In Washington, the State Department led the charge against Diem. As the crisis in South Vietnam deepened, officials at State sought to extend their critique beyond the specific grievances of the Buddhists to all of the regime's shortcomings. This list included old concerns, such as broadening the government politically and removing Nhu from office, and new ones, such as remedying problems with the hamlet program, extending the role of U.S. advisers in the countryside, and heading off the palace's contacts with North Vietnam.[82] Diem's chief critics at State were Averell Harriman, Roger Hilsman, and George Ball, who were joined by Michael Forrestal of the NSC staff. These anti-Diemists wanted to take a tough line with the regime; they also judged that the chances of a coup were at least even and argued that Washington should be prepared to consider Diem's replacement if a viable alternative presented itself.[83] In short, they were predisposed toward a change of government and even willing to lend a helping hand to push the teetering regime over the edge.

Their opportunity came a few days after Nhu ordered the raids on pagodas in Hue and Saigon. This was a clumsy attempt to settle the Buddhist crisis before Henry Cabot Lodge's arrival, and it convinced Diem's critics of the regime's bad faith and political ineptitude. On the morning of August 24, cables arrived in Washington from Saigon, reporting conversations with Secretary Thuan and Generals Le Van Kim and Tran Van Don. The Vietnamese described the situation as explosive and encouraged the United States to take action.[84] Since it was a Saturday, and most of the principal members of the administration were out of town, the anti-Diemists engaged in what Maxwell Taylor described as "an egregious 'end run,' " drafting a telegram and securing nominal concurrence for its dispatch to Saigon.[85] Cable 243 informed Lodge that "Diem must be given [a] chance to rid himself of Nhu and his coterie and replace them with [the] best military and political personalities available. If in spite of all your efforts, Diem remains obdurate and refuses, then we must face the possibility that Diem himself cannot be preserved." Lodge was also instructed to inform the ARVN generals of the U.S. position and explore "how we might bring about Diem's replacement if this should become necessary."[86]

Those policy makers cut out of the deliberations over cable 243 voiced their discontent at a White House meeting on the following Monday. The telegram exposed deep divisions between the anti-Diemists and other officials, such as McNamara and Taylor, who preferred to get Diem to make reforms and felt they were being bamboozled into backing a coup.[87] When an early coup failed to materialize in the wake of the cable's dispatch, Kennedy sent yet another fact-finding mission to Vietnam, this time led by McNamara and Taylor, in an attempt to reestablish a consensus within the administration. Following the McNamara-Taylor report of October 2, Washington settled on a series of selective aid cuts as well as an approach of not giving "active covert encouragement to a coup" but making an "urgent covert effort" to "build contacts with possible alternative leadership as and when it appears."[88] These were tortuous compromises, for the longer such policies were in force, the more likely they were to encourage instability and coup plotting. By the end of October, the administration's fragile consensus was clearly coming apart. William Bundy described the U.S. government in late 1963 as "more divided, more at sixes and sevens, than I can ever recall it."[89]

Political deadlock in Washington, however, did not stop events from moving forward in Saigon. The U.S. embassy's contacts with ARVN officers following the receipt of cable 243 clearly indicated to the generals that the United States no longer stood squarely behind Diem. The Kennedy administration's subsequent return to a policy of neither encouraging nor discouraging a coup could not put that particular genie back in the bottle. Given the clandestine nature of their enterprise, the South Vietnamese generals moved cautiously. Nevertheless, the direction of U.S. policy, especially the selective cuts in aid in October, encouraged their belief that the United States was prepared to condone the regime's overthrow.[90] The divisions in Washington, moreover, passed to the ambassador in Saigon the responsibility for translating the administration's indecision into concrete policy, and Henry Cabot Lodge seemed almost as anxious as the generals to rid the country of the Ngos.

When Lodge had arrived in Saigon in the wake of the August raids on the pagodas, he did not seem bent on promoting a coup. He expressed the need for caution in responding to the recent conversations with disgruntled RVN officials and later claimed that the receipt of cable 243, which represented a marked change in policy, surprised him. According to William Trueheart, however, the telegram was "not unwelcome" to the ambassador, who interpreted his orders in a typically creative fashion.[91] Quickly concluding that Diem could not be persuaded to dispense with Nhu's services, Lodge responded to the cable by proposing to "go straight to [the] Generals with our demands, without informing Diem. Would tell them we [are] prepared [to] have Diem without [the] Nhus but it is in effect up to them whether to keep him."[92]

As a Republican patrician, Lodge was not bound by the same constraints that might have inhibited a Democrat or a career diplomat. He adopted a freewheeling style of diplomacy, turning himself into a major player, not just a diplomatic conduit between the two countries. Egged on by the anti-Diemists in Washington, the new ambassador played a crucial role in fomenting a coup in Saigon.[93] Lodge displayed an unyielding hostility toward the palace, regularly describing the Ngos or their country as "medieval."[94] From August until November, he adopted a policy of silent disapproval, waiting for Diem to come to him rather than making the overtures. He poured cold water on the prospects for any meaningful reforms by the palace and ignored Washington's suggestions to see Diem by arguing that this would weaken his bargaining position. In the meantime, he assiduously cultivated contacts with the coup plotters through the CIA station in Saigon.[95] Lodge's approach was in stark contrast to that of his predecessor, who had always maintained close contact with the palace and sought to narrow U.S.–Vietnamese differences. Lodge played a very different role in late 1963, and it was a calculated, self-righteous, and, in the end, deadly performance.

The generals finally moved against the Ngos on November 1, in what proved to be a relatively bloodless affair. Its main victims were Captain Ho Tan Quyen, chief of naval operations, killed by one of his subordinates; Colonel Le Quang Tung, the special forces commander, executed after his surrender; and Diem and Nhu, of course, murdered in an armored personnel carrier en route to general staff headquarters on the morning after the coup. That there was no significant or prolonged fighting illustrated the extent of the palace's political isolation. As the Ngos desperately radioed for assistance on November 1, there was nobody out there except the unsympathetic and the hostile. "It wasn't a coup in the usual sense," commented Douglas Pike. "It was a collapse."[96]

There is little doubt that the political events in the second half of 1963 contributed to the deteriorating security situation, although U.S. assessments before the coup, especially military ones, tended to downplay the connection between the war and politics. General Krulak concluded after a trip to Vietnam in September that the battle was progressing well and the discipline of the armed forces was holding.[97] The State Department's Joseph Mendenhall, who accompanied Krulak on this visit, also reported that it was unclear whether the urban protests against the Diem regime had spread to the peasant population; he noted signs of rural Buddhist agitation only in the northern provinces of Quang Nam and Thua Thien.[98] Nevertheless, there was enough evidence in the reports of the period to suggest that the political crisis weakened the war effort in a number of ways, just at the moment when the insurgents were beginning to really test the regime's position in the countryside.

First, the crisis led to the gradual disintegration of the Diem regime. The palace lost key personnel during this period, such as Tran Kim Tuyen, exiled for political intrigue, and Vu Van Mau, who resigned in protest at the handling of the Buddhists. Nguyen Dinh Thuan, who had often served as a bridge between the Ngos and the Americans, stayed on but only out of fear; he informed Rufus Phillips that Nhu accused him of being a U.S. agent "and would certainly kill him if he tried to resign."[99] In general, an atmosphere of fear and anger pervaded the government's offices, especially in Saigon and other cities where many civil servants had family members who had suffered in the crackdown on the Buddhist-led protests. U.S. officials noted that their RVN counterparts were afraid to associate with them and many appeared to be "just going through the motions." Thuan told Mendenhall that he found the secretary for the economy "reading a detective story during office hours since the Ministry was not functioning." Things had reached the point, concluded the McNamara-Taylor report, "where it is uncertain that Diem can keep or enlist enough talent to run the war."[100]

The political crisis also resulted in a diversion of military resources, notably in the III Corps area around Saigon. This command, headed by the bombastic General Ton That Dinh, effectively became the "martial law corps," its attention focused primarily on events in the capital rather than the countryside. In August, for example, the PLAF succeeded in overrunning Ben Tuong, the flagship hamlet of Operation Sunrise, because Dinh had moved a unit protecting the area to participate in the suppression of the Buddhists.[101] Dinh's own interests were fixed firmly on the capital at this time, the general spending much of October there in the company of the other coup plotters. A U.S. adviser to the III Corps ran into him and General Tran Van Don at a Saigon restaurant in mid-October. Dinh, who was "obviously intoxicated," engaged the luckless adviser in a "somewhat incoherent" discussion, in which he explained that "he was without a doubt the greatest general officer in ARVN, the saviour of Saigon during the recent disturbance, and soon he would be the top military man in the country."[102] In the meantime, the NLF was systematically dismantling the III Corps' hamlet program.

General Dinh's incoherence and bravado offers a clue to some of the RVN's post-, as well as pre-, coup problems. The generals who orchestrated Diem's demise had been united by their ambitions and their distaste for the incumbent regime, but these qualities were not enough to put a listing ship of state back on an even keel after November 1. The new Military Revolutionary Council (MRC), chaired by General Duong Van Minh, began to flounder almost immediately. The generals were not politicians or administrators, nor did they have in hand a new political program to guide them. Minh's "only decisive act," William Colby noted derisively, "was to decide to kill Diem and Nhu." When the MRC did act decisively, its policies tended to backfire, notably its forthright attempts to purge the provinces of Diem's appointees, which paralyzed local administration and brought rural programs to a virtual standstill.[103]

This chaos was a serious blow to the hamlet program. The new government had initially been reluctant to endorse the scheme because of its association with the Ngos, but decided to proceed, as General Don explained, on the principle that they "had gone about the Strategic Hamlet program in the wrong way, even though the idea itself is excellent." In broad terms, Don's recipe for victory echoed that of the Ngos; the key was "winning the people's support, seducing them away from Communist influences, and enlisting their participation in a full-scale struggle." The MRC proposed a kinder, gentler version of the program, however, which would eliminate the coercive practices that had come to characterize the previous one.[104] On November 11, Saigon informed the provinces that it wished to continue strategic hamlets and would send detailed instructions of the new policy forthwith. Unfortunately, the MRC had only just completed these orders by the time General Nguyen Khanh overthrew it at the end of January 1964.[105] This new coup set back the war effort a second time. In the provinces, meanwhile, new hamlet construction ceased and existing settlements atrophied; in the absence of national direction, local officials, many of them new and inexperienced appointees, adopted a passive, wait-and-see approach.[106]

Whether they were conscious of it or not, the generals looked increasingly to the Americans to assist them with their problems. Indeed, from the outset, the MRC rejected the arm's-length approach to the alliance that had characterized the Diem regime; Minh even proposed to set up a U.S.–Vietnamese "brain trust" to guide the new government's efforts.[107] This receptivity began to look like helpless dependency, however, as the MRC continued to wallow in crisis. In turn, the United States felt bound to attempt to help sort out the mess left in the wake of the Diem regime's collapse. As William Bundy noted, America's role in the coup deepened its commitment to South Vietnam in a way that U.S. policy makers never anticipated. "The homespun analogy," he suggested, "is that of the parent who speaks up at PTA to oust an incompetent chairman; he or she cannot complain if the result is a job on the selection committee, or in the end as the new chairman."[108]

Diem's overthrow assumes an important place in the history of the Vietnam War because of its numerous consequences, including this deepening of America's involvement in the conflict. As a result, it has inevitably encouraged speculation about whether events might have turned out differently had the United States adopted an alternative policy in the second half of 1963 and not connived in a coup. A number of former U.S. and RVN officials have argued that the political turmoil in this period derailed the war effort, thus paving the way for the ill-fated Americanization of the conflict. While there were problems with strategic hamlets, they note, these were not insurmountable, but the Buddhist crisis and Diem's assassination dealt the program a fatal blow. "I believe to this day that this decision was one of the two most serious mistakes that the United States made in South Vietnam," observed John O'Donnell of the U.S. role in Diem's overthrow. "The other mistake was the introduction of American combat troops in 1965 and the subsequent Americanization of the war."[109]

During congressional hearings on the war in 1970, Daniel Ellsberg, the renegade Pentagon official, dismissed such arguments as a case of misplaced nostalgia. There were those, he noted sardonically, who suggested that "Diem would have won if only we had assassinated David Halberstam instead."[110] Ellsberg's skepticism seems well-founded, for although the insurgents experienced serious problems in the period 1962–1963, they had already begun to get the better of strategic hamlets before the Diem regime's political meltdown. Moreover, while U.S.–RVN forces might have responded more effectively to the guerrillas' counteroffensive if political events had not intervened, it is not clear that the insurgents could have been stopped from defeating the program. In short, the coup, and the crisis that preceded it, did affect the war effort, but whether their effect was decisive is another matter.

The Buddhist crisis actually appears to have been as much of a surprise to the communists as it was to Saigon and Washington, and they were slow to respond to the RVN's misfortunes.[111] It was not until late July that the NLF leadership began to issue instructions to its units to prepare to take advantage of the palace's plight and the likelihood of Diem's overthrow.[112] The guerrillas' burgeoning assault on strategic hamlets during the first few months of the political crisis seems to have been more a case of maintaining the momentum of the counteroffensive that was already under way, rather than a calculated attempt to put further pressure on Saigon.

NLF activity during this period was most pronounced in the vital Mekong Delta. The hamlet program was badly overextended there, and more aggressive PLAF tactics had begun to strip away the protective cover provided by RVN forces. Government troops could not be everywhere at once, nor did they dare to venture from their posts at night, just the time when the PLAF chose to operate. This left the defense of hamlets in the hands of the Self-Defense Corps and local militiamen, few of whom showed much stomach for a fight. As a result, the NLF could mobilize local residents to destroy strategic hamlets from the inside.[113] "The Viet Cong were invading in force," Rufus Phillips noted of their operations in Long An, "killing any hamlet defenders who opposed them, rousting the inhabitants from their homes, and making them take down and cut up the barbed-wire defenses and, in many cases, remove the corrugated metal roofs off their houses. This was happening in hamlet after hamlet." At a White House meeting on September 10, he described the war effort in the IV Corps as "going to pieces."[114]

While reports usually rated the situation as better in the rest of the country, the hamlet program was in some trouble in most areas. The U.S. consul in Hue, for example, reported that the formal expansion of the government's presence in the central and northern provinces did not necessarily denote real control. This problem became particularly clear after September when the ARVN Ninth Division moved to the Delta to bolster the IV Corps. In an oft-repeated pattern, once security forces left an area, the PLAF made a miraculous reappearance.[115] Support for the regime also appeared brittle among the Montagnards in highland areas. Even the Buon Enao experiment gradually fell apart after U.S. Special Forces began to turn the project over to Vietnamese control at the end of 1962. RVN heavy-handedness and ineptitude, together with careful guerrilla preparations, enabled the NLF to score some notable successes in penetrating hamlets in the area with the help of local inhabitants.[116]

What was most striking about the course of events in the summer and autumn of 1963 was the way in which the RVN's outwardly impressive security framework, the first line of defense for strategic hamlets, started to crumble under increased pressure from the insurgents. Government losses increased dramatically in 1963; they ran around two thousand per month by the end of the year, which approached the level claimed by the regime for the PLAF.[117] Unlike the guerrillas, however, government forces began to crack, especially the perennially unreliable Self-Defense Corps that bore the brunt of the fighting. In all, more than thirty-two thousand RVN troops deserted in 1963, about half of them from the SDC. In contrast, only around three thousand members of the NLF defected under the Diem regime's "Open Arms" program in 1963. Moreover, the defection rate tapered off after the summer and had slowed to a trickle by the end of the year. In short, as the war escalated, PLAF forces proved far more robust than their RVN counterparts.[118]

The rapid disintegration of the hamlet program following Diem's overthrow must be seen against this background and not simply as a consequence of the coup, although the insurgents did take full advantage of the ensuing chaos. PLAF units were ready for a coup and prepared to launch a new wave of attacks anyway if one did not materialize shortly. Hence, there was a dramatic surge in guerrilla activity in the week or so after Diem's demise. "It was something like a blind dog in a meat shop," reported General Harkins, "a bite here and a bite there."[119] MRC assessments of the impact on the hamlet program were sobering. With reports received from only half of the country's provinces, the number of hamlets attacked and damaged in the two weeks after the coup stood at 199. The NLF had virtually defeated the program in the III Corps, the new government concluded, as well as in large areas of the IV Corps.[120]

The collapse continued as the coup's initial shock proceeded to paralyze the RVN's political system. The process was well illustrated by events in Long An, the strategic gateway to the Delta. The war there had developed into a particularly fierce struggle in 1963. Because of the large size and intense activity of RVN forces, NLF plans and operations in Long An lagged somewhat behind those in neighboring provinces. As a result, the local insurgent leadership did not begin to plan an aggressive assault on the province's strategic hamlets until September. Meanwhile, it sought to beef up its military units, assisted by the arrival from the north of heavier weapons. When the offensive started in October, it coincided almost exactly with the coup and the chaos of the generals' new regime.[121] The guerrillas ran rampant in Long An, overrunning a military camp at Hiep Hoa, wrecking the RVN's security structure, and tearing apart the hamlet program. Two-thirds of the province's combat youth squads turned in their weapons, effectively announcing their withdrawal from the conflict. A U.S. report in December stated that no more than 35 of the 219 hamlets originally classed as completed could reasonably be considered effective. By the end of the year, observed General San, the NLF had smashed the program in Long An like a rotten egg.[122]

Perhaps another way to envision the collapse of strategic hamlets in Long An and elsewhere in South Vietnam is as a bursting dam. The hamlet program was a physically imposing structure, but one with weak foundations. Although it succeeded in 1962 in stemming the insurgents' advance, the buildup of guerrilla pressure from early 1963 placed enormous strain on that fragile base. In the summer and autumn, the Buddhist crisis and the November coup created fissures in the structure, and then the weight of NLF pressure brought

the entire edifice crashing down. Washed away in this collapse were the political ideas and aspirations of the Ngos as well as any foreseeable prospect of
there being a government in Saigon capable of controlling its own territory.
Bobbing amid the debris were American hopes of establishing a strong and
stable South Vietnam. It would soon dawn on U.S. policy makers that they
would have to launch a major rescue operation if they wanted to salvage anything from this wreckage.

"The psychology and outlook of the Ngo family were so completely alien to those of Washington," wrote David Halberstam, "that the alliance was almost doomed from the start." The Vietnamese and Americans "were talking about different problems, different beliefs, different worlds, and—despite their mutual fear of Communism—different enemies."[1] Even their one mutual interest turned into a running sore, for the growth and persistence of the insurgency exacerbated U.S.–Vietnamese differences as each partner insisted that its remedies for the RVN's difficulties represented the best solution. "In a sense," an official U.S. study later concluded, "Americans and Vietnamese were traveling in the same vehicle, but there was often considerable disagreement as to who was driving, what the destination was, and what route should be taken to get there. We were uncertain allies engaged in a joint but not common enterprise."[2]

Saigon and Washington clashed over the question of how to build a modern nation and simultaneously overcome the communist threat to South Vietnam. While the Americans sought to press their policy prescriptions on the palace, the Ngos possessed their own ideas about what constituted the best way forward. They resented U.S. pressure and regarded American advice as unsuitable for a newly independent, badly underdeveloped country, especially one at war. Indeed, they came to believe that the Americans represented almost as much of a threat to their Personalist revolution as the communists. Although they acknowledged the need for U.S. support in the short term, they argued that dependence on the Americans would stymie South Vietnam's development over the long run. To defeat their enemies—"Communism, Underdevelopment, and Disunity"—the Ngos believed that they had to mobilize the indigenous resources of the country and reduce South Vietnam's reliance on the United States.

In light of the palace's concerns, we need to revise the current image of Diem. In doing so, we get a much better sense of the dynamics of the conflict in Vietnam, as well as the sources of the tensions that plagued Washington's relations with Saigon. Diem was certainly no tool of the Americans, as communist propaganda asserted, but neither was he the "Last Confucian," the backward-looking mandarin who appears in the pages of most Western accounts of the war. Historians have tended to infer from their eventual triumph that the communists were the only contenders for the mantle of Vietnamese leadership with a discernibly forward-looking political agenda. Yet the Ngos clearly presented their own vision of a postcolonial state, giving expression to a noncommunist strain of modern Vietnamese nationalism that had stood in opposition to that of the communists since the 1920s. Diem did express "something real in Vietnamese history," observed Ken Post, "more so than any other regime in the South until 1975." His problem was that he could develop "no real social base" to sustain that vision.[3]

Given this latter failing, we can also gain a much better understanding of the evolution and outcome of the Vietnamese conflict by reexamining the Diem regime. As the history of its nation-building programs demonstrates, the palace ran into serious difficulties in attempting to promote its noncommunist revolution. The Ngos underestimated the task of mobilizing the rural population, their guiding philosophy of Personalism was vague and confusing, and the poor quality of the RVN's administrative apparatus exacerbated all of these other shortcomings. As a result, the Diem regime could not compete either ideologically or organizationally with its communist opponents. The latter, moreover, were not only more skilled and experienced in the business of political mobilization but also actively engaged in exploiting Saigon's weaknesses. Diem's government "probably was no worse than those of some other new Southeast Asian states emerging from colonialism," noted John Donnell, but it "was up against the particularly difficult challenge of an insurgent rival in the NLF which deliberately and systemically struggled to overload, erode and cripple it."[4]

Diem's inability to build a nation south of the Seventeenth Parallel put him on a collision course with American policy in Vietnam. In 1954–1955, the United States had swung into support of his fledgling regime in the hope that Diem would be able to establish a viable anticommunist state in the south. To assist him, Washington developed an advisory relationship, in which the Americans provided advice and support to Saigon but avoided colonial-style control. The course of events, however, constantly revealed the limits of this arm's-length relationship, for Diem neither listened to American advice nor proved capable of solving the RVN's problems. In response, U.S. officials sought to persuade, pressure, or bypass the palace in order to promote their own preferred policies; the more the goal of an anticommunist South Vietnam seemed in jeopardy, the more the United States sought to impose its policy agenda on Saigon. Ultimately, the Americans assumed the role of kingmaker in November 1963 in an attempt to find a more responsive and reliable client that would follow the U.S. recipe for nation building.

This step proved to be a most dangerous one because it was taken without devoting much attention to the question of what the United States would do if Diem's successors proved to be as uncooperative or ineffective as the Ngos. In a television interview on September 2, 1963, John Kennedy had told CBS correspondent Walter Cronkite that the United States could provide advice and support, but it was up to the South Vietnamese, not the Americans, to win or lose the war; however, he also informed the newsman that it would be a great mistake to withdraw from the conflict.[5] "What Kennedy never resolved," commented one historian, "because his administration was not forced to do so—was the U.S. response in the eventuality that the South Vietnamese could not win militarily on their own."[6] After all, while some of Diem's weaknesses were unique to his government, others were of a more general nature, notably the superior skills and appeal of the communist insurgents. Saigon's failings, especially some of the problems encountered in implementing the Strategic Hamlet program, offered plenty of evidence of the difficulties that any RVN government would face in establishing a secure and stable South Vietnam.

Rather than see these difficulties as deep-rooted, and perhaps insoluble, however, U.S. officials assumed that they could be overcome by continued American advice and an appropriate change of leadership at the top. From this perspective, the trouble with Diem was that he had carried out policies according to his own, rather than a U.S., design. Thus, the solution for Saigon's failings was to find the right sort of Vietnamese leaders who would implement the American blueprint.[7] The problem with this approach was that of finding the "right" Vietnamese, because Diem's demise replaced "bad leadership by no leadership at all."[8] The Diem government looked like a model of order and stability compared with the floundering, revolving-door regimes that followed in the period 1964–1965. In the absence of a functioning South Vietnamese government, Lyndon Johnson was forced to confront the eventuality that his predecessor had not: the prospect of the south's collapse without a dramatic increase in the U.S. commitment. Johnson's response was to send five hundred thousand U.S. troops to South Vietnam, in an attempt to overcome Saigon's political weaknesses by overwhelming the enemy militarily.

This move exposed the neocolonialism that never lay very far from the surface of the U.S. approach to the patron–client relationship with South Vietnam. If the American tendency to take charge had been kept in check for much of the Diem period, it burst forth in response to the political vacuum in Saigon. With the deployment of U.S. combat forces, the Americans elbowed the South Vietnamese out of the way and effectively took over the running of the war. Yet, in the process of trying to save the country from imminent defeat, the U.S. escalation of the conflict also undermined the long-term goal of American policy: the creation of a viable South Vietnam that would be capable one day of standing on its own two feet without the need for outside support. The expanded U.S. presence after 1965 undermined the political credibility of the Saigon government as well as encouraging a physically and morally corrosive reliance on American aid.[9] These dangers, of course, had been well understood by the Ngos. Whatever their other political failings, they had clearly recognized the neocolonial potential of the patron–client relationship and the problem of South Vietnam's dependence on the United States.

William Colby, who viewed LBJ's big-unit war as a big mistake, later contended that the United States should have stuck with Diem and the advisory relationship, come what may. He argued that the success of pacification and development programs in the period 1969–1972 demonstrated that U.S. advice and support to Saigon, rather than the use of raw firepower, could work and was the best way to lay the basis for a viable South Vietnam. It was "a chilling indictment of the lost years of the middle sixties," Colby noted, that U.S.–Vietnamese efforts at nation building after 1968—under the slogan "Local Self-Defense, Local Self-Government, and Local Self-Development"—bore a striking resemblance to the concerns of the earlier Strategic Hamlet program. "And in the worst case," he concluded, "if Diem had remained in office but fallen to the people's war of Ho Chi Minh in 1965, Vietnam, the United States, and the world as a whole would have suffered less in all ways than by postponing the event to Thieu's fall in 1975."[10]

Such what-ifs abound in discussions of the Vietnam War, but we need not stray too far into the realm of conjecture to appreciate that Diem's demise represented a critical turning point in the conflict. His overthrow brought to an end a nine-year effort to promote a noncommunist, and specifically Vietnamese, solution to the problem of nation building, thereby keeping Saigon's superpower patron at arm's length. With hindsight, it also presaged the failure of the U.S. policy of trying to save South Vietnam by providing advice and support to an indigenous client, rather than by the force of American arms. The chaos that followed the November 1963 coup sucked the Americans deeper and deeper into a political quagmire, foreshadowing the deployment of U.S. combat troops that would totally change the dimensions of the conflict and the scale of the destruction in Vietnam.

Notes

Introduction

1. Saigon to State, October 28, 1963, *Foreign Relations of the United States, 1961–1963,* vol. 4, *Vietnam* (Washington, D.C.: GPO, 1991), 442–46.

2. Ellen J. Hammer, *A Death in November: America in Vietnam, 1963* (New York: E. P. Dutton, 1987), 268; Saigon to State, October 28, 1963, *FRUS, 1961–1963,* vol. 4, 441–42; October 28, 1963, ibid., 442–46.

3. Denis Warner, *The Last Confucian: Vietnam, South-East Asia, and the West* (Harmondsworth, Middlesex: Penguin Books, 1964).

4. George C. Herring, "'Peoples Quite Apart': Americans, South Vietnamese, and the War in Vietnam," *Diplomatic History* (winter 1990): 1.

5. David Kaiser, *American Tragedy: Kennedy, Johnson, and the Origins of the Vietnam War* (Cambridge, Mass.: Belknap Press, 2000).

6. Huynh Kim Khanh, "The Making and Unmaking of 'Free Vietnam,'" *Pacific Affairs* (fall 1987): 474.

7. William J. Duiker, *The Communist Road to Power in Vietnam,* 2d ed. (Boulder, Colo.: Westview Press, 1996).

8. David Halberstam, *The Making of a Quagmire* (New York: Random House, 1965); Joseph Buttinger, *Vietnam: A Dragon Embattled,* vol. 2 (New York: Frederick A. Praeger, 1967); Frances FitzGerald, *Fire in the Lake: The Vietnamese and the Americans in Vietnam* (New York: Vintage Books, 1973); Stanley Karnow, *Vietnam: A History* (New York: Viking Press, 1983). For the popularity and influence of such accounts, see Sandra C. Taylor, "Reporting History: Journalists and the Vietnam War," *Reviews in American History* (September 1985): 451–61.

9. Robert Buzzanco, *Masters of War: Military Dissent and Politics in the Vietnam Era* (Cambridge: Cambridge University Press, 1997), 65.

10. Bernard B. Fall, *The Two Viet-Nams: A Political and Military Analysis,* 2d rev. ed. (New York: Frederick A. Praeger, 1967), 235.

1. A Shotgun Wedding

1. For secondary accounts, see David L. Anderson, *Trapped by Success: The Eisenhower Administration and Vietnam, 1953–1961* (New York: Columbia University Press,

1991); Lloyd C. Gardner, *Approaching Vietnam: From World War II through Dienbi-enphu, 1941–1954* (New York: W. W. Norton, 1988).

2. In the absence of a scholarly biography, the details of Diem's life remain patchy. The following paragraphs draw on Joseph Buttinger, *Vietnam: A Dragon Embattled*, vol. 2 (New York: Frederick A. Praeger, 1967), 1253–57; Bernard B. Fall, *The Two Viet-Nams: A Political and Military Analysis*, 2d rev. ed. (New York: Frederick A. Praeger, 1967), 234–45; Robert Shaplen, *The Lost Revolution: The U.S. in Vietnam, 1946–1966*, rev. ed. (New York: Harper & Row, 1966), 100–113; Denis Warner, *The Last Confucian: Vietnam, South-East Asia, and the West* (Harmondsworth, Middlesex: Penguin Books, 1964), 84–92.

3. Bruce McFarland Lockhart, *The End of the Vietnamese Monarchy* (New Haven: Yale Center for International and Area Studies, 1993), 59–92; Philippe Devillers, *Histoire du Viêt-Nam de 1940 à 1952*, 3d rev. et corr. (Paris: Editions du Seuil, n.d.), 61–64; Bao Dai, *Le Dragon D'Annam* (Paris: Plon, 1980), 57–61.

4. Stein Tønnesson, *The Vietnamese Revolution of 1945: Roosevelt, Ho Chi Minh, and de Gaulle in a World at War* (Oslo: International Peace Research Institute, 1991), 284–85; Masaya Shiraishi, "The Background to the Formation of the Tran Trong Kim Cabinet in April 1945: Japanese Plans for Governing Vietnam," in *Indochina in the 1940s and 1950s*, vol. 2, ed. Masaya Shiraishi and Motoo Furuta (Ithaca, N.Y.: Cornell University Southeast Asia Program, 1992), 113–41.

5. Diem told a number of people, including Ellen Hammer and Robert Shaplen, of an encounter with Ho at which he rejected the latter's overtures; the authenticity of the meeting, however, has been questioned by at least one commentator (Buttinger, vol. 1, 647).

6. Ellen J. Hammer, *The Struggle for Indochina, 1940–1955: Viet Nam and the French Experience* (Stanford: Stanford University Press, 1966), 203–45.

7. Memorandum of Conversation, May 7, 1953, *Foreign Relations of the United States, 1952–1954*, vol. 13, *Indochina*, pt. 1 (Washington, D.C.: GPO, 1982), 553–54.

8. Joseph G. Morgan, *The Vietnam Lobby: The American Friends of Vietnam, 1955–1975* (Chapel Hill: University of North Carolina Press, 1997), 2–14. For Diem's views at the time, see Memorandum of Conversation, May 7, 1953, *FRUS, 1952–1954*, vol. 13, 1, 553–54; Talk by Mr. Ngo Dinh Diem before Southeast Asia Seminar, Cornell University, February 20, 1953, Echols Collection, Cornell University Library; Indochina (enclosed in Douglas to Fisher, June 1953), Indo-China, Misc. Corres., Foreign Countries, Box 1717, William O. Douglas Papers, Library of Congress Manuscript Division; French Indo China as of the end of July 1953, Indo-China, Misc. Corres., Foreign Countries, Box 1717, ibid.; Diem to Douglas, November 19, 1953, Vietnam—Misc. Corres., Foreign Countries, Box 1731, ibid.

9. Anderson, 52–56; Morgan, 9–11; Cao Van Luan, *Ben Giong Lich Su, 1940–1965* (Saigon: Tri Dung, 1972), 246–50.

10. U.S. Del. to State, May 16, 1954, *Foreign Relations of the United States, 1952–1954*, vol. 16, *The Geneva Conference* (Washington, D.C.: GPO, 1981), 823–24;

May 17, 1954, ibid., 829–30; Memorandum of Conversation, May 18, 1954, ibid., 843–46; Bonsal to Smith, May 19, 1954, ibid., 848–49; Memorandum of Conversation, May 20, 1954, ibid., 859–62.

11. Saigon to State, January 30, 1952, *FRUS, 1952–1954,* vol. 13, 1, 22; June 1, 1952, ibid., 167; French Indo China as of the end of July 1953, Indo-China, Misc. Corres., Foreign Countries, Box 1717, Douglas Papers, LOCMD; Luan, 168–69, 210, 226.

12. Declaration of President Ngo-Dinh-Diem, June 18, 1954, Vietnam—Misc. Corres., Foreign Countries, Box 1731, Douglas Papers, LOCMD; Call to the People of President Ngo-Dinh-Diem, June 25, 1954, ibid.

13. State to U.S. Del., May 22, 1954, *FRUS, 1952–1954,* vol. 16, 892–94.

14. Memorandum of Conversation, May 22, 1954, ibid., 894–95; U.S. Del. to State, May 26, 1954, ibid., 936–37.

15. Memorandum of Conversation, May 18, 1954, ibid., 843–46; Paris to State, May 24, 1954, *FRUS, 1952–1954,* vol. 13, 2, 1608–9; May 26, 1954, ibid., 1614–15; June 15, 1954, ibid., 1695–96.

16. Paris to State, May 24, 1954, ibid., 1609; Saigon to State, June 11, 1954, ibid., 1681; July 23, 1954, ibid., 1873.

17. George McT. Kahin, *Intervention: How America Became Involved in Vietnam* (New York: Alfred A. Knopf, 1986), 81–82; State to Paris, September 28, 1954, *FRUS, 1952–1954,* vol. 13, 2, 2083; Robertson to Dulles, October 25, 1954, ibid., 2182–83; Paris to State, November 10, 1954, ibid., 2235–36; State to Paris, November 10, 1954, ibid., 2237.

18. Saigon to State, November 13, 1953, *FRUS 1952–1954,* vol. 13, 1, 862; Paris to State, May 24, 1954, *FRUS, 1952–1954,* vol. 13, 2, 1609; Saigon to State, July 4, 1954, ibid., 1783–84.

19. Edward Geary Lansdale, *In the Midst of Wars: An American's Mission to Southeast Asia* (New York: Harper & Row, 1972), 126–31, 154–59.

20. Robert Shaplen, "A Reporter in Vietnam," *The New Yorker,* September 22, 1962, 120.

21. Bernard B. Fall, "The Political-Religious Sects of Viet-Nam," *Pacific Affairs* (September 1955): 235–53.

22. Ronald H. Spector, *Advice and Support: The Early Years of the United States Army in Vietnam, 1941–1960* (New York: Free Press, 1985), 232–37.

23. Fishel to Weidner, August 25, 1954, Correspondence, Weidner, Edward W., 1954, Folder 101, M.S.U. Administration of the Project, Box 628, Vietnam Project, Michigan State University Archives and Historical Collections.

24. Saigon to State, July 16, 1954, *FRUS, 1952–1954,* vol. 13, 2, 1843; October 13, 1954, ibid., 2138. See also Neil L. Jamieson, *Understanding Vietnam* (Berkeley: University of California Press, 1995), 234–38.

25. Saigon to State, October 13, 1954, *FRUS, 1952–1954,* vol. 13, 2, 2138; October 22, 1954, ibid., 2151–53; November 7, 1954, ibid., 2221.

26. J. Lawton Collins, *Lightning Joe: An Autobiography* (Novato, Calif.: Presidio Press, 1994), 378–411; Memorandum of Discussion, January 27, 1955, *Foreign Relations of the United States, 1955–1957,* vol. 1, *Vietnam* (Washington, D.C.: GPO, 1985), 63–66; Saigon to State, March 31, 1955, ibid., 168–71; April 5, 1955, ibid., 205–8; April 7, 1955, ibid., 218–21.

27. State to Saigon, November 24, 1954, *FRUS, 1952–1954,* vol. 13, 2, 2303–4; Paris to State, December 19, 1954, ibid., 2401–4; State to Saigon, April 1, 1955, *FRUS, 1955–1957,* vol. 1, 179; April 4, 1955, ibid.,196–97; April 9, 1955, ibid., 229–31; April 16, 1955, ibid., 250–51; Dulles to Collins, April 20, 1955, ibid., 270–72.

28. Memorandum of Discussion, April 28, 1955, ibid., 307–12; Young to Robertson, April 30, 1955, ibid., 337–39.

29. Kahin, *Intervention,* 84; John Osborne, "The Tough Miracle Man of Asia," *Life,* May 13, 1957, 156–76.

30. State to Saigon, April 4, 1955, *FRUS, 1955–1957,* vol. 1, 196; May 1, 1955, ibid., 344–45.

31. Kahin, 92.

32. Eisenhower to Diem, October 25, 1954, *Public Papers of the Presidents of the United States: Dwight D. Eisenhower, 1954* (Washington, D.C.: GPO, 1960), 948–49.

33. Gardner, *Approaching Vietnam,* 342–43. See also Dulles to Collins, April 20, 1955, *FRUS, 1955-1957,* vol. 1, 271.

34. Henry Cabot Lodge, Oral History, 9–10, John F. Kennedy Library.

35. For analyses of the aid/intervention issue, see David A. Baldwin, "Foreign Aid, Intervention, and Influence," *World Politics* (April 1969): 425–47; Patrick Lloyd Hatcher, *The Suicide of an Elite: American Internationalists and Vietnam* (Stanford: Stanford University Press, 1990); Douglas J. Macdonald, *Adventures in Chaos: American Intervention for Reform in the Third World* (Cambridge: Harvard University Press, 1992).

36. Roy Jumper, "Problems of Public Administration in South Viet Nam," *Far Eastern Survey* (December 1957): 183; Nguyen Thai, *Is South Vietnam Viable?* (Manila: Carmelo & Bauermann, 1962), 15–16.

37. Saigon to State, July 30, 1956, 751G.03/7-3056, Central Decimal File 1955–1959, Record Group 59, U.S. National Archives. See also Jumper, 184–85; Fall, *The Two Viet-Nams,* 2d rev. ed., 259–68; J. A. C. Grant, "The Viet Nam Constitution of 1956," *American Political Science Review* (June 1958): 437–62.

38. Saigon to State, March 23, 1956, *FRUS, 1955–1957,* vol. 1, 662–66; April 16, 1956, 751G.00/4-1656, CDF 55-59, RG 59, USNA.

39. Saigon to State, August 28, 1959, *Foreign Relations of the United States, 1958–1960,* vol. 1, *Vietnam* (Washington, D.C.: GPO, 1986), 227–29; August 31, 1959, ibid., 229–30; September 2, 1959, ibid., 230–33. See also Thai, 138–45; Robert Scigliano, *South Vietnam: Nation under Stress* (Boston: Houghton Mifflin, 1964), 91–98; Nguyen Tuyet Mai, "Electioneering: Vietnamese Style," *Asian Survey* (November 1962): 11–18.

40. Scigliano, 39–46.

41. Ibid., 31–33; Thai, 64–70; Buttinger, *Vietnam*, vol. 2, 945–46; Saigon to State, November 6, 1956, 751G.022/11-656, CDF 55-59, RG 59, USNA.

42. John L. Sorenson and David K. Pack, *Unconventional Warfare and the Vietnamese Society* (China Lake, Calif.: U.S. Naval Ordnance Test Station, 1964), 79–80; Nicolaas Godfried Maria Luykx II, "Some Comparative Aspects of Rural Public Institutions in Thailand, the Philippines, and Viet-Nam" (Ph.D. diss., Cornell University, 1962), 810–13; John D. Donoghue, *My Thuan: A Mekong Delta Village in South Vietnam* (n.p.: MSU Viet Nam Advisory Group, 1961), 60–62.

43. Sorenson and Pack, 94–95; Luykx II, 798–810; Saigon to State, February 6, 1956, 751G.00/2-656, CDF 55-59, RG 59, USNA; July 23, 1956, 751G.00/7-2356, ibid.; July 30, 1956, 751G.00/7-3056, ibid.; Hue to State, October 4, 1957, 751G.00/10-457, ibid.; Saigon to State, February 28, 1958, 751G.00/2-2858, ibid.; Hue to State, March 19, 1958, 751G.00/3-1958, ibid.

44. Hue to State, March 19, 1958, 751G.00/3-1958, ibid.; Saigon to State, March 2, 1959, *FRUS, 1958–1960*, vol. 1, 144–70. See also Chu Bang Linh, *Dang Can Lao* (San Diego: Me Viet Nam, 1993).

45. Thai, 120.

46. Wesley R. Fishel, "Vietnam: Is Victory Possible?" *Foreign Policy Association*, Headline Series, February 1964, 21; Roy Jumper, "Mandarin Bureaucracy and Politics in South Viet Nam," *Pacific Affairs* (March 1957): 51, 55.

47. David G. Marr, *Vietnam 1945: The Quest for Power* (Berkeley: University of California Press, 1995), 445–46, 452–53.

48. Thai, *Is South Vietnam Viable?* 222–24; Warner, *The Last Confucian*, 120.

49. Thai, 218–22; Fishel, 19.

50. Sorenson and Pack, 96–97, identified Can's authority as covering only the central lowlands; the Hue consulate noted that his control also extended to the Central Highlands (*FRUS, 1958–1960*, vol. 1, 248–49).

51. Letter from Do Mau, December 7, 1995; Nguyen Tran, *Cong Va Toi: Nhung Su That Lich Su* (Los Alamitos, Calif.: Xuan Thu, 1992), 343–45; Luan, *Ben Giong Lich Su*, 181–83; Thai, 211–18; Fishel to Collins, March 7, 1955, *FRUS, 1955–1957*, vol. 1, 111–12; Hue to State, February 25, 1958, *FRUS, 1958–1960*, vol. 1, 17–20; November 19, 1959, ibid., 246–50.

52. Tran, 343-44; Luan, 181–89, 229–31; Saigon to State, August 30, 1955, 751G.00/8-3055, CDF 55-59, RG 59, USNA; Hue to State, October 4, 1957, 751G.00/10-457, ibid.; Saigon to State, February 28, 1958, 751G.00/2-2858, ibid.; Hue to State, March 19, 1958, 751G.00/3-1958, ibid.

53. Thai, 216–17; Tran Van Don, *Our Endless War: Inside Vietnam* (San Rafael, Calif.: Presidio Press, 1978), 52; Hoang Lac, "Blind Design," in *Prelude to Tragedy: Vietnam, 1960–1965*, ed. Harvey Neese and John O'Donnell (Annapolis: Naval Institute Press, 2001), 66; letter from Do Mau, December 7, 1995; Saigon to State, March 2, 1959, *FRUS, 1958–1960*, vol. 1, 145–56, 164–69.

54. Saigon to State, June 29, 1954, *FRUS, 1952–1954*, vol. 13, 2, 1762.

55. John C. Donnell, "Politics in South Vietnam: Doctrines of Authority in Conflict" (Ph.D. diss., University of California, Berkeley, 1964), 95–98; Buttinger, *Vietnam*, vol. 2, 785–87, 849–50, 1241; Luan, 229–30; Thai, 196–201; Saigon to State, March 2, 1959, *FRUS, 1958–1960*, vol. 1, 148–49. Diem was not entirely star-struck by his brother (see *FRUS, 1955–1957*, vol. 1, 111, 145).

56. Thai, 110–12, 202–9; Fishel, 16–17; Shaplen, *The Lost Revolution*, 106; Saigon to State, March 2, 1959, *FRUS, 1958–1960*, vol. 1, 152–53.

57. Shaplen, "A Reporter in Vietnam," 103–4.

58. Saigon to State, March 14, 1957, 851G.424/3-1457, CDF 55-59, RG 59, USNA; April 10, 1958, 851G.424/4-1058, ibid.; March 28, 1959, 851G.425/3-2859, ibid.

59. Thai, *Is South Vietnam Viable?* 178–95; John Mecklin, *Mission in Torment: An Intimate Account of the U.S. Role in Vietnam* (Garden City, N.Y.: Doubleday, 1965), 51; David Halberstam, *The Making of a Quagmire* (New York: Random House, 1965), 53–56; Buttinger, vol. 2, 956–58; Warner, *The Last Confucian*, 117–19; Don, 54–56; Mai, "Electioneering: Vietnamese Style," 11–18.

60. Halberstam, 53–54.

61. Thai, 125, 193; Mecklin, 49.

62. Buttinger, vol. 2, 956–57.

63. Paris to State, May 11, 1955, *FRUS, 1955–1957*, vol. 1, 397–98; Dulles to State, May 12, 1955, ibid., 400; May 13, 1955, ibid., 406–7.

64. Macdonald, *Adventures in Chaos*, 29–43.

65. State to Saigon, October 6, 1955, *FRUS, 1955–1957*, vol. 1, 559; Lansdale, *In the Midst of Wars*, 339–45; Anderson, *Trapped by Success*, 133. See also Young to Reinhardt, October 5, 1955, *FRUS, 1955–1957*, vol. 1, 552–53; Saigon to State, December 6, 1955, 751G.00/12-655, CDF 55-59, RG 59, USNA; December 7, 1959, *FRUS, 1958–1960*, vol. 1, 269.

66. Saigon to State, September 16, 1960, ibid., 579; December 4, 1960, ibid., 711; December 24, 1960, ibid., 744.

67. Arthur M. Schlesinger, Jr., *A Thousand Days: John F. Kennedy in the White House* (Boston: Houghton Mifflin, 1965), 543; Mark Philip Bradley, *Imagining Vietnam and America: The Making of Postcolonial Vietnam, 1919–1950* (Chapel Hill: University of North Carolina Press, 2000).

68. Scott L. Bills, *Empire and Cold War: The Roots of Third World Antagonism, 1945–47* (Basingstoke: Macmillan Education, 1990), 208–9; Michael H. Hunt, *The Making of a Special Relationship: The United States and China to 1914* (New York: Columbia University Press, 1983), 307.

69. Rostow to Kennedy, May 10, 1961, *Foreign Relations of the United States, 1961–1963*, vol. 1, *Vietnam* (Washington, D.C.: GPO, 1988), 131.

70. Lansdale, ix.

71. Stephen E. Ambrose, *Rise to Globalism: American Foreign Policy Since 1938*, 4th rev. ed. (New York: Viking Penguin, 1985), xviii.

72. Robert A. Packenham, *Liberal America and the Third World: Political Develop-*

ment Ideas in Foreign Aid and Social Science (Princeton: Princeton University Press, 1973); Michael E. Latham, *Modernization as Ideology: American Social Science and "Nation Building" in the Kennedy Era* (Chapel Hill: University of North Carolina Press, 2000).

73. Godfrey Hodgson, *The Gentleman from New York, Daniel Patrick Moynihan: A Biography* (Boston: Houghton Mifflin, 2000), 12.

74. W. W. Rostow, "Guerrilla Warfare in Underdeveloped Areas," in *The Guerrilla—And How to Fight Him*, ed. T. N. Greene (New York: Frederick A. Praeger, 1962), 54–61. See also Packenham, 61–63, 242–86; Latham, 3–8, 44–68.

75. Tony Smith, *America's Mission: The United States and the Worldwide Struggle for Democracy in the Twentieth Century* (Princeton: Princeton University Press, 1995), 179–84; Macdonald, *Adventures in Chaos*, 11–28; Packenham, 161–66.

76. Schlesinger, Jr., 769.

77. Macdonald, 270–72; Packenham, 109–10; Hatcher, *The Suicide of an Elite*, 16–22.

78. Saigon to State, December 5, 1957, *FRUS, 1955–1957*, vol. 1, 871.

79. Steeves to Durbrow, December 20, 1960, *FRUS, 1958–1960*, vol. 1, 737–38.

80. Saigon to State, December 6, 1955, 751G.00/12-655, CDF 55-59, RG 59, USNA.

81. Fishel, "Vietnam: Is Victory Possible?" 15, 20–22; Thai, *Is South Vietnam Viable?* 227–84; Paris to State, December 31, 1958, *FRUS, 1958–1960*, vol. 1, 114–17.

82. W. W. Rostow, *The Diffusion of Power: An Essay in Recent History* (New York: Macmillan, 1972), 292. For U.S. concerns about civil and military administration, see Saigon to State, December 5, 1957, *FRUS, 1955–1957*, vol. 1, 875–76; Williams to Lansdale, March 10, 1960, *FRUS, 1958–1960*, vol. 1, 321–24; Lansdale to Douglas, March 17, 1960, ibid., 336–37; Saigon to State, September 16, 1960, ibid., 575–77.

83. Saigon to State, February 6, 1956, 751G.00/2-656, CDF 55-59, RG 59, USNA; December 5, 1957, *FRUS, 1955–1957*, vol. 1, 875–81; December 7, 1959, *FRUS, 1958–1960*, vol. 1, 263–64; September 16, 1960, ibid., 575–79; December 24, 1960, ibid., 741–45; Truong Nhu Tang, with David Chanoff and Doan Van Toai, *A Viet Cong Memoir* (New York: Vintage Books, 1985), 34–39; Bui Diem, with David Chanoff, *In the Jaws of History* (Boston: Houghton Mifflin, 1987), 86–89.

84. Saigon to State, December 5, 1957, *FRUS, 1955–1957*, vol. 1, 869–84; September 16, 1960, *FRUS, 1958–1960*, vol. 1, 575–79; December 24, 1960, ibid., 741–45.

85. Mecklin, *Mission in Torment*, 33.

2. The Ngos, Nationalism, and Nation Building

1. Saigon to External Affairs, April 9, 1963, DV1015/24, Foreign Office 371/170090, Public Record Office.

2. Keith Weller Taylor, *The Birth of Vietnam* (Berkeley: University of California Press, 1983).

3. Saigon to State, August 13, 1958, 751G.11/8-1358, Central Decimal File 1955–1959, Record Group 59, U.S. National Archives; Mieczyslaw Maneli, *War of the Vanquished,* trans. Maria de Gorgey (New York: Harper & Row, 1971), 138.

4. Marguerite Higgins, *Our Vietnam Nightmare* (New York: Harper & Row, 1965), 168.

5. Talk by Mr. Ngo Dinh Diem before Southeast Asia Seminar, Cornell University, February 20, 1953, Echols Collection, Cornell University Library; Indochina (enclosed in Douglas to Fisher, June 1953), Indo-China, Misc. Corres., Foreign Countries, Box 1717, William O. Douglas Papers, Library of Congress Manuscript Division; French Indo China as of the end of July 1953, ibid.

6. Conversation with Dr. Tran Van Do, Saigon, April 14, 1971, Do, Tran Van—1966, Folder 1, Correspondence, Box 1185, Wesley R. Fishel Papers, Michigan State University Archives and Historical Collections.

7. William Henderson and Wesley R. Fishel, "The Foreign Policy of Ngo Dinh Diem," *Vietnam Perspectives* (August 1966): 9–12; Saigon to State, June 29, 1954, *Foreign Relations of the United States, 1952–1954,* vol. 13, *Indochina,* pt. 2 (Washington, D.C.: GPO, 1982), 1762–63; U.S. Del. to State, July 16, 1954, *Foreign Relations of the United States, 1952–1954,* vol. 16, *The Geneva Conference* (Washington, D.C.: GPO, 1981), 1386–87; July 17, 1954, ibid., 1418–19; July 18, 1954, ibid., 1432–34; Saigon to State, July 19, 1954, *FRUS, 1952–1954,* vol. 13, 2, 1853–55; U.S. Del. to State, July 19, 1954, *FRUS, 1952–1954,* vol. 16, 1464–65; July 20, 1954, ibid., 1477–78; July 21, 1954, ibid., 1497–99.

8. Sebald to Dulles, June 14, 1955, *Foreign Relations of the United States, 1955–1957,* vol. 1, *Vietnam* (Washington, D.C.: GPO, 1985), 451–52; Saigon to State, July 16, 1955, ibid., 489–90; *The Fight against the Subversive Communist Activities in Vietnam,* special ed. (Saigon: Review Horizons, 1957); *News from Viet-Nam,* August 9, 1957, 1–3.

9. Saigon to State, July 4, 1954, *FRUS, 1952–1954,* vol. 13, 2, 1782–84; August 26, 1955, 751G.13/8-2655, CDF 55-59, RG 59, USNA; John Mecklin, *Mission in Torment: An Intimate Account of the U.S. Role in Vietnam* (Garden City, N.Y.: Doubleday, 1965), 31; Cao Van Luan, *Ben Giong Lich Su, 1940–1965* (Saigon: Tri Dung, 1972), 241–51.

10. *The Fight against the Subversive Communist Activities in Vietnam;* Nguyen Van Chau, *Giong Lich Su* (Saigon: Nhom Van Chien, 1961). For Diem's view of Ho, see Frederick Nolting, *From Trust to Tragedy: The Political Memoirs of Frederick Nolting, Kennedy's Ambassador to Diem's Vietnam* (New York: Praeger Publishers, 1988), 33.

11. Presidency, *Major Policy Speeches by President Ngo Dinh Diem,* 3d ed. (Saigon, 1957), 34. For Catholic anticommunism, see David G. Marr, *Vietnamese Tradition on Trial, 1920–1945* (Berkeley: University of California Press, 1984), 84–85.

12. Tran Van Giau, *Mien Nam Giu Vung Thanh Dong: Luoc Su Dong Bao Mien Nam Dau Tranh Chong My Va Tay Sai,* vol. 1 (Hanoi: Khoa Hoc, 1964), 35–38; Tran Huy Lieu, "Theo Quan Diem Lich Su: Nhin Vao Cuoc Dao Chinh Vua Qua O Mien

Nam Viet-Nam Va So Kiep Ngo-Dinh-Diem," *Nghien cuu Lich su* (January 1964): 1–4; William J. Duiker, *Sacred War: Nationalism and Revolution in a Divided Vietnam* (Boston: McGraw-Hill, 1995), 143.

13. Robert Scigliano, *South Vietnam: Nation under Stress* (Boston: Houghton Mifflin, 1964), 158.

14. Presidency, *Ngo Dinh Diem of Viet-Nam* (Saigon, 1957), 26–29; Phan Thanh Nghi, *Dao-Duc Cach-Mang Cua Chi-Si Ngo-Dinh-Diem* (n.p., 1956); *Than-The va Su-Nghiep Tong-Thong Ngo-Dinh-Diem* (n.p.: T. T. Nam-Viet, 1956); Nguyen Huu Tiep, *Ngo-Dinh-Diem: Salazar Viet-Nam* (n.p.: Xa-Hoi An-Quan, 1957).

15. William Colby, with James McCargar, *Lost Victory: A Firsthand Account of America's Sixteen-Year Involvement in Vietnam* (Chicago: Contemporary Books, 1989), 110.

16. *News from Viet-Nam*, December 30, 1960, 12; Presidency, *Toward Better Mutual Understanding*, vol. 1, 2d ed. (Saigon, 1958), 55.

17. Henderson and Fishel, "The Foreign Policy of Ngo Dinh Diem," 7–9; Memorandum of Conversations, July 27, 1956, *FRUS, 1955–1957*, vol. 1, 730; Saigon to State, July 26, 1957, ibid., 829–31; December 5, 1957, ibid., 882.

18. Henderson and Fishel, 26; Diem to Douglas, November 19, 1953, Vietnam— Misc. Corres., Foreign Countries, Box 1731, Douglas Papers, LOCMD. See also Durbrow to Cumming, August 6, 1958, *Foreign Relations of the United States, 1958–1960*, vol. 1, *Vietnam* (Washington, D.C.: GPO, 1986), 69–70.

19. Dennis J. Duncanson, *Government and Revolution in Vietnam* (New York: Oxford University Press, 1968), 215.

20. Nguyen Van Chau, *Ngo Dinh Diem va No Luc Hoa Binh Dang Do*, trans. Nguyen Vy-Khanh (Los Alamitos, Calif.: Xuan Thu, 1989), 109; Malcolm W. Browne, *The New Face of War* (Indianapolis: Bobbs-Merrill, 1965), 267; Wesley R. Fishel, Internal Problems of the Southeast Asian Countries, National War College, March 2, 1964, Folder 54, Speeches, Box 1200, Fishel Papers, MSUAHC; letter from Do Mau, December 7, 1995.

21. Henderson and Fishel, 26; Hoang Lac, "Blind Design," in *Prelude to Tragedy: Vietnam, 1960–1965*, ed. Harvey Neese and John O'Donnell (Annapolis: Naval Institute Press, 2001), 70; Memorandum of Discussion, June 7, 1956, *FRUS, 1955–1957*, vol. 1, 697–703; Memorandum of Conversation, May 17, 1957, ibid., 820–22.

22. Saigon to State, October 8, 1957, 751G.00/10-857, CDF 55-59, RG 59, USNA; October 28, 1957, *FRUS, 1955–1957*, vol. 1, 854–55; Memorandum of Conversation, December 20, 1957, ibid., 890; Saigon to State, February 13, 1958, 751G.5-MSP/2-1358, CDF 55-59, RG 59, USNA.

23. Saigon to State, June 24, 1955, 751G.5-MSP/6-2455, ibid.; January 13, 1958, 751G.5-MSP/1-1358, ibid.; February 8, 1958, *FRUS, 1958–1960*, vol. 1, 14; June 10, 1958, 851G.00/6-1058, CDF 55-59, RG 59, USNA; Durbrow to Robertson, February 16, 1959, *FRUS, 1958–1960*, vol. 1, 140–41; Saigon to State, April 11, 1959, ibid., 181–82; Memorandum of Conversation, November 21, 1959, ibid., 251–54. See also Amos A. Jordan, Jr., *Foreign Aid and the Defense of Southeast Asia* (New York:

Frederick A. Praeger, 1962), 80–82, 102–5; John D. Montgomery, *The Politics of Foreign Aid: American Experience in Southeast Asia* (New York: Frederick A. Praeger,
1962), 85–93; George McT. Kahin, *Intervention: How America Became Involved in
Vietnam* (New York: Alfred A. Knopf, 1986), 85–88.

24. Ibid., 84–87; Duong Van Mai Elliott, *The Sacred Willow: Four Generations in
the Life of a Vietnamese Family* (New York: Oxford University Press, 1999), 260–61.

25. Stuart to Kattenburg, June 8, 1956, 751G.5-MSP/6-856, CDF 55-59, RG 59,
USNA; State to Saigon, June 27, 1956, 751G.5-MSP/6-2756, ibid.; Young to
Robertson, October 1, 1956, 751G.5-MSP/10-156, ibid.; Memorandum of Conversation, May 10, 1957, *FRUS, 1955–1957*, vol. 1, 814–15; Saigon to State, March
18, 1959, 751G.5-MSP/3-1859, CDF 55-59, RG 59, USNA; Scigliano, *South Vietnam*, 125.

26. Memorandum of Conversation, April 4, 1957, *FRUS, 1955–1957*, vol. 1, 770;
November 11, 1958, *FRUS, 1958–1960*, vol. 1, 97–98; Nhu's comments, February 2,
1962, *Ban Ghi Chep: Nhung Buoi Noi Chuyen Than Mat Cua Ong Co Van Chinh Tri
Ve Ap Chien Luoc*, vol. 1, Tai Lieu Do So Luu Tru Va Cong Bao Phu Thu Tuong Viet
Nam Cong Hoa, SC.04 8676, Cuc Luu Tru II; Bien-Ban so 16 Uy-Ban Lien-Bo Dac-
Trach Ap Chien-Luoc, July 13, 1962, GVN Strat Hams, Vietnam Archive.

27. Saigon to State, July 30, 1957, 751G.11/7-3057, CDF 55-59, RG 59, USNA.

28. Young to Robertson, October 1, 1956, 751G.5-MSP/10-156, ibid.; Memorandum of Conversation, April 4, 1957, *FRUS, 1955–1957*, vol. 1, 770–72; January 30,
1958, *FRUS, 1958–1960*, vol. 1, 8.

29. Saigon to State, February 14, 1959, 751G.5-MSP/2-1459, CDF 55-59, RG 59,
USNA; Durbrow to Robertson, February 16, 1959, *FRUS, 1958–1960*, vol. 1, 141.

30. Reinhardt to Young, December 20, 1956, *FRUS, 1955–1957*, vol. 1, 759–60.

31. Mecklin, *Mission in Torment*, 46.

32. Memorandum of Conversation, August 1, 1957, *FRUS, 1955–1957*, vol. 1, 836.

33. Ibid., 833–36; Nguyen Thai, *Is South Vietnam Viable?* (Manila: Carmelo &
Bauermann, 1962), 45–57, 71–82.

34. Ellen J. Hammer, *A Death in November: America in Vietnam, 1963* (New York:
E. P. Dutton, 1987), 130–33; Ronald H. Spector, *Advice and Support: The Early Years
of the United States Army in Vietnam, 1941–1960* (New York: Free Press, 1985),
278–80; Saigon to State, December 7, 1959, *FRUS, 1958–1960*, vol. 1, 265–66; Lansdale to McGarr, August 11, 1960, ibid., 534–35.

35. Enclosed in Burrows to Secondé, May 30, 1962, DV1201/24, FO371/166748,
PRO.

36. Memorandum of Conversation, June 24, 1960, *FRUS, 1958–1960*, vol. 1,
507–8; Higgins, *Our Vietnam Nightmare*, 169–70; Scigliano, *South Vietnam*, 48–51;
Denis Warner, *The Last Confucian: Vietnam, South-East Asia, and the West* (Harmondsworth, Middlesex: Penguin Books, 1964), 94, 108.

37. Colby, *Lost Victory*, 105–6; Saigon to Foreign Office, December 7, 1961,
DV103145/36, FO371/160129, PRO.

38. *Press Interviews with President Ngo Dinh Diem, Political Counselor Ngo Dinh Nhu* (n.p., 1963), 63.

39. William S. Turley, *The Second Indochina War: A Short Political and Military History, 1954–1975* (New York: Mentor, 1987), 13; George C. Herring, *America's Longest War: The United States and Vietnam, 1950–1975,* 2d ed. (New York: Alfred A. Knopf, 1986), 49.

40. Jean Lacouture, *Vietnam: Between Two Truces,* trans. Konrad Kellen and Joel Carmichael (New York: Vintage Books, 1966), 19; Frances FitzGerald, *Fire in the Lake: The Vietnamese and the Americans in Vietnam* (New York: Vintage Books, 1973), 132–34.

41. Higgins, 166.

42. Alexander B. Woodside, *Community and Revolution in Modern Vietnam* (Boston: Houghton Mifflin, 1976), 171.

43. Hans Rogger and Eugen Weber, eds., *The European Right: A Historical Profile* (London: Weidenfeld & Nicholson, 1965), 24, 588.

44. David G. Marr, *Vietnamese Anticolonialism, 1885–1925* (Berkeley: University of California Press, 1971); Marr, *Vietnamese Tradition on Trial* (60, 292 for quotations); Hue-Tam Ho Tai, *Radicalism and the Origins of the Vietnamese Revolution* (Cambridge: Harvard University Press, 1996); Woodside, esp. 5–8.

45. Marr, *Vietnamese Tradition on Trial,* 2, 31.

46. Woodside, 8.

47. Ibid., esp. 5–8, 95–100; Marr, *Vietnamese Tradition on Trial,* esp. 115–20.

48. Wm. Theodore de Bary, *Asian Values and Human Rights: A Confucian Communitarian Perspective* (Cambridge: Harvard University Press, 1998), 87.

49. *Major Policy Speeches,* 3; Wesley R. Fishel, "Problems of Democratic Growth in Free Vietnam," in *Problems of Freedom: South Vietnam Since Independence,* ed. Wesley R. Fishel (New York: Free Press of Glencoe, 1961), 16–17; Call to the People of President Ngo-Dinh-Diem, June 25, 1954, Vietnam—Misc. Corres., Foreign Countries, Box 1731, Douglas Papers, LOCMD.

50. Reinhardt to Young, December 20, 1956, *FRUS, 1955–1957,* vol. 1, 760.

51. *Major Policy Speeches,* 5–6, 21–22; Memorandum of Conversation, April 5, 1957, *FRUS, 1955–1957,* vol. 1, 773–75.

52. Saigon to State, December 7, 1959, *FRUS, 1958–1960,* vol. 1, 256.

53. *President Ngo-Dinh-Diem's Political Philosophy,* special ed. (Saigon: Review Horizons, 1956), 13.

54. *News from Viet-Nam,* December 8, 1958, 3; *Chi-Dao,* October 1961, 6–7; Nguyen Van Chau, *Con Duong Song* (Saigon: Nhom Van Chien, 1961); Departments and Ministries National Defense Report, "Fundamental Theory of Strategic Hamlets" 1962, Folder 75, Public Administration, Box 675, Vietnam Project, MSUAHC; Higgins, *Our Vietnam Nightmare,* 166–76.

55. Saigon to State, July 11, 1959, 751G.11/7-1159, CDF 55-59, RG 59, USNA; *Chan-Hung Kinh-Te,* May 30, 1963, 7–9; *Chi Dao,* National Day issue, 1963, 57.

56. *Major Policy Speeches,* 14–15; *News from Viet-Nam,* October 16, 1959, 3–4.

57. Lloyd D. Musolf, "Public Enterprise and Development Perspectives in South Vietnam," *Asian Survey* (August 1963): 357–71; Maneli, *War of the Vanquished*, 144–45; Memorandum of Conversation, January 30, 1958, *FRUS, 1958–1960*, vol. 1, 5–7; *News from Viet-Nam*, February 29, 1960, 3.

58. *Toward Better Mutual Understanding*, vol. 1, 59–60; Saigon to State, November 19, 1957, 751G.11/11-1957, CDF 55-59, RG 59, USNA.

59. Saigon to State, July 11, 1959, 751G.11/7-1159, ibid.

60. *News from Viet-Nam*, January 25, 1957, 2–3, and March 2, 1959, 2–4. See also Saigon to State, November 19, 1959, 751G.00/11-1959, CDF 55-59, RG 59, USNA.

61. Higgins, 166.

62. *News from Viet-Nam*, October 18, 1957, 10; Saigon to State, January 20, 1958, 751G.11/1-2058, CDF 55-59, RG 59, USNA; John C. Donnell, "Politics in South Vietnam: Doctrines of Authority in Conflict" (Ph.D. diss., University of California, Berkeley, 1964), 80.

63. Marr, *Vietnamese Tradition on Trial*, 8–13, 106–15, 275–76, 331–35; Woodside, *Community and Revolution*, 85, 90–92, 102–8.

64. *News from Viet-Nam*, January 25, 1957, 3.

65. *Toward Better Mutual Understanding*, vol. 2, 13–16.

66. Ngo Dinh Diem, "Democratic Development in Vietnam," *Free China Review* (June 1955): 25–36. See also Higgins, *Our Vietnam Nightmare*, 173.

67. *News from Viet-Nam*, January 25, 1957, 2–3; Saigon to State, December 19, 1957, 751G.11/12-1957, CDF 55-59, RG 59, USNA; John C. Donnell, "National Renovation Campaigns in Vietnam," *Pacific Affairs* (March 1959): 76–78.

68. *Toward Better Mutual Understanding*, vols. 1 and 2.

69. Emmanuel Mounier, *Personalism*, trans. Philip Mairet (Notre Dame: University of Notre Dame Press, 1952), vii–xxviii; Jacques Maritain, *Redeeming the Time*, trans. Harry Lorin Binsse (London: Centenary Press, 1943), 182–84; John T. Marcus, "Social Catholicism in Postwar France," *South Atlantic Quarterly* (summer 1957): 304; Mario Einaudi and Francois Goguel, *Christian Democracy in Italy and France* (Hamden, Conn.: Archon Books, 1969), 109–16; John Hellman, *Emmanuel Mounier and the New Catholic Left, 1930–1950* (Toronto: University of Toronto Press, 1981), 3–11.

70. Mounier, xxvi, 18–19, 32, 52. See also Jacques Maritain, *The Person and the Common Good*, trans. John J. FitzGerald (Notre Dame: University of Notre Dame Press, 1966), 91–97.

71. Mounier, 18–21; Jacques Maritain, *Christianity and Democracy & The Rights of Man and Natural Law*, trans. Doris C. Anson (San Francisco: Ignatius Press, 1986), 88–106.

72. Ibid., 171–80; Mounier, 39–40, 103–4, 111–16.

73. Donnell, "Politics in South Vietnam," 80–81, 92–97.

74. Ibid., 99–101; Donnell, "National Renovation Campaigns in Vietnam," 79–80; Thai, *Is South Vietnam Viable?* 127–31.

75. *News from Viet-Nam*, July 1961, 2–3.

76. John C. Donnell, "Personalism in Vietnam," in *Problems of Freedom*, ed. Fishel, 40–41; Saigon to State, January 20, 1958, 751G.11/1-2058, CDF 55–59, RG 59, USNA.

77. Donnell, "Politics in South Vietnam," 109; de Bary, *Asian Values and Human Rights*, 22–29.

78. Nguyen Khac Vien, *Tradition and Revolution in Vietnam*, trans. Linda Yarr, Jayne Werner, and Tran Tuong Nhu (Berkeley: Indochina Resource Center, 1975), 45–52; Marr, *Vietnamese Tradition on Trial*, 130–34; William J. Duiker, *Ho Chi Minh* (New York: Hyperion, 2000), 62–63, 75, 135–36, 555.

79. Donnell, "Personalism in Vietnam," 55–56; *News from Viet-Nam*, October 13, 1956, 8, and November 10, 1958, 19–20; Marr, *Vietnamese Tradition on Trial*, esp. 93–95, for prewar thinking about the issue of Confucianism and citizenship (includes the term "family morality written large").

80. *News from Viet-Nam*, December 30, 1960, 11.

81. Wesley R. Fishel, "Vietnam's War of Attrition," *New Leader*, December 7, 1959, 20–21; Saigon to State, July 30, 1957, 751G.11/7-3057, CDF 55–59, RG 59, USNA; November 19, 1959, 751G.00/11-1959, ibid.

82. Donnell, "Politics in South Vietnam," 93; Robert Shaplen, *The Lost Revolution: The U.S. in Vietnam, 1946–1966*, rev. ed. (New York: Harper & Row, 1966), 131; Nhu's address, *Dan Thang*, April 2, 1963.

83. Marr, *Vietnamese Tradition on Trial*, esp. 299, 357–58.

84. Donnell, "Politics in South Vietnam," 224–85; Charles A. Joiner and Roy Jumper, "Organizing Bureaucrats: South Viet Nam's National Revolutionary Civil Servants' League," *Asian Survey* (April 1963): 203–15 (includes the term "intermediate social structures").

85. Saigon to State, July 20, 1959, 851G.20/7-2059, CDF 55–59, RG 59, USNA; Nicolaas Godfried Maria Luykx II, "Some Comparative Aspects of Rural Public Institutions in Thailand, the Philippines, and Viet-Nam" (Ph.D. diss., Cornell University, 1962), 813–17; Tran Ngoc Lien, "The Growth of Agricultural Credit and Cooperatives in Vietnam," in *Problems of Freedom*, ed. Fishel, 177–89.

86. Most thoroughly elaborated by Nhu in Donnell, "Politics in South Vietnam," 578–83; Saigon to State, November 19, 1959, 751G.00/11-1959, CDF 55–59, RG 59, USNA.

87. *President Ngo-Dinh-Diem's Political Philosophy*, 8–10.

88. Press releases, July 6 and 7, 1955, Subject File, Vietnam General, 1953–62, Box 351, Records of Moral Re-Armament, Inc., LOCMD; Diem to Buchman, June 25, 1956, Frank N. D. Buchman, General Correspondence, Ngo, Dinh Diem 1956, 1958, Box 66, ibid.

89. *Major Policy Speeches*, 19; Donnell, "Personalism in Vietnam," 32–34, 38–54; Donnell, "Politics in South Vietnam," 579.

90. Ibid., 118–21, 579–81; *Chan-Hung Kinh-Te*, May 30, 1963, 3–7.

91. Donnell, "Politics in South Vietnam," 114–16.

92. *News from Viet-Nam*, August 18, 1956, 2–3, and October 18, 1957, 10; Memo-

randum of Conversation, April 5, 1957, *FRUS, 1955–1957*, vol. 1, 774; May 9, 1957, ibid., 795; May 10, 1957, ibid., 808; Saigon to State, July 1, 1957, ibid., 825.

93. Joseph Buttinger, *Vietnam: A Dragon Embattled*, vol. 2 (New York: Frederick A. Praeger, 1967), 1139.

94. Nhu's comments on Personalism's popularity, Saigon to State, November 19, 1959, 751G.00/11-1959, CDF 55–59, RG 59, USNA. For contrary views, see Saigon to State, January 7, 1963, 751K.00/1-763, CDF 60–63, ibid.; Nguyen Qui Hung, *Neuf Ans de Dictatures au Sud Vietnam: Témoignages Vivants sur Mme Nhu et les Ngo* (Saigon: n.p., 1964), 79–80; Luan, *Ben Giong Lich Su*, 262–63; David Halberstam, *The Making of a Quagmire* (New York: Random House, 1965), 50.

95. Shaplen, *The Lost Revolution*, 131; Buttinger, 1139.

96. Saigon to State, December 22, 1958, *FRUS, 1958–1960*, vol. 1, 109–13.

97. Saigon to State, October 9, 1963, *Foreign Relations of the United States, 1961–1963*, vol. 4, *Vietnam* (Washington, D.C.: GPO, 1991), 392.

98. Mecklin, *Mission in Torment*, 33–34.

99. Donnell, "National Renovation Campaigns in Vietnam," 88.

100. Bien-Ban so 9, April 13, 1962, GVN Strat Hams, VA; Bien-Ban so 16, July 13, 1962, ibid.; Maneli, *War of the Vanquished*, 144.

101. Donnell, "Politics in South Vietnam," 494–95. See also Ernst Nolte, *Three Faces of Fascism*, trans. Leila Vennewitz (New York: Holt, Rinehart and Winston, 1966), 113.

102. Richard L. Park, "Second Thoughts on Asian Democracy," *Asian Survey* (April 1961): 26–27.

103. *Toward Better Mutual Understanding*, vol. 1, 20–21, 30–31; Higgins, *Our Vietnam Nightmare*, 166, 173; Colby, *Lost Victory*, 32; Memorandum for Record, June 8, 1963, Folder 1373, Subject File, Box 49, Edward G. Lansdale Papers, Hoover Institute. See also Jan Breman, *The Shattered Image: Construction and Deconstruction of the Village in Colonial Asia* (Dordrecht–Holland: Forbis Publications, 1988), 38.

104. Higgins, 166, 173; Saigon to State, August 8, 1956, 751G.00/8-856, CDF 55–59, RG 59, USNA.

105. Saigon to State, November 19, 1959, 751G.00/11-1959, ibid.

106. Presidency, *Interviews of Ngo Dinh Diem* (Saigon, 1960) (Scripps-Howard interview, June 25, 1959); Luan, *Ben Giong Lich Su*, 260; Thai, *Is South Vietnam Viable?* 113–16; Saigon to State, December 13, 1955, 751G.00/12-1355, CDF 55–59, RG 59, USNA; December 17, 1955, 751G.00/12-1755, ibid.; August 8, 1956, 751G.00/8-856, ibid.

107. Saigon to State, August 8, 1956, 751G.00/8-856, ibid.

3. Land Reform, Land Development, and Agrovilles

1. Edward Geary Lansdale, *In the Midst of Wars: An American's Mission to Southeast Asia* (New York: Harper & Row, 1972), 354.

2. Lansdale to Gilpatric, April 25, 1961, *United States–Vietnam Relations, 1945–1967,* bk. 11 (Washington, D.C.: GPO, 1971), 39.

3. John D. Montgomery, *The Politics of Foreign Aid: American Experience in Southeast Asia* (New York: Frederick A. Praeger, 1962), 121–28; Saigon to State, July 30, 1954, *Foreign Relations of the United States, 1952–1954,* vol. 13, *Indochina,* pt. 2 (Washington, D.C.: GPO, 1982), 1894–95; Collins to Reinhardt, May 10, 1955, *Foreign Relations of the United States, 1955–1957,* vol. 1, *Vietnam* (Washington, D.C.: GPO, 1985), 391.

4. Ladejinsky to Reinhardt, June 7, 1955, *Agrarian Reform as Unfinished Business: The Selected Papers of Wolf Ladejinsky,* ed. Louis J. Walinsky (New York: Oxford University Press, 1977), 239; State to Saigon, August 25[?], 1955 (Tel. 664), 751G.00/6-1555, Central Decimal File 1955–1959, Record Group 59, U.S. National Archives; Saigon to State, December 7, 1955, 851G.411/12-755, ibid.

5. Wolf Ladejinsky, "Agrarian Reform in the Republic of Vietnam," in *Problems of Freedom: South Vietnam Since Independence,* ed. Wesley R. Fishel (New York: Free Press of Glencoe, 1961), 159–71; Gittinger's report, Saigon to State, July 23, 1960, 851K.16/7-2360, CDF 60-63, RG 59, USNA (inc. Delta figures). For landholding patterns, and the outlook of landlords, in the Delta, see Alexander B. Woodside, *Community and Revolution in Modern Vietnam* (Boston: Houghton Mifflin, 1976), 120–24.

6. Saigon to State, July 12, 1956, 851G.20/7-1256, CDF 55-59, RG 59, USNA.

7. *News from Viet-Nam,* October 18, 1957, 2.

8. Saigon to State, July 9, 1956, *FRUS, 1955–1957,* vol. 1, 715; *Chan-Hung Kinh-Te,* December 20, 1962, 25, and January 17, 1963, 10–11.

9. Saigon to State, July 12, 1956, 851G.20/7-1256, CDF 55-59, RG 59, USNA; Jeffrey Race, *War Comes to Long An: Revolutionary Conflict in a Vietnamese Province* (Berkeley: University of California Press, 1973), 98; Truong Nhu Tang, with David Chanoff and Doan Van Toai, *A Viet Cong Memoir* (New York: Vintage Books, 1985), 325–26.

10. Saigon to State, July 12, 1956, 851G.20/7-1256, CDF 55-59, RG 59, USNA; Young to Robertson, October 1, 1956, 751G.5-MSP/10-156, ibid.; State to Saigon, June 10, 1958, 851G.00/6-1058, ibid.

11. Roy L. Prosterman, "Land Reform in Vietnam," *Current History* (December 1969): 328–30; William Bredo, "Agrarian Reform in Vietnam: Vietcong and Government of Vietnam Strategies in Conflict," *Asian Survey* (August 1970): 741–43; Ladejinsky to Diem, October 9, 1956, ed. Walinsky, 271–72; Ladejinsky, 168. Compare Ordinance 57 with the Thieu government's more far-reaching Land-to-the-Tiller program: Charles Stuart Callison, *Land-to-the-Tiller in the Mekong Delta: Economic, Social, and Political Effects of Land Reform in Four Villages of South Vietnam* (Lanham, Md.: University Press of America, 1983), 81–83, 327–28; Nhan Thi Huong, "So-Sanh Du 57 Ngay 22-10-1956 Va Luat 003/70 Ngay 26-3-1970" (Hoc-Vien Quoc-Gia Hanh-Chanh, Luan-Van Tot-Nghiep, 1972).

12. Race, 57–61.

13. William Colby, Oral History, Interview 1, 21–23, Lyndon B. Johnson Library; Ladejinsky, 168.

14. Ladejinsky's reports, Saigon to State, March 25, 1955, 851G.16/3-2555, CDF 55-59, RG 59, USNA; and ed. Walinsky, 255, 263–64. See also Tran Van Don, *Our Endless War: Inside Vietnam* (San Rafael, Calif.: Presidio Press, 1978), 68.

15. Saigon to State, July 12, 1956, 851G.20/7-1256, CDF 55-59, RG 59, USNA; *Land Reform in Free Vietnam*, special ed. (Saigon: Review Horizons, 1956); *So Sanh Cai Cach Dien Dia Tai Mien Nam Cua Chinh Phu Cong Hoa Voi Cai Cach Ruong Dat Cua Viet Cong Tai Mien Bac* (Saigon: Van Huu A Chau, 1960). For the DRVN's program, see Edwin E. Moise, *Land Reform in China and North Vietnam: Consolidating the Revolution at the Village Level* (Chapel Hill: University of North Carolina Press, 1983), 178–236.

16. Ladejinsky's reports, *Agrarian Reform as Unfinished Business*, ed. Walinsky, 224–27, 232–33, 237; Gittinger's report, Saigon to State, July 23, 1960, 851K.16/7-2360, CDF 60-63, RG 59, USNA.

17. Ladejinsky's report, ed. Walinsky, 255, 262–63.

18. Saigon to State, March 25, 1955, 851G.16/3-2555, CDF 55-59, RG 59, USNA.

19. Saigon to State, January 26, 1957, 851G.16/1-2657, ibid.

20. Ladejinsky's report, ed. Walinsky, 255, 263–64.

21. Ladejinsky's reports, ibid., esp. 223, 230, 233–37, 244, 247–55, 259, 264; Nguyen Tran, *Cong Va Toi: Nhung Su That Lich Su* (Los Alamitos, Calif.: Xuan Thu, 1992), 210–11; Woodside, *Community and Revolution*, 302.

22. Saigon to State, December 7, 1955, 851G.411/12-755, CDF 55-59, RG 59, USNA; July 5, 1957, 851G.00/7-557, ibid.; December 20, 1958, 851G.00/12-2058, ibid.; February 18, 1959, 851G.00/2-1859, ibid.; April 13, 1959, 851G.20/4-1359, ibid.; December 18, 1959, 851G.00/12-1859, ibid.; Gittinger's report, July 23, 1960, 851K.16/7-2360, CDF 60-63, ibid. (a rather upbeat summation).

23. For an official description, see Commissariat General for Land Development, *The Work of Land Development in Viet Nam Up to June 30, 1959* (n.p., n.d.). Good secondary accounts are Montgomery, *The Politics of Foreign Aid*, 72–83; William Henderson, "Opening of New Lands and Villages: The Republic of Vietnam Land Development Program," in *Problems of Freedom*, ed. Fishel, 123–37. For the Montagnards, see Gerald Cannon Hickey, *Free in the Forest: Ethnohistory of the Vietnamese Central Highlands, 1954–1976* (New Haven: Yale University Press, 1982), 1–46.

24. Secretariat of State for Information, *Cai San: The Dramatic Story of Resettlement and Land Reform in the "Rice Bowl" of the Republic of Viet-Nam* (Saigon, n.d.).

25. Paris to State, March 24, 1959, 751G.00/3-2459, CDF 55-59, RG 59, USNA (summary of *Le Figaro* interview); Presidency, *Toward Better Mutual Understanding*, vol. 1, 2d ed. (Saigon, 1958), 30. See also Ngo Dinh Diem, "Democratic Development in Vietnam," *Free China Review* (June 1955): 33–34; Fishel to Diem, December 30,

1958, Ngo Dinh Diem 1951–1962, Folder 33, Correspondence, Box 1184, Wesley R. Fishel Papers, Michigan State University Archives and Historical Collections.

26. Charles A. Joiner, "Administration and Political Warfare in the Highlands," *Vietnam Perspectives* (November 1965): 21–23; Cao Van Luan, *Ben Giong Lich Su, 1940–1965* (Saigon: Tri Dung, 1972), 165–68.

27. Saigon to State, August 9, 1957, 751G.11/8-957, CDF 55-59, RG 59, USNA; Hickey, 5–8.

28. Le Thanh Khoi, *Le Viet-Nam: Histoire et Civilisation* (Paris: Editions de Minuit, 1955), 359.

29. Saigon to State, March 22, 1955, 751G.00/3-2255, CDF 55-59, RG 59, USNA; December 7, 1955, 851G.411/12-755, ibid. (memoranda of November 16 and 30); August 28, 1956, 751G.5-MSP/8-2856, ibid.; February 9, 1957, 851G.00/2-957, ibid.; Memorandum of Conversation, May 10, 1957, *FRUS, 1955–1957,* vol. 1, 813–14.

30. *The Work of Land Development,* 10–25; Saigon to State, January 6, 1958, 751G.11/1-658, CDF 55-59, RG 59, USNA; Gittinger's report, Saigon to State, July 23, 1960, 851K.16/7-2360, CDF 60-63, ibid.

31. *The Work of Land Development,* 26–28, and attached graphs and maps; *Times of Viet Nam Magazine,* January 6, 1963, 18–19.

32. Memorandum of Conversation, April 4, 1957, *FRUS, 1955–1957,* vol. 1, 770–71.

33. Saigon to State, August 30, 1957, ibid., 842–43; September 12, 1957, 751G.00/9-1257, CDF 55-59, RG 59, USNA; October 8, 1957, 751G.00/10-857, ibid.; November 19, 1957, 751G.11/11-1957, ibid.

34. Saigon to State, December 7, 1955, 851G.411/12-755, ibid. (memo of conversation, November 16); April 29, 1957, 751G.00/4-2957, ibid.; Memorandum of Conversation, May 9, 1957, *FRUS, 1955–1957,* vol. 1, 801; Saigon to State, August 30, 1957, ibid., 841–43; September 12, 1957, 751G.00/9-1257, CDF 55-59, RG 59, USNA; October 8, 1957, 751G.00/10-857, ibid.; November 19, 1957, 751G.11/11-1957, ibid.; Memorandum of Conversation, December 20, 1957, *FRUS, 1955–1957,* vol. 1, 889–94.

35. Saigon to State, February 27, 1957, 751G.5/2-2757, CDF 55-59, RG 59, USNA; May 23, 1957, 751G.00/5-2357, ibid.

36. Saigon to State, February 27, 1957, 751G.5/2-2757, ibid.; *News from Viet-Nam,* August 30, 1957, 7; Saigon to State, November 19, 1957, 751G.11/11-1957, CDF 55-59, RG 59, USNA; *The Work of Land Development,* 5–6, 19; *Times of Viet Nam Magazine,* May 14, 1960, 14. Despite Saigon's declared intent, neither settlers nor Montagnards had received title to their land by the end of 1959; they were, in effect, working government-owned lands on a rent-free basis.

37. *The Work of Land Development,* 4, 17–18; Gittinger's report, Saigon to State, July 23, 1960, 851K.16/7-2360, CDF 60-63, RG 59, USNA.

38. Saigon to State, January 6, 1958, 751G.11/1-658, CDF 55-59, ibid.; *News from*

Viet-Nam, January 17, 1958, 2–4; *Vietnam Press*, w/e March 8, 1959, 1. See also ibid., w/e October 4, 1959, 19.

39. Diem, 34; *News from Viet-Nam*, January 17, 1958, 4.

40. *The Work of Land Development*, 15–18, 25; Gittinger's report, Saigon to State, July 23, 1960, 851K.16/7-2360, CDF 60-63, RG 59, USNA; Vu Van Thai, "Vietnam's Concept of Development," in *Problems of Freedom*, ed. Fishel, 72–73.

41. Saigon to State, September 26, 1957, 751G.11/9-2657, CDF 55-59, RG 59, USNA. See also August 30, 1957, *FRUS, 1955–1957*, vol. 1, 842; November 19, 1957, 751G.11/11-1957, CDF 55-59, RG 59, USNA.

42. Montgomery, *The Politics of Foreign Aid*, 74–75.

43. Saigon to State, May 23, 1957, 751G.00/5-2357, CDF 55-59, RG 59, USNA; Hue to State, August 20, 1959, 751G.00/8-2059, ibid.; Hickey, *Free in the Forest*, 19–20, 32–45.

44. For how the program was supposed to work, see *The Work of Land Development*, 14–15; Nicolaas Godfried Maria Luykx II, "Some Comparative Aspects of Rural Public Institutions in Thailand, the Philippines, and Viet-Nam" (Ph.D. diss., Cornell University, 1962), 830–31. Coercive practices are noted in Saigon to State, May 8, 1958, 851G.00/5-858, CDF 55-59, RG 59, USNA; Hue to State, March 2, 1959, 751G.00/3-259, ibid.; July 6, 1959, 851G.411/7-659, ibid.; August 20, 1959, 751G.00/8-2059, ibid.; Ngo Dinh Quy, "Tu Chinh-Sach Dinh-Dien Den Chuong-Trinh Khan-Hoang Lap-Ap" (Truong Quoc-Gia Hanh-Chanh, Luan-Van Tot Nghiep, 1974), 18–19.

45. Saigon to State, March 14, 1957, 851G.424/3-1457, CDF 55-59, RG 59, USNA; May 9, 1957, 851G.413/5-957, ibid.; January 21, 1958, 751G.00/1-2158, ibid.; Hue to State, July 6, 1959, 851G.411/7-659, ibid.

46. Memorandum of Conversation, July 2, 1959, Jonas, Gilbert Correspondence, 1959, Folder 25, Vietnam Project/MSU Advisory Group, Box 1207, Fishel Papers, MSUAHC. Henderson, "Opening of New Lands and Villages," 128–29, argues that Saigon "chose on the whole to rely on persuasion rather than coercion."

47. Saigon to State, May 23, 1957, 751G.00/5-2357, CDF 55-59, RG 59, USNA.

48. Saigon to State, May 23, 1957, ibid.; June 10, 1957, 851G.00/6-1057, ibid.; September 12, 1957, 751G.00/9-1257, ibid.; January 6, 1958, 851G.16/1-658, ibid.; Gardiner's testimony, Hearings before the Subcommittee on the Far East and the Pacific of the Committee on Foreign Affairs, House of Representatives, Eighty-sixth Congress, First Session, Current Situation in the Far East, July–August 1959 (Washington, D.C.: GPO, 1959), 324; Montgomery, 73–79; Henderson, 127–30, 134–35.

49. Saigon to State, December 5, 1957, *FRUS, 1955–1957*, vol. 1, 874–75; January 13, 1958, 751G.5 MSP/1-1358, CDF 55-59, RG 59, USNA; February 8, 1958, 751G.5 MSP/2-858, CDF 55-59, ibid.

50. Saigon to State, February 8, 1958, 751G.5 MSP/2-858, CDF 55-59, ibid.; Memorandum of Conversation, January 7, 1960, 751K.5-MSP/1-760, CDF 60-63, ibid.; Montgomery, 72–82.

51. Memorandum of Conversation, December 20, 1957, *FRUS, 1955–1957,* vol. 1, 889–94; January 30, 1958, *FRUS, 1958–1960,* vol. 1, 8; Durbrow to Robertson, February 16, 1959, ibid., 141–42; Memorandum of Conversation, November 21, 1959, ibid., 251–54.

52. Memorandum of Conversation, September 25, 1956, *FRUS, 1955–1957,* vol. 1, 740.

53. Montgomery, *The Politics of Foreign Aid,* 178–81.

54. Bo-Truong Phu Tong-Thong [to] Tinh-Truong, April 13, 1959, Van-Phong Bo-Truong Phu Tong-Thong, BT 517/1, Cuc Luu Tru II; Tong Giam-Doc Kien-Thiet va Thiet-Ke Do-Thi [to] Bo-Truong PTT, October 15, 1959, BT 517/1, ibid.; Tong-Thong [to] Dai-Bieu Chanh-Phu Mien Dong Nam-Phan [et al.], June 2, 1960, Tai Lieu Do So Luu Tru Va Cong Bao Phu Thu Tuong Viet Nam Cong Hoa, SC.05 10074, ibid.; Nguyen Khac Nhan, "Policy of Key Rural Agrovilles," *Asian Culture* (July–December 1961): 35–41.

55. Nguyen Cong Vien, *Seeking the Truth: The Inside Story of Viet Nam after the French Defeat by a Man Who Served in Dai's Cabinet* (New York: Vantage Press, 1966), 7, 18–34.

56. Saigon to State, October 5, 1960, 751K.5-MSP/10-560, CDF 60-63, RG 59, USNA.

57. Race, *War Comes to Long An,* 97–104; Ronald H. Spector, *Advice and Support: The Early Years of the United States Army in Vietnam, 1941–1960* (New York: Free Press, 1985), 325–27; William S. Turley, *The Second Indochina War: A Short Political and Military History* (New York: Mentor, 1987), 26–28; Nguyen Thi Dinh, *No Other Road to Take: Memoirs of Mrs. Nguyen Thi Dinh,* trans. Mai V. Elliott (Ithaca, N.Y.: Cornell University Southeast Asia Program, 1976), 48–59.

58. War Experiences Recapitulation Committee of the High-Level Military Institute, *The Anti–U.S. Resistance War for National Salvation, 1954–1975: Military Events,* trans. JPRS 80968 (Washington, D.C.: GPO, 1982), 29–31; Carlyle A. Thayer, *War by Other Means: National Liberation and Revolution in Viet-Nam, 1954–1960* (Sydney: Allen & Unwin, 1989); Bui Tin, *Following Ho Chi Minh: The Memoirs of a North Vietnamese Colonel,* trans. and adapted by Judy Stowe and Do Van (London: Hurst, 1995), 41–42; William J. Duiker, *Ho Chi Minh* (New York: Hyperion, 2000), 470–73, 491–519.

59. Telephone interview with Tran Ngoc Chau, July 18, 1997; Tran Ngoc Chau, "My War Story: From Ho Chi Minh to Ngo Dinh Diem," in *Prelude to Tragedy: Vietnam, 1960–1965,* ed. Harvey Neese and John O'Donnell (Annapolis: Naval Institute Press, 2001), 188–89, 205–6; Saigon to State, July 23, 1956, 751G.00/7-2356, CDF 55-59, RG 59, USNA.

60. Letter from Tran Ngoc Chau, August 27, 1997. See also: *The American Syndrome: An Interview with the BBC* (1991), 9–10, Folder 1, Box 62, Vann-Sheehan Vietnam War Collection, Library of Congress Manuscript Division; Hue to State, February 20, 1958, 751G.00/2-2058, CDF 55-59, RG 59, USNA; Saigon to State, March 7, 1960, *FRUS, 1958–1960,* vol. 1, 312–13.

61. Race, 111–12; Turley, 28; Dinh, 63.

62. Saigon to State, May 10, 1960, 751K.00/5-1060, CDF 60-63, RG 59, USNA; Milton E. Osborne, *Strategic Hamlets in South Viet-Nam: A Survey and a Comparison* (Ithaca, N.Y.: Cornell University Southeast Asia Program, 1965), 21.

63. Nhan, 29–32; Joseph J. Zasloff, *Rural Resettlement in Vietnam: An Agroville in Development* (n.p., MSU Vietnam Advisory Group, 1963), 6–8. See also documents in SC.05 10.102, CLT II.

64. Memorandum of Conversation, April 24, 1959, *FRUS, 1958–1960,* vol. 1, 188–90; Saigon to State, May 14, 1959, ibid., 195. See also Robert Shaplen, "The Cult of Diem," *New York Times Magazine,* May 14, 1972, 50.

65. Uy Ban Lanh-Dao Hoc Tap Trung Uong [to] Truong Ban Huong Dan Hoc Tap Cac Don Vi Quan Chinh, May 16, 1959, BT 576, CLT II.

66. Saigon to State, May 14, 1959, *FRUS, 1958–1960,* vol. 1, 195.

67. Nhan, "Policy of Key Rural Agrovilles," 32–33; Zasloff, 7.

68. Bo-Truong PTT [to] Tong Giam-Doc Kien-Thiet va Thiet-Ke Do-Thi [et al.], May 25, 1959, SC.05 9696B, CLT II; Saigon to State, July 1, 1959, *FRUS, 1958–1960,* vol. 1, 214–15; May 10, 1960, 751K.00/5-1060, CDF 60-63, RG 59, USNA.

69. For regional settlement patterns, see Maynard Weston Dow, *Nation Building in Southeast Asia* (Boulder, Colo.: Pruett Press, 1966), 158–63.

70. Bo-Truong PTT [to] Pho TT, May 25, 1959, SC.05 9696B, CLT II; Saigon to State, July 1, 1959, *FRUS, 1958–1960,* vol. 1, 214; Bo-Truong Bo Thong-Tin va Thanh-Nien, July 20, 1959, SC.05 9696B, CLT II; *Times of Viet Nam Magazine,* May 7, 1960, 14. Zasloff, 4, mentions the construction of fences and guard posts, but this is one of the few references to physical defenses.

71. Dai-Bieu Chanh-Phu MDNP [to] Tinh Truong, June 30, 1960, SC.05 10074, CLT II; *Khu Tru Mat* (Saigon: Van Huu A Chau, 1960); description of Vi Thanh-Hoa Luu, Saigon to State, June 6, 1960, 751K.00/6-660, CDF 60-63, RG 59, USNA; Diem's address at Vi Thanh, So Bao Chi Phu Tong Thong, *Con Duong Chinh Nghia: Nhan-Vi, Cong-Dong, Dong-Tien,* vol. 6 (Saigon, n.d.), 93.

72. Nhan, 40–41; Nghiem Dang, *Viet-Nam: Politics and Public Administration* (Honolulu: East-West Center Press, 1966), 157–59.

73. *Con Duong Chinh Nghia,* vol. 6, 95–97; *News from Viet-Nam,* October 26, 1960, 4; Zasloff, 10.

74. Memorandum of Conversation, April 8, 1960, 751K.5-MSP/4-860, CDF 60-63, RG 59, USNA.

75. *Con Duong Chinh Nghia,* vol. 6, 95–97.

76. Chester L. Cooper et al., *The American Experience with Pacification in Vietnam,* vol. 3 (Arlington, Va.: Institute for Defense Analyses, 1972), 139; Saigon to State, June 6, 1960, 751K.00/6-660, CDF 60-63, RG 59, USNA; *Times of Viet Nam Magazine,* October 29, 1961, 13.

77. Saigon to State, February 16, 1960, 751K.5/2-1660, CDF 60-63, RG 59, USNA; June 6, 1960, 751K.00/6-660, ibid.; July 14, 1960, 751K.00/7-1460, ibid.

78. Saigon to State, March 10, 1960, 751K.00/3-1060, ibid.

79. Saigon to State, May 10, 1960, 751K.00/5-1060, ibid. See Zasloff, *Rural Resettlement in Vietnam*, 16–19, for labor practices in neighboring Vinh Long.

80. Dai Bieu Chanh Phu Tay Nam Nam Phan [to] Tinh Truong TNNP, October 15, 1959, SC.05 9696/1, CLT II; March 4, 1960, BT 517/1, ibid. See also Bo-Truong Noi-Vu [to] Tinh-Truong, March 25, 1960, BT 517/1, ibid.; Phien hop Hoi-Dong Noi-Cac, April 30, 1960, SC.05 10001, ibid.

81. Dai Bieu Chanh Phu TNNP [to] Tinh Truong TNNP, October 15, 1959, BT 517/1, ibid. Long An's province chief put the cost of the Duc Hue agroville at 2,820,000 piasters—Long An [to] Tong-Thong, October 9, 1959, ibid.—although estimates of agroville costs made by U.S. aid officials suggest that this figure is too low—John C. Donnell, "Politics in South Vietnam: Doctrines of Authority in Conflict" (Ph.D. diss., University of California, Berkeley, 1964), 188.

82. Jason L. Finkle and Tran Van Dinh, *Provincial Government in Viet Nam: A Study of Vinh Long Province* (Saigon: MSU Viet Nam Advisory Group and NIA, 1961), 19–21, 71–72, 87. See also Hoang Lac, Ha Mai Viet, *Nam-Viet-Nam, 1954–1975: Nhung Su That Chua He Nhac Toi* (Alief, Tex.: Hoang Lac, 1990), 245–46; Donnell, 71–72.

83. Zasloff, 18, 20–21, 24–25, 29–31.

84. Ibid., 21–22, 26–27; Race, *War Comes to Long An,* 173; VC docs. 1033, 1042, Race Collection, Center for Research Libraries; Bo-Truong Noi-Vu [to] Tinh-Truong, March 25, 1960, BT 517/1, CLT II; Kien-Tuong [to] Tong Giam-Doc Kien-Thiet va Thiet-Ke Do-Thi, November 29, 1960, SC.05 9694, ibid.

85. Dinh, *No Other Road to Take,* 59–61. There are photographs of a visit by Diem to Thanh Thoi (in dossier 156, Van-Phong Bi-Thu-Truong Phu Tong-Thong, CLT II), but no signs or mention of demonstrations.

86. Cooper et al., vol. 3, 151–53. For Ba's death, see Finkle and Dinh, 11; Vinh Long [to] Dong-Ly Van-Phong PTT, August 23, 1960, SC.05 9694, CLT II.

87. Dinh, 62–77; Bo Chi Huy Quan Su Tinh Ben Tre, *Ben Tre: 30 Nam Khang Chien Chong Phap, Chong My, 1945–1975* (n.p., 1990), 127–38.

88. Race, 113–16; Nguyen Huu Nguyen, "Hinh Thai Chien Tranh Nhan Dan O Long An Trong Khang Chien Chong My Tren Chien Truong Nam Bo (1960–1975)" (TP Ho Chi Minh, Luan An Pho Tien Sy, 1994), 48–51; Tran Van Giau, *Long An: 21 Nam Danh My* (n.p.: Long An, 1988), 98–104.

89. Saigon to State, March 7, 1960, *FRUS, 1958–1960,* vol. 1, 300–20; War Experiences Recapitulation Committee, *The Anti–U.S. Resistance War,* 38–39; John D. Donoghue, *My Thuan: A Mekong Delta Village in South Vietnam* (n.p.: MSU Viet Nam Advisory Group, 1961), 15–17; Joseph J. Zasloff and Nguyen Khac Nhan, *A Study of Administration in Binh Minh District* (Saigon: MSU Viet Nam Advisory Group and NIA, 1961), 49–51.

90. Phien hop Hoi-Dong Noi-Cac, February 2, 1960, SC.05 10.001, CLT II; Saigon to State, March 7, 1960, *FRUS, 1958–1960,* vol. 1, 316.

234 Diem's Final Failure

91. Saigon to State, March 2, 1960, ibid., 294–97; March 7, 1960, ibid., 312, 315–16; July 12, 1960, 751K.5/7-1260, CDF 60-63, RG 59, USNA.

92. Saigon to State, March 7, 1960, *FRUS, 1958–1960,* vol. 1, 316; March 10, 1960, 751K.00/3-1060, CDF 60-63, RG 59, USNA; Bo-Truong Noi-Vu [to] Tinh-Truong, March 25, 1960, BT 517/1, CLT II.

93. Memorandum of Conversation, April 8, 1960, 751K.5-MSP/4-860, CDF 60-63, RG 59, USNA; Saigon to State, September 1, 1960, 851K.00/9-160, ibid.

94. Saigon to State, October 7, 1960, 751K.5/10-760, ibid.

4. Origins of the Strategic Hamlet Program

1. Saigon to State, January 24, 1961, 751K.00/1-2461, Central Decimal File 1960–1963, Record Group 59, U.S. National Archives; March 4, 1961, 751K.00/3-461, ibid.; April 6, 1961, 751K.00/4-661, ibid.

2. Robert K. Brigham, *Guerrilla Diplomacy: The NLF's Foreign Relations and the Viet Nam War* (Ithaca, N.Y.: Cornell University Press, 1999), 10–13; William S. Turley, *The Second Indochina War: A Short Political and Military History, 1954–1975* (New York: Mentor, 1987), 28–32; Jeffrey Race, *War Comes to Long An: Revolutionary Conflict in a Vietnamese Province* (Berkeley: University of California Press, 1973), 121–23; Truong Nhu Tang, with David Chanoff and Doan Van Toai, *A Viet Cong Memoir* (New York: Vintage Books, 1985), 63–80, 320.

3. Draft notes of meeting, April 24, 1961, *Foreign Relations of the United States, 1961–1963,* vol. 1, *Vietnam* (Washington, D.C.: GPO, 1988), 78.

4. Race, 130.

5. Saigon to State, September 20, 1961, 751K.00/9-2061, CDF 60-63, RG 59, USNA; William J. Rust and the editors of U.S. News Books, *Kennedy in Vietnam* (New York: Charles Scribner's Sons, 1985), 37; *Mien Dong Nam Bo Khang Chien (1945–1975),* vol. 2 (Hanoi: Quan Doi Nhan Dan, 1993), 108–12.

6. Saigon to State, September 5, 1961, *FRUS, 1961–1963,* vol. 1, 292; McGarr to Felt, September 10, 1961, ibid., 296–98; McGarr to McNamara, October 30, 1961, ibid., 449; Hue to State, October 12, 1961, 751K.00/10-1261, CDF 60-63, RG 59, USNA.

7. McGarr to Felt, September 10, 1961, *FRUS, 1961–1963,* vol. 1, 296–98; Saigon to State, October 10, 1961, ibid., 333–35; October 10, 1961, 751K.00/10-1061, CDF 60-63, RG 59, USNA; October 10, 1961, 751K.5811/10-1061, ibid.; *News from Viet-Nam,* October 1961, 12.

8. Memorandum for Record, October 20, 1961, *FRUS, 1961–1963,* vol. 1, 404.

9. Wood to Steeves, November 14, 1961, 751K.00/11-1461, CDF 60-63, RG 59, USNA. See also Department of State, *A Threat to the Peace: North Viet-Nam's Effort to Conquer South Viet-Nam* (Washington, D.C.: GPO, 1961).

10. War Experiences Recapitulation Committee of the High-Level Military Insti-

tute, *The Anti-U.S. Resistance War for National Salvation, 1954–1975: Military Events,* trans. JPRS 80968 (Washington, D.C.: GPO, 1982), 46–47; Memorandum for Record, October 20, 1961, *FRUS, 1961–1963,* vol. 1, 403–4; Saigon to State, November 27, 1961, 751K.5/11-2761, CDF 60-63, RG 59, USNA.

11. Johnson to Rostow, October 5, 1961, Johnson, Sept. 1–Dec. 31, 1961, Lot 67D548, Records of the Policy Planning Staff 1957–1961, Box 178, ibid.

12. Saigon to State, November 27, 1961, 751K.5/11-2761, CDF 60-63, ibid.; Nguyen Tran, *Cong Va Toi: Nhung Su That Lich Su* (Los Alamitos, Calif.: Xuan Thu, 1992), 379.

13. Ronald H. Spector, *Advice and Support: The Early Years of the United States Army in Vietnam, 1941–1960* (New York: Free Press, 1985), 361–71; Country team paper, January 1961, *FRUS, 1961–1963,* vol. 1, 1–12.

14. Weiss to Bell, January 10, 1961, 751K.00/1-1061, CDF 60-63, RG 59, USNA.

15. Saigon to State, October 15, 1960, 751K.00/10-1560, ibid.; October 15, 1960, *Foreign Relations of the United States, 1958–1960,* vol. 1, *Vietnam* (Washington, D.C.: GPO, 1986), 595–96.

16. Rust, *Kennedy in Vietnam,* 1–20; William Colby, with James McCargar, *Lost Victory: A Firsthand Account of America's Sixteen-Year Involvement in Vietnam* (Chicago: Contemporary Books, 1989), 76–79; Tran Tuong, ed., *Bien Co 11: Tu Dao Chanh Den Tu Day* (reprint of unspecified edition, 1986).

17. Saigon to State, December 24, 1960, *FRUS, 1958–1960,* vol. 1, 739–41; State to Saigon, December 31, 1960, 751K.00/12-2960, CDF 60-63, RG 59, USNA; Memorandum for Files, January 10, 1961, 751K.00/1-1061, ibid.

18. James N. Giglio, *The Presidency of John F. Kennedy* (Lawrence: University Press of Kansas, 1991), 221–22. Ike-JFK meeting in Clark Clifford Memorandum, September 29, 1967, *United States–Vietnam Relations, 1945–1967,* bk. 10 (Washington, D.C.: GPO, 1971), 1360–62 (see also Fred I. Greenstein and Richard H. Immerman, "What Did Eisenhower Tell Kennedy about Indochina? The Politics of Misperception," *Journal of American History* [September 1992]: 568–87).

19. Lansdale's report, *United States–Vietnam Relations, 1945–1967,* bk. 11, 1–12; *FRUS, 1961–1963,* vol. 1, 16 (note 2).

20. Records of meeting, *FRUS, 1961–1963,* vol. 1, 13–15, 16–19; John M. Newman, *JFK and Vietnam: Deception, Intrigue, and the Struggle for Power* (New York: Warner Books, 1992), 4–6; Gary R. Hess, "Commitment in the Age of Counterinsurgency: Kennedy's Vietnam Options and Decisions, 1961–1963," in *Shadow on the White House: Presidents and the Vietnam War, 1945–1975,* ed. David L. Anderson (Lawrence: University Press of Kansas, 1993), 63–70; Orrin Schwab, *Defending the Free World: John F. Kennedy, Lyndon Johnson, and the Vietnam War, 1961–1965* (Westport, Conn.: Praeger Publishers, 1998), 1–10.

21. State to Saigon, February 3, 1961, *United States–Vietnam Relations, 1945–1967,* bk. 11, 14–16 (Washington's instructions); Saigon to State, February 14, 1961, 751K.5-MSP/2-1461, CDF 60-63, RG 59, USNA (copy of plan handed to Diem).

For key U.S.–Vietnamese encounters, see Saigon to State, February 13, 1961, *FRUS, 1961–1963*, vol. 1, 31–32; February 28, 1961, ibid., 37–40; March 11, 1961, 751K.5-MSP/3-1161, CDF 60-63, RG 59, USNA; March 16, 1961, *FRUS, 1961–1963*, vol. 1, 47–51; April 13, 1961, 751K.00/4-1361, CDF 60-63, RG 59, USNA; April 14, 1961, 751K.00/4-1461, ibid.; May 3, 1961, 751K.5-MSP/5-361, ibid.; Memorandum of Conversation, March 27, 1961, *FRUS, 1961–1963*, vol. 1, 52–57.

22. Washington to Foreign Office, February 20, 1961, DV1015/10, Foreign Office 371/160108, Public Record Office; Anderson to Parsons, March 10, 1961, Viet-Nam 1961, Geographic Files: Malaya to Vietnam, Ass. Sec. for Far Eastern Affairs: Subject, Personal Name, and Country Files—1960–1963, Bureau of Far Eastern Affairs, Box 6 1961, RG 59, USNA; Lemnitzer to JCS, May 8, 1961, *FRUS, 1961–1963*, vol. 1, 126–28.

23. Rust, 28–34; Newman, 9–20, 46–56; David Kaiser, *American Tragedy: Kennedy, Johnson, and the Origins of the Vietnam War* (Cambridge, Mass.: Belknap Press, 2000), 36–57.

24. *The Pentagon Papers: The Defense Department History of United States Decisionmaking on Vietnam*, vol. 2, Gravel ed. (Boston: Beacon Press, 1971), 30–55 (report's drafting process); *United States–Vietnam Relations, 1945–1967*, bk. 11, 42–56, 69–130, and *FRUS, 1961–1963*, vol. 1, 92–115 (main drafts); NSAM 52, *United States–Vietnam Relations, 1945–1967*, bk. 11, 136–37; State to Saigon, May 20, 1961, *FRUS, 1961–1963*, vol. 1, 140–43.

25. A Program of Action, *United States–Vietnam Relations, 1945–1967*, bk. 11, 69–130.

26. Frederick Nolting, *From Trust to Tragedy: The Political Memoirs of Frederick Nolting, Kennedy's Ambassador to Diem's Vietnam* (New York: Praeger Publishers, 1988), 14–15; JCS (Historical Division), *The History of the Joint Chiefs of Staff: The Joint Chiefs of Staff and the War in Vietnam, 1960–1968*, pt. 1, chs. 2, 8.

27. Saigon to State, May 26, 1961, 033.1100-JO/5-2661, CDF 60-63, RG 59, USNA; Kennedy letter, May 8, 1961, *United States–Vietnam Relations, 1945–1967*, bk. 11, 132–35.

28. Stanley Karnow, *Vietnam: A History* (New York: Viking Press, 1983), 214.

29. Saigon to State, November 11, 1960, *FRUS, 1958–1960*, vol. 1, 634–36; McGarr to Felt, November 12, 1960, ibid., 647; Saigon to State, November 12, 1960, ibid., 649–50; Mendenhall and Colby comments, ibid., 662–63.

30. Saigon to State, December 1, 1960, 611.51K/12-160, CDF 60-63, RG 59, USNA; December 1, 1960, 751K.00/12-160, ibid.; Stanley Karnow, "Diem Defeats His Own Best Troops," *The Reporter*, January 19, 1961, 28; George McT. Kahin, *Intervention: How America Became Involved in Vietnam* (New York: Alfred A. Knopf, 1986), 125; *Times of Viet Nam Magazine*, November 26, 1960, 6.

31. Erskine to Parsons, January 9, 1961, 751K.00/1-961, CDF 60-63, RG 59, USNA.

32. *News from Viet-Nam*, February 1961, 4–7.

33. Saigon to State, September 17, 1956, *Foreign Relations of the United States*,

1955–1957, vol. 1, *Vietnam* (Washington, D.C.: GPO, 1985), 737–38; October 5, 1960, 751K.5-MSP/10-560, CDF 60-63, RG 59, USNA. After U.S. concessions, agreement was finally reached at the end of June regarding the financing of the increase (Saigon to State, June 29, 1961, 751K.5-MSP/6-2961, ibid.).

34. Diem to Kennedy, May 15, 1961, *United States–Vietnam Relations, 1945–1967*, bk. 11, 155.

35. *Cach Mang Quoc Gia*, January 2–20, 1961; Harriman to Washington, May 4, 1961, General, 5/3/61–5/7/61, Countries: VN, Box 193, National Security Files, John F. Kennedy Library.

36. Arthur M. Schlesinger, Jr., *A Thousand Days: John F. Kennedy in the White House* (Boston: Houghton Mifflin, 1965), 329–40, 512–15; Newman, *JFK and Vietnam*, 107–15; Rudy Abramson, *Spanning the Century: The Life of W. Averell Harriman, 1891–1986* (New York: William Morrow, 1992), 582–87. Although eschewing armed intervention, Kennedy supported an extensive covert effort in Laos—see Timothy N. Castle, *At War in the Shadow of Vietnam: U.S. Military Aid to the Royal Lao Government, 1955–1975* (New York: Columbia University Press, 1993), 26–61.

37. *News from Viet-Nam*, July 1961, 8–10.

38. *Vietnam Press*, w/e May 21, 1961, 1–2; Lansdale to Taylor, October 21, 1961, *FRUS, 1961–1963*, vol. 1, 411–12; Saigon to Foreign Office, August 1, 1962, DV1015/166, FO371/166706, PRO. See also Lansdale to Gilpatric, July 12, 1961, *United States–Vietnam Relations, 1945–1967*, bk. 11, 176.

39. Diem to Kennedy, June 9, 1961, ibid., 167–70.

40. Kennedy to Diem, August 5, 1961, *FRUS, 1961–1963*, vol. 1, 263–67; Saigon to State, August 8, 1961, ibid., 269–73.

41. Saigon to State, August 8, 1961, ibid., 269, 272; CIA Information Report, November 29, 1961, ibid., 692–93.

42. Saigon to State, October 10, 1961, 751K.5811/10-1061, CDF 60-63, RG 59, USNA; October 13, 1961, 751K.5-MSP/10-1361, ibid.

43. Cottrell to McConaughy, July 8, 1961, *FRUS, 1961–1963*, vol. 1, 201–3; Rostow to Kennedy, July 29, 1961, ibid., 256–57.

44. Research Memorandum, September 29, 1961, *United States–Vietnam Relations, 1945–1967*, bk. 11, 259–61.

45. Maxwell D. Taylor, *Swords and Plowshares* (New York: W. W. Norton, 1972), 221–44; Taylor to Kennedy, November 3, 1961, *FRUS, 1961–1963*, vol. 1, 477–532.

46. Ibid. (specific information and quotations, 480–81, 488–89, 491–94, 501–2).

47. Schlesinger, Jr., 547; W. W. Rostow, *The Diffusion of Power: An Essay in Recent History* (New York: Macmillan, 1972), 278. See also Fredrik Logevall, *Choosing War: The Lost Chance for Peace and the Escalation of War in Vietnam* (Berkeley: University of California Press, 1999), 22–33; Kaiser, *American Tragedy*, 108–21.

48. State to Saigon, November 15, 1961, 751K.00/11-1561, CDF 60-63, RG 59, USNA; November 15, 1961, *United States–Vietnam Relations, 1945–1967*, bk. 11, 400–405. William Bundy stated that inclusion of a quid pro quo "had the President's

own imprint, as well as that of Rusk" (Bundy manuscript, ch. 4, 32, William P. Bundy Papers, Lyndon B. Johnson Library).

49. Even Nolting only received confirmation of the Taylor visit *after* a VOA broadcast announcing the mission (State to Saigon, October 11, 1961, 120.1551K/10-1161, CDF 60-63, RG 59, USNA; Saigon to State, October 12, 1961, 120.1551K/10-1261, ibid.).

50. Saigon to State, October 18, 1961, 120.1551K/10-1861, ibid.; October 25, 1961 (Tel. 540), 751K.00/10-256, ibid.; October 25, 1961 (Tel. 541), 751K.00/10-2561, ibid.; Taylor to State, October 25, 1961, *FRUS, 1961–1963*, vol. 1, 427–29.

51. CIA Information Report, November 22, 1961, General, 11/21/61–11/23/61, Countries: VN, Box 195, NSF, JFK. An undated/sanitized document lists Diem, Tho, Thuan, and Khanh as supporters of a U.S. troop deployment; Nhu favored technical and logistical forces, not combat troops (Security 1961, Countries: VN, Box 128a, Presidential Office Files, JFK).

52. Saigon to State, October 25, 1961, 751K.00/10-2561, CDF 60-63, RG 59, USNA; November 22, 1961, 751K.00/11-2261, ibid.

53. Saigon to State, November 18, 1961, 751K.00/11-1861, ibid.; November 25, 1961, 751K.5/11-2561, ibid.; CIA Information Report, November 29, 1961, *FRUS, 1961–1963*, vol. 1, 692–93.

54. Saigon to State, November 25, 1961 (Tel. 707), 751K.00/11-2561, CDF 60-63, RG 59, USNA; November 25, 1961, 751K.5/11-2561, ibid.; November 25, 1961 (Tel. 709), 751K.00/11-2561, ibid.; November 27, 1961, 751K.5/11-2761, ibid.; November 29, 1961, 751K.5/11-2961, ibid.; Memorandum for Record, December 1, 1961, *FRUS, 1961–1963*, vol. 1, 704–6.

55. State to Saigon, November 27, 1961, ibid., 676–77.

56. Taylor to Kennedy, November 3, 1961, ibid., 491; USDEL HAKONE to State, November 1, 1961, 751K.00/11-161, CDF 60-63, RG 59, USNA; Johnson's paper, November 28, 1961, *FRUS, 1961–1963*, vol. 1, 683–87.

57. Saigon to State, December 1, 1961, 751K.00/12-161, CDF 60-63, RG 59, USNA; December 3, 1961, 751K.00/12-361, ibid.; December 4, 1961, 751K.00/12-461, ibid. Nolting had already cautioned against expecting Diem's ready compliance with U.S. proposals (Saigon to State, November 6, 1961, 751K.00/11-661, ibid.; November 7, 1961, 751K.00/11-761, ibid.).

58. State to Saigon, December 4, 1961, 751K.00/12-461, ibid.; Battle to Bundy, December 6, 1961, General 12/6/61–12/7/61, Countries: VN, Box 195, NSF, JFK.

59. Bundy manuscript, ch. 4, 40–41, Bundy Papers, LBJ; Taylor, *Swords and Plow-shares*, 248–49; Kahin, *Intervention*, 94; USDEL HAKONE to State, November 1, 1961, 751K.00/11-161, CDF 60-63, RG 59, USNA.

60. Memorandum for Record, October 19, 1961, *FRUS, 1961–1963*, vol. 1, 395–98.

61. Battle to Bundy, November 29, 1961, 751K.00/11-2961, CDF 60-63, RG 59, USNA.

62. CIA Information Report, November 22, 1961, General 11/21/61–11/23/61, Countries: VN, Box 195, NSF, JFK.

63. CIA Information Report, November 28, 1961, *FRUS, 1961–1963*, vol. 1, 690–91. See also Lansdale to Taylor, October 21, 1961, ibid., 412–13; Paris to State, December 2, 1961, 611.51K/12-261, CDF 60-63, RG 59, USNA.

64. Saigon to State, December 19, 1961, 751K.00/12-1961, ibid.

65. Saigon to State, June 8, 1954, *Foreign Relations of the United States, 1952–1954*, vol. 13, *Indochina*, pt. 2 (Washington, D.C.: GPO, 1982), 1666–67; November 4, 1955, 751G.00/11-455, CDF 55-59, RG 59, USNA; Stuart to Kattenburg, January 24, 1956, 751G.001/1-2456, ibid.

66. Hoyt to Weidner, September 30, 1955, Correspondence, Edward W. Weidner, October 1955, Folder 2, M.S.U. Administration of the Project, Box 629, Vietnam Project, Michigan State University Archives and Historical Collections.

67. Saigon to State, February 3, 1955, *FRUS, 1955–1957*, vol. 1, 76–78; September 30, 1955, 751G.00/9-3055, CDF 55-59, RG 59, USNA; Weidner to Barrows (and enclosed memos), October 5, 1955, Correspondence, Edward W. Weidner, October 1955, Folder 2, M.S.U. Administration of the Project, Box 629, Vietnam Project, MSUAHC; Weidner to Barrows, October 11, 1955, ibid.; Saigon to State, November 17, 1955, *FRUS, 1955–1957*, vol. 1, 581–84; December 4, 1955, 751G.00(W)/12-455, CDF 55-59, RG 59, USNA; December 5, 1955, *FRUS, 1955–1957*, vol. 1, 596–97; Memorandum of Conversation, December 28, 1955, ibid., 603–5 (includes quotation); Memorandum for Record, ibid., 611–12.

68. Bo-Truong Phu Tong-Thong [to] Do-Truong, Tinh-Truong, September 6, 1957, Tai Lieu Do So Luu Tru Va Cong Bao Phu Thu Tuong Viet Nam Cong Hoa, SC.02 3470/1, Cuc Luu Tru II; Bo-Truong PTT [to] Tinh-Truong, December 30, 1957, ibid.; Saigon to State, September 30, 1958, *FRUS, 1958–1960*, vol. 1, 82–83; September 25, 1959, 751G.00/9-2559, CDF 55-59, RG 59, USNA.

69. Dai-Bieu Chanh-Phu Mien-Dong Nam-Phan [to] Tinh-Truong, May 31, 1960, SC.02 4308/3, CLT II; Dai-Bieu Chanh-Phu MDNP [to] Dong-Ly Van-Phong PTT, August 1, 1960, SC.02 4308/2, ibid.

70. John L. Sorenson and David K. Pack, *Unconventional Warfare and the Vietnamese Society* (China Lake, Calif.: U.S. Naval Ordnance Test Station, 1964), 106–7; Saigon to State, October 20, 1960, 751K.00/10-2060, CDF 60-63, RG 59, USNA; Burns to Chief, CATO, March 26, 1960, Folder 1182, Correspondence, Box 42, Edward G. Lansdale Papers, Hoover Institute; Memorandum of Conversation, April 6, 1960, *FRUS, 1958–1960*, vol. 1, 371.

71. Saigon to State, October 20, 1960, 751K.00/10-2060, CDF 60-63, RG 59, USNA; November 26, 1960, *FRUS, 1958–1960*, vol. 1, 688–89; March 18, 1961, 751K.00/3-1861, CDF 60-63, RG 59, USNA; June 15, 1961, 751K.5-MSP/6-1561, ibid.

72. Phien Hop Hoi-Dong Noi-Cac, December 1, 1960, SC.05 10.001, CLT II; Saigon to State, December 15, 1960, *FRUS, 1958–1960*, vol. 1, 732–33; *News from Viet-Nam*, June 1961, 6–7; John C. Donnell, "Politics in South Vietnam: Doctrines of Authority in Conflict" (Ph.D. diss., University of California, Berkeley, 1964), 267–70.

73. Phien Hop Hoi-Dong Noi-Cac, May 30, 1961, SC.05 10.001, CLT II.

74. Saigon to State, February 16, 1960, 751K.5/2-1660, CDF 60-63, RG 59, USNA.

75. *News from Viet-Nam*, October 26, 1960, 8; Donnell, 270–74.

76. *Cach Mang Quoc Gia*, November 19 and 20, 1960; *News from Viet-Nam*, June 1961, 7.

77. Colby, *Lost Victory*, 32–33, 85–86, 99; William Colby and Peter Forbath, *Honorable Men: My Life in the CIA* (New York: Simon and Schuster, 1978), 155–56; Lansdale to Taylor, October 21, 1961, *FRUS, 1961–1963*, vol. 1, 412–15; CIA Information Report, November 28, 1961, ibid., 690–91; interview with Douglas Pike, November 19, 1996. For the influence of Marxism-Leninism, see Donnell, 224–28. See Tran, *Cong Va Toi*, 258–69, for an insight into Nhu's earlier thinking about security.

78. Colby, *Lost Victory*, 31–34, 88–92; Colby, *Honorable Men*, 154–55, 161–62, 165–69. For Buon Enao, see Francis J. Kelly, *The Green Berets in Vietnam, 1961–71* (New York: Brassey's, 1991), 19–29; Gerald Cannon Hickey, *Free in the Forest: Ethnohistory of the Vietnamese Central Highlands, 1954–1976* (New Haven: Yale University Press, 1982), 73–79.

79. Colby, *Lost Victory*, 85–86, 99–100. For "combat villages," see Michael Charles Conley, *The Communist Insurgent Infrastructure in South Vietnam: A Study of Organization and Strategy* (Washington, D.C.: Department of the Army, 1967), 348–60.

80. Saigon to State, January 24, 1961, 751K.00/1-2461, CDF 60-63, RG 59, USNA; March 23, 1961, 751K.5/3-2361, ibid.

81. Interview with Nguyen Van Dam (pseudonym), March 17 and 27, 1997.

82. Saigon to Foreign Office, January 30, 1963, DV1017/4, FO371/170100, PRO.

83. Tay-Ninh [to] Van-Phong Pho TT, February 28, 1962, SC.25 951, CLT II.

84. Quang-Ngai [to] Bo-Truong PTT, June 20, 1961, SC.02 3562, ibid.; Hue to State, August 31, 1961, 751K.00/8-3161, CDF 60-63, RG 59, USNA.

85. Letter from Tran Ngoc Chau, August 27, 1997.

86. Vinh Long [to] Bo-Truong PTT, September 8, 1961, Van-Phong Bo-Truong Phu Tong-Thong, BT 577, CLT II. For an eyewitness account, see Vien Lang (Nguyen Lien), *Duong ve Ap Chien Luoc: Hoi-Ky cua Vien-Lang (Nguyen-Lien)* (Saigon: n.p., 1962).

87. Vinh Long, Phieu-Trinh, October 21, 1961, SC.03 5571/23, CLT II; Saigon to State, February 12, 1962, 751K.00/2-1262, CDF 60-63, RG 59, USNA.

88. *Vietnam Press*, w/e July 30, 1961, 11.

89. Saigon to State, March 18, 1961, 751K.00/3-1861, CDF 60-63, RG 59, USNA; Phien Hop Hoi-Dong Noi-Cac, June 19, 1961, SC.05 10.001, CLT II; An Giang [to] Bo-Truong Dac-Nhiem Phoi-Hop An-Ninh, July 31, 1961, SC.06 10618, ibid.; Saigon to State, August 4, 1961, 751K.00/8-461, CDF 60-63, RG 59, USNA.

90. *Vietnam Press*, w/e July 24, 1961, 6, and w/e July 30, 1961, 4; *Times of Viet Nam*, August 3, 1961, 2.

91. *Vietnam Press*, w/e August 13, 1961, 15.

92. Saigon to State, August 29, 1961, 751K.00/8-2961, CDF 60-63, RG 59, USNA.

93. Bo-Truong Noi-Vu [to] Tinh-Truong, October 5, 1961, BT 576, CLT II; Bien Ban phien hop cua Uy-Ban Lien-Bo dac trach ve ap chien luoc, January 20, 1962, BT 491, ibid.

94. Doan-Them, *Hai Muoi Nam Qua: Viec tung ngay (1945–1964)* (Los Alamitos, Calif.: Xuan Thu, n.d.), 310; *Khom Chien-Luoc*, 1962, SC.25 952, CLT II.

95. Binh-Long [to] Tong Thong, January 6, 1961, SC.05 9696/4, ibid.; Tay Ninh [to] Dong-Ly Van Phong PTT, January 13, 1961, SC.05 9696/8, ibid.; Binh-Thuan, Bien Ban Hoi Nghi An-Ninh Thuong Ky Thang 4-1961, SC.02 3563, ibid.; Kien-Tuong [to] Van-Phong Pho TT [et al.], July 15, 1961, SC.06 10618, ibid.

96. Thuan to Wood, July 18, 1961, *FRUS, 1961–1963*, vol. 1, 230. See also Dong-Ly Van-Phong PTT [to] Bo-Truong Cai-Tien Nong-Thon [et al.], August 21, 1961, SC.05 9696D, CLT II.

97. Dai-Bieu Chanh-Phu MDNP [to] Tinh-Truong, June 8, 1960, SC.05 10074, ibid.; Ap Kien Thiet, March 15, 1962, SC.25 956, ibid.; Nhu's address, March 17, 1962, *Ban Ghi Chep: Nhung Buoi Noi Chuyen Than Mat Cua Ong Co Van Chinh Tri Ve Ap Chien Luoc*, vol. 1, SC.04 8676, ibid. For a sense of the relative financial costs of agrovilles, agro-hamlets, and strategic hamlets, see Kien-Tuong [to] Bo-Truong Noi-Vu, December 9, 1961, SC.25 877, ibid.

98. Basic Counterinsurgency Plan, *FRUS, 1961–1963*, vol. 1, 5; Saigon to State, January 25, 1961, 751K.5-MSP/1-2561, CDF 60-63, RG 59, USNA.

99. State to Saigon, May 20, 1961, *FRUS, 1961–1963*, vol. 1, 142; Kennedy to Diem, May 8, 1961, *United States–Vietnam Relations, 1945–1967*, bk. 11, 134–35.

100. Staley-Thuc program, ibid., 183, 196, 216. See also Lansdale to Gilpatric, July 12, 1961, ibid., 176.

101. Memorandum of Discussion, July 28, 1961, *FRUS, 1961–1963*, vol. 1, 255–56; Rostow to Kennedy, August 4, 1961, ibid., 259–60.

102. Kennedy to Diem, August 5, 1961, ibid., 263–67; Saigon to State, August 8, 1961, ibid., 269–73.

103. Saigon to State, March 8, 1961, 751K.5-MSP/3-861, CDF 60-63, RG 59, USNA; March 23, 1961, 751K.5/3-2361, ibid.; McGarr to Diem, August 2[?], 1961, *United States–Vietnam Relations, 1945–1967*, bk. 11, 227–38; Saigon to State, August 14, 1961, 751K.00/8-1461, CDF 60-63, RG 59, USNA; McGarr to Felt, September 1, 1961, 268 Training–Viet Nam Armed Forces, MAAG Vietnam, Adjutant General Division 1961, Box 26, RG 334, USNA; Kennedy to Diem, August 5, 1961, *FRUS, 1961–1963*, vol. 1, 264.

104. McGarr to Diem, August 2[?], 1961, *United States–Vietnam Relations, 1945–1967*, bk. 11, 231–32.

105. White to Schlesinger, August 1961, Arthur M. Schlesinger 8/61–10/61, Staff Memoranda, Meetings and Memoranda, Box 326-27, NSF, JFK.

106. Point made by Pham Ngoc Thao—see Milton E. Osborne, *Strategic Hamlets in*

South Viet-Nam: A Survey and a Comparison (Ithaca, N.Y.: Cornell University Southeast Asia Program, 1965), 26.

107. McGarr to Felt, September 1, 1961, 268 Training–Viet Nam Armed Forces, MAAG Vietnam, AGD 1961, Box 26, RG 334, USNA.

108. Saigon to State, August 29, 1961, 751K.00/8-2961, CDF 60–63, RG 59, ibid. See also Colby, *Lost Victory*, 101–2.

109. Saigon to Foreign Office, August 5, 1960, DV1631/4, FO371/152790, PRO; *United States–Vietnam Relations, 1945–1967*, bk. 11, 345–58 ("Delta Plan"); Robert Thompson, *Make for the Hills: Memories of Far Eastern Wars* (London: Leo Cooper, 1989), 122–29.

110. Frances FitzGerald, *Fire in the Lake: The Vietnamese and the Americans in Vietnam* (New York: Vintage Books, 1973), 165–66; Kahin, *Intervention*, 140–41; George C. Herring, *America's Longest War: The United States and Vietnam, 1950–1975*, 2d ed. (New York: Alfred A. Knopf, 1986), 85–86; Marilyn B. Young, *The Vietnam Wars, 1945–1990* (New York: HarperCollins, 1991), 82; Kaiser, *American Tragedy*, 167.

111. Memorandum of Conversation, June 24, 1960, *FRUS, 1958–1960*, vol. 1, 504–5. See also Tran Ngoc Chau, "My War Story: From Ho Chi Minh to Ngo Dinh Diem," in *Prelude to Tragedy: Vietnam, 1960–1965*, ed. Harvey Neese and John O'Donnell (Annapolis: Naval Institute Press, 2001), 194–95. For a comparative study of strategic hamlets and "New Villages," see Osborne, *Strategic Hamlets in South Viet-Nam*.

112. Thompson to Denson, February 26, 1962, DV1015/43, FO371/166700, PRO; Saigon to Foreign Office, February 28, 1962, DV1015/64, FO371/166701, ibid.; June 12, 1962, DV1201/30, FO371/166748, ibid.; Saigon to War Office, July 26, 1962, DV1201/47, FO371/166749, ibid. See also Colby, *Lost Victory*, 100.

113. Saigon to State, November 30, 1961, *FRUS, 1961–1963*, vol. 1, 698–700; London to State, December 4, 1961, 751K.00/12-461, CDF 60–63, RG 59, USNA; Senior Officers Oral History Program, vol. 3, 135, W. B. Rosson Papers, U.S. Army Military History Institute; Dennis J. Duncanson, *Government and Revolution in Vietnam* (New York: Oxford University Press, 1968), 314.

114. PTT [to] Dai Bieu Chanh Phu Cao-Nguyen Trung-Phan, October 14, 1961, SC.03 5570/13, CLT II; Nhu's address, October 16, *Ban Ghi Chep*, vol. 1, SC.04 8676, ibid.

115. Rostow, *The Diffusion of Power*, 276–77.

116. Saigon to State, December 19, 1961, 751K.00/12-1961, CDF 60–63, RG 59, USNA.

117. Bo-Truong Noi-Vu [to] Bo-Truong PTT [et al.], January 8, 1962, BT 576, CLT II; Tong Thu-Ky Thuong-Truc Quoc Phong [to] Bo-Truong PTT, January 8, 1962, BT 576, ibid.; Tom Trinh ve Ap chien luoc, SC.04 8676, ibid.

118. Sac-Lenh so 11/TTP, February 3, 1962, SC.14 1073, ibid.; *Press Interviews with President Ngo Dinh Diem, Political Counselor Ngo Dinh Nhu* (n.p., 1963), 69; Hoang Lac, "Blind Design," in *Prelude to Tragedy*, ed. Neese and O'Donnell, 69–70.

5. Theory and Practice

1. Robert Thompson, *Make for the Hills: Memories of Far Eastern Wars* (London: Leo Cooper, 1989), 130, 139; Roger Hilsman, *To Move a Nation: The Politics of Foreign Policy in the Administration of John F. Kennedy* (Garden City, N.Y.: Doubleday, 1967), 580. An earlier version of this chapter appeared as "Counter-Insurgency and Nation-Building: The Strategic Hamlet Programme in South Vietnam, 1961–1963," *International History Review* (December 1999): 918–40.

2. Bo-Truong Noi-Vu [to] Bo-Truong Phu Tong-Thong, December 15, 1961, Tai Lieu Do So Luu Tru Va Cong Bao Phu Thu Tuong Viet Nam Cong Hoa, SC.03 5571/23, Cuc Luu Tru II. See also Nhu's address, March 17, 1962, *Ban Ghi Chep: Nhung Buoi Noi Chuyen Than Mat Cua Ong Co Van Chinh Tri Ve Ap Chien Luoc*, vol. 1, SC.04 8676, ibid.

3. Hoang Lac, "Blind Design," in *Prelude to Tragedy: Vietnam, 1960–1965*, ed. Harvey Neese and John O'Donnell (Annapolis: Naval Institute Press, 2001), 70; letter from Hoang Van Lac, February 13, 1996.

4. John Mecklin, *Mission in Torment: An Intimate Account of the U.S. Role in Vietnam* (Garden City, N.Y.: Doubleday, 1965), 45.

5. *Press Interviews with President Ngo Dinh Diem, Political Counselor Ngo Dinh Nhu* (n.p., 1963), 72.

6. Directorate General of Information, *Viet Nam's Strategic Hamlets*, 2d rev. ed. (Saigon, 1963), 26–28; *Times of Viet Nam Magazine*, October 28, 1962, 34–37; Dinh Ro Vi-Tri Chinh-Sach Ap Chien-Luoc, September 25, 1962, SC.25 956, CLT II; Rufus Phillips, "Before We Lost in South Vietnam," in *Prelude to Tragedy*, ed. Neese and O'Donnell, 30.

7. *Viet Nam's Strategic Hamlets*, 2d rev. ed., 25–38; *Times of Viet Nam Magazine*, April 21, 1963, 2.

8. Douglas Pike, *Viet Cong: The Organization and Techniques of the National Liberation Front of South Vietnam* (Cambridge, Mass.: MIT Press, 1967), 85–99; Nguyen Van Chau, *Giong Lich-Su* (Saigon: Nhom Van Chien, 1961), 7–9.

9. *Chien Si*, January and February 1962, 14, and March 1962, 7; Bien-Ban so 1 Uy-Ban Lien-Bo Dac-Trach Ap Chien-Luoc, February 12, 1962, GVN Strat Hams, Vietnam Archive.

10. Hoang Khanh, *Tim Hieu Quoc Sach Ap Chien Luoc* (Saigon: Nguyen ba Tong, 1962), 103–4; *Viet Nam's Strategic Hamlets*, 2d rev. ed., 16.

11. Nhu's comments, February 2, 1962, *Ban Ghi Chep*, vol. 1, SC.04 8676, CLT II; Bien-Ban so 1, February 12, 1962, GVN Strat Hams, VA; Nhu's talk, March 17, 1962, *Ban Ghi Chep*, vol. 1, SC.04 8676, CLT II; Nhu's talk, March 19, 1962, *Ban Ghi Chep*, vol. 2, SC.03 5570, ibid.; Bien-Ban so 16, July 13, 1962, GVN Strat Hams, VA.

12. Bien-Ban so 16, July 13, 1962, ibid.

13. Neil Sheehan, *A Bright Shining Lie: John Paul Vann and America in Vietnam* (New York: Random House, 1988), 50.

14. Nhu's talk, March 19, 1962, *Ban Ghi Chep*, vol 2, SC.03 5570, CLT II; Directorate General of Information, *Viet Nam's Strategic Hamlets* (Saigon, 1963), 19.

15. *Viet Nam's Strategic Hamlets*, 2d rev. ed., 7–9, 17; Hoang Khanh, 73–98; Nhu's talk, October 1961, *Ban Ghi Chep*, vol. 1, SC.04 8676, CLT II; "How to Beat the Reds in Southeast Asia: Interview with President Diem of South Vietnam," *U.S. News & World Report*, February 18, 1963, 71.

16. Nhu's address, October 1962, *Ban Ghi Chep*, vol. 2, SC.03 5570, CLT II; his talk, July 1963, *Nhung Huan Thi Cua Ong Co Van Chinh Tri Ve Quoc Sach Ap Chien Luoc tai Suoi Lo O*, vol. 5, SC.04 8676, ibid.; *Times of Viet Nam Magazine*, October 28, 1962, 38–39; Saigon to External Affairs, April 9, 1963, DV1015/24, Foreign Office 371/170090, Public Record Office.

17. Bien-Ban so 6, March 23, 1962, GVN Strat Hams, VA.

18. Bien-Ban so 26, November 1, 1962, ibid.; Bo Cong Dan Vu, Tai-Lieu Hoc-Tap: Ap Chien Luoc, SC.03 5570/8, CLT II (under cover of memo from Ban Huong-dan Hoc-tap, March 27, 1962); Hoang Khanh, 19–22, 87, 102–4; *Times of Viet Nam Magazine*, October 28, 1962, 3.

19. Bien-Ban so 6, March 23, 1962, GVN Strat Hams, VA.

20. Bien Ban phien hop cua Uy-Ban Lien-Bo dac trach ve ap chien luoc, January 20, 1962, Van-Phong Bo-Truong Phu Tong-Thong, BT 491, CLT II; Bien-Ban so 5, March 16, 1962, GVN Strat Hams, VA.

21. Suzanne Labin, *Vietnam: An Eye-Witness Account* (Springfield, Va.: Crestwood Books, 1964), 55.

22. *Viet Nam's Strategic Hamlets*, 2d rev. ed., 14–15; Khanh, *Tim Hieu Quoc Sach Ap Chien Luoc*, 136–61.

23. Bien-Ban so 9, April 13, 1962, GVN Strat Hams, VA. See also *Chi-Dao*, April 1962, 1–3; *Chan-Hung Kinh-Te*, December 20, 1962, 25, and January 17, 1963, 10–11; *Viet Nam's Strategic Hamlets*, 19.

24. Nhu's comments, August 2, 1962, *Ban Ghi Chep*, vol. 2, SC.03 5570, CLT II; Pham Chung, *An Analysis of the Long-Range Military, Economic, Political, and Social Effects of the Strategic Hamlet Program in Viet Nam* (Washington, D.C.: Advanced Research Projects Agency, 1965), 238–41.

25. Nhu's talk, March 19, 1962, *Ban Ghi Chep*, vol. 2, SC.03 5570, CLT II; *Times of Viet Nam Magazine*, May 27, 1962, 17.

26. Elections occurred in tandem with the spread of the hamlet program, although the regime did not establish official electoral guidelines until May 1963 (Saigon to State, June 20, 1963, POL 26-1 S VIET, Subject-Numeric File, Record Group 59, U.S. National Archives). For an account of a hamlet election, see Richard Tregaskis, *Vietnam Diary* (New York: Holt, Rinehart and Winston, 1963), 381–88.

27. Bien-Ban so 9, April 13, 1962, GVN Strat Hams, VA.

28. Bien-Ban so 4, March 9, 1962, ibid.; Nhu's talk, March 17, 1962, *Ban Ghi Chep*, vol 1, SC.04 8676, CLT II.

29. Bien-Ban so 6, March 23, 1962, GVN Strat Hams, VA; Bo Cong-Dan-Vu, *Tu Ap Chien-Luoc Den Xa Tu-Ve* (Saigon, 1962), 57–58, 65–66.

30. Burrows to Secondé, May 30, 1962, DV1201/24, FO371/166748, PRO (includes a translation, identical in most respects, of *Tu Ap Chien-Luoc Den Xa Tu-Ve*); Robert Scigliano, *South Vietnam: Nation under Stress* (Boston: Houghton Mifflin, 1964), 186.

31. Nhu's talk, March 17, 1962, *Ban Ghi Chep*, vol. 1, SC.04 8676, CLT II; Bien-Ban so 6, March 23, 1962, GVN Strat Hams, VA; Bien-Ban so 9, April 13, 1962, ibid.; Bien-Ban so 24, October 12, 1962, ibid.; Phillips to Fippin, June 25, 1962, *Foreign Relations of the United States, 1961–1963*, vol. 2, *Vietnam* (Washington, D.C.: GPO, 1990), 470–71.

32. *Huong Uoc* (Saigon, n.d.); Hue to State, April 17, 1963, POL 26-1 S VIET, SNF, RG 59, USNA; Saigon to State, December 13, 1962, 751K.5/12-1362, Central Decimal File 1960–1963, ibid.

33. Nhu's talk, March 19, 1962, *Ban Ghi Chep*, vol. 2, SC.03 5570, CLT II; Bien-Ban so 9, April 13, 1962, GVN Strat Hams, VA; Phillips to Fippin, June 25, 1962, *FRUS, 1961–1963*, vol. 2, 470; *Viet Nam's Strategic Hamlets*, 19.

34. Saigon to Foreign Office, January 17, 1962, DV1015/26, FO371/166699, PRO.

35. Nhu's talk, March 19, 1962, *Ban Ghi Chep*, vol. 2, SC.03 5570, CLT II. See also Bien-Ban so 7, March 30, 1962, GVN Strat Hams, VA; *Times of Viet Nam Magazine*, May 27, 1962, 4.

36. See draft plans, esp. Ap Kien Thiet, March 15, 1962, SC.25 956, CLT II.

37. Tong Thu-Ky Thuong-Truc Quoc Phong [to] Bo-Truong PTT, January 8, 1962, BT 576, ibid.; Nhu's comments, February 2, 1962, *Ban Ghi Chep*, vol. 1, SC.04 8676, ibid.; Bien-Ban so 3, March 2, 1962, GVN Strat Hams, VA.

38. Bien-Ban so 16, July 13, 1962, ibid.; Bien-Ban so 31, December 7, 1962, ibid.

39. Bien-Ban so 26, November 1, 1962, ibid.; Tong Thu-Ky Ban Thuong-Vu [to] Co-Van Chanh-Tri, December 15, 1962, BT 576, CLT II.

40. *Chan-Hung Kinh-Te*, May 9, 1963, 3–6, and May 30, 1963, 3–9.

41. Pike, *Viet Cong*, 66–67.

42. Bien-Ban so 5, March 16, 1962, GVN Strat Hams, VA; Bien-Ban so 16, July 13, 1962, ibid.; *Chan-Hung Kinh-Te*, April 17, 1963, 22; Tong Thu-Ky Ban Thuong-Vu [to] Co-Van Chanh-Tri, December 15, 1962, BT 576, CLT II.

43. *Viet Nam's Strategic Hamlets*, 11–12; *Chan-Hung Kinh-Te*, April 17, 1963, 22; Truong Tieu-Ban Thuong-Vu [to] Dong-Ly Van-Phong PTT, May 30, 1963, BT 576, CLT II.

44. Nguyen Dang Thuc, "Democracy in Traditional Vietnamese Society," *Vietnam Culture Series*, No. 4, Department of National Education, 1961, 5–6. See also *Viet Nam's Strategic Hamlets*, 3. For a critique of this "myth of the village," see Jan Breman, *The Shattered Image: Construction and Deconstruction of the Village in Colonial Asia* (Dordrecht–Holland: Forbis Publications, 1988).

45. Marguerite Higgins, *Our Vietnam Nightmare* (New York: Harper & Row, 1965), 166–67, 173. See also Thompson to McGhie, November 27, 1961, DV1015/258, FO371/160119, PRO; Saigon to Foreign Office, August 1, 1962, DV1015/166, FO371/166706, ibid.

46. *Press Interviews*, 56–57; *Times of Viet Nam Magazine,* October 13, 1963, 2–3.

47. William Colby, with James McCargar, *Lost Victory: A Firsthand Account of America's Sixteen-Year Involvement in Vietnam* (Chicago: Contemporary Books, 1989), 86.

48. Memorandum for Record, September 14, 1962, *FRUS, 1961–1963,* vol. 2, 637.

49. William J. Rust and the editors of U.S. News Books, *Kennedy in Vietnam* (New York: Charles Scribner's Sons, 1985), 66–67.

50. Saigon to State, September 18, 1962, 751K.00/9-1862, CDF 60-63, RG 59, USNA.

51. John C. Donnell, "Politics in South Vietnam: Doctrines of Authority in Conflict" (Ph.D. diss., University of California, Berkeley, 1964), 273, 528. See also the summary of the interministerial meeting, March 1, 1963, POL 26-1 S VIET, SNF, RG 59, USNA.

52. Saigon to State, July 20, 1959, 851G.20/7-2059, CDF 55-59, ibid.; October 20, 1960, 751K.00/10-2060, CDF 60-63, ibid.; CIA Information Report, November 29, 1962, General 11/26/62–11/30/62, Countries: VN, Box 197, National Security Files, John F. Kennedy Library. For the communists' organizational framework, see David G. Marr, *Vietnamese Tradition on Trial, 1920–1945* (Berkeley: University of California Press, 1984), 402.

53. Bien-Ban so 5, March 16, 1962, GVN Strat Hams, VA.

54. Saigon to Foreign Office, August 1, 1962, DV1015/166, FO371/166706, PRO; Mieczyslaw Maneli, *War of the Vanquished,* trans. Maria de Gorgey (New York: Harper & Row, 1971), 145.

55. Philippe C. Schmitter, "Still the Century of Corporatism?" *Review of Politics* (January 1974): 85–131.

56. Colby, 99–100.

57. Donnell, 544–49.

58. *Times of Viet Nam Magazine,* October 28, 1962, 30–32; *Viet Nam's Strategic Hamlets,* 21; Bien-Ban so 20, September 7, 1962, GVN Strat Hams, VA.

59. Ho Quy Ba, *Quoc Sach Ap Chien Luoc cua My-Diem* (Hanoi: Quan Doi Nhan Dan, 1962), 31–40; Liberation Editions, *Outlines of "Strategic Hamlets"* (n.p., 1963).

60. Tran Van Giau, *Mien Nam Giu Vung Thanh Dong: Luoc Su Dong Bao Mien Nam Dau Tranh Chong My Va Tay Sai,* vol. 2 (Hanoi: Khoa Hoc, 1966), 157–65.

61. Frances FitzGerald, *Fire in the Lake: The Vietnamese and the Americans in Vietnam* (New York: Vintage Books, 1973), 166–67; George McT. Kahin, *Intervention: How America Became Involved in Vietnam* (New York: Alfred A. Knopf, 1986), 140–41; George C. Herring, *America's Longest War: The United States and Vietnam, 1950–1975,* 2d ed. (New York: Alfred A. Knopf, 1986), 89; D. Michael Shafer, *Deadly Paradigms: The Failure of U.S. Counterinsurgency Policy* (Princeton: Princeton University Press, 1988), 267–68; Marilyn B. Young, *The Vietnam Wars, 1945–1990* (New York: HarperCollins, 1991), 84–86.

62. Frederick Nolting, *From Trust to Tragedy: The Political Memoirs of Frederick Nolting, Kennedy's Ambassador to Diem's Vietnam* (New York: Praeger Publishers,

1988), 54; Cao Van Luan, *Ben Giong Lich Su, 1940–1965* (Saigon: Tri Dung, 1972), 309, 338–40; Memo in Sullivan to Harriman, December 31, 1963, Vietnam General, December 1963, Special Files: Public Service, JFK-LBJ Ads, Subject File, Box 519, W. Averell Harriman Papers, Library of Congress Manuscript Division.

63. Johnson to Rostow, October 16, 1962, Vietnam 1962, Lot File 69D121, Records of the Policy Planning Staff 1962, Box 219, RG 59, USNA; Douglas S. Blaufarb, *The Counterinsurgency Era: U.S. Doctrine and Performance, 1950 to the Present* (New York: Free Press, 1977), 112–13.

64. Chinh Sach Ap Chien Luoc, February 25, 1962, and Loi Noi Dau, March 15, 1962, SC.25 956, CLT II. See also *Tu Ap Chien-Luoc Den Xa Tu-Ve,* 6–7.

65. Bien-Ban so 8, April 6, 1962, SC.25 951, CLT II.

66. Bien-Ban so 6, March 23, 1962, GVN Strat Hams, VA; Ap Chien-Luoc: Bien-Ban so 25, October 19, 1962, SC.25 963, CLT II; Pike, *Viet Cong,* 67.

67. Bien-Ban so 19, August 31, 1962, GVN Strat Hams, VA; Bien-Ban so 20, September 7, 1962, ibid.; Bien-Ban so 23, October 5, 1962, ibid.; Bien-Ban so 30, November 30, 1962, ibid.; Nhu's address, March 26, 1963, *Ban Ghi Chep,* vol. 4, SC.25 939, CLT II; *Viet Nam's Strategic Hamlets,* 2d rev. ed., 32–35.

68. Chu-Tich, Ban Chap-Hanh Trung-Uong [to] Dong-Ly Van-Phong PTT, August 8, 1962, SC.03 5570/10, CLT II.

69. Nhu's address, March 26, 1963, *Ban Ghi Chep,* vol. 4, SC.25 939, ibid.

70. Bien-Ban so 1, February 12, 1962, GVN Strat Hams, VA; Bien-Ban so 6, March 23, 1962, ibid.; Bien-Ban so 8, April 6, 1962, ibid.; Bien-Ban so 10, April 20, 1962, ibid.; *Tu Ap Chien-Luoc Den Xa Tu-Ve,* 80–81.

71. Bien-Ban, January 20, 1962, BT 491, CLT II.

72. Earl Young's paper, July 31, 1964, Box 8, Charles T. R. Bohannan Papers, Hoover Institute. Accurate totals for numbers resettled are difficult to find. USOM's *Notes on Strategic Hamlets* (Saigon, 1963), 18–19, gives a total for "relocation and resettlement" of over 150,000, yet the figure for Long An is only 1,200, which would appear to be a vast underestimation. The scale of resettlement was subsequently criticized in Phieu Trinh Thu-Tuong Chinh-Phu Viet-Nam Cong-Hoa, December 4, 1963, SC.04 7704, CLT II.

73. Bien-Ban so 1, February 12, 1962, GVN Strat Hams, VA; Bien-Ban so 3, March 2, 1962, ibid.; So Mat-Ma PTT [to] Do-Truong [et al.], July 4, 1962, SC.03 5570/23, CLT II; Saigon to State, July 19, 1962, 751K.00/7-1962, CDF 60-63, RG 59, USNA.

74. Saigon to State, January 3, 1963, 751K.5/1-363, ibid.; Hue to State, January 24, 1963, 751K.5/1-2463, ibid.

75. Phillips to Brent, March 25, 1963, Box 34, Bohannan Papers, HI; Bien-Ban so 43, April 5, 1963, GVN Strat Hams, VA; Phillips, "Before We Lost in South Vietnam," in *Prelude to Tragedy,* ed. Neese and O'Donnell, 34–35.

76. Bien-Ban so 20, September 7, 1962, GVN Strat Hams, VA; Bien-Ban so 21, September 14, 1962, ibid.; Phieu Trinh Thu-Tuong Chinh-Phu Viet-Nam Cong-Hoa, December 4, 1963, SC.04 7704, CLT II.

77. CIA Information Report, November 29, 1962, General 11/26/62–11/30/62, Countries: VN, Box 197, NSF, JFK; Heavner Report, December 11, 1962, *FRUS, 1961–1963,* vol. 2, 767; Saigon to State, March 11, 1963, POL 18-1 S VIET, SNF, RG 59, USNA; Phieu Trinh Thu-Tuong Chinh-Phu Viet-Nam Cong-Hoa, December 4, 1963, SC.04 7704, CLT II.

78. Phieu Trinh Thu-Tuong Chinh-Phu Viet-Nam Cong-Hoa, December 4, 1963, SC.04 7704, ibid.

79. Bien Ban, January 20, 1962, BT 491, ibid.

80. Bien-Ban so 6, March 23, 1962, GVN Strat Hams, VA; Nhu's comments, March 27, 1962, *Ban Ghi Chep,* vol. 1, SC.04 8676, CLT II.

81. *Times of Viet Nam Magazine,* December 30, 1962, 18; Tong Thu-Ky Ban Thuong-Vu [to] Co-Van Chanh-Tri, December 15, 1962, BT 576, CLT II. By April 1963, the completion date had evidently been set back again, to the end of 1963 (Tai-Lieu Tom-Tat Ve Chuong-Trinh Xay-Dung Ap Chien-Luoc Sau Mot Nam Hoat-Dong, undated, SC.25 957, ibid.). Figures need to be treated with care: there were frequent discrepancies in those put out by the regime; moreover, provincial reports did not give an accurate picture of the state of the program.

82. Stanley Karnow, *Vietnam: A History* (New York: Viking Press, 1983), 257; Truong Nhu Tang, with David Chanoff and Doan Van Toai, *A Viet Cong Memoir* (New York: Vintage Books, 1985), 42–62. See also Pham Ngoc Thao, Biographical File, VA.

83. Bui Tin, *Following Ho Chi Minh: The Memoirs of a North Vietnamese Colonel,* trans. and adapted by Judy Stowe and Do Van (London: Hurst, 1995), 58–60, 83–84.

84. David Halberstam, *The Making of a Quagmire* (New York: Random House, 1965), 204.

85. *Ban Ghi Chep,* vol. 1, SC.04 8676, CLT II; Bien-Ban so 23, October 5, 1962, GVN Strat Hams, VA.

86. Saigon to Foreign Office, July 31, 1962, DV1015/165, FO371/166706, PRO; Warner to Thompson, October 4, 1963, DV1017/41, FO371/170102, ibid.

87. Bien Ban, January 20, 1962, BT 491, CLT II; Bien-Ban phien hop cua Ban Thuong-Vu dac trach ve ap chien luoc, April 14, 1962, SC.25 951, ibid.

88. Stanley Karnow, "The Edge of Chaos," *Saturday Evening Post,* September 28, 1963, 35. On the eve of the regime's overthrow, Nhu showed some concern for slowing the pace of the program (Thompson to Warner, October 29, 1963, DV1017/41, FO371/170102, PRO).

89. Memorandum for Record, June 8, 1963, Folder 1373, Subject File, Box 49, Edward G. Lansdale Papers, HI. See also Bien-Ban so 16, July 13, 1962, GVN Strat Hams, VA; Bien-Ban so 18, August 10, 1962, ibid.

90. Jeffrey Race, *War Comes to Long An: Revolutionary Conflict in a Vietnamese Province* (Berkeley: University of California Press, 1973), 132; telephone interview with Tran Ngoc Chau, July 18, 1997; John B. O'Donnell, "The Strategic Hamlet Program in Kien Hoa Province, South Vietnam: A Case Study of Counter-Insurgency,"

in *Southeast Asian Tribes, Minorities, and Nations*, vol. 2, ed. Peter Kunstadter (Princeton: Princeton University Press, 1967), 721.

91. Saigon to State, September 30, 1963, DEF 19 US-S VIET, SNF, RG 59, USNA.

92. Nguyen Thai, *Is South Vietnam Viable?* (Manila: Carmelo & Bauermann, 1962), 250–56.

93. Giam-Doc Trung-Tam Huan-Luyen [to] Bo-Truong PTT, November 13, 1962, BT 576, CLT II (for a specific example, see Long An [to] Bo-Truong PTT, October 1, 1962, SC.02 3565, ibid.); Heavner to Nolting, April 27, 1962, *FRUS, 1961–1963,* vol. 2, 358.

94. Lac, "Blind Design," 70.

95. Colby, *Lost Victory*, 101. See also *Tu Ap Chien-Luoc Den Xa Tu-Ve,* 7, 81–82.

96. Bien-Ban so 16, July 13, 1962, GVN Strat Hams, VA.

97. For an earlier observation of this tendency, see John D. Donoghue, *My Thuan: A Mekong Delta Village in South Vietnam* (n.p.: MSU Viet Nam Advisory Group, 1961), 58.

98. Race, 12–24, 44–64, 130–32, 151–55, 193–209; Scigliano, *South Vietnam,* 11, 37–39, 48–50; John C. Donnell, "The War, the Gap, and the Cadre," *Asia Magazine* (winter 1966): 53; Saigon to War Office, July 19, 1962, DV1201/43, FO371/166749, PRO (see also Saigon to State, September 6, 1962, 751K.00/9-662, CDF 60-63, RG 59, USNA).

99. O'Donnell, "The Strategic Hamlet Program in Kien Hoa Province, South Vietnam," 703–44; Tran Ngoc Chau, "My War Story: From Ho Chi Minh to Ngo Dinh Diem," in *Prelude to Tragedy,* ed. Neese and O'Donnell, 192–96; telephone interview with Tran Ngoc Chau, July 18, 1997. See also Zalin Grant, *Facing the Phoenix* (New York: W. W. Norton, 1991).

100. Saigon to State, September 6, 1962, 751K.00/9-662, CDF 60-63, RG 59, USNA.

101. Denis Warner, *The Last Confucian: Vietnam, South-East Asia, and the West* (Harmondsworth, Middlesex: Penguin Books, 1964), 30.

102. Dai-Bieu Chanh-Phu Mien-Dong Nam-Phan [to] Phuoc-Thanh, February 24, 1962, SC.08 15266, CLT II.

103. Interview with Nguyen Van No and Nguyen Van Ben, p.15, Race Collection, Center for Research Libraries; Long An Province Survey, January[?] 1964, Folder 569A, Subject File, Box 23, Lansdale Papers, HI; George K. Tanham, with W. Robert Warne, Earl J. Young, and William A. Nighswonger, *War without Guns: American Civilians in Rural Vietnam* (New York: Frederick A. Praeger, 1966), 104, 109, 117.

104. Giam-Doc Trung-Tam Huan-Luyen [to] Bo-Truong PTT, November 13, 1962, BT 576, CLT II.

105. Bien ban phien hop Ap Chien-Luoc, November 16, 1963, SC.03 5067, ibid.

106. Bien-Ban so 19, August 31, 1962, GVN Strat Hams, VA; W. P. Davison, *Some Observations on Viet Cong Operations in the Villages* (Santa Monica, Calif.: RAND, 1968), 164.

107. Long An Province Survey, January[?] 1964, Folder 569A, Subject File, Box 23, Lansdale Papers, HI; Ban Nghien-Cuu Dac-Biet–Uoc tinh Cac Kha-Nang Chong Pha Ap Chien-Luoc Cua V.C., June 22, 1962, SC.25 955, CLT II; interview with Nguyen Van Cu, 31–32, Race Collection, CRL.

108. Saigon to State, April 25, 1963, POL 18 S VIET, SNF, RG 59, USNA.

109. VCD 93 [trans.], 34, Pike Collection, CRL (see also VCD 15 [trans.], ibid.).

110. Ban Nghien-Cuu Dac-Biet, June 22, 1962, SC.25 955, CLT II. See also VCD 34 [trans.], 2–3, Pike Collection, CRL.

111. Giam-Doc Trung-Tam Huan-Luyen [to] Bo-Truong PTT, November 13, 1962, BT 576, CLT II; Phieu Trinh Thu-Tuong Chinh-Phu Viet-Nam Cong-Hoa, December 4, 1963, SC.04 7704, ibid.

112. Interview with Ha Chi, 20–22, Race Collection, CRL; Race, *War Comes to Long An*, 181.

113. Heavner's report, December 11, 1962, *FRUS, 1961–1963*, vol. 2, 767; Saigon to State, March 11, 1963, POL 18-1 S VIET, SNF, RG 59, USNA; Hue to State, April 17, 1963, POL 26-1 S VIET, ibid.

114. Breman, *The Shattered Image*, 38.

115. James B. Hendry, *The Small World of Khanh Hau* (Chicago: Aldine Publishing, 1964), 6–7, 248–62; Gerald C. Hickey, *Village in Vietnam* (New Haven: Yale University Press, 1964), 276–85. See also Pierre Brocheux, *The Mekong Delta: Ecology, Economy, and Revolution, 1860–1960* (Madison: Center for Southeast Asian Studies, University of Wisconsin-Madison, 1995). For the corporate identity of a northern village, see Hy V. Luong, *Revolution in the Village: Tradition and Transformation in North Vietnam, 1925–1988* (Honolulu: University of Hawaii Press, 1992).

116. Bien-Ban so 9, April 13, 1962, GVN Strat Hams, VA.

117. Alexander B. Woodside, *Community and Revolution in Modern Vietnam* (Boston: Houghton Mifflin, 1976), 178–79.

118. Race, 179–80.

119. Davison, *Some Observations on Viet Cong Operations in the Villages*, 10–29; Race, 141–209; William J. Duiker, *Sacred War: Nationalism and Revolution in a Divided Vietnam* (Boston: McGraw-Hill, 1995), 141–50, 251–53. For a survey of the literature on the NLF, see David Hunt, "U.S. Scholarship and the National Liberation Front," in *The American War in Vietnam*, ed. Jayne Werner and David Hunt (Ithaca, N.Y.: Cornell University Southeast Asia Program, 1993), 93–108.

6. Competitive Cooperation

1. *The Pentagon Papers: The Defense Department History of United States Decisionmaking on Vietnam*, vol. 2, Gravel ed. (Boston: Beacon Press, 1971), 149.

2. William Colby, with James McCargar, *Lost Victory: A Firsthand Account of America's Sixteen-Year Involvement in Vietnam* (Chicago: Contemporary Books, 1989), 101–2.

3. Saigon to State, March 8, 1961, 751K.5-MSP/3-861, Central Decimal File 1960–1963, Record Group 59, U.S. National Archives; McGarr to Felt, September 1, 1961, 268 Training–Viet Nam Armed Forces, MAAG, Adjutant General Division 1961, Box 26, RG 334, ibid. See also Memorandum for Rostow, March 28, 1961, Guerrilla and Unconventional Warfare, 3/20/61–3/29/61, Walt W. Rostow, Staff Memoranda, Meetings and Memoranda, Box 324-25, National Security Files, John F. Kennedy Library.

4. MAAG Vietnam to JCS, November 8, 1961, 9155.3/9105 (8 Nov. 61), CDF, RG 218, USNA; *Pentagon Papers,* vol. 2, 137–38.

5. Saigon to State, August 31, 1961, 751K.5-MSP/8-3161, CDF 60-63, RG 59, USNA; April 16, 1962, 751K.5/4-1662, ibid.; introduction to plan, minus annexes, in *Foreign Relations of the United States, 1961–1963,* vol. 2, *Vietnam* (Washington, D.C.: GPO, 1990), 17–21.

6. Saigon to State, November 27, 1961, 751K.5/11-2761, CDF 60-63, RG 59, USNA.

7. Roger Hilsman, *To Move a Nation: The Politics of Foreign Policy in the Administration of John F. Kennedy* (Garden City, N.Y.: Doubleday, 1967), 427–39.

8. Strategic Concept for South Vietnam, February 2, 1962, *FRUS, 1961–1963,* vol. 2, 73–75, 82–90.

9. JCS paper, January 4, 1962, ibid., 7–10.

10. Memorandum for President, April 4, 1962, General 4/1/62–4/10/62, Countries: VN, Box 196, NSF, JFK.

11. Cleveland to Harriman, January 25, 1962, Viet-Nam 1962, 1962 Geographic Files, Ass. Sec. for Far Eastern Affairs: Subject, Personal Name, and Country Files—1960–1963, Bureau of Far Eastern Affairs, Box 13, RG 59, USNA; DOD draft memorandum, January 26, 1962, *FRUS, 1961–1963,* vol. 2, 60–65; Memorandum for Record, March 19, 1962, Countries: VN 3/1/62–7/27/62, Box 3, Roger Hilsman Papers, JFK.

12. Bundy manuscript, ch. 5, 1–2, William P. Bundy Papers, Lyndon B. Johnson Library; John M. Newman, *JFK and Vietnam: Deception, Intrigue, and the Struggle for Power* (New York: Warner Books, 1992), 145–47, 154–56.

13. Martin to Cottrell, December 18, 1961, *Foreign Relations of the United States, 1961–1963,* vol. 1, *Vietnam* (Washington, D.C.: GPO, 1988), 742–43.

14. Report of McNamara's visit, *FRUS, 1961–1963,* vol. 2, 381.

15. Carl W. Schaad, "The Strategic Hamlet Program in Vietnam: The Role of the People in Counterinsurgency Warfare," March 1964, 1, 67–71, U.S. Army Military History Institute; CHMAAG to State, November 27, 1962, 751K.5/11-2762, CDF 60-63, RG 59, USNA.

16. Phillips's two memoranda, July 20, 1962, Folder 1373, Subject File, Box 49, Edward G. Lansdale Papers, Hoover Institute; Saigon to State, August 3, 1962, *FRUS, 1961–1963,* vol. 2, 576–79; Administrative History of the Agency for International Development, vol. 2, 391–94, LBJ; George K. Tanham, with W. Robert

Warne, Earl J. Young, and William A. Nighswonger, *War without Guns: American Civilians in Rural Vietnam* (New York: Frederick A. Praeger, 1966), 23–26; Rufus Phillips, "Before We Lost in South Vietnam," in *Prelude to Tragedy: Vietnam, 1960–1965,* ed. Harvey Neese and John O'Donnell (Annapolis: Naval Institute Press, 2001), 25–31; Bert Fraleigh, "Counterinsurgency in South Vietnam," in ibid., 95–110.

17. State to Saigon, April 4, 1962, *FRUS, 1961–1963,* vol. 2, 304–5; Saigon to State, April 11, 1962, ibid., 322–23.

18. Schaad, 66–67; *Pentagon Papers,* vol. 2, 146.

19. For an analysis of the U.S. view of the hamlet program, see Michael E. Latham, *Modernization as Ideology: American Social Science and "Nation Building" in the Kennedy Era* (Chapel Hill: University of North Carolina Press, 2000), 151–207.

20. Johnson's paper, July 27, 1962, Vietnam 1962, Lot File 69D121, Records of the Policy Planning Staff 1962, Box 219, RG 59, USNA; Johnson to Rostow, September 21, 1962, Johnson, R. Chron 1962, PPS 1962, Box 235, ibid.; Johnson to Rice, October 18, 1962, ibid.

21. Forrestal to Bundy, September 8, 1962, General 9/1/62–9/14/62, Countries: VN, Box 196, NSF, JFK; Hilsman/Forrestal to Kennedy, January 25, 1963, *Foreign Relations of the United States, 1961–1963,* vol. 3, *Vietnam* (Washington, D.C.: GPO, 1991), 51.

22. Strategic Concept for South Vietnam, February 2, 1962, *FRUS, 1961–1963,* vol. 2, 78; Memorandum on Substance of a Discussion, February 9, 1962, ibid., 113–14; Hilsman to Rusk, April 1963, *FRUS, 1961–1963,* vol. 3, 189–90.

23. W. W. Rostow, "Guerrilla Warfare in Underdeveloped Areas," in *The Guerrilla— And How to Fight Him,* ed. T. N. Greene (New York: Frederick A. Praeger, 1962), 55–56.

24. Saigon to Foreign Office, February 28, 1962, DV1015/64, Foreign Office 371/166701, Public Record Office (see also Saigon to War Office, July 26, 1962, DV1201/47, FO371/166749, ibid.); Saigon to State, March 23, 1962, *FRUS, 1961–1963,* vol. 2, 268.

25. Saigon to State, March 23, 1962, ibid., 269.

26. USOM/Rural Affairs, *Notes on Strategic Hamlets* (Saigon, 1963), 6–12, 16.

27. Outline Plan of COIN Operations, January 10, 1962, *FRUS, 1961–1963,* vol. 2, 17–21; Strategic Concept for South Vietnam, February 2, 1962, ibid., 73–90.

28. Saigon to State, April 16, 1962, 751K.5/4-1662, CDF 60-63, RG 59, USNA.

29. Tanham to Rostow, September 21, 1961, General 9/61, Countries: VN, Box 194, NSF, JFK.

30. For example: State to Saigon, April 4, 1962, *FRUS, 1961–1963,* vol. 2, 304–5; Saigon to State, April 11, 1962, ibid., 322–23.

31. Trueheart to Cottrell, February 12, 1962, ibid., 120–21 (Thompson's modified proposal, ibid., 102–9).

32. Diem's decree, March 16, 1962, ibid., 238-44; Saigon to War Office, April 12, 1962, DV1201/12, FO371/166747, PRO.

33. Bien Ban phien hop Uy-Ban Lien Bo dac-trach ve Ap Chien-Luoc, April 13, 1962, Tai Lieu Do So Luu Tru Va Cong Bao Phu Thu Tuong Viet Nam Cong Hoa, SC.25 951, Cuc Luu Tru II (Trueheart's summary of meeting, Saigon to State, April 27, 1962, 751K.5/4-2762, CDF 60-63, RG 59, USNA). See also Memorandum of Conversation, May 24, 1962, *FRUS, 1961–1963*, vol. 2, 428–30.

34. Strategic Concept for South Vietnam, February 2, 1962, ibid., 77–78; Memorandum for Record, March 19, 1962, Countries: VN 3/1/62–7/27/62, Box 3, Hilsman Papers, JFK; Saigon to State, March 23, 1962, *FRUS, 1961–1963*, vol. 2, 265–66; Bagley to Taylor, April 27, 1962, ibid., 348; Heavner to Nolting, April 27, 1962, ibid., 359–60; Bagley to Taylor, May 9, 1962, ibid., 377–78.

35. Report on Counter-Insurgency in Vietnam, August 31, 1962, Folder 1373, Subject File, Box 49, Lansdale Papers, HI; Robert Thompson, *Defeating Communist Insurgency: The Lessons of Malaya and Vietnam* (New York: Frederick A. Praeger, 1967), 129.

36. Saigon to State, June 11, 1962, 751K.5/6-1162, CDF 60-63, RG 59, USNA; Report on Counter-Insurgency in Vietnam, August 31, 1962, Folder 1373, Subject File, Box 49, Lansdale Papers, HI; Phillips, "Before We Lost in South Vietnam," 27; Denis Warner, *The Last Confucian: Vietnam, South-East Asia, and the West* (Harmondsworth, Middlesex: Penguin Books, 1964), 203–16.

37. Saigon to State, May 23, 1962, *FRUS, 1961–1963*, vol. 2, 419.

38. Phillips, 31.

39. Status Report on the Instructions to Ambassador Nolting, May 2, 1962, Viet-Nam Task Force 1962, 1962 Geographic Files, Ass. Sec. FE: Subject, Personal Name, and Country Files—1960–1963, BFE, Box 13, RG 59, USNA; Saigon to State, May 23, 1962, *FRUS, 1961–1963*, vol. 2, 425; Forrestal to Bundy, May 29, 1962, ibid., 430–31; JCS Team Report, January 1963, *FRUS, 1961–1963*, vol. 3, 75.

40. Phillips, 28–29; Fraleigh, "Counterinsurgency in South Vietnam," 97–98.

41. Saigon to State, June 7, 1962, 751K.00/6-762, CDF 60-63, RG 59, USNA; Administrative History of AID, vol. 2, 395, LBJ.

42. Saigon to State, June 6, 1962, *FRUS, 1961–1963*, vol. 2, 437–41; June 6, 1962, ibid., 441–42; June 14, 1962, ibid., 454–55; State to Saigon, June 15, 1962, ibid., 460–61; Forrestal to Kennedy, June 20, 1962, ibid., 463–66; Saigon to State, July 20, 1962, ibid., 539–40; August 23, 1962, 751K.5/8-2362, CDF 60-63, RG 59, USNA; Administrative History of AID, vol. 2, 400–2, LBJ.

43. Saigon to State, July 19, 1962, 751K.00/7-1962, CDF 60-63, RG 59, USNA. This arrangement represented an extension to the rest of the country of the operational framework that Thompson had proposed in the "Delta Plan."

44. Saigon to State, August 9, 1962, 751K.5/8-962, CDF 60-63, RG 59, USNA.

45. Saigon to State, February 21, 1963, DEF 19 S VIET, Subject-Numeric File, ibid.; John B. O'Donnell, "The Strategic Hamlet Program in Kien Hoa Province, South Vietnam: A Case Study of Counter-Insurgency," in *Southeast Asian Tribes, Minorities, and Nations,* vol. 2, ed. Peter Kunstadter (Princeton: Princeton University Press, 1967), 713–15.

46. Saigon to State, February 21, 1963, DEF 19 S VIET, SNF, RG 59, USNA.

47. State paper, undated, *FRUS, 1961–1963,* vol. 2, 685.

48. Memorandum of Conversation, June 19, 1962, 751K.00/6-1962, CDF 60-63, RG 59, USNA; Saigon to State, September 18, 1962, 751K.00/9-1862, ibid.; State paper, undated, *FRUS, 1961–1963,* vol. 2, 679–87; Saigon to State, November 16, 1962, 751K.00/11-1662, CDF 60-63, RG 59, USNA.

49. Mendenhall to Rice, August 16, 1962, *FRUS, 1961–1963,* vol. 2, 596–601.

50. Southeast Asia–Viet Nam, December 18, 1962, 751K.00/12-1862, CDF 60-63, RG 59, USNA.

51. Senior Officers Oral History Program, vol. 2, 295–96, and vol. 3, 155, 164, William B. Rosson Papers, USAMHI.

52. Memorandum of Conversation, June 26, 1962, *FRUS, 1961–1963,* vol. 2, 477.

53. Undated report on implementing II Corps hamlet program, II CTZ Index of Problems, Wilbur Wilson Papers, USAMHI.

54. Phillips to York, January 24, 1963, Box 34, Charles T. R. Bohannan Papers, HI.

55. Neil Sheehan, *A Bright Shining Lie: John Paul Vann and America in Vietnam* (New York: Random House, 1988), 277.

56. Saigon to State, August 9, 1962, 751K.5/8-962, CDF 60-63, RG 59, USNA.

57. Hilsman/Forrestal to Kennedy, January 25, 1963, *FRUS, 1961–1963,* vol. 3, 49–59.

58. Bien-Ban so 7 Uy-Ban Lien-Bo Dac-Trach Ap Chien-Luoc, March 30, 1962, GVN Strat Hams, Vietnam Archive; Bien-Ban so 8, April 6, 1962, ibid.; Saigon to State, May 23, 1962, *FRUS, 1961–1963,* vol. 2, 421.

59. Bien-Ban so 6, March 23, 1962, GVN Strat Hams, VA; Bien-Ban so 7, March 30, 1962, ibid.; Bien-Ban so 8, April 6, 1962, ibid.

60. Report on Counter-Insurgency in Vietnam, August 31, 1962, Folder 1373, Subject File, Box 49, Lansdale Papers, HI; Memorandum for Record, June 8, 1963, ibid.

61. Saigon to State, September 4, 1962, 751K.00/9-462, CDF 60-63, RG 59, USNA; Paris to State, October 18, 1962, 751K.00/10-1862, ibid.; Saigon to State, October 29, 1962, 751K.00/10-2962, ibid.; January 2, 1963, 611.51K/1-263, ibid.

62. Saigon to State, April 5, 1963, *FRUS, 1961–1963,* vol. 3, 210; May 23, 1963, ibid., 325.

63. Bien-Ban so 8, April 6, 1962, GVN Strat Hams, VA; Bien-Ban so 32, December 14, 1962, ibid.; Nolting to Harriman, November 19, 1962, *FRUS, 1961–1963,* vol. 2, 738–39; Saigon to External Affairs, April 9, 1963, DV1015/24, FO371/170090, PRO.

64. Bien-Ban so 7, March 30, 1962, GVN Strat Hams, VA; Bien-Ban so 21, September 14, 1962, ibid.; Bien-Ban so 31, December 7, 1962, ibid.; Colby, *Lost Victory,* 99–100.

65. Saigon to State, April 5, 1963, *FRUS, 1961–1963,* vol. 3, 209, 211; George McT. Kahin, *Intervention: How America Became Involved in Vietnam* (New York: Alfred A. Knopf, 1986), 143.

66. Darlac [to] Bo-Truong Phu Tong-Thong, March 13, 1962, Van-Phong Bo-

Truong Phu Tong-Thong, BT 577, CLT II; Bien-Ban so 5, March 16, 1962, GVN Strat Hams, VA.

67. Francis J. Kelly, *The Green Berets in Vietnam, 1961–71* (New York: Brassey's, 1991), 24–44; Gerald Cannon Hickey, *Free in the Forest: Ethnohistory of the Vietnamese Central Highlands, 1954–1976* (New Haven: Yale University Press, 1982), 79–82; CIA Information Report, April 22, 1963, *FRUS, 1961–1963*, vol. 3, 246–47.

68. Saigon to State, June 22, 1962, 751K.00/6-2262, CDF 60-63, RG 59, USNA.

69. Saigon to External Affairs, April 9, 1963, DV1015/24, FO371/170090, PRO. See also Saigon to State, April 5, 1963, *FRUS, 1961–1963*, vol. 3, 209.

70. Saigon to State, June 25, 1962, *FRUS, 1961–1963*, vol. 2, 468–69; April 5, 1963, *FRUS, 1961–1963*, vol. 3, 209. U.S. adviser numbers are from Guenter Lewy, *America in Vietnam* (New York: Oxford University Press, 1978), 24.

71. Memorandum for Record, July 31, 1962, *FRUS, 1961–1963*, vol. 2, 530; Saigon to State, April 5, 1963, *FRUS, 1961–1963*, vol. 3, 209.

72. Bien-Ban so 20, September 7, 1962, GVN Strat Hams, VA; Bien-Ban so 21, September 14, 1962, ibid; *Ban Ghi Chep: Nhung Buoi Noi Chuyen Than Mat Cua Ong Co Van Chinh Tri Ve Ap Chien Luoc*, vol. 3, SC.04 8676, CLT II.

73. Bien-Ban so 1, February 12, 1962, GVN Strat Hams, VA.

74. Saigon to State, June 11, 1962, 751K.5/6-1162, CDF 60-63, RG 59, USNA; June 22, 1962, 751K.00/6-2262, CDF 60-63, ibid.; January 19, 1963, 751K.00/1-1963, CDF 60-63, ibid.; February 21, 1963, AID (US) S VIET, SNF, ibid.

75. Bien-Ban so 21, September 14, 1962, GVN Strat Hams, VA. See also Memorandum for Record, April 12, 1963, *FRUS, 1961–1963*, vol. 3, 222.

76. Saigon to State, January 15, 1963, 751K.5/1-1563, CDF 60-63, RG 59, USNA; State to Saigon, February 16, 1963, AID (US) S VIET, SNF, ibid.; Saigon to State, February 21, 1963, AID (US) S VIET, ibid.; Nolting to Thuan, March 18, 1963, *FRUS, 1961–1963*, vol. 3, 156–61. For a breakdown of the piaster fund, see the latter document and an unidentified one entitled VIET-NAM, Doc. 14, National Security Council (I), Box 4, Vice Presidential Security File, LBJ.

77. Phillips, "Before We Lost in South Vietnam," 28.

78. Saigon to State, February 21, 1963, AID (US) S VIET, SNF, RG 59, USNA; February 28, 1963, AID (US) S VIET, ibid.; March 9, 1963, POL 23 S VIET, ibid.; March 28, 1963, *FRUS, 1961–1963*, vol. 3, 183–84.

79. For Saigon's reaction, see editorial note, *FRUS, 1961–1963*, vol. 3, 124; Mecklin to Manell, March 15, 1963, ibid., 152–55; Saigon to State, March 30, 1963, POL 23 S VIET, SNF, RG 59, USNA. For expressions of concern about Laos, see Saigon to Foreign Office, August 1, 1962, DV1015/166, FO371/166706, PRO; Saigon to State, August 16, 1962, 751K.00/8-1662, SNF, RG 59, USNA; Memorandum for Record, October 21, 1962, *FRUS, 1961–1963*, vol. 2, 714.

80. Saigon to State, March 28, 1963, *FRUS, 1961–1963*, vol. 3, 183–84; Memorandum of Conversation, July 17, 1963, ibid., 509.

81. Saigon to External Affairs, April 9, 1963, DV1015/24, FO371/170090, PRO;

Memorandum for Record, April 12, 1963, *FRUS, 1961–1963*, vol. 3, 223–24; *Washington Post*, May 12, 1963.

82. Saigon to State, April 5, 1963, *FRUS, 1961–1963*, vol. 3, 207–13; Phien Hop Hoi-Dong Noi-Cac, March 19, 1963, SC.05 10.001, CLT II.

83. Saigon to State, April 5, 1963, *FRUS, 1961–1963*, vol. 3, 207–13 (for items subject to an aid cutoff, see State to Saigon, April 1, 1963, ibid., 195); Saigon to State, April 7, 1963, ibid., 213.

84. *Pentagon Papers*, vol. 2, 160–200. The Americans seemed reluctant to confide in their ally about these withdrawal plans (Saigon to State, April 7, 1963, *FRUS, 1961–1963*, vol. 3, 214; State to Saigon, April 18, 1963, ibid., 235), although a Saigon newspaper mentioned them in May (Saigon to State, May 13, 1963, POL 27 S VIET-US, SNF, RG 59, USNA).

85. Saigon to State, April 7, 1963, *FRUS, 1961–1963*, vol. 3, 213–14; State to Saigon, April 8, 1963, ibid., 215–16.

86. Saigon to State, April 9, 1963, ibid., 216–18; April 17, 1963, ibid., 227–29.

87. Saigon to State, April 26, 1963, ibid., 254–56; Nolting to Thuan, May 10, 1963, ibid., 289–90; U.S.–RVN joint communiqué, May 17, ibid., 307–8.

88. Bo-Truong Noi-Vu [to] Do-Truong, [et al.], May 4, 1963, SC.25 939, CLT II. For certain CIA activities in the provinces, see Douglas Valentine, *The Phoenix Program* (New York: William Morrow, 1990), 43–46.

89. Saigon to State, April 26, 1963, *FRUS, 1961–1963*, vol. 3, 254–56.

90. Phillips, "Before We Lost in South Vietnam," 35–38; Memorandum for Record, April 30, 1963, Folder 1079, Correspondence, Box 40, Lansdale Papers, HI; Janow to Phillips, May 15, 1963, *FRUS, 1961–1963*, vol. 3, 301–3.

91. Saigon to State, June 7, 1963, ibid., 360–61; July 22, 1963, DEF 19 US-S VIET, SNF, RG 59, USNA.

92. Phillips, 38; Memorandum for Record, June 8, 1963, Folder 1373, Subject File, Box 49, Lansdale Papers, HI.

93. Saigon to State, April 9, 1963, *FRUS, 1961–1963*, vol. 3, 218.

94. Saigon to State, October 14, 1963, DEF 19 US-S VIET, SNF, RG 59, USNA; October 21, 1963, ibid.; October 28, 1963, ibid.

7. Binh Duong Province: Case Study of a Program in Trouble

1. Bundy manuscript, ch. 9, 18, William P. Bundy Papers, Lyndon B. Johnson Library.

2. The choice of case study was also influenced by the author's terms of reference for working in the Vietnamese archives.

3. Bo-Truong Phu Tong-Thong [to] Van-Thanh-Cao [et al.], May 9, 1961, Tai Lieu Do So Luu Tru Va Cong Bao Phu Thu Tuong Viet Nam Cong Hoa, SC.04 8070, Cuc Luu Tru II.

4. Dai Bieu Chanh-Phu Mien-Dong Nam-Phan [to] Thieu-Tuong Tu-Linh Vung Chien-Thuat III, July 14, 1961, SC.07 13851, ibid.

5. Pham Cuong, "Cu Chi, a Guerilla Base," *Vietnamese Studies* 20 (1968): 268–71; Tom Mangold and John Penycate, *The Tunnels of Cu Chi* (New York: Random House, 1985); Eric M. Bergerud, *The Dynamics of Defeat: The Vietnam War in Hau Nghia Province* (Boulder, Colo.: Westview Press, 1991).

6. *Times of Viet Nam Magazine,* April 15, 1962, 16–17 (based on an official report, Dai Bieu Chanh-Phu MDNP [to] Dong-Ly Van-Phong PTT, April 4, 1962, Van-Phong Bo-Truong Phu Tong-Thong, BT 577, CLT II); Bien-Ban buoi hop thuong nguyet, August 16, 1961, SC.02 3563, ibid.

7. Bien-Ban buoi hop thuong-nguyet, September 18, 1961, and October 16, 1961, ibid.; *Times of Viet Nam Magazine,* April 15, 1962, 17–20.

8. Dai Bieu Chanh-Phu MDNP [to] Tinh-Truong, August 31, 1961, SC.07 13851, CLT II; September 8, 1961, BT 577, ibid.

9. *Times of Viet Nam Magazine,* April 15, 1962, 18, 20; Saigon to State, April 12, 1962, 751K.00/4-1262, Central Decimal File 1960–1963, Record Group 59, U.S. National Archives.

10. Saigon to Foreign Office, April 4, 1962, DV1015/100, Foreign Office 371/166702, Public Record Office.

11. Bien-Ban so 8 Uy-Ban Lien-Bo Dac-Trach Ap Chien-Luoc, April 6, 1962, GVN Strat Hams, Vietnam Archive.

12. Saigon to State, April 12, 1962, 751K.00/4-1262, CDF 60-63, RG 59, USNA; Gloria Emerson, *Winners and Losers: Battles, Retreats, Gains, Losses, and Ruins from the Vietnam War* (New York: Harcourt Brace Jovanovich, 1976), 285.

13. Heavner to Wood, March 19, 1962, *Foreign Relations of the United States, 1961–1963,* vol. 2, *Vietnam* (Washington, D.C.: GPO, 1990), 250; John C. Donnell, "Politics in South Vietnam: Doctrines of Authority in Conflict" (Ph.D. diss., University of California, Berkeley, 1964), 260.

14. Bien Ban buoi hop thuong-nguyet, September 18, 1961, SC.02 3563, CLT II; Nguyen Tran, *Cong Va Toi: Nhung Su That Lich Su* (Los Alamitos, Calif.: Xuan Thu, 1992), 218.

15. Heavner to Wood, March 19, 1962, *FRUS, 1961–1963,* vol. 2, 249–50.

16. John C. Donnell and Gerald C. Hickey, *The Vietnamese "Strategic Hamlets": A Preliminary Report* (Santa Monica, Calif.: RAND, 1962), 7, 11–19, 24.

17. This is also the essence of Race's analysis of events in Long An—see Jeffrey Race, *War Comes to Long An: Revolutionary Conflict in a Vietnamese Province* (Berkeley: University of California Press, 1973), 151–55.

18. Ban Tong Ket Chien Tranh Thanh Uy Thanh Pho Ho Chi Minh, *Lich Su Sai Gon–Cho Lon–Gia Dinh Khang Chien (1945–1975)* (Ho Chi Minh: n.p., 1994), 346–50; Phuc Trinh cua Thuong-si Nguyen Huu Hue, Tieu Doi Truong Hien-Binh Q. G., September 9, 1961, Tham-Muu Biet Bo, Tong-Thong Phu, TM 622, CLT II; *Times of Viet Nam Magazine,* April 15, 1962, 18.

19. Bien-Ban so 33, December 21, 1962, GVN Strat Hams, VA. See also Cu Chi district reports, November 1962, SC.05 10.357, CLT II.

20. Serong to Harkins, October 1962, Doc. 51, #1 (History Backup) 30 Mar. 62–Nov. 63 (I), Box 1, William C. Westmoreland Papers, LBJ.

21. See November 1962 reports, SC.05 10.357, CLT II.

22. Bergerud, *The Dynamics of Defeat,* 52; MAAG, Vietnam, Lessons Learned Number 10, May 1, 1962, Doc. 21, #1 (History Backup) 30 Mar. 62–Nov. 63 (I), Box 1, Westmoreland Papers, LBJ.

23. Bien-Ban buoi hop thuong-nguyet, October 16, 1961, SC.02 3563, CLT II. See Race, 193–96, for the same arguments used by officials in Long An.

24. Bien ban phien hop Ap Chien-Luoc, November 16, 1963, SC.03 5067, CLT II.

25. *Mien Dong Nam Bo Khang Chien (1945–1975),* vol. 1 (Hanoi: Quan Doi Nhan Dan, 1990), 177–182.

26. Toa Dai-Bieu Chanh-Phu MDNP, To-Trinh, February 13, 1962, TM 459/58, CLT II.

27. There was apparently some confusion over titles. The term "Sunrise campaign" applied to activities in all ten provinces of the eastern region; "Operation Sunrise I" referred to the operation in northern Binh Duong. To avoid overly complicating matters, the use of the terms "Operation Sunrise" or "Sunrise" refers here to the activities in northern Binh Duong.

28. McGarr to Thuan, December 18, 1961, 9155.3/9105 (13 October 1961) Sec. 2, CDF, RG 218, USNA; Martin to Cottrell, December 18, 1961, *Foreign Relations of the United States, 1961–1963,* vol. 1, *Vietnam* (Washington, D.C.: GPO, 1988), 742–43; Felt to McGarr, December 23, 1961, ibid., 758; Memorandum for Record, January 12, 1962, *FRUS, 1961–1963,* vol. 2, 24–27; JCS (Historical Division), *The History of the Joint Chiefs of Staff: The Joint Chiefs of Staff and the War in Vietnam, 1960–1968,* pt. 1, ch. 4, 5–7; *The Pentagon Papers: The Defense Department History of United States Decisionmaking on Vietnam,* vol. 2, Gravel ed. (Boston: Beacon Press, 1971), 143.

29. Saigon to State, December 7, 1961, 751K.5/12-761, CDF 60-63, RG 59, USNA; Memorandum for Record, January 12, 1962, *FRUS, 1961–1963,* vol. 2, 26–27; March 1, 1962, ibid., 192; *Pentagon Papers,* vol. 2, 143–44.

30. Dai Bieu Chanh-Phu MDNP [to] Bo-Truong Noi-Vu, January 31, 1962, SC.03 5570/12, CLT II.

31. Toa Dai-Bieu Chanh-Phu MDNP, To-Trinh, February 13, 1962, TM 459/58, ibid.; Ke-Hoach Hanh-Quan Binh-Minh, March 1962, SC.06 10586, ibid.; Bagley to Taylor, March 10, 1962, *FRUS, 1961–1963,* vol. 2, 212–13.

32. Hung's reports, SC.05 10.357, CLT II; Giam-Doc Trung-Tam Huan-Luyen [to] Bo-Truong PTT, November 13, 1962, BT 576, ibid.

33. *Ap Chien Luoc,* July 1962, 11.

34. Memorandum for Record, March 1, 1962, *FRUS, 1961–1963,* vol. 2, 192; Binh-Tuy [to] Bo-Truong PTT Kiem Bo-Truong Dac Nhiem An-Ninh, June 1,

1962, SC.02 3565, CLT II; Bernard B. Fall, *The Two Viet-Nams: A Political and Military Analysis*, 2d rev. ed. (New York: Frederick A. Praeger, 1967), 380.

35. Roger Hilsman, *To Move a Nation: The Politics of Foreign Policy in the Administration of John F. Kennedy* (Garden City, N.Y.: Doubleday, 1967), 440–41; Hilsman to Taylor, March 31, 1962, *FRUS, 1961–1963*, vol. 2, 245–46.

36. Dai Bieu Chanh-Phu MDNP, To-Trinh, April 10, 1962, SC.08 15266, CLT II; *New York Times*, March 29, 1962.

37. R. M. Rhotenberry, "Pacification, Binh Duong Province, RVN (1962–1967)," March 1970, 10–11, U.S. Army Military History Institute.

38. *New York Times*, March 29, 1962; Dai Bieu Chanh-Phu MDNP, To-Trinh, April 10, 1962, SC.08 15266, CLT II.

39. *Time*, April 6, 1962.

40. MAAG, Vietnam, Lessons Learned Number 19, July 31, 1962, Doc. 41, #1 (History Backup) 30 Mar. 62–Nov. 63 (I), Box 1, Westmoreland Papers, LBJ.

41. *New York Times*, March 29, and April 8, 1962; *Kien Quoc*, April 2, and May 28, 1962.

42. Interview with Douglas Pike, November 19, 1996.

43. William Prochnau, *Once upon a Distant War* (New York: Random House, 1995), 74; MAAG, Vietnam, Lessons Learned Number 19, July 31, 1962, Doc. 41, #1 (History Backup) 30 Mar. 62–Nov. 63 (I), Box 1, Westmoreland Papers, LBJ.

44. Dai Bieu Chanh-Phu MDNP, To-Trinh, April 10, 1962, SC.08 15266, CLT II; *New York Times*, March 29, and April 8, 1962; Rhotenberry, 11.

45. Dai Bieu Chanh-Phu MDNP, To-Trinh, April 10, 1962, SC.08 15266, CLT II; *New York Times*, March 29, and April 8, 1962; COMUSMACV to State, July 12, 1962, 751K.5/7-1262, CDF 60-63, RG 59, USNA.

46. Senior Officers Oral History Program, vol. 3, 130, William B. Rosson Papers, USAMHI.

47. Saigon to War Office, August 2, 1962, DV1201/51, FO371/166749, PRO; COMUSMACV to AIG 924, September 8, 1962, General 9/1/62–9/14/62, Countries: VN, Box 196, National Security Files, John F. Kennedy Library.

48. Phu Dac-Uy Trung-Uong Tinh-Bao, Phieu Tinh-Bao, April 7, 1962, TM 598/628, CLT II.

49. *Mien Dong Nam Bo Khang Chien (1945–1975)*, vol. 2 (Hanoi: Quan Doi Nhan Dan, 1993), 118–19; VCD 302 and 303 [trans.], Pike Collection, Center for Research Libraries; Southeast Asia Situation Report No. 18-62, May 2, 1962, Michael Forrestal 1/62–5/62, Staff Memoranda, Meetings and Memoranda, Box 320, NSF, JFK.

50. Rhotenberry, "Pacification, Binh Duong Province," 12–13; Status Report on Southeast Asia, July 11, 1962, Subjects, Status Reports 4/4/62–7/11/62, Countries: VN, Box 202-03, NSF, JFK; Saigon to State, August 21, 1962, 751K.00/8-2162, CDF 60-63, RG 59, USNA; Saigon to War Office, August 2, 1962, DV1201/51, FO371/166749, PRO.

51. COMUSMACV to AIG 924, September 8, 1962, General 9/1/62–9/14/62,

Countries: VN, Box 196, NSF, JFK; Truong Phong Nhi Bo Tong Tham Muu/QDVNCH, Phieu Trinh, April 17, 1962, TM 598/628, CLT II.

52. *New York Times,* June 17, 1962; McCone to Kennedy, undated, Security 1962, Countries: VN, Box 128a, Presidential Office Files, JFK.

53. Ke-Hoach Hanh-Quan Binh-Minh, March 1962, SC.06 10586, CLT II.

54. Forrestal to Bundy, May 8, 1962, Michael Forrestal 1/62–5/62, Staff Memo- randa, Meetings and Memoranda, Box 320, NSF, JFK; Senior Officers Oral History Program, vol. 3, 130, Rosson Papers, USAMHI; Dai Bieu Chanh-Phu MDNP, To- Trinh, April 10, 1962, SC.08 15266, CLT II; COMUSMACV to AIG 924, June 29, 1962, General 6/24/62–6/30/62, Countries: VN, Box 196, NSF, JFK; Binh Duong, Phieu Kinh De Trinh, July 14, 1963, SC.03 5571/3, CLT II.

55. Prochnau, *Once upon a Distant War,* 74–75.

56. Toa Dai-Bieu Chanh-Phu MDNP, To-Trinh, February 13, 1962, TM 459/58, CLT II; Saigon to War Office, April 5, 1962, DV103145/105, FO371/166722, PRO; Saigon to Foreign Office, May 16, 1962, DV1015/129, FO371/166704, ibid.; Chi- Huy-Truong Chien-Dich Xay Dung Nong-Thon [to] Dai-Ta Tu-Lenh Khu Chien- Thuat 31, July 11, 1962, SC.06 10586, CLT II.

57. Status Report on Southeast Asia, October 31, 1962, Subjects, T. Force Status Reports 10/21/62–10/31/62, Regional Security, SEA, Box 231A, NSF, JFK.

58. Bien-Ban so 15, June 29, 1962, GVN Strat Hams, VA; Bien-Ban so 16, July 13, 1962, ibid.; Bien-Ban so 19, August 31, 1962, ibid.; Bien-Ban so 21, September 14, 1962, ibid.

59. Phillips to Fippin, June 25, 1962, *FRUS, 1961–1963,* vol. 2, 471; Bien-Ban so 19, August 31, 1962, GVN Strat Hams, VA.

60. Saigon to War Office, September 27, 1962, DV1201/70, FO371/166750, PRO.

61. Dai Bieu Chanh-Phu MDNP [to] Bo-Truong Noi-Vu, February 12, 1963, SC.08 15266, CLT II.

62. *New York Times,* August 21, 1963; *Mien Dong Nam Bo Khang Chien (1945–1975),* vol. 2, 138; Rhotenberry, "Pacification, Binh Duong Province," 17.

63. Saigon to State, August 9, 1962, 751K.5/8-962, CDF 60-63, RG 59, USNA; Bo-Truong PTT [to] Van-Thanh-Cao, September 11, 1962, SC.06 12365, CLT II; Status Report on Southeast Asia, September 19, 1962, Subjects, T. Force Status Reports 9/1/62–9/30/62, Regional Security, SEA, Box 231A, NSF, JFK.

64. Saigon to State, August 9, 1962, 751K.5/8-962, CDF 60-63, RG 59, USNA.

65. Bien-Ban so 15, June 29, 1962, GVN Strat Hams, VA; Dai-Bieu Chanh-Phu MDNP [to] Chanh Van-Phong, July 24, 1962, SC.08 15266, CLT II.

66. Binh Duong [to] Bo-Truong Noi-Vu, April 28, 1962, TM 598/628, ibid.; Dai- Bieu Chanh-Phu MDNP [to] Chanh Van-Phong, July 24, 1962, SC.08 15266, ibid.; November 1962 district reports, SC.05 10357, ibid.

67. Binh Duong [to] Dong-Ly Van-Phong PTT, November 14, 1962, TM 489/149, ibid.; November 29, 1962, ibid.; Saigon to State, January 19, 1963, 751K.00/1-1963, CDF 60-63, RG 59, USNA.

68. Wilson to Senior Advisor, 5th Inf. Div. [et al.], May 20, 1963, Memorandums for Senior and Sector Advisers 1963, Wilbur Wilson Papers, USAMHI; Binh Duong [to] Dong-Ly Van-Phong PTT, December 4, 1962, TM 489/149, CLT II.

69. Krulak report, undated, *Foreign Relations of the United States, 1961–1963*, vol. 3, *Vietnam* (Washington, D.C.: GPO, 1991), 457.

70. U.S. MAAG, III Corps, Special Evaluation Team Report, June 30, 1963, Memorandums for Senior and Sector Advisers 1963, Wilson Papers, USAMHI.

71. Wilson to Senior Advisor, 5th Infantry Division [et al.], May 20, 1963, Memorandums for Senior and Sector Advisers 1963, ibid.; U.S. MAAG, III Corps, Progress Report OPLAN BINH DUONG, July 1, 1963, Memorandums for CHUSASEC, ibid.

72. Saigon to State, March 25, 1963, DEF 19 US-S VIET, Subject-Numeric File, RG 59, USNA; Binh Duong, Phieu, September 17, 1963, SC.03 5571/3, CLT II.

73. Bien-Ban so 6, March 23, 1962, GVN Strat Hams, VA.

74. Binh-Duong [to] Tham Muu Biet Bo PTT, September 21, 1962, TM 598/628, CLT II; Tai lieu So-Luoc, October 9, 1962, TM 489/149, ibid.; Tong Thu-ky Thuong-Truc Quoc-Phong [to] Bo-Truong Noi-Vu, October 12, 1962, TM 489/149, ibid.; Hoi-nghi Lien-Bo, November 14, 1962, SC.03 5159, ibid.; Bien-Ban so 29, November 23, 1962, BT 491, ibid.

75. Dong-Ly Van-Phong PTT [to] Bo-Truong Cai-Tien Nong-Thon, December 19, 1962, SC.03 5958, ibid.

76. Bo-Truong CTNT, Phieu-Trinh, January 15, 1963, SC.03 5958, ibid. (also the plain copy with Diem's handwritten comments); Dong-Ly Van-Phong PTT [to] Bo-Truong CTNT, January 30, 1963, SC.03 5958, ibid.

77. Binh Duong, Phieu Kinh De-Trinh, June 17, 1963, SC.03 5571/3, ibid.; Binh Duong, Phieu, September 17, 1963, ibid.; Rhotenberry, "Pacification, Binh Duong Province," 16.

78. U.S. MAAG, III Corps, Progress Report OPLAN BINH DUONG, July 1, 1963, Memorandums for CHUSASEC, Wilson Papers, USAMHI.

79. Binh Duong, Nguyet-De "A," October 24, 1963, BT 644, CLT II; Wilson to Dinh, October 7, 1963, III Corps Estimate of the Situation, Wilson Papers, USAMHI. The revised hamlet total probably reflected a reassessment of the number required, rather than any lowering of expectations. Figures need to be used with care because, besides the potential for reporting inaccuracies, different sources often give quite widely varying numbers.

80. Binh Duong, Phieu, September 17, 1963, SC.03 5571/3, CLT II; Wilson to Dinh, October 7, 1963, III Corps Estimate of the Situation, Wilson Papers, USAMHI.

81. U.S. MAAG, III Corps, Progress Report OPLAN BINH DUONG, July 1, 1963, Memorandums for CHUSASEC, ibid.

82. Binh Duong, Phieu Kinh De Trinh, July 14, 1963, SC.03 5571/3, CLT II; Binh Duong, Phieu, September 17, 1963, ibid.; U.S. MAAG, III Corps, Progress Report OPLAN BINH DUONG, July 1, 1963, Memorandums for CHUSASEC, Wilson

Papers, USAMHI; Wilson to Dinh, October 7, 1963, III Corps Estimate of the Situation, ibid.

83. Dai-Bieu Chanh-Phu MDNP [to] Binh Duong, June 20, 1963, SC.08 15266, CLT II.

84. Wilson to Dinh, October 7, 1963, III Corps Estimate of the Situation, Wilson Papers, USAMHI.

85. Rhotenberry, 16–17.

86. District reports, SC.05 10357, CLT II; Binh-Duong [to] Bo-Truong Noi-Vu, March 19, 1963, SC.05 10357, ibid.; Binh Duong, Nguyet-De "A," October 24, 1963, BT 644, ibid.; Nguyet-De "B," October 5, 1963, ibid.

87. Letter from Tran Ngoc Chau, August 27, 1997; Race, *War Comes to Long An,* 70–71.

88. Phillips to York, January 24, 1963, Box 34, Charles T. R. Bohannan Papers, Hoover Institute.

8. The Reckoning

1. Wilfred G. Burchett, *Vietnam: Inside Story of the Guerilla War* (New York: International Publishers, 1965), 189–90.

2. *Times of Viet Nam Magazine,* October 28, 1962.

3. Bundy manuscript, ch. 8, 2, William P. Bundy Papers, Lyndon B. Johnson Library.

4. Status Report on Southeast Asia, October 3, 1962, Subjects, T. Force Status Reports 10/1/62–10/20/62, Regional Security, SEA, Box 231A, National Security Files, John F. Kennedy Library; Heavner Report, December 11, 1962, *Foreign Relations of the United States, 1961–1963,* vol. 2, *Vietnam* (Washington, D.C.: GPO, 1990), 764; Current Intelligence Memorandum, January 11, 1963, *Foreign Relations of the United States, 1961–1963,* vol. 3, *Vietnam* (Washington, D.C.: GPO, 1991), 22; Burris to Johnson, January 24, 1963, Doc. 83, Memos to the VP from Col. Burris, July 1962–April 1963, Box 6, Vice Presidential Security Files, LBJ.

5. COMUSMACV to State, June 15, 1962, 751K.00/6-1562, Central Decimal File 1960–1963, Record Group 59, U.S. National Archives; State Department Paper, October 1962, *FRUS, 1961–1963,* vol. 2, 679–87; Saigon to State, November 16, 1962, 751K.00/11-1662, CDF 60–63, RG 59, USNA; Heavner Report, December 11, 1962, *FRUS, 1961–1963,* vol. 2, 764–65; Hilsman/Forrestal to Kennedy, January 25, 1963, *FRUS, 1961–1963,* vol. 3, 49–52.

6. Saigon to State, August 3, 1962, *FRUS, 1961–1963,* vol. 2, 576–77; Hilsman/Forrestal to Kennedy, January 25, 1963, *FRUS, 1961–1963,* vol. 3, 49-62; NIE, April 17, 1963, ibid., 232–35.

7. Douglas Pike, Oral History, Interview 1, 18, LBJ.

8. War Experiences Recapitulation Committee of the High-Level Military Insti-

tute, *The Anti-U.S. Resistance War for National Salvation, 1954–1975: Military Events,* trans. JPRS 80968 (Washington, D.C.: GPO, 1982), 49; Robert K. Brigham, *Guerrilla Diplomacy: The NLF's Foreign Relations and the Viet Nam War* (Ithaca, N.Y.: Cornell University Press, 1999), 15–16.

9. Nguyen Chi Thanh, "Who Will Win in South Vietnam?" *Vietnamese Studies* 1 (1964): 15.

10. Tran Van Giau, *Long An: 21 Nam Danh My* (n.p.: Long An, 1988), 141; Douglas Pike, *Viet Cong: The Organization and Techniques of the National Liberation Front of South Vietnam* (Cambridge, Mass.: MIT Press, 1967), 116.

11. Giau, 140–41; Nguyen Huu Nguyen, "Hinh Thai Chien Tranh Nhan Dan O Long An Trong Khang Chien Chong My Tren Chien Truong Nam Bo (1960–1975)" (TP Ho Chi Minh, Luan An Pho Tien Sy, 1994), 66–68; Le Quoc San, *Cuoc Do Suc Than Ky* (Hanoi: Quan Doi Nhan Dan, 1991), 144; Hilsman to Harriman, June 18, 1962, Countries: VN 3/1/62–7/27/62, Box 3, Roger Hilsman Papers, JFK.

12. Saigon to State, August 25, 1962, *FRUS, 1961–1963,* vol. 2, 612–13; September 18, 1962, 751K.00/9-1862, CDF 60-63, RG 59, USNA; November 21, 1962, *FRUS, 1961–1963,* vol. 2, 741; December 15, 1962, 751K.00/12-1562, CDF 60-63, RG 59, USNA; *Lich Su Khu 6 (Cuc Nam Trung Bo Nam Tay Nguyen) Khang Chien Chong My (1954–1975)* (Hanoi: Quan Doi Nhan Dan, 1995), 78–97.

13. Saigon to State, October 16, 1962, 751K.00/10-1662, CDF 60-63, RG 59, USNA; Heavner to Wood, October 29, 1962, 751K.5/10-2962, ibid.; Saigon to State, November 16, 1962, 751K.00/11-1662, ibid.

14. Saigon to State, September 29, 1962, 751K.00/9-2962, ibid.; Status Report on Southeast Asia, October 3, 1962, Subjects, T. Force Status Reports 10/1/62–10/20/62, Regional Security, SEA, Box 231A, NSF, JFK; *Mien Dong Nam Bo Khang Chien (1945–1975),* vol. 2 (Hanoi: Quan Doi Nhan Dan, 1993), 136; Giau, 143; William R. Andrews, *The Village War: Vietnamese Communist Revolutionary Activities in Dinh Tuong Province, 1960–1964* (Columbia: University of Missouri Press, 1973), 125.

15. Hilsman/Forrestal to Kennedy, January 25, 1963, *FRUS, 1961–1963,* vol. 3, 49–50; JCS Team Report, January 1963, ibid., 75–78.

16. San, 96–99; Saigon to State, December 15, 1962, 751K.00/12-1562, CDF 60-63, RG 59, USNA.

17. Saigon to State, June 19, 1962, 751K.00/6-1962, CDF 60-63, ibid.; September 18, 1962, 751K.00/9-1862, CDF 60-63, ibid.; December 8, 1962, 751K.00/12-862, CDF 60-63, ibid.; January 25, 1963, 751K.00/1-2563, CDF 60-63, ibid.; June 12, 1963, POL 18 S VIET, Subject-Numeric File, ibid.

18. Saigon to State, June 6, 1963, POL 27-7 VIET, ibid.; Giau, 141.

19. Saigon to State, March 11, 1963, DEF 19 US-S VIET, SNF, RG 59, USNA; Andrews, 126–27; W. P. Davison, *Some Observations on Viet Cong Operations in the Villages* (Santa Monica, Calif.: RAND, 1968), 164–69; RAND, Interviews Concerning the National Liberation Front of South Vietnam, File No. DT-188 (I), Folder 647,

Subject File, Box 29, Edward G. Lansdale Papers, Hoover Institute (the chronology here is not entirely clear, but the description of popular attitudes is consonant with what other sources note was happening in this period).

20. VCD 35 [trans.], 2, 6, and VCD 48A, 4, Pike Collection, Center for Research Libraries; Giau, 144.

21. Serong to Harkins, October 1962, Doc. 51, #1 (History Backup) 30 Mar. 62–Nov. 63 (I), Box 1, William C. Westmoreland Papers, LBJ; Pacification Plan, Autumn 1962, Folder 1570, Subject File, Box 60, Lansdale Papers, HI; JCS Team Report, January 1963, *FRUS, 1961–1963*, vol. 3, 79. Not all officials were convinced that the flow of intelligence had improved significantly (Johnson to Rostow, October 16, 1962, Vietnam 1962, Lot File 69D121, Records of the Policy Planning Staff 1962, Box 219, RG 59, USNA).

22. *Vietnam Press,* w/e April 28, 1963, 7–8; Saigon to State, April 29, 1963, DEF 19 US-S VIET, SNF, RG 59, USNA; *Times of Viet Nam Magazine,* May 5, 1963, 2–3; USOM, *Operational Report, 1963–1964* (n.p., n.d.), 9–11; Lu Lan, "The People's War or War on the People?" in *Prelude to Tragedy: Vietnam, 1960–1965,* ed. Harvey Neese and John O'Donnell (Annapolis: Naval Institute Press, 2001), 146–49.

23. VCD 93 [trans.], 20–22, and VCD 257 [trans.], 12–15, Pike Collection, CRL.

24. Saigon to State, January 25, 1963, 751K.00/1-2563, CDF 60-63, RG 59, USNA.

25. VCD 35 [trans.], 2 (see also VCD 93 [trans.], 32, and VCD 257 [trans.], 30), Pike Collection, CRL.

26. Esp. VCD 257 [trans.], and VCD 636 [trans.], ibid.

27. Saigon to State, December 8, 1962, 751K.00/12-862, CDF 60-63, RG 59, USNA; Serong to Harkins, March 14, 1963, Doc. 61, #1 (History Backup) 30 Mar. 62–Nov. 63 (II), Box 1, Westmoreland Papers, LBJ.

28. Current Intelligence Memorandum, January 11, 1963, *FRUS, 1961–1963,* vol. 3, 20. RVN figures for NLF casualties were notoriously unreliable; one historian also argues that U.S. figures for PLAF forces were far too low because MACV manipulated estimates—John M. Newman, *JFK and Vietnam: Deception, Intrigue, and the Struggle for Power* (New York: Warner Books, 1992), 240–44.

29. William S. Turley, *The Second Indochina War: A Short Political and Military History, 1954–1975* (New York: Mentor, 1987), 44; a recent communist summary of northern support states that infiltration from 1961–1963 included forty thousand personnel and 165,000 weapons—Ban Chi Dao Tong Ket Chien Tranh Truc Thuoc Bo Chinh Tri, *Tong Ket Cuoc Khang Chien Chong My, Cuu Nuoc: Thang Loi va Bai Hoc* (Hanoi: Chinh Tri Quoc Gia, 1995), 48–49, 311.

30. VCD 93 [trans.], 21–22, VCD 138 [trans.], 1, 8, VCD 257 [trans.], 19, and VCD 636 [trans.], 36–37, Pike Collection, CRL.

31. VCD 3 [trans.], 8–12, VCD 93 [trans.], 32–42, VCD 257 [trans.], 19, and VCD 636 [trans.], 33–38, ibid.; M. N., " 'Ba Mui Giap Cong' Trong Cuoc Chien Tranh Nhan Dan Chong My Va Tay Sai O Mien Nam," *Nghien cuu Lich su* (May 1966): 5–14, 62.

32. Nguyen Van Vinh, "May Diem Chinh Ve Tinh Hinh Mien Nam Nam 1962," in *Cach Mang Mien Nam Nhat Dinh Thang Loi Nhung Phuc Tap, Lau Dai* (Hanoi: Su That, 1963), 56–57.

33. War Experiences Recapitulation Committee, *The Anti-U.S. Resistance War,* 49–50.

34. San, *Cuoc Do Suc Than Ky,* 98–127; Neil Sheehan, *A Bright Shining Lie: John Paul Vann and America in Vietnam* (New York: Random House, 1988), 203–65. For U.S. reaction, see editorial, *FRUS, 1961–1963,* vol. 3, 1–3; Harkins to Dodge, January 4, 1963, General 1/10/63–1/30/63, Countries: VN, NSF, JFK; Saigon to State, January 8, 1963, 751K.5/1-863, CDF 60-63, RG 59, USNA. For the NLF view, see VCD 777 [trans.], Pike Collection, CRL; Tran Van Giau, *Mien Nam Giu Vung Thanh Dong: Luoc Su Dong Bao Mien Nam Dau Tranh Chong My Va Tay Sai,* vol. 2 (Hanoi: Khoa Hoc, 1966), 128–34.

35. Walton to "I" + Toussaint, September 17, 1962, Box 35, Charles T. R. Bohannan Papers, HI; Johnson to Rostow, October 16, 1962, Vietnam 1962, Lot File 69D121, PPS 1962, Box 219, RG 59, USNA; Saigon to State, January 12, 1963, 751K.00/1-1263, CDF 60-63, ibid.; Hue to State, April 18, 1963, POL 23 S VIET, SNF, ibid.

36. Giam-Doc Trung Tam Huan-Luyen [to] Bo-Truong Phu Tong-Thong, November 13, 1962, Van-Phong Bo-Truong Phu Tong-Thong, BT 576, Cuc Luu Tru II; Binh-Thuan [to] Bo-Truong PTT, June 12, 1963, Tai Lieu Do So Luu Tru Va Cong Bao Phu Thu Tuong Viet Nam Cong Hoa, SC.02 3566, ibid.

37. San, 129–36. See also Giau, *Long An,* 144–45; Air Force message, December 21, 1963, Doc. 3, Vietnam Cables vol. 2, 12/63–1/64, Country File—Vietnam, Box 1, National Security File, LBJ; CIA Special Report, January 17, 1964, Doc. 21, Southeast Asia vol. 1, Special Intell. Material 12/63–7/64, Country File—Vietnam, Box 48, ibid. For examples of NLF learning documents about strategic hamlets, see VCD 14 [trans.], VCD 35 [trans.], VCD 48A, and VCD 302 [trans.], Pike Collection, CRL.

38. For communist commentary: Bo Chi Huy Quan Su Tinh Ben Tre, *Ben Tre: 30 Nam Khang Chien Chong Phap, Chong My, 1945–1975* (n.p., 1990), 192–97; *Lich Su Khu 6,* 107-8; *Mien Dong Nam Bo Khang Chien (1945–1975),* vol. 2, 136–44; Giau, *Mien Nam Giu Vung Thanh Dong,* vol. 2, 131–34, 367-71; San, 129–36, 143–47; Vuong Thanh Dien, *7 Tran Thang Lon O Mien Nam* (Hanoi: Quan Doi Nhan Dan, 1964). For U.S. reports: Saigon to State, March 30, 1963, POL 23 S VIET, SNF, RG 59, USNA; May 4, 1963, DEF 19 US-S VIET, ibid.; Air Force message, December 21, 1963, Doc. 3, Vietnam Cables vol. 2, 12/63–1/64, Country File—Vietnam, Box 1, NSF, LBJ; CIA Special Report, January 17, 1964, Doc. 21, Southeast Asia vol. 1, Special Intell. Material 12/63–7/64, Country File—Vietnam, Box 48, ibid.

39. For example: Nguyen Qui Hung, *Neuf Ans de Dictatures au Sud Vietnam: Témoignages Vivants sur Mme Nhu et les Ngo* (Saigon: n.p., 1964), 149–50, 172–73; Hoanh Linh Do Mau, *Viet-Nam Mau Lua Que Huong Toi: Hoi-Ky Chinh-Tri* (Mission Hills, Calif.: Que Huong, 1988), 557, 685. Catholics in South Vietnam, who numbered about one million out of a population of fifteen million, did wield disproportionate

influence, but Diem favored his coreligionists principally because of their anticommunism, not their faith.

40. For secondary accounts of the period: George McT. Kahin, *Intervention: How America Became Involved in Vietnam* (New York: Alfred A. Knopf, 1986), 146–81; Ellen J. Hammer, *A Death in November: America in Vietnam, 1963* (New York: E. P. Dutton, 1987), 103–311; Newman, *JFK and Vietnam*, 331–416; David Kaiser, *American Tragedy: Kennedy, Johnson, and the Origins of the Vietnam War* (Cambridge, Mass.: Belknap Press, 2000), 213–83.

41. Phien Hop Hoi-Dong Noi-Cac, May 13, 1963, SC.05 10.001, CLT II. See also Hughes to Acting Secretary, August 21, 1963, General 8/21/63–8/23/63, Countries: VN, Box 198, NSF, JFK; Saigon to State, August 29, 1963, *Foreign Relations of the United States, 1961–1963*, vol. 4, *Vietnam* (Washington, D.C.: GPO, 1991), 18.

42. CIA Information Report, July 8, 1963, *FRUS, 1961–1963*, vol. 3, 473–78; Saigon to Agency, September 10, 1963, *FRUS, 1961–1963*, vol. 4, 147; Ken Post, *Revolution, Socialism, and Nationalism in Viet Nam*, vol. 4 (Aldershot, Hants: Dartmouth Publishing, 1990), 181–90.

43. Saigon to State, June 22, 1963, *FRUS, 1961–1963*, vol. 3, 409–10; Special NIE, July 10, 1963, Doc. 3, 53 South Vietnam, National Intelligence Estimates, Boxes 6-7, NSF, LBJ; David Halberstam, *The Making of a Quagmire* (New York: Random House, 1965), 212–13.

44. Saigon to State, June 25, 1963, *FRUS, 1961–1963*, vol. 3, 413–14; Special NIE, July 10, 1963, Doc. 3, 53 South Vietnam, National Intelligence Estimates, Boxes 6-7, NSF, LBJ.

45. Saigon to State, August 29, 1963, *FRUS, 1961–1963*, vol. 4, 19; Halberstam, 74–75.

46. Helms to Bundy, October 22, 1963, General 10/15/63–10/28/63 Memos and Misc., Countries: VN, Box 200-01, NSF, JFK.

47. Saigon to State, August 30, 1963, POL S VIET-US, SNF, RG 59, USNA; *Times of Viet Nam*, September 2, 1963.

48. Memorandum of Conversation, July 17, 1963, *FRUS, 1961–1963*, vol. 3, 501.

49. CIA Information Report, August 27, 1963, General 8/24/63–8/31/63 TDC's (CIA Info. Reports), Countries: VN, Box 198, NSF, JKF. See also Phien Hop Hoi-Dong Noi-Cac, July 31, 1963, SC.05 10.001, CLT II; Saigon to State, October 16, 1963, Subjects, Top Secret Cables, Tabs A-B 10/63, Countries: VN, NSF, JFK; Cline to Bundy, October 19, 1963, General 10/15/63–10/28/63 Memos and Misc., Countries: VN, Box 200-01, ibid.

50. Frederick Nolting, *From Trust to Tragedy: The Political Memoirs of Frederick Nolting, Kennedy's Ambassador to Diem's Vietnam* (New York: Praeger Publishers, 1988), 117–18.

51. Saigon to Agency, September 2, 1963, *FRUS, 1961–1963*, vol. 4, 89–90; Memorandum for McCone, September 26, 1963, ibid., 295–98.

52. Hammer, *A Death in November*, 221–22; Mieczyslaw Maneli, *War of the Van-*

107. Saigon to State, November 30, 1963, *FRUS, 1961–1963*, vol. 4, 646.

108. Bundy manuscript, ch. 10, 5–7, Bundy Papers, LBJ.

109. Pike, OH, Interview 1, 10–11, LBJ; Senior Officers Debriefing Program, 60–61, Harkins Papers, USAMHI; William Colby, with James McCargar, *Lost Victory: A Firsthand Account of America's Sixteen-Year Involvement in Vietnam* (Chicago: Contemporary Books, 1989), 168–69; comments by Rufus Phillips, Lu Lan, and John O'Donnell in Neese and O'Donnell eds., 41, 55–56, 150–51, 227–28, 231–32.

110. Hearings before the Committee on Foreign Relations, United States Senate, Ninety-first Congress, Second Session, on Impact of the War in Southeast Asia on the U.S. Economy, Part 2, April 28 and 29, May 13 and 19, June 2, and August 13, 1970, 317.

111. Pike, *Viet Cong*, 352–53; NLF document, June 29, 1963, VC Docs 1962–63, Box 5, Bohannan Papers, HI.

112. NLF document, July 28, 1963, ibid.; Saigon to State, October 28, 1963, DEF 19 US-S VIET, SNF, RG 59, USNA; Monthly Intelligence Analysis, III Corps Army Advisory Group, December 5, 1963, Senior Advisors' Conference, 7–8 December 1963, Wilson Papers, USAMHI.

113. Serong to Harkins, March 14, 1963, Doc. 61, #1 (History Backup) 30 Mar. 62–Nov. 63 (II), Box 1, Westmoreland Papers, LBJ; Second Informal Appreciation of the Status of the Strategic Hamlet Program, September 1, 1963, Folder 1372, Subject File, Box 49, Lansdale Papers, HI; Saigon to State, December 7, 1963, *FRUS, 1961–1963*, vol. 4, 687–89; interview with Nguyen Van Cu, 31–33, Race Collection, CRL; C. V. Sturdevant, J. M. Carrier, and J. I. Edelman, *An Examination of the Viet Cong Reaction to the Vietnamese Strategic Hamlet Program* (Santa Monica, Calif.: RAND, 1964).

114. Phillips, "Before We Lost in South Vietnam," 45; Memorandum of Conference, September 10, 1963, Meetings on VN 9/1/63–9/10/63, Meetings and Memoranda, Box 316, NSF, JFK.

115. Hue to State, April 18, 1963, POL 23 S VIET, SNF, RG 59, USNA; October 10, 1963, ibid.; CIA Information Report, October 14, 1963, *FRUS, 1961–1963*, vol. 4, 401; CIA Memorandum, February 14, 1964, Doc. 84, Vietnam Memos and Misc. vol. 4, 2/64–3/64, Country File—Vietnam, Box 2, NSF, LBJ.

116. For the turnover, see Colby, 163–66; Francis J. Kelly, *The Green Berets in Vietnam, 1961–71* (New York: Brassey's, 1991), 35–44; Wilson to COMUSMACV, January 17, 1963 (inc. attached memo), A-113 General Correspondence May 1962–January 1963, Box 6, RG 472, USNA. For NLF successes, see *Lich Su Khu 6*, 107–8; Wilson to COMUSMACV, July 29, 1963, Memorandums for COMUSMACV 1963, Wilson Papers, USAMHI.

117. CIA Special Report, January 17, 1964, Doc. 21, Southeast Asia, vol. 1, Special Intell. Material 12/63–7/64, Country File—Vietnam, Box 48, NSF, LBJ.

118. CIA Memorandum, February 20, 1964, Doc. 86, Vietnam Memos and Misc., vol. 4, 2/64–3/64, Country File—Vietnam, Box 2, ibid. For the pressure on SDC forces, see the Dinh Tuong reports for September and October 1963, BT 644, CLT II.

119. San, *Cuoc Do Suc Than Ky*, 137–38; Harkins to Taylor, November 15, 1963, POL 27 S VIET, SNF, RG 59, USNA; Honolulu Meeting Briefing Book, 11/20/63, Part I, Countries: VN, Box 204, NSF, JFK.

120. Bien ban phien hop Ap Chien-Luoc, November 16, 1963, SC.03 5067, CLT II.

121. Bien-Ban Ban Giao Quyen Quan-Su Thuoc Tinh Long-An, July 15, 1963, SC.04 8175, ibid.; Nguyen Huu Nguyen, "Hinh Thai Chien Tranh Nhan Dan O Long An," 67–70; Giau, *Long An*, 138–48, 156–58.

122. San, 139–43; Giau, *Long An*, 157–66; Saigon to State, December 7, 1963, *FRUS, 1961–1963*, vol. 4, 687–89; Report on Long An, December 20, 1963, ibid., 714.

Conclusion

1. David Halberstam, *The Making of a Quagmire* (New York: Random House, 1965), 209.

2. Chester L. Cooper et al., *The American Experience with Pacification in Vietnam*, vol. 1 (Arlington, Va.: Institute for Defense Analyses, 1972), 9.

3. Ken Post, *Revolution, Socialism, and Nationalism in Viet Nam*, vol. 4 (Aldershot, Hants: Dartmouth Publishing, 1990), 206–12.

4. John C. Donnell, "Expanding Political Participation—The Long Haul from Villagism to Nationalism," *Asian Survey* (August 1970): 692.

5. *Foreign Relations of the United States, 1961–1963*, vol. 4, *Vietnam* (Washington, D.C.: GPO, 1991), 93–94.

6. Gary R. Hess, "Commitment in the Age of Counterinsurgency: Kennedy's Vietnam Options and Decisions, 1961–1963," in *Shadow on the White House: Presidents and the Vietnam War, 1945–1975*, ed. David L. Anderson (Lawrence: University Press of Kansas, 1993), 81–83.

7. Draft Memorandum for President, undated, 12/20/63–12/31/63, Countries: VN, Roger Hilsman Papers, John F. Kennedy Library; Phillips to Poats, January 9, 1964, Vietnam General, 1964, Special Files: Public Service, JFK–LBJ Ads, Subject File, Box 519, W. Averell Harriman Papers, Library of Congress Manuscript Division.

8. Frances FitzGerald, *Fire in the Lake: The Vietnamese and the Americans in Vietnam* (New York: Vintage Books, 1973), 351.

9. George C. Herring, " 'Peoples Quite Apart': Americans, South Vietnamese, and the War in Vietnam," *Diplomatic History* (winter 1990): 3–14.

10. William Colby, with James McCargar, *Lost Victory: A Firsthand Account of America's Sixteen-Year Involvement in Vietnam* (Chicago: Contemporary Books, 1989), 227–378. For a critical assessment of U.S./RVN efforts in 1969–1972, see Richard A. Hunt, *Pacification: The American Struggle for Vietnam's Hearts and Minds* (Boulder, Colo.: Westview Press, 1995).

Bibliography

Archival Collections

Center for Research Libraries, Chicago
    Pike Collection
    Race Collection
Cuc Luu Tru II [National Archives II], Ho Chi Minh City
    Tai Lieu Do So Luu Tru Va Cong Bao Phu Thu Tuong Viet Nam Cong Hoa
    Tham-Muu Biet Bo, Tong-Thong Phu
    Van-Phong Bi-Thu-Truong Phu Tong-Thong
    Van-Phong Bo-Truong Phu Tong-Thong
Hoover Institute, Stanford, California
    Bohannan, Charles T. R., Papers
    Lansdale, Edward G., Papers
Lyndon B. Johnson Library, Austin, Texas
    Administrative History of the Agency for International Development
    Bundy, William P., Papers
    Johnson, Lyndon B., Papers
        National Security File
        Vice Presidential Security Files
    Oral History Interviews
        Ball, George W.
        Bundy, William P.
        Colby, William
        Pike, Douglas
        Trueheart, William C.
    Westmoreland, William C., Papers
John F. Kennedy Library, Boston, Massachusetts
    Kennedy, John F., Papers
        National Security Files
        Presidential Office Files
    Hilsman, Roger, Papers
    Oral History Interviews
        Gilpatric, Roswell
        Harriman, W. Averell

Lodge, Henry Cabot
Sorensen, Theodore
Library of Congress Manuscript Division, Washington, D.C.
Douglas, William O., Papers
Harriman, W. Averell, Papers
Records of Moral Re-Armament, Inc.
Vann-Sheehan Vietnam War Collection
Massachusetts Historical Society, Boston, Massachusetts
Lodge, Henry Cabot II, Papers
Michigan State University Archives and Historical Collections, East Lansing, Michigan
Fishel, Wesley R., Papers
Vietnam Project
National Archives, College Park, Maryland
RG 59, Records of the Department of State
RG 218, Records of the Joint Chiefs of Staff
RG 334, Records of Interservice Agencies
RG 472, Records of A and B Detachments
Public Record Office, London
FO 371 Foreign Office Records
U.S. Army Military History Institute, Carlisle Barracks, Pennsylvania
Harkins, Paul D., Papers
Rosson, William B., Papers
Wilson, Wilbur, Papers
Vietnam Archive, Lubbock, Texas
Biographical Files
GVN Strat Hams

Interviews and Correspondence

Do Mau. Letter of December 7, 1995
Hoang Van Lac. Letter of February 13, 1996
Nguyen Van Dam (pseudonym). Interviews of March 17 and 27, 1997
Pike, Douglas. Interview of November 19, 1996
Tran Ngoc Chau. Telephone interview of July 18, 1997; letter of August 27, 1997

Published Collections

Foreign Relations of the United States, 1952–1954. Vol. 13. *Indochina.* Pts. 1 and 2. Washington, D.C.: GPO, 1982.

Foreign Relations of the United States, 1952–1954. Vol. 16. *The Geneva Conference.* Washington, D.C.: GPO, 1981.

Foreign Relations of the United States, 1955–1957. Vol. 1. *Vietnam.* Washington, D.C.: GPO, 1985.

Foreign Relations of the United States, 1958–1960. Vol. 1. *Vietnam.* Washington, D.C.: GPO, 1986.

Foreign Relations of the United States, 1961–1963. Vols. 1–4. *Vietnam.* Washington, D.C.: GPO, 1988-1991.

Public Papers of the Presidents of the United States: Dwight D. Eisenhower, 1954. Washington, D.C.: GPO, 1960.

United States–Vietnam Relations, 1945–1967. Washington, D.C.: GPO, 1971.

Walinsky, Louis J., ed. *Agrarian Reform as Unfinished Business: The Selected Papers of Wolf Ladejinsky.* New York: Oxford University Press, 1977.

Government Publications

Bo Cong-Dan-Vu. *Tu Ap Chien-Luoc Den Xa Tu-Ve* [*From the Strategic Hamlet to the Self-Defense Village*]. Saigon, 1962.

Commissariat General for Land Development. *The Work of Land Development in Viet Nam Up to June 30, 1959.* N.p., n.d.

Department of State. *A Threat to the Peace: North Viet-Nam's Effort to Conquer South Viet-Nam.* Washington, D.C.: GPO, 1961.

Directorate General of Information. *Viet Nam's Strategic Hamlets.* Saigon, 1963.

———. *Viet Nam's Strategic Hamlets.* 2d rev. ed. Saigon, 1963.

Hearings before the Committee on Foreign Relations, United States Senate, Ninety-first Congress, Second Session, on Impact of the War in Southeast Asia on the U.S. Economy, Part 2, April 28 and 29, May 13 and 19, June 2, and August 13, 1970.

Hearings before the Subcommittee on the Far East and the Pacific of the Committee on Foreign Affairs, House of Representatives, Eighty-sixth Congress, First Session, Current Situation in the Far East, July–August 1959. Washington, D.C.: GPO, 1959.

Huong Uoc [*Communal Rules*]. Saigon, n.d.

Nguyen Dang Thuc. "Democracy in Traditional Vietnamese Society." *Vietnam Culture Series* 4, Department of National Education, 1961.

Presidency. *Ngo Dinh Diem of Viet-Nam.* Saigon, 1957.

———. *Major Policy Speeches by President Ngo Dinh Diem.* 3d ed. Saigon, 1957.

———. *Toward Better Mutual Understanding.* Vols. 1 and 2. 2d ed. Saigon, 1958.

———. *Interviews of Ngo Dinh Diem.* Saigon, 1960.

Press Interviews with President Ngo Dinh Diem, Political Counselor Ngo Dinh Nhu. N.p., 1963.

Secretariat of State for Information. *Cai San: The Dramatic Story of Resettlement and Land Reform in the "Rice Bowl" of the Republic of Viet-Nam.* Saigon, n.d.

So Bao Chi Phu Tong Thong. *Con Duong Chinh Nghia: Nhan-Vi, Cong-Dong, Dong-Tien* [*The Pursuit of the Just Cause: Personalism, Community, Collective Advance*]. Vol. 6. Saigon, n.d.

USOM. *Operational Report, 1963–1964.* N.p., n.d.

USOM/Rural Affairs. *Notes on Strategic Hamlets.* Saigon, 1963.

Vietnamese-Language Books and Articles

Ban Chi Dao Tong Ket Chien Tranh Truc Thuoc Bo Chinh Tri. *Tong Ket Cuoc Khang Chien Chong My, Cuu Nuoc: Thang Loi va Bai Hoc* [*Recapitulating the Anti-U.S. Resistance War for National Salvation: Victories and Lessons*]. Hanoi: Chinh Tri Quoc Gia, 1995.

Ban Tong Ket Chien Tranh Thanh Uy Thanh Pho Ho Chi Minh. *Lich Su Sai Gon–Cho Lon–Gia Dinh Khang Chien (1945–1975)* [*The History of Saigon–Cholon–Gia Dinh in the Resistance War (1945–1975)*]. Ho Chi Minh: n.p., 1994.

Bo Chi Huy Quan Su Tinh Ben Tre. *Ben Tre: 30 Nam Khang Chien Chong Phap, Chong My, 1945–1975* [*Ben Tre: Thirty Years of the Anti-French and Anti-U.S. Resistance War, 1945–1975*]. N.p., 1990.

Cao Van Luan. *Ben Giong Lich Su, 1940–1965* [*In the Course of History, 1940–1965*]. Saigon: Tri Dung, 1972.

Chu Bang Linh. *Dang Can Lao* [*The Can Lao Party*]. San Diego: Me Viet Nam, 1993.

Doan Them. *Hai Muoi Nam Qua: Viec tung ngay (1945–1964)* [*Twenty Years Past: Events Day by Day (1945–1964)*]. Los Alamitos, Calif.: Xuan Thu, n.d.

Ho Quy Ba. *Quoc Sach Ap Chien Luoc cua My-Diem* [*The Strategic Hamlet Policy of American-Diem*]. Hanoi: Quan Doi Nhan Dan, 1962.

Hoang Khanh. *Tim Hieu Quoc Sach Ap Chien Luoc* [*Understanding the National Policy of Strategic Hamlets*]. Saigon: Nguyen ba Tong, 1962.

Hoang Lac, Ha Mai Viet. *Nam-Viet-Nam, 1954–1975: Nhung Su That Chua He Nhac Toi* [*South Vietnam, 1954–1975: Truths Never Told*]. Alief, Tex.: Hoang Lac, 1990.

Hoanh Linh Do Mau. *Viet-Nam Mau Lua Que Huong Toi: Hoi-Ky Chinh-Tri* [*Vietnam the Blood and Fire of My Country: Political Memoirs*]. Mission Hills, Calif.: Que Huong, 1988.

Khu Tru Mat [*Agrovilles*]. Saigon: Van Huu A Chau, 1960.

Le Quoc San. *Cuoc Do Suc Than Ky* [*The Glorious Test of Strength*]. Hanoi: Quan Doi Nhan Dan, 1991.

Lich Su Khu 6 (Cuc Nam Trung Bo Nam Tay Nguyen) Khang Chien Chong My (1954–1975) [*The History of Zone 6 (Deep Southern Central Southern Western Highlands) in the Anti-U.S. Resistance War (1954–1975)*]. Hanoi: Quan Doi Nhan Dan, 1995.

M. N. " 'Ba Mui Giap Cong' Trong Cuoc Chien Tranh Nhan Dan Chong My Va Tay Sai O Mien Nam" [" 'Three Front Attack' in the People's War against the Americans and their Lackeys in the South"]. *Nghien cuu Lich su* [*Historical Studies*] (May 1966): 5–14, 62.

Mien Dong Nam Bo Khang Chien (1945–1975) [*The Resistance War in the Eastern Region of the South (1945–1975)*]. Vols. 1 and 2. Hanoi: Quan Doi Nhan Dan, 1990, 1993.

Nguyen Huu Tiep. *Ngo-Dinh-Diem: Salazar Viet-Nam* [*Ngo Dinh Diem: The Salazar of Vietnam*]. N.p.: Xa-Hoi An-Quan, 1957.

Nguyen Tran. *Cong Va Toi: Nhung Su That Lich Su* [*Actions and Crimes: Historical Truths*]. Los Alamitos, Calif.: Xuan Thu, 1992.

Nguyen Van Chau. *Con Duong Song* [*The Way of Existence*]. Saigon: Nhom Van Chien, 1961.

———. *Giong Lich Su* [*The Course of History*]. Saigon: Nhom Van Chien, 1961.

———. *Ngo Dinh Diem va No Luc Hoa Binh Dang Do* [*Ngo Dinh Diem and the Unfinished Struggle for Peace*]. Trans. Nguyen Vy-Khanh. Los Alamitos, Calif.: Xuan Thu, 1989.

Nguyen Van Vinh. "May Diem Chinh Ve Tinh Hinh Mien Nam 1962" ["Essential Points about the Situation in the South 1962"]. In *Cach Mang Mien Nam Nhat Dinh Thang Loi Nhung Phuc Tap, Lau Dai* [*The Southern Revolution Will Win but It Will Be Hard and Prolonged*]. Hanoi: Su That, 1963, 40–64.

Phan Thanh Nghi. *Dao-Duc Cach-Mang Cua Chi-Si Ngo-Dinh-Diem* [*The Revolutionary Morality of the Virtuous Ngo Dinh Diem*]. N.p., 1956.

So Sanh Cai Cach Dien Dia Tai Mien Nam Cua Chinh Phu Cong Hoa Voi Cai Cach Ruong Dat Cua Viet Cong Tai Mien Bac [*Comparing Land Reform in the South by the Republican Government with Land Reform by the Viet Cong in the North*]. Saigon: Van Huu A Chau, 1960.

Than-The va Su-Nghiep Tong-Thong Ngo-Dinh-Diem [*The Life and Work of President Ngo Dinh Diem*]. N.p.: T. T. Nam-Viet, 1956.

Tran Huy Lieu. "Theo Quan Diem Lich Su: Nhin Vao Cuoc Dao Chinh Vua Qua O Mien Nam Viet-Nam Va So Kiep Ngo-Dinh-Diem" ["From a Historical Standpoint: Looking into the Recent Coup in South Vietnam and the Fate of Ngo Dinh Diem"]. *Nghien cuu Lich su* [*Historical Studies*] (January 1964): 1–4.

Tran Tuong, ed. *Bien Co 11: Tu Dao Chanh Den Tu Day* [*The Events of November 11: The Coup and Its Aftermath*]. Reprint of unspecified edition, 1986.

Tran Van Giau. *Mien Nam Giu Vung Thanh Dong: Luoc Su Dong Bao Mien Nam Dau Tranh Chong My Va Tay Sai* [*The South Maintaining a Bulwark: A Brief History of the Southern Compatriots in the Struggle against the Americans and their Lackeys*]. Vols. 1 and 2. Hanoi: Khoa Hoc, 1964, 1966.

———. *Long An: 21 Nam Danh My* [*Long An: Twenty-one Years of Fighting the Americans*]. N.p.: Long An, 1988.

Vien Lang (Nguyen Lien). *Duong ve Ap Chien Luoc: Hoi-Ky cua Vien-Lang (Nguyen-*

Lien) [*The Way to Strategic Hamlets: Memoirs of Vien Lang (Nguyen Lien)*]. Saigon: n.p., 1962.

Vuong Thanh Dien. *7 Tran Thang Lon O Mien Nam* [*Seven Big Victorious Battles in the South*]. Hanoi: Quan Doi Nhan Dan, 1964.

Western-Language Books and Articles

Abramson, Rudy. *Spanning the Century: The Life of W. Averell Harriman, 1891–1986*. New York: William Morrow, 1992.

Ambrose, Stephen E. *Rise to Globalism: American Foreign Policy Since 1938*. 4th rev. ed. New York: Viking Penguin, 1985.

Anderson, David L. *Trapped by Success: The Eisenhower Administration and Vietnam, 1953–1961*. New York: Columbia University Press, 1991.

Andrews, William R. *The Village War: Vietnamese Communist Revolutionary Activities in Dinh Tuong Province, 1960–1964*. Columbia: University of Missouri Press, 1973.

Baldwin, David A. "Foreign Aid, Intervention, and Influence." *World Politics* (April 1969): 425–47.

Ball, George W. *The Past Has Another Pattern*. New York: W. W. Norton, 1982.

Bao Dai. *Le Dragon D'Annam*. Paris: Plon, 1980.

Bergerud, Eric M. *The Dynamics of Defeat: The Vietnam War in Hau Nghia Province*. Boulder, Colo.: Westview Press, 1991.

Bills, Scott L. *Empire and Cold War: The Roots of Third World Antagonism, 1945–47*. Basingstoke: Macmillan Education, 1990.

Blair, Anne E. *Lodge in Vietnam: A Patriot Abroad*. New Haven: Yale University Press, 1995.

Blaufarb, Douglas S. *The Counterinsurgency Era: U.S. Doctrine and Performance, 1950 to the Present*. New York: Free Press, 1977.

Bradley, Mark Philip. *Imagining Vietnam and America: The Making of Postcolonial Vietnam, 1919–1950*. Chapel Hill: University of North Carolina Press, 2000.

Bredo, William. "Agrarian Reform in Vietnam: Vietcong and Government of Vietnam Strategies in Conflict." *Asian Survey* (August 1970): 738–50.

Breman, Jan. *The Shattered Image: Construction and Deconstruction of the Village in Colonial Asia*. Dordrecht–Holland: Forbis Publications, 1988.

Brigham, Robert K. *Guerrilla Diplomacy: The NLF's Foreign Relations and the Viet Nam War*. Ithaca, N.Y.: Cornell University Press, 1999.

Brocheux, Pierre. *The Mekong Delta: Ecology, Economy, and Revolution, 1860–1960*. Madison: Center for Southeast Asian Studies, University of Wisconsin-Madison, 1995.

Browne, Malcolm W. *The New Face of War*. Indianapolis: Bobbs-Merrill, 1965.

Bui Diem, with David Chanoff. *In the Jaws of History*. Boston: Houghton Mifflin, 1987.

Bui Tin. *Following Ho Chi Minh: The Memoirs of a North Vietnamese Colonel*. Trans. and adapted by Judy Stowe and Do Van. London: Hurst, 1995.

Burchett, Wilfred G. *Vietnam: Inside Story of the Guerilla War*. New York: International Publishers, 1965.

Buttinger, Joseph. *Vietnam: A Dragon Embattled*. Vols. 1 and 2. New York: Frederick A. Praeger, 1967.

Buzzanco, Robert. *Masters of War: Military Dissent and Politics in the Vietnam Era*. Cambridge: Cambridge University Press, 1997.

Callison, Charles Stuart. *Land-to-the-Tiller in the Mekong Delta: Economic, Social, and Political Effects of Land Reform in Four Villages of South Vietnam*. Lanham, Md.: University Press of America, 1983.

Castle, Timothy N. *At War in the Shadow of Vietnam: U.S. Military Aid to the Royal Lao Government, 1955–75*. New York: Columbia University Press, 1993.

Catton, Philip E. "Counter-Insurgency and Nation-Building: The Strategic Hamlet Programme in South Vietnam, 1961–1963." *International History Review* (December 1999): 918–40.

Chaffard, Georges. *Les Deux Guerres Du Vietnam: De Valluy A Westmoreland*. Paris: La Table Ronde, 1969.

Colby, William, and Peter Forbath. *Honorable Men: My Life in the CIA*. New York: Simon and Schuster, 1978.

Colby, William, with James McCargar. *Lost Victory: A Firsthand Account of America's Sixteen-Year Involvement in Vietnam*. Chicago: Contemporary Books, 1989.

Collins, J. Lawton. *Lightning Joe: An Autobiography*. Novato, Calif.: Presidio Press, 1994.

Conley, Michael Charles. *The Communist Insurgent Infrastructure in South Vietnam: A Study of Organization and Strategy*. Washington, D.C.: Department of the Army, 1967.

Cooper, Chester L. *The Lost Crusade: America in Vietnam*. New York: Dodd, Mead, 1970.

Cooper, Chester L., et al. *The American Experience with Pacification in Vietnam*. Arlington, Va.: Institute for Defense Analyses, 1972.

Davison, W. P. *Some Observations on Viet Cong Operations in the Villages*. Santa Monica, Calif.: RAND, 1968.

De Bary, Wm. Theodore. *Asian Values and Human Rights: A Confucian Communitarian Perspective*. Cambridge: Harvard University Press, 1998.

Devillers, Philippe. *Histoire du Viêt-Nam de 1940 à 1952*. 3d rev. et. corr. Paris: Editions du Seuil, n.d.

Donnell, John C. "National Renovation Campaigns in Vietnam." *Pacific Affairs* (March 1959): 73–88.

———. "Personalism in Vietnam." In *Problems of Freedom: South Vietnam Since Independence*. Ed. Wesley R. Fishel. New York: Free Press of Glencoe, 1961, 29–67.

———. "The War, the Gap, and the Cadre." *Asia Magazine* (winter 1966): 49–71.

————. "Expanding Political Participation—The Long Haul from Villagism to Nationalism." *Asian Survey* (August 1970): 688–704.

Donnell, John C., and Gerald C. Hickey. *The Vietnamese "Strategic Hamlets": A Preliminary Report.* Santa Monica, Calif.: RAND, 1962.

Donoghue, John D. *My Thuan: A Mekong Delta Village in South Vietnam.* N.p.: MSU Viet Nam Advisory Group, 1961.

Dow, Maynard Weston. *Nation Building in Southeast Asia.* Boulder, Colo.: Pruett Press, 1966.

Duiker, William J. *Sacred War: Nationalism and Revolution in a Divided Vietnam.* Boston: McGraw-Hill, 1995.

————. *The Communist Road to Power in Vietnam.* 2d ed. Boulder, Colo.: Westview Press, 1996.

————. *Ho Chi Minh.* New York: Hyperion, 2000.

Duncanson, Dennis J. *Government and Revolution in Vietnam.* New York: Oxford University Press, 1968.

Duong Van Mai Elliott. *The Sacred Willow: Four Generations in the Life of a Vietnamese Family.* New York: Oxford University Press, 1999.

Einaudi, Mario, and Francois Goguel. *Christian Democracy in Italy and France.* Hamden, Conn.: Archon Books, 1969.

Emerson, Gloria. *Winners and Losers: Battles, Retreats, Gains, Losses, and Ruins from the Vietnam War.* New York: Harcourt Brace Jovanovich, 1976.

Fall, Bernard B. "The Political-Religious Sects of Viet-Nam." *Pacific Affairs* (September 1955): 235–53.

————. *The Two Viet-Nams: A Political and Military Analysis.* 2d rev. ed. New York: Frederick A. Praeger, 1967.

The Fight against the Subversive Communist Activities in Vietnam. Special ed. Saigon: Review Horizons, 1957.

Finkle, Jason L., and Tran Van Dinh. *Provincial Government in Viet Nam: A Study of Vinh Long Province.* Saigon: MSU Viet Nam Advisory Group and NIA, 1961.

Fishel, Wesley R. "Vietnam's War of Attrition." *New Leader,* December 7, 1959, 16–21.

————. "Problems of Democratic Growth in Free Vietnam." In *Problems of Freedom: South Vietnam Since Independence.* Ed. Wesley R. Fishel. New York: Free Press of Glencoe, 1961, 9–28.

————. "Vietnam: Is Victory Possible?" *Foreign Policy Association,* Headline Series, February 1964.

FitzGerald, Frances. *Fire in the Lake: The Vietnamese and the Americans in Vietnam.* New York: Vintage Books, 1973.

Fraleigh, Bert. "Counterinsurgency in South Vietnam." In *Prelude to Tragedy: Vietnam, 1960–1965.* Ed. Harvey Neese and John O'Donnell. Annapolis: Naval Institute Press, 2001, 86–128.

Gardner, Lloyd C. *Approaching Vietnam: From World War II through Dienbienphu, 1941–1954.* New York: W. W. Norton, 1988.

Giglio, James N. *The Presidency of John F. Kennedy.* Lawrence: University Press of Kansas, 1991.

Grant, J. A. C. "The Viet Nam Constitution of 1956." *American Political Science Review* (June 1958): 437–62.

Grant, Zalin. *Facing the Phoenix.* New York: W. W. Norton, 1991.

Greenstein, Fred I., and Richard H. Immerman. "What Did Eisenhower Tell Kennedy about Indochina? The Politics of Misperception." *Journal of American History* (September 1992): 568–87.

Halberstam, David. *The Making of a Quagmire.* New York: Random House, 1965.

Hammer, Ellen J. *The Struggle for Indochina, 1940–1955: Viet Nam and the French Experience.* Stanford: Stanford University Press, 1966.

———. *A Death in November: America in Vietnam, 1963.* New York: E. P. Dutton, 1987.

Hatcher, Patrick Lloyd. *The Suicide of an Elite: American Internationalists and Vietnam.* Stanford: Stanford University Press, 1990.

Hellman, John. *Emmanuel Mounier and the New Catholic Left, 1930–1950.* Toronto: University of Toronto Press, 1981.

Henderson, William. "Opening New Lands and Villages: The Republic of Vietnam Land Development Program." In *Problems of Freedom: South Vietnam Since Independence.* Ed. Wesley R. Fishel. New York: Free Press of Glencoe, 1961, 123–37.

Henderson, William, and Wesley R. Fishel. "The Foreign Policy of Ngo Dinh Diem." *Vietnam Perspectives* (August 1966): 3–30.

Hendry, James B. *The Small World of Khanh Hau.* Chicago: Aldine Publishing, 1964.

Herring, George C. *America's Longest War: The United States and Vietnam, 1950–1975.* 2d ed. New York: Alfred A. Knopf, 1986.

———. " 'Peoples Quite Apart': Americans, South Vietnamese, and the War in Vietnam." *Diplomatic History* (winter 1990): 1–23.

Hersh, Seymour. *The Dark Side of Camelot.* Boston: Little, Brown, 1997.

Hess, Gary R. "Commitment in the Age of Counterinsurgency: Kennedy's Vietnam Options and Decisions, 1961–1963." In *Shadow on the White House: Presidents and the Vietnam War, 1945–1975.* Ed. David L. Anderson. Lawrence: University Press of Kansas, 1993, 63–86.

Hickey, Gerald C. *Village in Vietnam.* New Haven: Yale University Press, 1964.

———. *Free in the Forest: Ethnohistory of the Vietnamese Central Highlands, 1954–1976.* New Haven: Yale University Press, 1982.

Higgins, Marguerite. *Our Vietnam Nightmare.* New York: Harper & Row, 1965.

Hilsman, Roger. *To Move a Nation: The Politics of Foreign Policy in the Administration of John F. Kennedy.* Garden City, N.Y.: Doubleday, 1967.

Hoang Lac. "Blind Design." In *Prelude to Tragedy: Vietnam, 1960–1965.* Ed. Harvey Neese and John O'Donnell. Annapolis: Naval Institute Press, 2001, 58–85.

Hodgson, Godfrey. *The Gentleman from New York, Daniel Patrick Moynihan: A Biography.* Boston: Houghton Mifflin, 2000.

Hue-Tam Ho Tai. *Radicalism and the Origins of the Vietnamese Revolution.* Cambridge: Harvard University Press, 1996.

Hunt, David. "U.S. Scholarship and the National Liberation Front." In *The American War in Vietnam.* Ed. Jayne Werner and David Hunt. Ithaca, N.Y.: Cornell University Southeast Asia Program, 1993, 93–108.

Hunt, Michael H. *The Making of a Special Relationship: The United States and China to 1914.* New York: Columbia University Press, 1983.

Hunt, Richard A. *Pacification: The American Struggle for Vietnam's Hearts and Minds.* Boulder, Colo.: Westview Press, 1995.

Huynh Kim Khanh. "The Making and Unmaking of 'Free Vietnam.'" *Pacific Affairs* (fall 1987): 473–81.

Hy V. Luong. *Revolution in the Village: Tradition and Transformation in North Vietnam, 1925–1988.* Honolulu: University of Hawaii Press, 1992.

Jamieson, Neil L. *Understanding Vietnam.* Berkeley: University of California Press, 1993.

Joiner, Charles A. "Administration and Political Warfare in the Highlands." *Vietnam Perspectives* (November 1965): 19–37.

Joiner, Charles A., and Roy Jumper. "Organizing Bureaucrats: South Viet Nam's National Revolutionary Civil Servants' League." *Asian Survey* (April 1963): 203–15.

Jordan, Amos A., Jr. *Foreign Aid and the Defense of Southeast Asia.* New York: Frederick A. Praeger, 1962.

Jumper, Roy. "Mandarin Bureaucracy and Politics in South Viet Nam." *Pacific Affairs* (March 1957): 47–58.

———. "Problems of Public Administration in South Viet Nam." *Far Eastern Survey* (December 1957): 183–90.

Kahin, George McT. *Intervention: How America Became Involved in Vietnam.* New York: Alfred A. Knopf, 1986.

Kaiser, David. *American Tragedy: Kennedy, Johnson, and the Origins of the Vietnam War.* Cambridge, Mass.: Belknap Press, 2000.

Karnow, Stanley. "Diem Defeats His Own Best Troops." *The Reporter,* January 19, 1961, 24–29.

———. "The Edge of Chaos." *Saturday Evening Post,* September 28, 1963.

———. "Lost Chance in Vietnam." *New Republic,* February 2, 1974, 17–19.

———. *Vietnam: A History.* New York: Viking Press, 1983.

Kelly, Francis J. *The Green Berets in Vietnam, 1961–71.* New York: Brassey's, 1991.

Labin, Suzanne. *Vietnam: An Eye-Witness Account.* Springfield, Va.: Crestwood Books, 1964.

Lacouture, Jean. *Vietnam: Between Two Truces.* Trans. Konrad Kellen and Joel Carmichael. New York: Vintage Books, 1966.

Ladejinsky, Wolf. "Agrarian Reform in the Republic of Vietnam." In *Problems of Freedom: South Vietnam Since Independence.* Ed. Wesley R. Fishel. New York: Free Press of Glencoe, 1961, 153–75.

Land Reform in Free Vietnam. Special ed. Saigon: Review Horizons, 1956.

Lansdale, Edward Geary. *In the Midst of Wars: An American's Mission to Southeast Asia.* New York: Harper & Row, 1972.

Latham, Michael E. *Modernization as Ideology: American Social Science and "Nation Building" in the Kennedy Era.* Chapel Hill: University of North Carolina Press, 2000.

Le Thanh Khoi. *Le Viet-Nam: Histoire et Civilisation.* Paris: Editions de Minuit, 1955.

Lewy, Guenter. *America in Vietnam.* New York: Oxford University Press, 1978.

Liberation Editions. *Outlines of "Strategic Hamlets."* N.p., 1963.

Lockhart, Bruce McFarland. *The End of the Vietnamese Monarchy.* New Haven: Yale Center for International and Area Studies, 1993.

Logevall, Fredrik. *Choosing War: The Lost Chance for Peace and the Escalation of War in Vietnam.* Berkeley: University of California Press, 1999.

Lu Lan. "The People's War or War on the People?" In *Prelude to Tragedy: Vietnam, 1960–1965.* Ed. Harvey Neese and John O'Donnell. Annapolis: Naval Institute Press, 2001, 129–54.

Macdonald, Douglas J. *Adventures in Chaos: American Intervention for Reform in the Third World.* Cambridge, Mass.: Harvard University Press, 1992.

Maneli, Mieczyslaw. *War of the Vanquished.* Trans. Maria de Gorgey. New York: Harper & Row, 1971.

Mangold, Tom, and John Penycate. *The Tunnels of Cu Chi.* New York: Random House, 1985.

Marcus, John T. "Social Catholicism in Postwar France." *South Atlantic Quarterly* (summer 1957): 299–313.

Maritain, Jacques. *Redeeming the Time.* Trans. Harry Lorin Binsse. London: Centenary Press, 1943.

———. *The Person and the Common Good.* Trans. John J. FitzGerald. Notre Dame: University of Notre Dame Press, 1966.

———. *Christianity and Democracy & The Rights of Man and Natural Law.* Trans. Doris C. Anson. San Francisco: Ignatius Press, 1986.

Marr, David G. *Vietnamese Anticolonialism, 1885–1925.* Berkeley: University of California Press, 1971.

———. *Vietnamese Tradition on Trial, 1920–1945.* Berkeley: University of California Press, 1984.

———. *Vietnam 1945: The Quest for Power.* Berkeley: University of California Press, 1995.

Masaya Shiraishi. "The Background to the Formation of the Tran Trong Kim Cabinet in April 1945: Japanese Plans for Governing Vietnam." In *Indochina in the 1940s and 1950s.* Vol. 2. Ed. Masaya Shiraishi and Motoo Furuta. Ithaca, N.Y.: Cornell University Southeast Asia Program, 1992, 113–41.

Maurer, Harry. *Strange Ground: Americans in Vietnam, 1945–1975, an Oral History.* New York: Henry Holt & Company, 1989.

Mecklin, John. *Mission in Torment: An Intimate Account of the U.S. Role in Vietnam.* Garden City, N.Y.: Doubleday, 1965.

Moise, Edwin E. *Land Reform in China and North Vietnam: Consolidating the Revolution at the Village Level.* Chapel Hill: University of North Carolina Press, 1983.

Montgomery, John D. *The Politics of Foreign Aid: American Experience in Southeast Asia.* New York: Frederick A. Praeger, 1962.

Morgan, Joseph G. *The Vietnam Lobby: The American Friends of Vietnam, 1955–1975.* Chapel Hill: University of North Carolina Press, 1997.

Mounier, Emmanuel. *Personalism.* Trans. Philip Mairet. Notre Dame: University of Notre Dame Press, 1952.

Musolf, Lloyd D. "Public Enterprise and Development Perspectives in South Vietnam." *Asian Survey* (August 1963): 357–71.

Newman, John M. *JFK and Vietnam: Deception, Intrigue, and the Struggle for Power.* New York: Warner Books, 1992.

Nghiem Dang. *Viet-Nam: Politics and Public Administration.* Honolulu: East-West Center Press, 1966.

Ngo Dinh Diem. "Democratic Development in Vietnam." *Free China Review* (June 1955): 25–36.

Nguyen Chi Thanh. "Who Will Win in South Vietnam?" *Vietnamese Studies* 1 (1964).

Nguyen Cong Vien. *Seeking the Truth: The Inside Story of Viet Nam after the French Defeat by a Man Who Served in Dai's Cabinet.* New York: Vantage Press, 1966.

Nguyen Khac Nhan. "Policy of Key Rural Agrovilles." *Asian Culture* (July–December 1961): 29–49.

Nguyen Khac Vien. *Tradition and Revolution in Vietnam.* Trans. Linda Yarr, Jayne Werner, and Tran Tuong Nhu. Berkeley: Indochina Resource Center, 1975.

Nguyen Qui Hung. *Neuf Ans de Dictatures au Sud Vietnam: Témoignages Vivants sur Mme Nhu et les Ngo.* Saigon: n.p., 1964.

Nguyen Thai. *Is South Vietnam Viable?* Manila: Carmelo & Bauermann, 1962.

Nguyen Thi Dinh. *No Other Road to Take: Memoirs of Mrs. Nguyen Thi Dinh.* Trans. Mai V. Elliott. Ithaca, N.Y.: Cornell University Southeast Asia Program, 1976.

Nguyen Tuyet Mai. "Electioneering: Vietnamese Style." *Asian Survey* (November 1962): 11–18.

Nolte, Ernst. *Three Faces of Fascism.* Trans. Leila Vennewitz. New York: Holt, Rinehart and Winston, 1996.

Nolting, Frederick. *From Trust to Tragedy: The Political Memoirs of Frederick Nolting, Kennedy's Ambassador to Diem's Vietnam.* New York: Praeger Publishers, 1988.

O'Donnell, John B. "The Strategic Hamlet Program in Kien Hoa Province, South Vietnam: A Case Study of Counter-Insurgency." In *Southeast Asian Tribes, Minorities, and Nations.* Vol. 2. Ed. Peter Kunstadter. Princeton: Princeton University Press, 1967, 703–44.

Osborne, John. "The Tough Miracle Man of Asia." *Life,* May 13, 1957, 156–76.

Osborne, Milton E. *Strategic Hamlets in South Viet-Nam: A Survey and a Comparison.* Ithaca, N.Y.: Cornell University Southeast Asia Program, 1965.

Packenham, Robert A. *Liberal America and the Third World: Political Development*

Ideas in Foreign Aid and Social Science. Princeton: Princeton University Press, 1973.

Park, Richard L. "Second Thoughts on Asian Democracy." *Asian Survey* (April 1961): 24-27.

Parmet, Herbert S. *JFK: The Presidency of John F. Kennedy.* New York: Dial Press, 1983.

The Pentagon Papers: The Defense Department History of United States Decisionmaking on Vietnam. Vol. 2. Gravel ed. Boston: Beacon Press, 1971.

Pham Chung. *An Analysis of the Long-Range Military, Economic, Political, and Social Effects of the Strategic Hamlet Program in Viet Nam.* Washington, D.C.: Advanced Research Projects Agency, 1965.

Pham Cuong. "Cu Chi, a Guerilla Base." *Vietnamese Studies* 20 (1968).

Phillips, Rufus. "Before We Lost in South Vietnam." In *Prelude to Tragedy: Vietnam, 1960–1965.* Ed. Harvey Neese and John O'Donnell. Annapolis: Naval Institute Press, 2001, 7–57.

Pike, Douglas. *Viet Cong: The Organization and Techniques of the National Liberation Front of South Vietnam.* Cambridge, Mass.: MIT Press, 1967.

Post, Ken. *Revolution, Socialism, and Nationalism in Viet Nam.* Vol. 4. Aldershot, Hants: Dartmouth Publishing, 1990.

President Ngo-Dinh-Diem's Political Philosophy. Special ed. Saigon: Review Horizons, 1956.

Prochnau, William. *Once upon a Distant War.* New York: Random House, 1995.

Prosterman, Roy L. "Land Reform in Vietnam." *Current History* (December 1969): 327-68.

Race, Jeffrey. *War Comes to Long An: Revolutionary Conflict in a Vietnamese Province.* Berkeley: University of California Press, 1973.

Rogger, Hans, and Eugen Weber, eds. *The European Right: A Historical Profile.* London: Weidenfeld & Nicholson, 1965.

Rostow, W. W. "Guerrilla Warfare in Underdeveloped Areas." In *The Guerrilla—And How to Fight Him.* Ed. T. N. Greene. New York: Frederick A. Praeger, 1962, 54–61.

———. *The Diffusion of Power: An Essay in Recent History.* New York: Macmillan, 1972.

Rusk, Dean, as told to Richard Rusk. *As I Saw It.* New York: Penguin Books, 1991.

Rust, William J., and the editors of U.S. News Books. *Kennedy in Vietnam.* New York: Charles Scribner's Sons, 1985.

Schlesinger, Arthur M., Jr. *A Thousand Days: John F. Kennedy in the White House.* Boston: Houghton Mifflin, 1965.

———. *Robert Kennedy and His Times.* New York: Ballantine Books, 1978.

Schmitter, Philippe C. "Still the Century of Corporatism?" *Review of Politics* (January 1974): 85–131.

Schwab, Orrin. *Defending the Free World: John F. Kennedy, Lyndon Johnson, and the Vietnam War, 1961–1965.* Westport, Conn.: Praeger Publishers, 1998.

Scigliano, Robert. *South Vietnam: Nation under Stress.* Boston: Houghton Mifflin, 1964.

Shafer, D. Michael. *Deadly Paradigms: The Failure of U.S. Counterinsurgency Policy.* Princeton: Princeton University Press, 1988.

Shaplen, Robert. "A Reporter in Vietnam." *The New Yorker,* September 22, 1962, 103–31.

———. *The Lost Revolution: The U.S. in Vietnam, 1946–1966.* Rev. ed. New York: Harper & Row, 1966.

———. "The Cult of Diem." *New York Times Magazine,* May 14, 1972, 16–17, 40–58.

Sheehan, Neil. *A Bright Shining Lie: John Paul Vann and America in Vietnam.* New York: Random House, 1988.

Smith, Tony. *America's Mission: The United States and the Worldwide Struggle for Democracy in the Twentieth Century.* Princeton: Princeton University Press, 1995.

Sorenson, John L., and David K. Pack. *Unconventional Warfare and the Vietnamese Society.* China Lake, Calif.: U.S. Naval Ordnance Test Station, 1964.

Spector, Ronald H. *Advice and Support: The Early Years of the United States Army in Vietnam, 1941–1960.* New York: Free Press, 1985.

Sturdevant, C. V., J. M. Carrier, and J. I. Edelman. *An Examination of the Viet Cong Reaction to the Vietnamese Strategic Hamlet Program.* Santa Monica, Calif.: RAND, 1964.

Tanham, George K., with W. Robert Warne, Earl J. Young, and William A. Nighswonger. *War without Guns: American Civilians in Rural Vietnam.* New York: Frederick A. Praeger, 1966.

Taylor, Keith Weller. *The Birth of Vietnam.* Berkeley: University of California Press, 1983.

Taylor, Maxwell D. *Swords and Plowshares.* New York: W. W. Norton, 1972.

Taylor, Sandra C. "Reporting History: Journalists and the Vietnam War." *Reviews in American History* (September 1985): 451–61.

Thayer, Carlyle A. *War by Other Means: National Liberation and Revolution in Viet-Nam, 1954–1960.* Sydney: Allen & Unwin, 1989.

Thompson, Robert. *Defeating Communist Insurgency: The Lessons of Malaya and Vietnam.* New York: Frederick A. Praeger, 1967.

———. *Make for the Hills: Memories of Far Eastern Wars.* London: Leo Cooper, 1989.

Tønnesson, Stein. *The Vietnamese Revolution of 1945: Roosevelt, Ho Chi Minh, and de Gaulle in a World at War.* Oslo: International Peace Research Institute, 1991.

Tran Ngoc Chau. "My War Story: From Ho Chi Minh to Ngo Dinh Diem." In *Prelude to Tragedy: Vietnam, 1960–1965.* Ed. Harvey Neese and John O'Donnell. Annapolis: Naval Institute Press, 2001, 180–209.

Tran Ngoc Lien. "The Growth of Agricultural Credit and Cooperatives in Vietnam." In *Problems of Freedom: South Vietnam Since Independence.* Ed. Wesley R. Fishel. New York: Free Press of Glencoe, 1961, 177–89.

Tran Van Don. *Our Endless War: Inside Vietnam.* San Rafael, Calif.: Presidio Press, 1978.

Tregaskis, Richard. *Vietnam Diary.* New York: Holt, Rinehart and Winston, 1963.

Truong Nhu Tang, with David Chanoff and Doan Van Toai. *A Viet Cong Memoir.* New York: Vintage Books, 1985.

Turley, William S. *The Second Indochina War: A Short Political and Military History, 1954–1975.* New York: Mentor, 1987.

U.S. News & World Report. "How to Beat the Reds in Southeast Asia: Interview with President Diem of South Vietnam." February 18, 1963, 70–72.

Valentine, Douglas. *The Phoenix Program.* New York: William Morrow, 1990.

Vu Van Thai. "Vietnam's Concept of Development." In *Problems of Freedom: South Vietnam Since Independence.* Ed. Wesley R. Fishel. New York: Free Press of Glencoe, 1961, 69–73.

War Experiences Recapitulation Committee of the High-Level Military Institute. *The Anti-U.S. Resistance War for National Salvation, 1954–1975: Military Events.* Trans. JPRS 80968. Washington, D.C.: GPO, 1982.

Warner, Denis. *The Last Confucian: Vietnam, South-East Asia, and the West.* Harmondsworth, Middlesex: Penguin Books, 1964.

Warner, Geoffrey. "The United States and the Fall of Diem I: The Coup That Never Was." *Australian Outlook* (December 1974): 245–58.

———. "The United States and the Fall of Diem Part II: The Death of Diem." *Australian Outlook* (March 1975): 3–17.

Winters, Francis X. *The Year of the Hare: America in Vietnam, January 25, 1963–February 15, 1964.* Athens: University of Georgia Press, 1997.

Woodside, Alexander B. *Community and Revolution in Modern Vietnam.* Boston: Houghton Mifflin, 1976.

Young, Marilyn B. *The Vietnam Wars, 1945–1990.* New York: HarperCollins, 1991.

Zasloff, Joseph J. *Rural Resettlement in Vietnam: An Agroville in Development.* N.p.: MSU Vietnam Advisory Group, 1963.

Zasloff, Joseph J., and Nguyen Khac Nhan. *A Study of Administration in Binh Minh District.* Saigon: MSU Viet Nam Advisory Group and NIA, 1961.

Dissertations, Unpublished Works

Donnell, John C. "Politics in South Vietnam: Doctrines of Authority in Conflict." Ph.D. diss., University of California, Berkeley, 1964.

JCS (Historical Division). *The History of the Joint Chiefs of Staff: The Joint Chiefs of Staff and the War in Vietnam, 1960–1968.*

Luykx, Nicolaas Godfried Maria II. "Some Comparative Aspects of Rural Public Institutions in Thailand, the Philippines, and Viet-Nam." Ph.D. diss., Cornell University, 1962.

Ngo Dinh Diem. Talk by Mr. Ngo Dinh Diem before Southeast Asia Seminar. Cornell University, February 20, 1953, Echols Collection, Cornell University Library.

Ngo Dinh Quy. "Tu Chinh-Sach Dinh-Dien Den Chuong-Trinh Khan-Hoang Lap-Ap [From the Land Development Policy to the Land Clearance and Settlement Program]." Truong Quoc-Gia Hanh-Chanh, Luan-Van Tot-Nghiep, 1974.

Nguyen Huu Nguyen. "Hinh Thai Chien Tranh Nhan Dan O Long An Trong Khang Chien Chong My Tren Chien Truong Nam Bo (1960–1975) [The Shape of People's War in Long An during the Anti-U.S. Resistance War on the Southern Battlefield (1960–1975)]." TP Ho Chi Minh, Luan An Pho Tien Sy, 1994.

Nhan Thi Huong. "So-Sanh Du 57 Ngay 22-10-1956 Va Luat 003/70 Ngay 26-3-1970 [Comparing Decree 57 of 22-10-1956 and Law 003/70 of 26-3-1970]." Hoc Vien Quoc-Gia Hanh-Chanh, Luan-Van Tot-Nghiep, 1972.

Rhotenberry, R. M. "Pacification, Binh Duong Province, RVN (1962–1967)." U.S. Army War College, Carlisle Barracks, Pennsylvania, March 1970.

Schaad, Carl W. "The Strategic Hamlet Program in Vietnam: The Role of the People in Counterinsurgency Warfare." U.S. Army War College, Carlisle Barracks, Pennsylvania, March 1964.

Index

Agency for International Development (AID), 21, 53, 144, 148, 149, 159
Agglomeration Centers, 65–66
Agroville program, 51, 60, 71, 73, 87, 89, 91, 92, 98, 131, 168
  agro–hamlets, 63, 93, 94
  aims and implementation of, 66–70
  comparison with strategic hamlets, 93–96
  guerrilla response to, 69–70
  lack of U.S. involvement in, 67
  origins of, 63–66
  peasant reaction to, 69
  settlement characteristics, 63
  Staley-Thuc report, 94
  suspension of, 70
  U.S. views of, 67–68, 94
An Nhon Tay, 169
Anderson, Daniel, 13
Ap Bac, 152, 191, 192
Army of the Republic of Vietnam (ARVN), 161, 169, 170, 178, 181
  coup plots, 201
  expansion of, 75, 79–80, 94–95, 188
  opposition to regime, 83, 85
  palace's view of, 33, 87, 95, 120–21
  tactics of, 120, 176–77
  units: Eighth Regiment, 175, 178; Fifth Division, 178; Ninth Division, 206; Seventh Division, 87; Twenty-fifth Division, 189
Associated State of Vietnam, 5, 6, 7, 26, 27

Ball, George, 200
Bao Dai, 5–10, 26, 64
Barbour, Robert, 15
Bau Bang, 174–75
Bay of Pigs, 77
Ben Cat, 170–80, 183
Ben Dong So, 174–75
Ben Tre. *See* Kien Hoa
Ben Tuong, 172–78, 203
Bigart, Homer, 172, 173
Binh Dinh, 149
Binh Duong, 148, 185, 186
  case study of Strategic Hamlet program, 163–83
  map, 164
Binh Long, 170
Binh Xuyen, 9, 10–11
British Advisory Mission (BRIAM), 96–97, 117, 147, 189. *See also* Thompson, Robert
Browne, Malcolm, 200
Buchman, Frank, 45
Buddhism, 43
Buddhist crisis, 141, 186, 199, 205, 207
  impact on countryside of, 203
  origins of, 192–93
  regime's raids on the pagodas, 200
  self-immolations, 2, 17, 200
Budget and Foreign Aid, 48
Bui Diem, 23
Bui Van Luong, 57, 67, 92, 97, 118, 123, 147
Bundy, William, 85, 163, 185, 199, 201, 204
Buon Enao, 90, 155–56, 206

Burchett, Wilfred, 185
Bureau of Intelligence and Research, 81, 187
Burns, Paul, 87
Buttinger, Joseph, 2, 17
Buu Hoi, 8

Cable no. 243, 200–2
Cach Mang Quoc Gia, 80, 89
Cai San, 56
Cambodia, 58, 165
Can Lao (Revolutionary Personalist Workers' Party), 14, 16, 18, 90
Cao Dai, 9, 49, 56
Cao Van Luan, 27, 57, 130, 196
Catholics in Vietnam, 61, 85, 192, 265–66n. 39. *See also* Refugees, northern
Cau Dinh, 179–80
Central Highlands, 132, 151, 155, 170
    Land Development in, 57–63
Central Intelligence Agency (CIA), 8, 160, 190, 194, 198
    Buddhist crisis/1963 coup, 193, 202
    Nhu, 70, 90, 155, 196, 197
    See also Buon Enao; Montagnards
Chams, 49
Chau Thanh, 178–79
Chiang Kai-shek, 19, 37, 84
Chi-Dao, 38
Chinh nghia (just cause), 26
Citizens Group, 14
Civil Guard, 75, 181, 188
Colby, William, 28, 90, 127, 128, 135, 141, 204, 212
Collins, J. Lawton, 10–11, 12, 17
Combat hamlet *(ap chien dau)*, 91, 118, 131, 171, 177
Commander-in-Chief Pacific (CINCPAC), 81, 96, 170
Commodity Import Program, 30–31, 153

Communist-led insurgency, 92, 98, 117, 118, 130, 133, 171, 179, 180, 186, 193, 194, 199, 210
    1960 uprising, 69–70, 73–74, 87
    Agroville program, 69, 93
    BRIAM's view of, 198, 199
    Cau Dinh, 179
    Cu Chi, 165–66, 168–70, 181–82
    development of PLAF, 75, 182, 190, 264n. 29
    Diem regime's repression of, 64–66
    Diem's view of, 70, 80–81, 86–89, 120, 133–34, 170–71, 197–98
    DRVN, 64, 73–75, 186, 190–91
    founding of NLF, 74
    Nhu's view of, 89–91, 120–22, 133–34, 156, 196–98
    Operation Sunrise, 172–76, 178, 203
    political mobilization, 140, 210
    Strategic Hamlet program, 129, 137, 138, 140, 141, 179, 180, 181–82, 186, 187–92, 203, 205–7
    U.S. views of, 74–75, 142–43, 145, 151–53, 163, 183, 185–86, 198–99
    Vang Huong/Pho Binh, 180–81
    War Zones, 165, 170, 174
    See also Viet Minh
Community Development, 44, 59, 67, 68
Conein, Lucius, 155
Confucianism, 40, 43–44
Counterinsurgency fund, 150, 157–60
Counterinsurgency Plan, 75, 77–78, 79–80, 83, 94
Coup against Diem, 200–2
    ARVN generals in, 201, 204
    effects on the war effort of, 202–8, 212
Coups, attempted, rumored, 33, 76, 79, 85
Cronkite, Walter, 211
Cu Chi, 165–70, 173, 175, 177, 178, 182, 183

Darlac province. *See* Buon Enao
Dau tranh (struggle), 45
de Gaulle, Charles, 194
"Delta Plan," 96, 142, 147. *See also*
   Thompson, Robert
Diem regime (government)
   Buddhist protests against, 192–93,
      200
   characteristics of officials, 22, 32–33,
      55, 64–65, 68–69, 70, 131, 134–36,
      156
   disintegration of, 203
   elections, local, 13–14, 88, 123–24,
      127–28, 132
   elections, national, 13
   establishment of, 8–10
   overthrow of, 202
   plots against, 9, 33, 76
   political characteristics of, 12–17,
      22–23, 32–34, 54, 56, 210
   weaknesses in the countryside, 56,
      64–66, 86
Dien Bien Phu, 5, 7, 27, 94
Dillon, Douglas C., 8
Dinh Tuong, 187–88, 191, 192
Do Van Giong, 188
Doan ket (unity), 36
Doan the (cohesion), 36
Domenach, Jean-Marie, 47
Dong Quan, 64
Donnell, John C., 43, 48, 127, 168, 169,
   210
Douglas, William O., 7, 29
DRVN (Democratic Republic of
   Vietnam), 26, 28, 194–95
   North-South relations, 194–95
   See also Communist-led insurgency
Dulles, John Foster, 7, 10–11, 18, 29
Duong Thai Dong, 148
Duong Van Minh, 85, 204
Durbrow, Elbridge, 25, 32, 60, 66, 68,
   70, 78, 88
   view of, relationship with, Diem, 18,
      21, 62, 67, 76, 77, 79

Eisenhower, Dwight D., 11, 76–77
Eisenhower administration, 17–18
Ellsberg, Daniel, 205
Esprit, 41, 47

Fall, Bernard, 3
Farmers' associations, 45, 128
Federation of Vietnamese Landowners,
   55
Felt, Harry, 81. *See also* Commander-
   in-Chief Pacific (CINCPAC)
Figaro, Le, 57
First Indochina War, 5, 53, 64, 90, 156,
   165, 167, 170
Fishel, Wesley, 9, 29, 30, 32, 36
FitzGerald, Frances, 2, 34
Force Populaire, 130
Forrestal, Michael, 200
   Hillsman-Forrestal Report, 145, 153,
      186
Fraleigh, Bert, 144
France
   colonialism, 5–6, 57, 156
   Diem's premiership, 6–10, 18
   First Indochina War, 5, 64

Galbraith, John Kenneth, 143
Geneva Conference (1954), 5, 7, 23,
   26–27
Geneva Conference (1961), 80
Goburdhun, Ramchundur, 194
Group 559, 64

Halberstam, David, 2, 17, 47, 133, 205,
   209
Harkins, Paul D., 172, 189, 191, 198,
   207
Harriman, W. Averell, 80, 143, 199, 200
Heath, Donald R., 8, 9, 10
Heavner, Theodore, 132
Helble, John, 91
Hellman, John, 41
Henderson, William, 29, 30
Hendry, James, 139

Herring, George, 34
Hickey, Gerald, 168, 169
Hiep Hoa, 207
Higgins, Marguerite, 26, 35, 49, 127
Hilsman, Roger, 142
　criticism of Diem regime, 117, 199,
　　200
　Hillsman-Forrestal report, 145, 153,
　　186
　Operation Sunrise, 172, 174
　"Strategic Concept for South
　　Vietnam, A," 142–43
Hinduism, 43
Ho Chi Minh, 5, 26, 27, 46, 156, 212
Ho Tan Quyen, 202
Ho Van Hung, 171, 177
Hoa Hao, 9, 49, 56
Hoang Van Lac, 118, 135, 147
Hodgson, Godfrey, 20
Hohler, Harry, 80, 91, 146
Hoyt, Howard, 86
Hue. See Buddhist crisis

Interagency Committee for Province
　Rehabilitation, 144, 150
Interministerial Committee for
　Strategic Hamlets, 97, 130,
　150
International Control Commission
　(ICC), 58, 128, 194
Israeli kibbutz, 91

Johnson, Lyndon, 78, 80, 211, 212
Johnson, Robert, 145
Jonas, Gilbert, 61

Karnow, Stanley, 2, 78, 133,134
Kattenburg, Paul, 27
Kennedy, John F., 76
　Bay of Pigs, 77
　Counterinsurgency Plan, 77, 80
　Lansdale report, 77
　Laos, 77, 80
　preinaugural briefing, 76–77

Staley-Thuc report, 94
　Taylor mission/report, 82–83
Kennedy administration
　Buddhist crisis, 192, 193, 199–200
　cable no. 243, 200–202
　coup against Diem, 201–202
　Counterinsurgency Plan, 77–78, 94
　McNamara-Taylor mission/report,
　　201
　"Presidential Program," 77–78
　Strategic Hamlet program, 141–42
　Taylor mission/report, 81–85,
　　237–38n. 48
　withdrawal plan, 159, 256n. 84
Khuu Van Ba, 68–69, 91
Kien Hoa, 65, 69, 133, 134, 136, 187
Kien Quoc, 173
Kissinger, Henry, 195
Kontum, 73–74
Krulak, Victor, 179, 202

Lacouture, Jean, 34
Ladejinsky, Wolf, 52, 53, 54, 55–56, 65,
　66
Lai Thieu, 178–79
Lalouette, Roger, 194, 197
Land Development, 51, 79, 89, 98
　aims of, 56, 57, 58–60
　Diem's interest in, 56–57
　implementation of, 58, 60–61
　popular reaction to, 60–61
　settlement characteristics, 57
　success of, 63, 71
　U.S. role in, 57, 61–62
Land reform, 52
　Diem's approach to, 52–54
　failure of, 53–56
　landlord reaction to, 54–55
　ordinances, 52, 53, 54–55
　peasant reaction to, 54–56
　U.S. views of, 51–52, 62
Lansdale, Edward, 18, 20, 77, 80, 90,
　144, 149
　Diem, 8, 51, 78, 79

Laos, 58, 74, 77, 80, 158
Law 10/59, 66
Le Duc Tho, 195
Le Quang Tung, 202
Le Quoc San, 188, 191, 207
Le Van Dong, 65
Le Van Kim, 200
Le Van Phuoc, 91, 136
Lodge, Henry Cabot, 193, 195, 196,
    198
  on alliance diplomacy, 11–12
  role in coup, 202
  view of the Diem regime, 1, 47–48,
    200, 201–2
Long An, 138, 140, 182
  guerrilla activities in, 69–70, 187,
    206, 207
  land reform in, 54
  Strategic Hamlet program in, 131,
    134, 187, 206, 207
Long Cau, 174–75
Long Nguyen forest, 170

Malayan Emergency, 90, 96–97
  "New Villages," 64, 66, 91, 96
Maneli, Mieczyslaw, 128, 194–95, 197,
    198
Mansfield, Mike, 152, 158
Maritain, Jacques, 42
Marr, David, 35, 36
Marshall, George, 84
Maryknoll Mission Society, 6
McClintock, Robert, 8, 16, 27
McGarr, Lionel C., 74, 79, 94, 95, 96,
    142, 170
McNamara, Robert, 163, 171
  McNamara-Taylor mission/report,
    163, 201, 203
  Strategic Hamlet program, 141, 143,
    170, 176
  view on coup, 143, 201
Mecklin, John, 17, 24, 48, 118, 198
Mekong Delta, 56, 63, 66, 71, 73, 74,
    82, 132, 165, 170, 187, 191, 206–7

landownership in, 52
settlement characteristics in, 131, 139
See also individual provinces
Mendenhall, Joseph, 151, 152, 203
Michigan State University Vietnam
    Advisory Group, 13, 86, 139
Military Assistance Advisory Group
    (MAAG), 21, 31, 74, 87, 96
  counterinsurgency operations, 94–95,
    142, 170
  Strategic Hamlet program, 149, 150,
    152, 159
Military Assistance Command, Vietnam
    (MACV), 144, 151, 191
Military Revolutionary Council (MRC),
    204, 207
Montagnards, 49, 151, 187, 206
  Land Development, 56, 57, 58, 60,
    62
  See also Buon Enao
Moral Re-Armament, 45
Mounier, Emmanuel, 41, 42
"Mutual-aid family groups," 14, 86
My Tho, 191
My-Diem ("American Diem"), 28

National Front for the Liberation of
    South Vietnam (NLF). See
    Communist-led insurgency
National Revolutionary Movement, 14,
    45, 80, 131
National Security Action
    Memorandum No. 52, 77–78
Nehru, Jawaharlal, 39
New York Times, 172, 178
News from Viet-Nam, 59, 88, 89
Ngo Dinh Can, 15, 16, 65, 89, 130,
    217n. 50
Ngo Dinh Diem
  anticommunism, 8, 27–28, 38–39
  appointment as premier, 5, 6–8
  assassination, 202. See also Coup
    against Diem
  assassination attempts, 33, 58

Ngo Dinh Diem, *continued*
  attitude toward urban elite, 33, 49,
    127, 128
  Bao Dai, 6, 7, 26
  Buddhist crisis, 192–93
  concern about dependency on U.S.,
    25–26, 31, 33, 34, 155–56, 209
  concern about nationalist credentials,
    26, 28
  conservatism, 34–37
  critical of number of U.S. advisors,
    158, 196
  criticism of U.S. support, 30–34,
    62–63, 78–81, 83–84, 85, 154, 209
  doubts about U.S. reliability, 29–30
  French, 6–7, 9, 26, 27, 28
  Geneva accords, 26–27
  historians' views of, 2–3, 34, 209–10
  Ho Chi Minh, 5, 6, 27, 214n. 5
  Japanese occupation, 6, 28
  Lansdale, Edward, 9, 149
  monologues of, 1
  nation building, 2, 37–41, 45–47,
    49–50, 51, 58, 66, 88–89, 118–19,
    126–30, 209, 210. *See also*
    Personalism
  North-South relations, 26–27, 31–32,
    46–47, 58, 60
  Operation Sunrise, 172, 177
  opposition to neutralism, 29
  personal characteristics of, 5, 8, 9–10,
    27
  political background of, 5–6
  as premier, 8–11
  rapprochement with Hanoi, 194, 197
  regional prejudices of, 27
  relationship with Nhu, 16–17, 218n.
    55
  time in the U.S., 6
  U.S. views of, 5, 6, 8, 10–11
  view of Madame Nhu, 17
  view of the peasantry, 49–50
  See also British Advisory Mission
    (BRIAM); Malayan Emergency;

    see under Communist-led
    insurgency; Land Development;
    Land Reform; Viet Minh
Ngo Dinh Kha, Mrs., 16
Ngo Dinh Khoi, 15
Ngo Dinh Luyen, 7, 15
Ngo Dinh Nhu
  assassination, 202
  attitude toward rural elite, 124–25
  attitude toward urban elite, 33, 49,
    127, 128
  Buddhist crisis, 193, 200
  concern about dependency on U.S.,
    31, 33, 34, 125–26, 154–56, 157,
    158, 209
  critical of number of U.S. advisors,
    158
  criticism of U.S. support, 30–34, 80,
    84, 85–86, 95, 153–54, 193–94, 209
  doubts about U.S. reliability, 29, 80,
    86, 158, 194
  influence with Diem, 15–17, 89
  Marxism-Leninism, 89–90
  nation building, 37–41, 45–47,
    49–50, 58, 90, 118–19, 122,
    126–30, 209, 210
  Operation Sunrise, 171, 177
  personal characteristics of, 29
  as prime mover of the Strategic
    Hamlet program, 97, 117–19
  rapprochement with Hanoi, 194–97
  relationship with Diem, 16–17
  U.S. views of, 76, 143, 160, 200–201,
    202
  view of the peasantry, 49–50
  view of U.S.-Vietnamese relations,
    25, 29
  visit to Cu Chi, 166–67, 169
  See also Republican Youth Movement;
    see under Central Intelligence
    Agency (CIA); Communist-led
    insurgency; Personalism
Ngo Dinh Nhu, Madame (Tran Le
  Xuan), 17, 61, 122, 193, 200

Ngo Dinh Thuc, 15, 39, 91
Ngo Trong Hieu, 92, 96
Nguyen Chi Thanh, 187
Nguyen Dinh Thuan, 67, 70, 93, 159,
    193, 196, 200, 203
Nguyen Huu Bai, 5
Nguyen Huu Chau, 15
Nguyen Huy Bao, 44
Nguyen Khac Vien, 43
Nguyen Khanh, 204
Nguyen Ngoc Tho, 65, 152, 159
Nguyen Thai, 14
Nguyen Thi Dinh, 69
Nguyen Tran, 56
Nguyen Van Binh, 168, 169, 170
Nguyen Van Chau, 29, 38, 119
Nguyen Van Hinh, 9, 33
Nguyen Van Tat, 91
Nguyen Van Thieu, 56, 212
Nguyen Van Thoi, 56
Nguyen Van Vinh, 190
Nguyen Viet Thanh, 74, 134
Ninh Thuan, 15
Nixon, Richard, 52, 53
Nolting, Frederick, 94, 96, 130, 154,
    155, 160, 172, 179, 186, 194
  appointment of, 78
  approach to Diem regime, 84, 202
  counterinsurgency fund, 150, 158–60
  Taylor report, 83–85

O'Daniel, John W., 31, 32, 53
O'Donnell, John, 205
Office of Rural Affairs, 144. *See also*
    Phillips, Rufus; Agency for
    International Development
    (AID)
"Open Arms" program, 188, 206
Operation Ben San, 180
Operation Forward Together, 149
Operation Royal Phoenix, 149
Operation Sea Swallow II, 148, 157
Operation Sunrise, 148, 170–78, 179,
    181, 183, 203

Packenham, Robert, 21
Partial Test Ban Treaty, 194
Pentagon Papers, 171
People's Liberation Armed Forces
    (PLAF). *See under* Communist-led
    insurgency
Personalism, 73, 90, 128, 209, 210
  Agroville program, 66
  critics of, 47–48, 146
  Land Development, 59
  Land Reform, 52, 54
  Nhu, 42
  origins and tenets, 41–42
  palace's interest in, 42–46, 48–49
  Strategic Hamlet program, 118, 122,
    140
Pham Ngoc Thao, 66, 133
Pham Quynh, 40
Pham Van Dong, 195
Pham Xuan An, 133
Phillips, Rufus, 124, 148, 149, 152, 183,
    203, 206
  counterinsurgency fund, 157, 160
  Office of Rural Affairs, 144
Pho Binh, 180–81
Phong Dinh, 65, 68
Phu My Hung, 169
Phu Yen, 148, 149
Phuoc Hiep, 166, 168
Phuoc Thanh, 74, 180
Phuoc Tuy, 165
Pike, Douglas, 126, 173, 202
Plain of Reeds, 58
Post, Ken, 210
"Presidential Program," 77–78, 94
Price, Marvin, 174

Quang Nam, 203
Quang Ngai, 91, 92, 93, 149, 189
Quang Tri, 15

Race, Jeffrey, 136, 140, 182
Radford, Arthur, 29
RAND Corporation, 147, 168, 169

Refugees, northern, 46–47, 56, 58, 60–61, 167
Reinhardt, Frederick, 18, 22, 32, 37
Republic of Vietnam (RVN) National Assembly, 13, 50
Constitution, 13, 42
See also Diem regime (government)
Republican Youth Movement, 45, 87–88, 89, 123, 124–25, 127, 146, 161, 169
Rhade tribe, 90. See also Buon Enao
Rhee, Syngman, 79
Rhotenberry, R. M., 172, 175
Richardson, John, 196
Rose, Jerry, 173
Rosson, William B., 152, 174
Rostow, Walt, 20, 22, 81, 83, 97, 125
Rubber plantations, 170, 180
"Rural Consolidation" campaign, 87
Rural Reconstruction Campaign, 165
Rusk, Dean, 83, 84, 85, 199

Schaad, Carl W., 144
Schlesinger, Arthur Jr., 19, 82
Scigliano, Robert, 13, 28, 136
SECDEF (secretary of defense's) conference, 143, 170
Self-Defense Corps, 75, 87, 88, 135, 178, 179, 182, 188, 206
Serong, Francis P., 169, 189, 199
Service for Political and Social Research, 16, 91
Shaplen, Robert, 17, 44, 47
Soc Trang, 55
Southeast Asia Treaty Organization (SEATO), 80
Soviet Union, 194
Sparkman, John, 60
Staley, Eugene, 94
Staley-Thuc report, 81, 94
Strategic Hamlet program, 3, 32, 49, 51, 58, 60, 73, 86, 199, 211, 212
adopted as national policy, 97
Binh Duong, case study of, 163–83

collapse of, 204, 205–8
communal rules, 124, 132
comparison with Agroville program, 93–94, 95–96
criteria for completion of hamlets, 130
early local experiments, 91–93
elections in, 123–24, 127–28, 132, 244n. 26
genesis of, 89–91
hamlet militia, 120–22, 138–39, 154–55, 175–76, 177, 181, 206, 207
Military Revolutionary Council, 204
Nhu as prime mover, 97, 117–19
palace's belief in success of, 185, 194, 196, 197–98
palace's concern about U.S. involvement in, 153–61
palace's reluctance to consult with U.S./BRIAM, 94–97, 117
popular self-sufficiency, 119
problems with implementation of, 129–40
province rehabilitation committees, 150–51
purposes of, 98, 118, 119–29
strategic quarters, 93
U.S. views of, role in, 117, 126, 141–53, 160, 185–86
See also individual operations; Communist-led insurgency
Sullivan, William H., 130

Tan An, 91
Tan An Hoi, 166, 167, 168
Tan Phu Trung, 166
Tanham, George, 147
Taoism, 43
Tay Ninh, 91, 92, 93, 136, 165, 167
Taylor, Maxwell, 200
McNamara-Taylor mission/report, 163, 201, 203
Taylor mission/report, 82–86, 95, 97, 141, 143, 149, 151
views on coup, 201

Thanh Thoi, 69
Thi Nghe, 136, 137
Thich Quang Duc, 2, 200
Thich Tri Quang, 193
Thompson, Robert, 96, 117, 137, 142, 147, 148, 189, 198
Thua Thien, 203
Time, 173
Times of Viet Nam, 32, 193
Times of Viet Nam Magazine, 79, 129, 185
Ton That Dinh, 155, 203–4
Tran Chanh Thanh, 15
Tran Cuu Thien, 65, 66, 68
Tran Kim Tuyen, 15, 16, 83, 91, 203
Tran Le Xuan. *See* Ngo Dinh Nhu, Madame
Tran Ngoc Chau, 64, 134, 136
Tran Ngoc Lien, 45
Tran Quoc Buu, 15, 16
Tran Trong Kim, 40
Tran Tu Oai, 130, 137
Tran Van Chuong, 31
Tran Van Dinh, 195
Tran Van Do, 15, 26
Tran Van Don, 200, 203
Tran Van Giau, 129, 188
Tran Van Lam, 86
Tran Van Minh, 178, 179, 181
Tri Tam, 170, 171, 180
Trueheart, William C., 144, 146, 147, 150, 202
Trung Lap, 169
Trung Sisters, 17
Truong Cong Cuu, 193
Truong Nhu Tang, 23, 133
Turley, William, 34

United States
    bureaucratic differences over policy, 21–22, 75–76, 144, 199
    calls to replace Diem, 10, 18, 76, 143, 151–52
    criticism, proposed reform, of Diem
        regime, 22–23, 61–62, 68, 75–76, 78, 81–83, 94–95, 144–53, 158–60, 192–93, 198, 199–200
    expanded military support for Diem regime, 75, 79–80, 81, 82, 144, 149, 156, 188
    nation building, 20–22, 144–47, 160
    nature of relationship with Diem regime, 1, 3–4, 5, 9, 11–12, 17–20, 23–24, 25, 73, 83, 84, 161, 209, 210–11
    negative views of Vietnamese, 19–20
    post-Diem South Vietnam, 4, 204–5, 211–212
    press, 156, 172, 173, 174, 178, 193, 199–200
    role in coup against Diem, 1, 4, 200–202, 210–11
    start of relationship with Diem, 5, 6–11
    view of regime's programs. *See under* Agroville Program; Land Development; Land Reform; Strategic Hamlet program
United States Information Service (USIS), 43, 149, 173
United States Operations Mission (USOM), 9, 52, 62, 63, 124, 134, 154
    Strategic Hamlet program, 144, 146, 148, 150, 152, 159
United States Special Forces, 155, 188, 206

Van Thanh Cao, 136
    operations in Binh Duong, 165, 166, 167, 171, 172, 174, 175, 176, 177, 178
Vang Huong, 180, 181
Vann, John Paul, 120, 152, 168
Vi Thanh, 66, 68
Viet Cong (VC). *See* Communist-led insurgency

Viet Minh, 5, 8, 60, 86, 91, 136, 167
  Diem's view of, 6, 26, 27
  land reform, 54–55
  regime's treatment of former
    members, 64–66
Vietnam Press, 14
Vietnam Task Force, 75, 93
Vietnam Working Group, 132
Vietnamese Catholicism, 27
Vietnamese nationalism, 25, 35–36,
  210
Vinh Long, 15, 47, 68–69, 91–92, 93,
  132
Vo Van Hai, 15
Vu Ngoc Nha, 133

Vu Quoc Thuc, 94
Vu Van Mau, 28, 31, 37, 44, 80, 203
Vu Van Thai, 59
Vung Tau, 165

Weidner, Ed, 86
Weiss, Seymour, 76
White, Theodore, 95
Williams, Samuel T., 21, 30, 87, 88
Wilson, Wilbur, 179–80
Wood, Ben, 93
Wood, Chalmers, 75

Xa Hoi, 16, 42
Xom-Hue, 168